Masterworks of Modern Art
from The Museum of Modern Art, New York

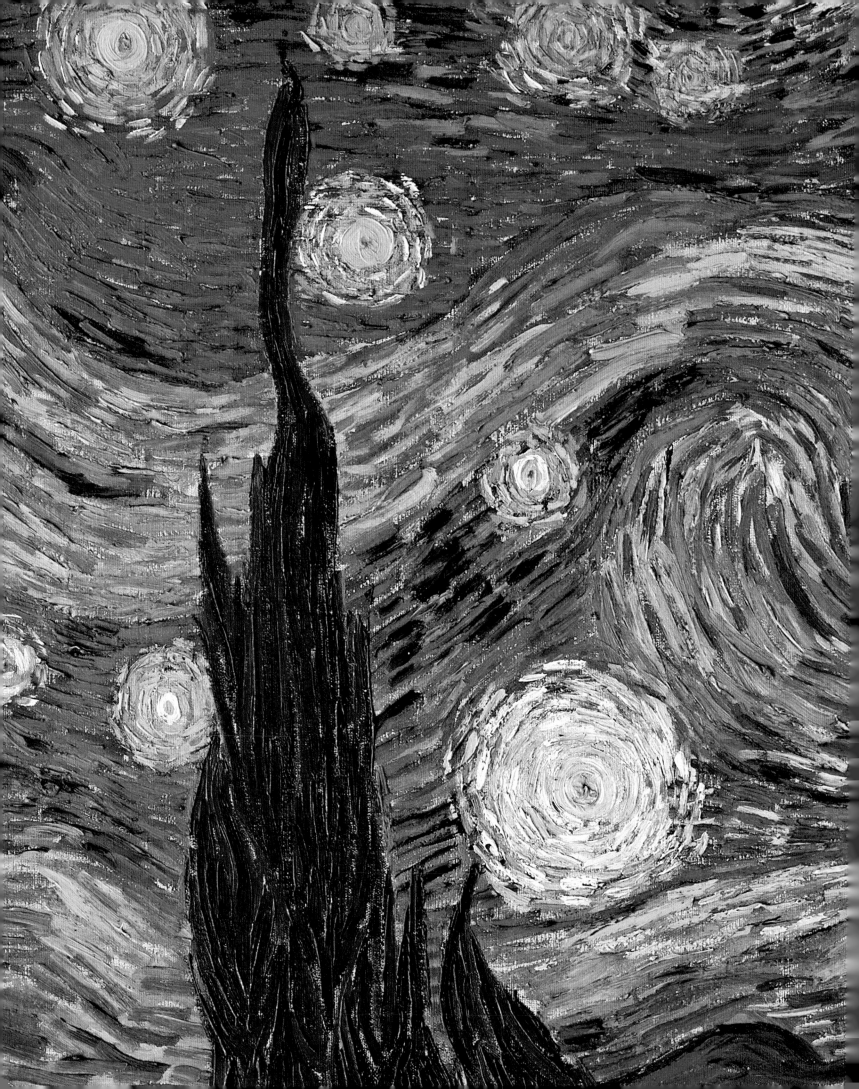

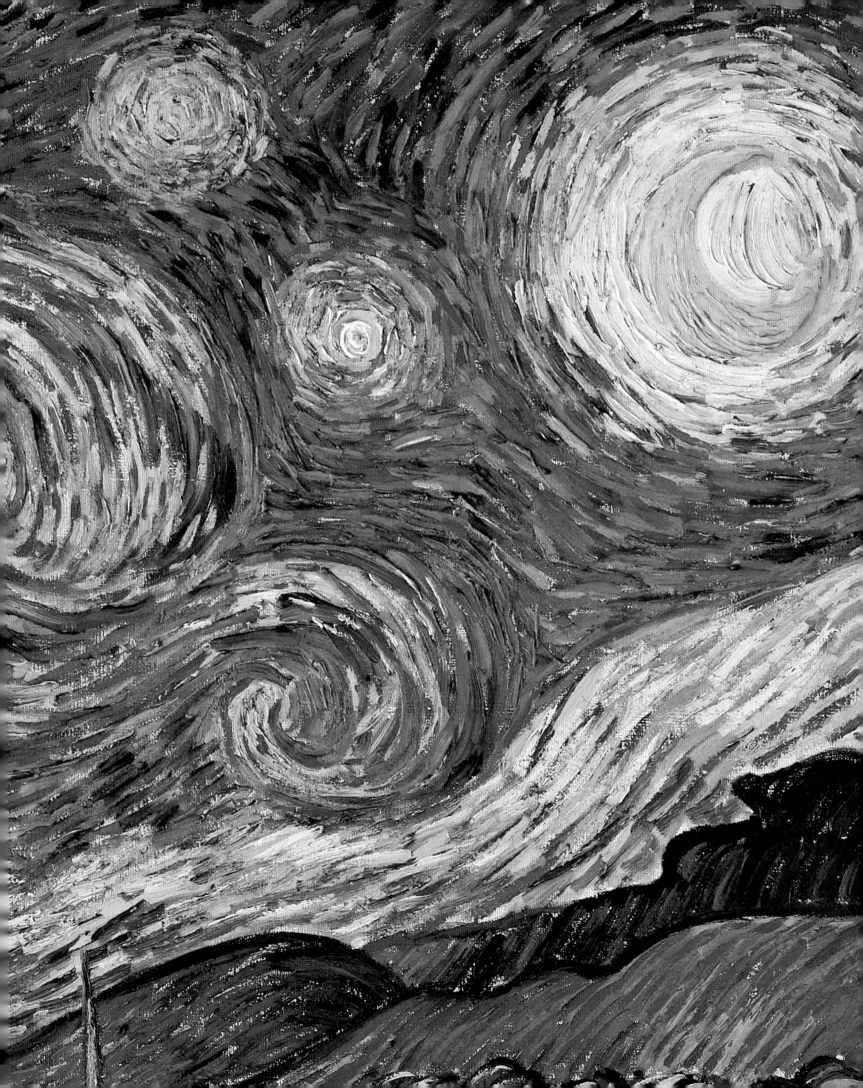

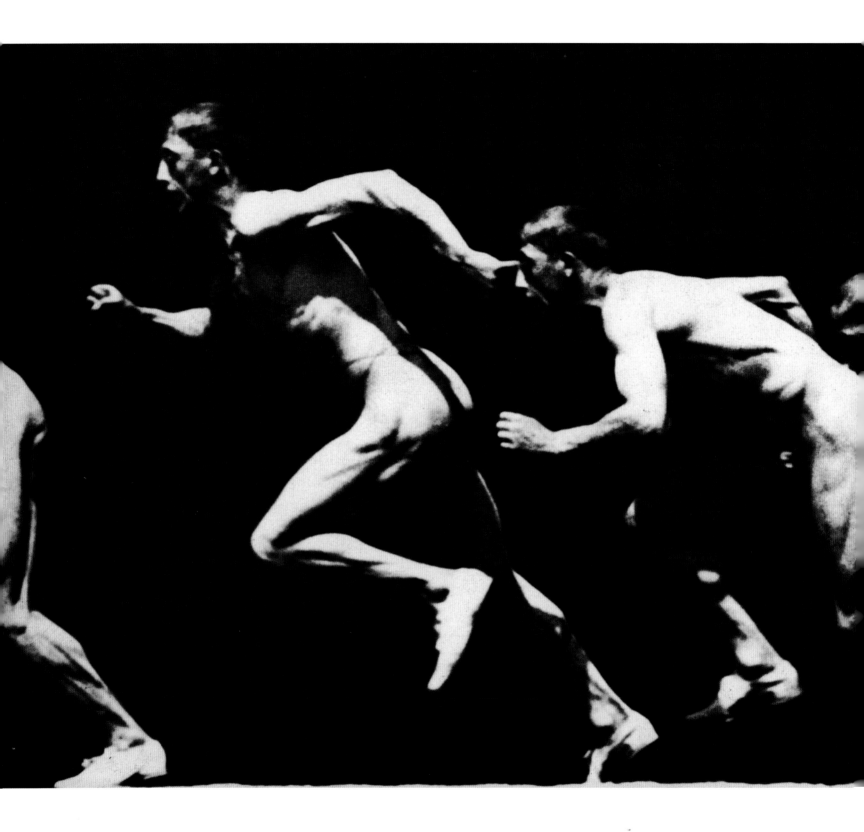

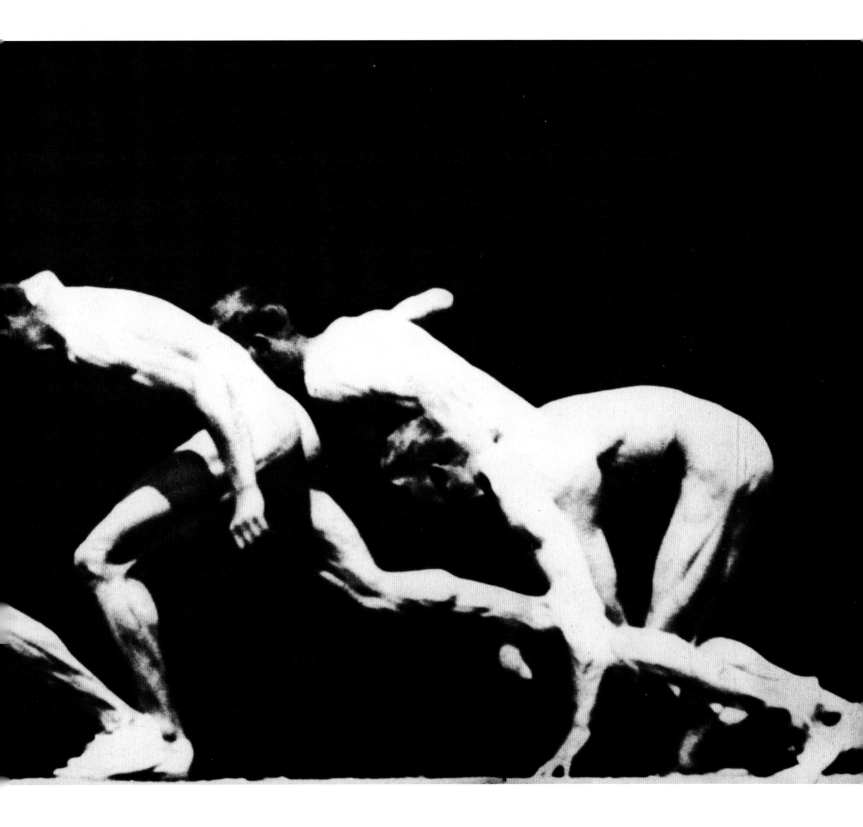

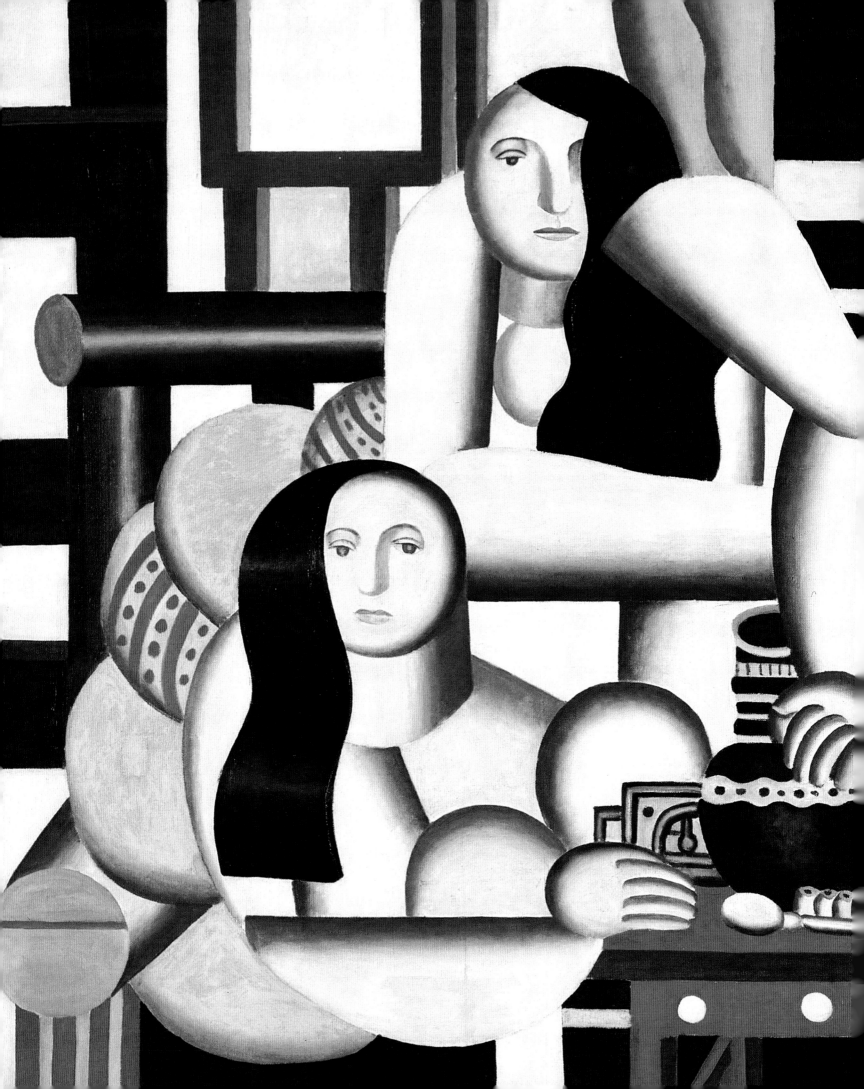

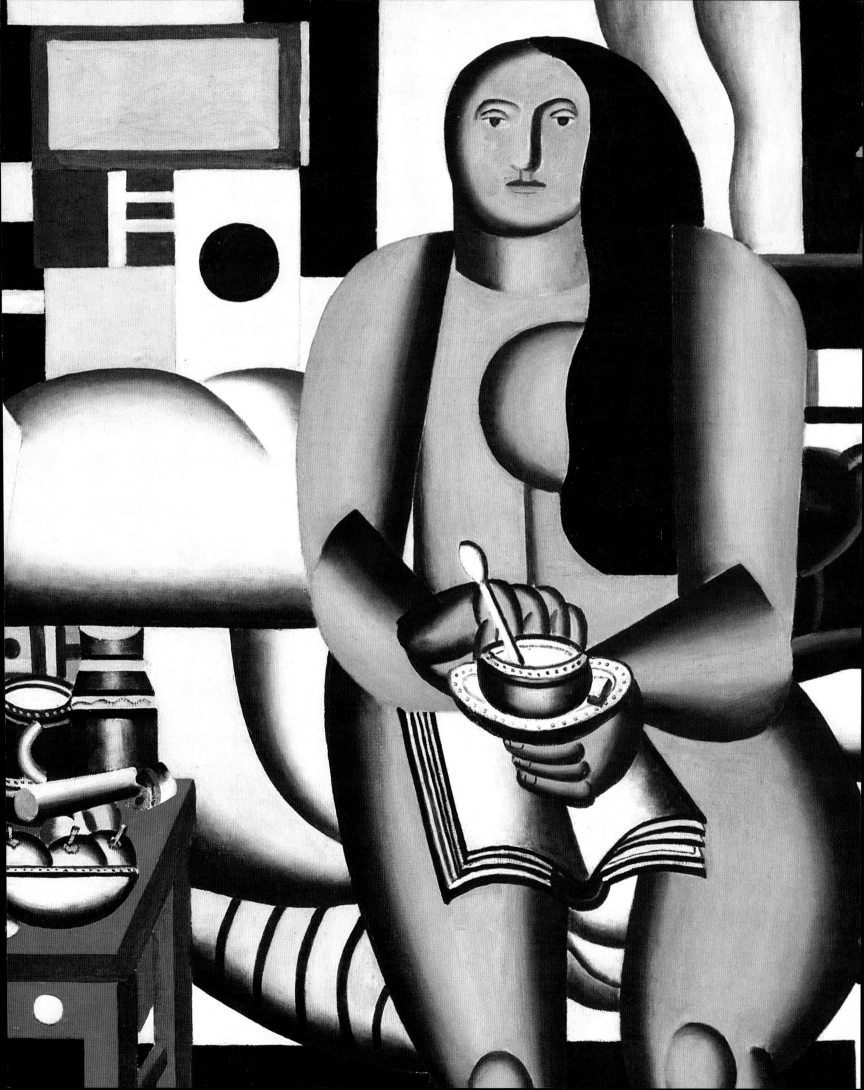

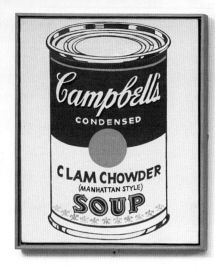

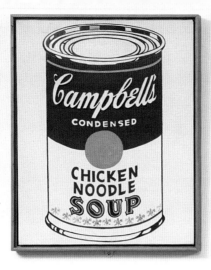

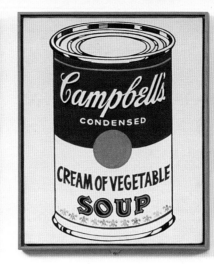

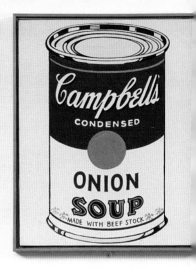

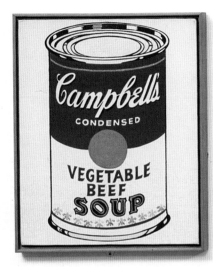

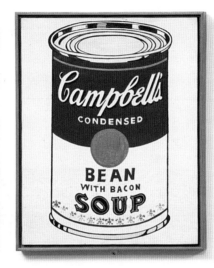

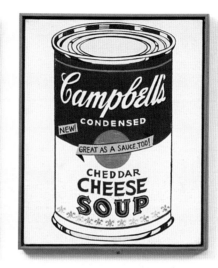

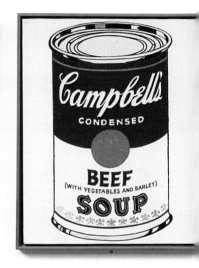

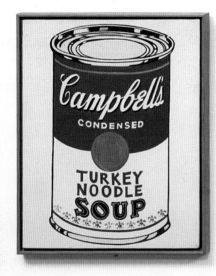

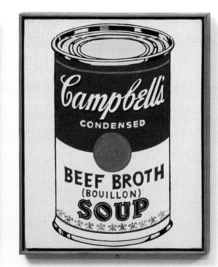

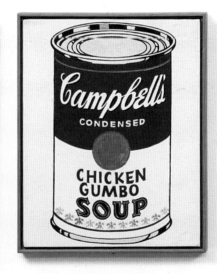

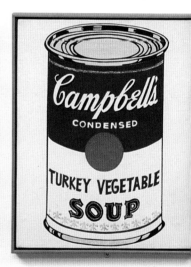

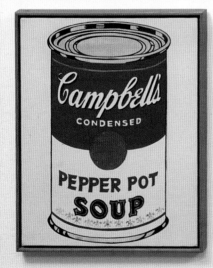

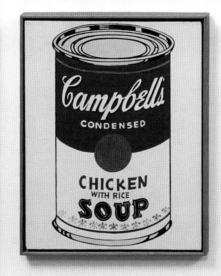

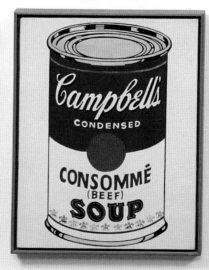

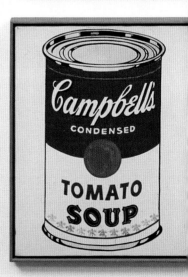

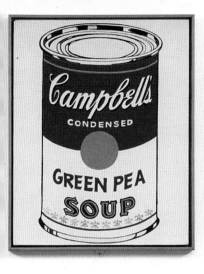

Campbell's CONDENSED GREEN PEA SOUP

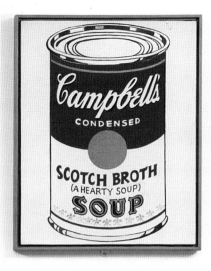

Campbell's CONDENSED SCOTCH BROTH (A HEARTY SOUP) SOUP

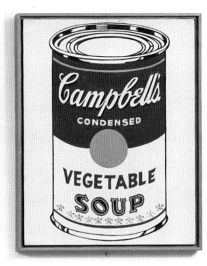

Campbell's CONDENSED VEGETABLE SOUP

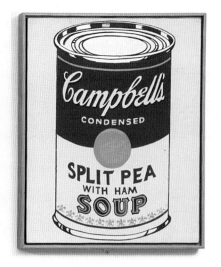

Campbell's CONDENSED SPLIT PEA WITH HAM SOUP

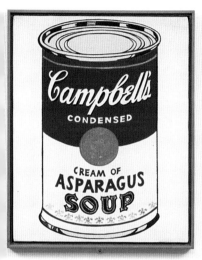

Campbell's CONDENSED CREAM OF ASPARAGUS SOUP

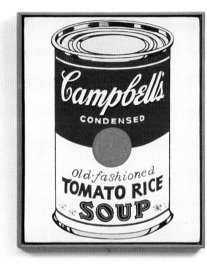

Campbell's CONDENSED Old-fashioned TOMATO RICE SOUP

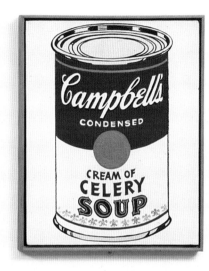

Campbell's CONDENSED CREAM OF CELERY SOUP

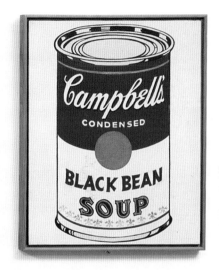

Campbell's CONDENSED BLACK BEAN SOUP

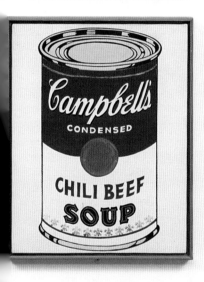

Campbell's CONDENSED CHILI BEEF SOUP

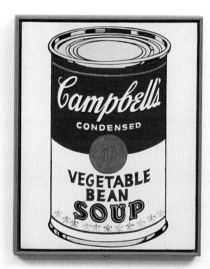

Campbell's CONDENSED VEGETABLE BEAN SOUP

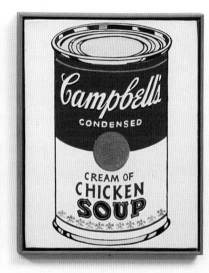

Campbell's CONDENSED CREAM OF CHICKEN SOUP

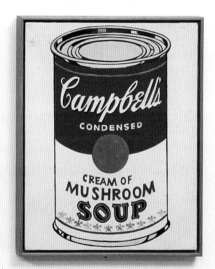

Campbell's CONDENSED CREAM OF MUSHROOM SOUP

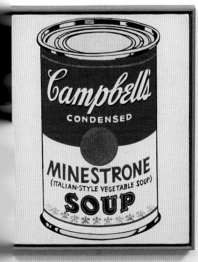

Campbell's CONDENSED MINESTRONE (ITALIAN-STYLE VEGETABLE SOUP) SOUP

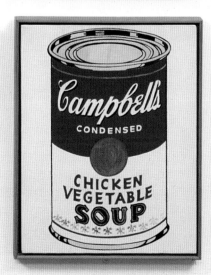

Campbell's CONDENSED CHICKEN VEGETABLE SOUP

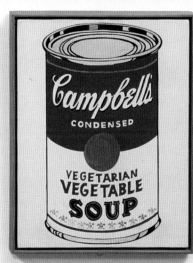

Campbell's CONDENSED VEGETARIAN VEGETABLE SOUP

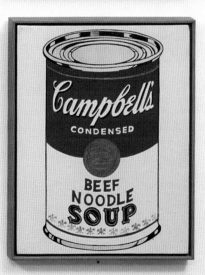

Campbell's CONDENSED BEEF NOODLE SOUP

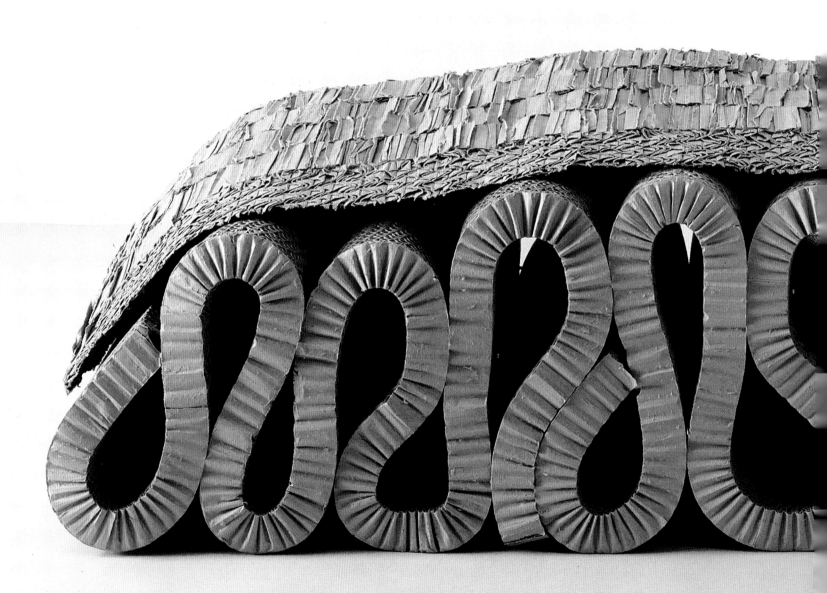

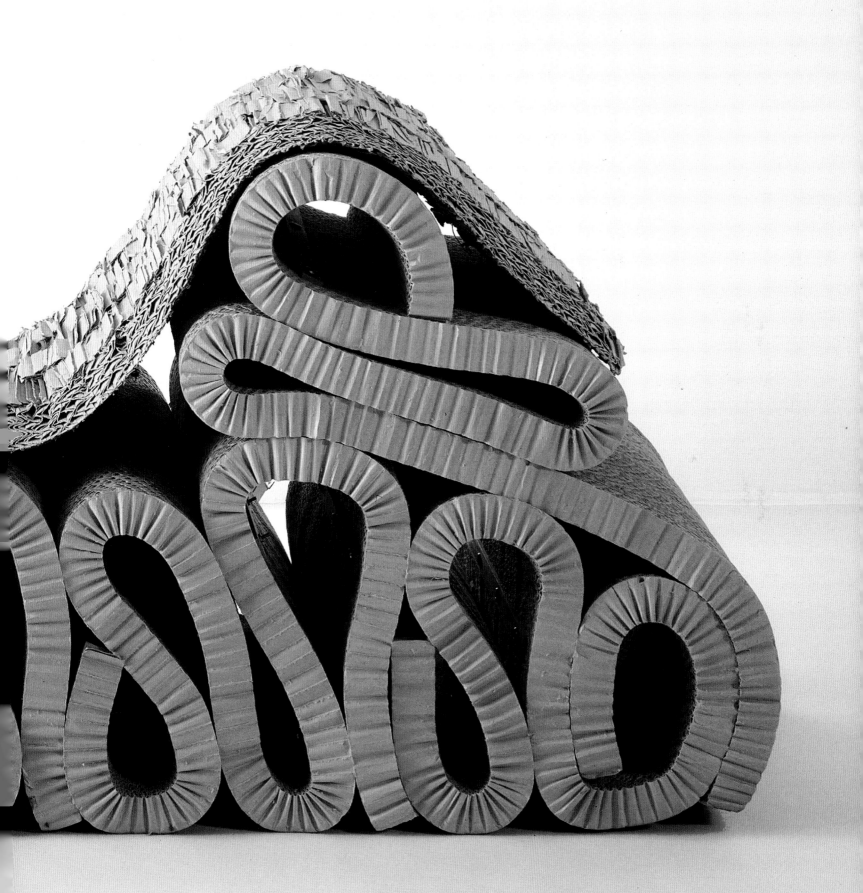

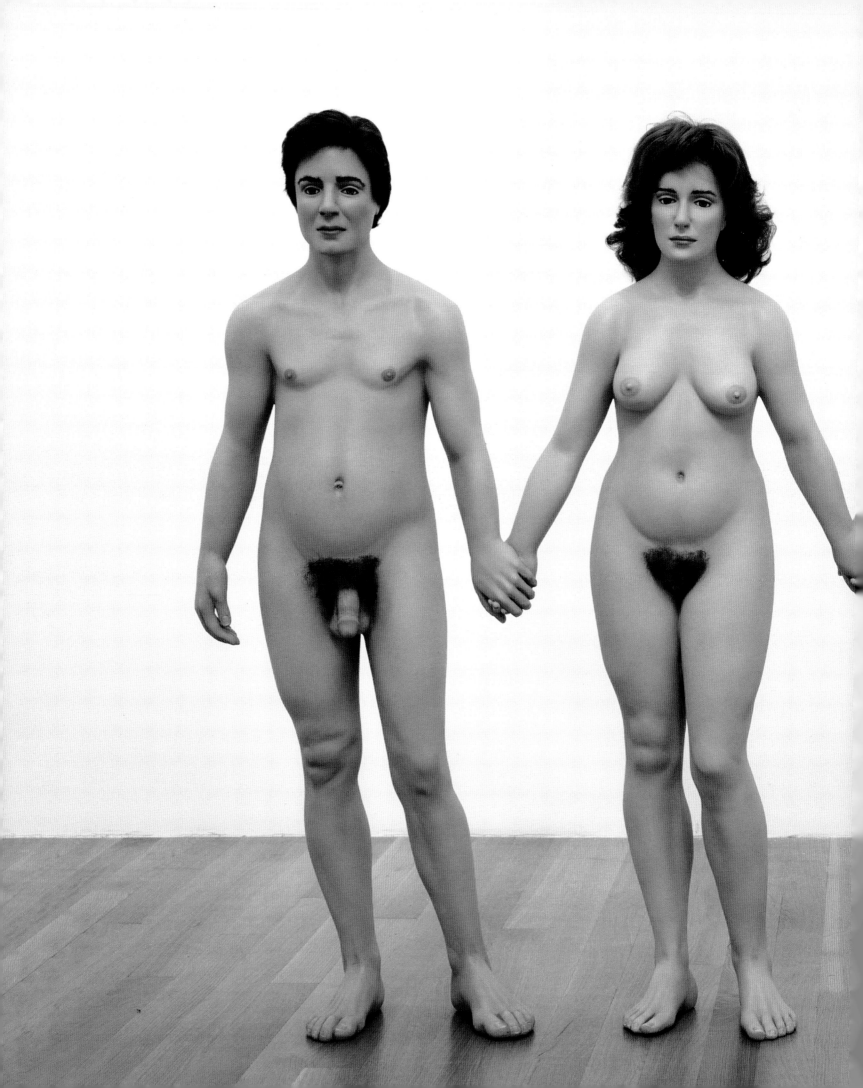

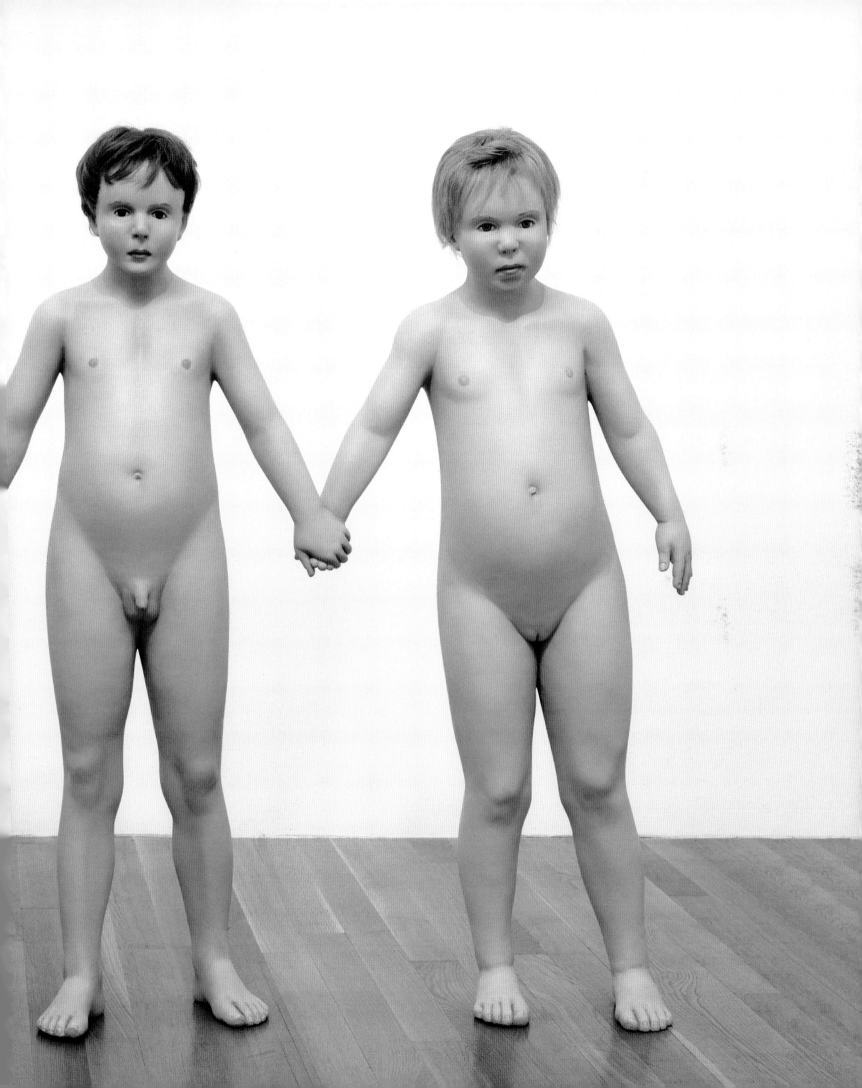

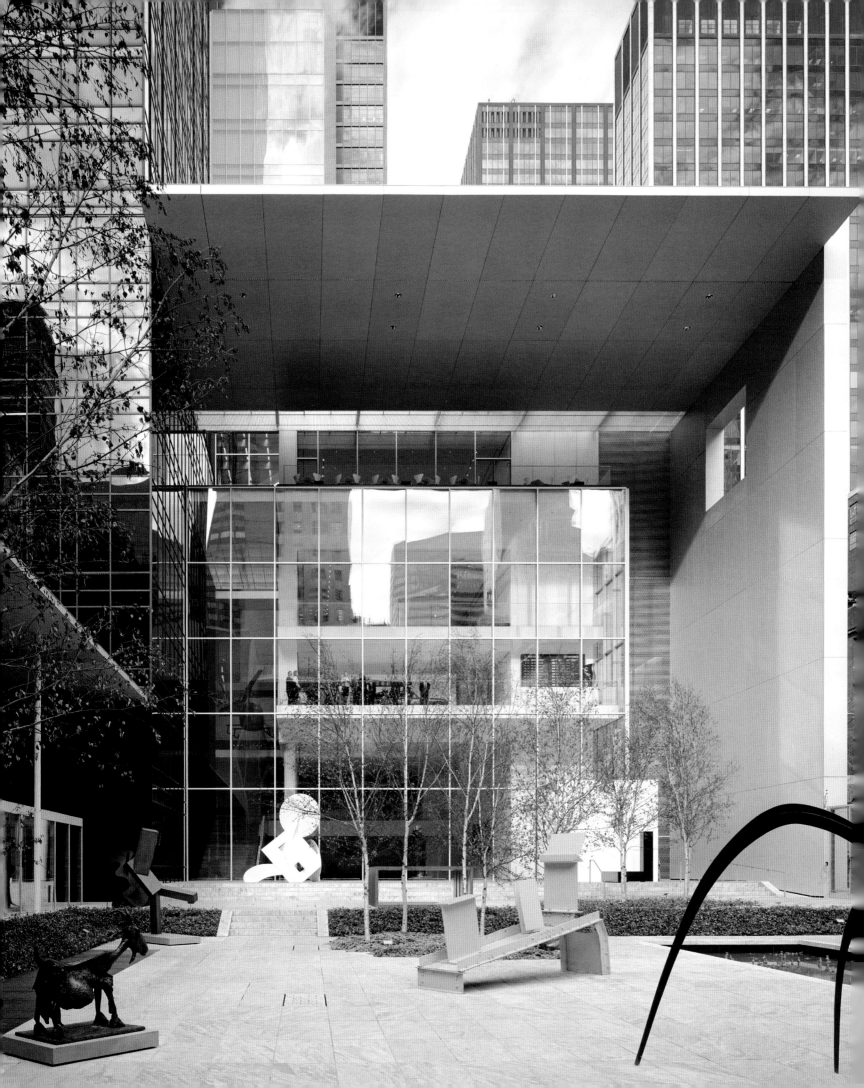

Masterworks of Modern Art
from The Museum of Modern Art, New York

Introduced by

Glenn D. Lowry, Director of the MoMA

SCALA VISION

Publisher's Note

This sweeping anthology of modern and contemporary art, unique in its comprehensive-ness and quality, covers over a century of painting and sculpture, design and architecture, photography and books by artists. It is arranged in strictly chronological order, so as to of-fer readers a perspective that will allow them to look at a work and compare different ap-proaches and intuitions in others that were produced that same year and over the course of time.

A "timeline" of modern and contemporary art, drawing on the most authoritative and famous collection in the world.

© 2005 SCALA Group S.p.A., Florence
© 2005 SCALAVISION/ibooks for the North American & UK editions
© 2005 The Museum of Modern Art, New York for the English texts
Digital Images © 2005 The Museum of Modern Art, New York / SCALA, Florence
Certain illustrations are covered by claims to copyright noted in the Photograph Credits
All rights reserved

ISBN 978-88-8117-298-6

Published by SCALAVISION/ibooks, Inc.
24 West 25ᵗʰ Street, New York, NY 10010

Distributed in North America by D.A.P./Distributed Art Publishers, Inc.
155 Sixth Avenue, New York

Distributed outside North America and Italy by Thames & Hudson
181a High Holborn, London WC1V 7QX
United Kingdom

Printed in China

Pages 2–3: Vincent van Gogh, *The Starry Night*, 1889, detail (see p. 34)
Pages 4–5: Étienne-Jules Marey or Georges Demenÿ, Untitled, c. 1890–1900 (see p. 40)
Pages 6–7: Fernand Léger, *Three Women*, 1921, detail (see p. 112)
Pages 8–9: Andy Warhol, *Campbell's Soup Cans*, 1962 (see p. 227)
Pages 10–11: Frank O. Gehry, Bubbles Chaise Longue, 1987 (see p. 275)
Pages 12–13: Charles Ray, *Family Romance*, 1993 (see p. 285)
Pages 14, 18–19: The Museum of Modern Art, the Sculpture Garden and, beyond it, the new gallery building by Yoshio Taniguchi, 2004
Page 27: Hilaire-Germain-Edgar Degas, *At the Milliner's*, c. 1882, detail (see p. 29)
Page 55: Pablo Picasso, *Les Demoiselles d'Avignon*, 1907, detail (see p. 64)

CONTENTS

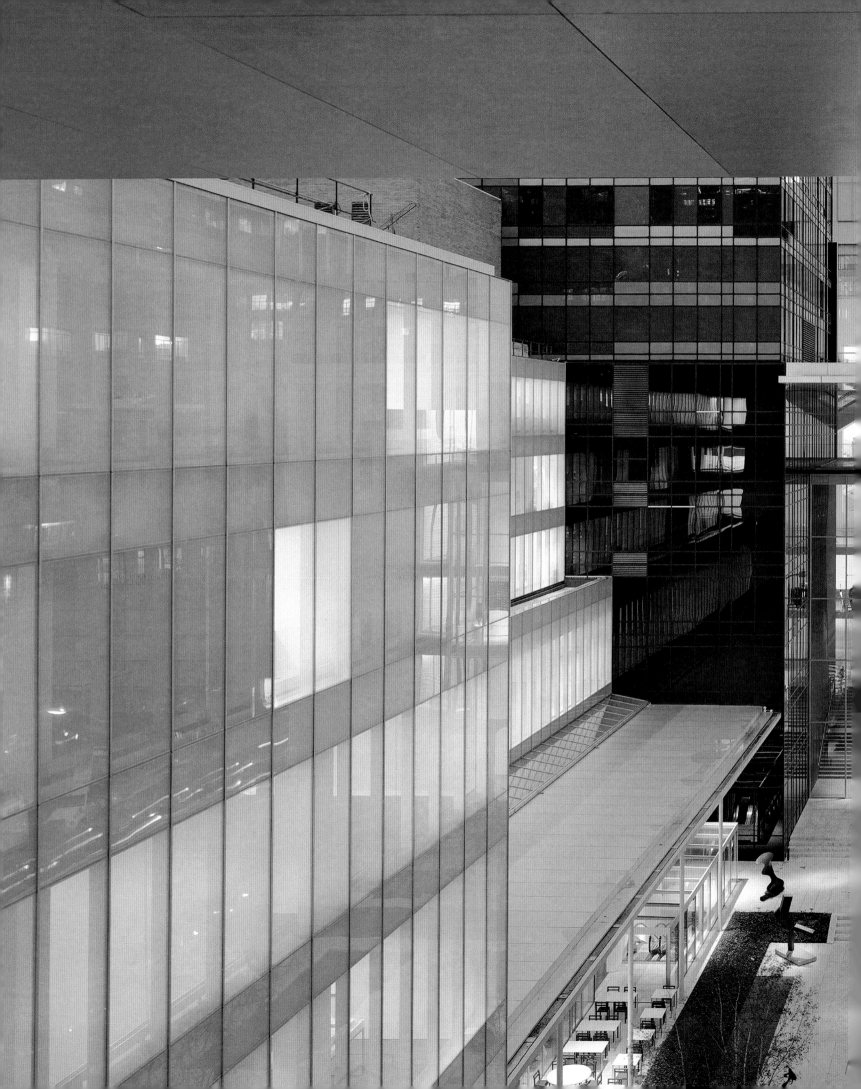

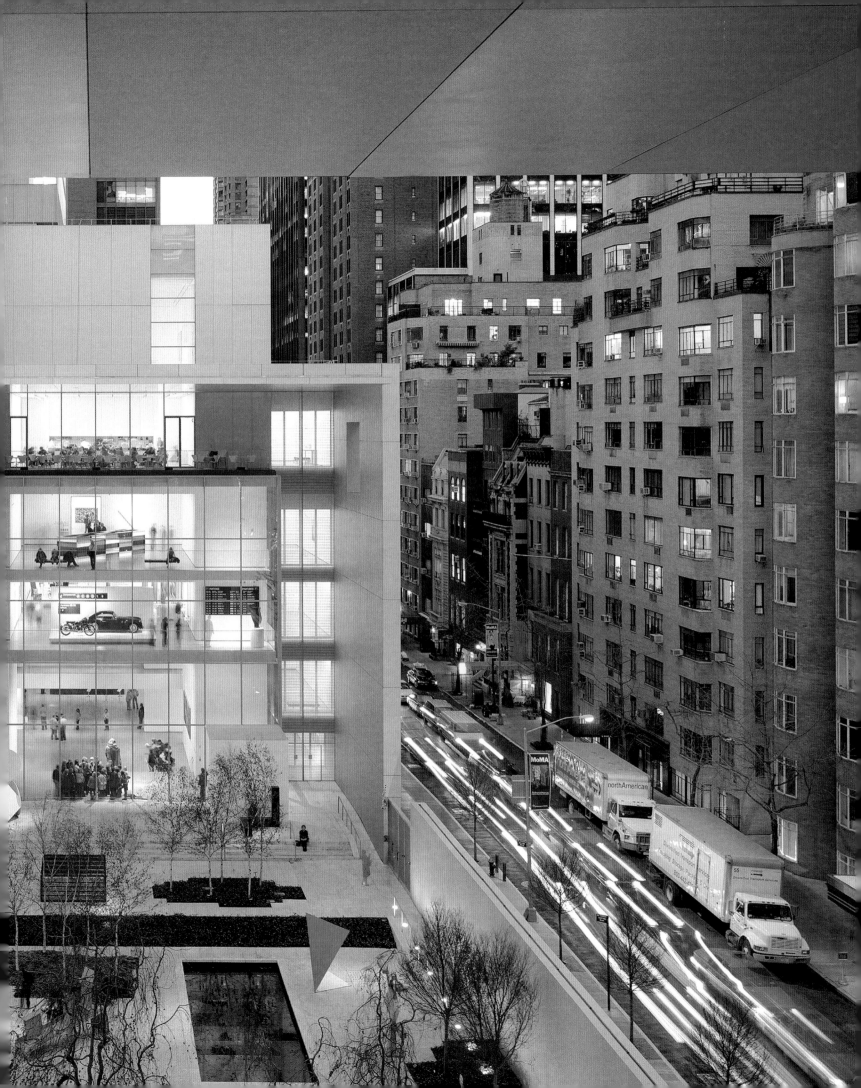

INTRODUCTION

Masterworks of Modern Art. From The Museum of Modern Art, New York presents 240 works chosen to offer a panoramic overview of the Museum's remarkable collection, now numbering over 100,000 works of art. From the Museum's founding, in 1929, it recognized that its ability to make available to the public the finest works of modern and contemporary art would be a unique and singularly important contribution not only to the cultural life of New York City but to the life of art around the world. With a determination that at times can border on the fanatical, the Museum has gone about developing and refining its collection to the point that today that collection is widely recognized as the finest of its kind in the world. The publication of *Masterworks of Modern Art* both reflects this achievement and happily coincides with the celebration of the Museum's seventy-fifth anniversary year. In anticipation of this event, The Museum of Modern Art underwent a $425 million expansion and renovation designed by Yoshio Taniguchi, one of Japan's foremost architects, that have produced virtually a new museum.

The Museum has also marked this important milestone in its history with the publication of a number of books on the collection, which, however, are principally dedicated to one or the other of the Museum's six curatorial departments: Architecture and Design, Drawings, Film and Media, Painting and Sculpture, Photography, and Prints and Illustrated Books. *Masterworks of Modern Art* represents an effort to look at the collection synthetically, or whole, in all its breadth and quality, much as it was conceived by the Museum's founding director, Alfred H. Barr, Jr. And unlike *Highlights*, the existing gallery guide, *Masterworks of Modern Art* is in a large format that creates the possibility of much richer illustrations, resulting in a book to be enjoyed for many years both for the lucidity of its essays and entries and for its visual quality.

What is The Museum of Modern Art? At first glance, this seems a relatively straightforward question. But the answer is neither simple nor straightforward, and any attempt to answer it almost immediately reveals a complex institution that, from its inception, has engendered a variety of meanings. For some, the Museum is a cherished place, a sanctuary in the heart of midtown Manhattan. For others, it is an idea represented by its collection and amplified by its exhibition program. For still others, the Museum is a laboratory of learning, a place where the most challenging and difficult art of our time can be measured against the achievements of the immediate past.

The Museum of Modern Art is, of course, all of this and more. Yet, in 1929, its founders dreamed, and its friends, trustees, and staff have dreamed since, that its multiple meanings and potential would ultimately be resolved into some final, fully formed equilibrium. In 1939, for instance, in his preface to the catalogue of the Museum's tenth anniversary exhibition, the Museum's president, A. Conger Goodyear, proudly proclaimed that the institution had finally reached maturity. As we now realize, in spite of the achievements of the Museum's initial years, he could not have anticipated the challenges to come. The Museum was still at the beginning of an adventure, an evolution that continues to unfold more than half a century later. At the age of ten the Museum was (and at more than seven times ten moves onward as) an exploratory enterprise whose parameters and possibilities remain open.

From small temporary quarters at 730 Fifth Avenue to its new building occupying most of a city block at 11 West 53 Street, from a single curatorial department to seven (six of which are collecting departments), and from a program without a permanent collection to a collection of over 100,000 objects, The Museum of Modern Art has grown, changed, and rethought itself on a regular basis. In doing so, it has undergone seven major architectural expansions and renovations since the completion of its first building in 1939—with its most recent expansion, designed by the celebrated Japanese architect Yoshio Taniguchi, finished in late 2004. This virtually continuous process of physical growth reflects the institution's ongoing efforts to honor its own changing programmatic and intellectual needs by constantly adjusting, and frequently rethinking, the topography of its space. Each evolution of the Museum has opened up the possibility for the next iteration of the institution, creating a kind of permanent self-renewing debate within The Museum of Modern Art about its future as well as its relationship to the past. With each change have come new expectations and challenges for the Museum, and this is especially true today as the Museum enters a new millennium.

The Museum of Modern Art is predicated on a relatively simple proposition, that the art of our time—modern art—is as vital and important as the art of the past. A corollary of this proposition is that the aesthetic and intellectual interests that shape modern art can be seen in mediums as different as painting and sculpture, film and media, photography, architecture and design, prints and illustrated books, and drawings—the current curatorial departments of the Museum.

From the outset, The Museum of Modern Art has been a laboratory for the study of the ways in which modernity has manifested itself in the visual arts. There has been, of course, and there will continue to be, a great deal of debate over what is actually meant by the term modern. Does it connote a moment in time, an idea, or a particular set of values? Whatever definition is favored, it seems clear that any discussion of the concept must take into account the role The Museum of Modern Art has played in attempting to define, by its selective focus and the intellectual arguments of its staff, a canon of modern and contemporary art. These efforts at definition have often been controversial, as the Museum has sought to navigate between the interests of the avant-garde, which it seeks to promote, and the general public, which it seeks to serve.

The story of how The Museum of Modern Art came to be so intimately associated with the history of modern art forms a rich narrative that, over time, has acquired the potency of a founding myth. Like all such myths, it is part truth and part fiction, built upon the reality of the Museum's unparalleled collection. Various accounts—from Russell Lynes's book of 1973, *Good Old Modern*, to the Museum's own volume of 1984, *The Museum of Modern Art, New York: The History and the Collection*—give the details of The Museum of Modern Art's story at length, and this is not the place to repeat or enlarge upon it. What is worth considering, however, is that seventy-five years after the Museum first opened its doors, many of those associated with the beginnings of the Museum—Abby Aldrich Rockefeller, a founding trustee; Alfred H. Barr, Jr.; Philip Johnson, who established the department of architecture and design; and Dorothy C. Miller, one of the Museum's first curators, to name only a few—remain vivid figures whose ideas and personalities continue to reverberate throughout the institution. This is true, in part, because there are still many people involved with the Museum who knew them, and have preserved and burnished their memories, but it is also because they are such fascinating figures, whose vision and drive gave birth to an institution that was the first, and rapidly became the foremost, museum of its kind in the world.

Given the resonance of this founding legacy, the challenge for The Museum of Modern Art today is to build upon this past without being delimited or constrained by it. This is by no means a simple task. To keep the Museum open to new ideas and new possibilities also means reevaluating and changing its perception of its past. As The Museum of Modern Art has become increasingly successful, established, and respected, its sense of responsibility to its own prior achievements has grown. In many ways, the Museum has become an agent implicated in the growth of the very tradition it seeks to explore and explicate: through its pioneering exhibitions, often based upon the Museum's permanent collection; its International Program, which has helped promote modern art around the world by circulating exhibitions to Europe, South America, and Asia; and through its acquisitions, publications, and public programs. Thus, it must constantly seek an appropriate critical distance, one that allows it to be an observer as well as the observed. While this distance may, in fact, be impossible to achieve fully, the effort to do so has resulted in a commitment to an intense internal debate, and an openness to sharing ideas with the public in a quest to promote an ever deeper engagement with modern art for the largest possible audience.

Any understanding of The Museum of Modern Art must begin with the recognition that the very idea of a museum of modern art implies an institution that is forever willing to take risks and court controversy. The challenge for the Museum is to periodically reinvent itself, to map new space, metaphorically as well as practically; to do this it must be its own severest critic. Programmed, therefore, into the Museum and its history—and by implication its future—are a series of contradictions and conflicts. These have often given rise to fierce divisions within, as well as outside, the Museum, over such diverse issues, for example, as the importance of abstract art, how to deal with the representation of alternative modernisms within the collection, and whether the Museum should continue to collect contemporary art. But, rather than resolve such divisions, the Museum has had the strength to live with them. This has insured that the Museum remains an extremely lively place, where issues and ideas are argued over with an often startling intellectual intensity.

Working within its current configuration of six curatorial departments that collect, the Museum has built an unparalleled collection of art that now spans more than 150 years, from the mid-nineteenth century to the present. Defined by their focus on different mediums, the curatorial departments reflect the Museum's interest in examining the various ways modern ideas and ideals have manifested themselves across different disciplines. While the roles of the departments were initially relatively fluid, during the late 1960s and 1970s they became more codified, as each department became responsible for developing its collection independently of the other departments.

This approach has enabled The Museum of Modern Art to study and organize the vast array of art that it owns. It has led, as well, to the layout of the Museum's galleries in recent times by department. But this fundamentally taxonomic approach has resulted, in many instances, in a relatively static reading of modern art by the Museum, with a clearly defined set of physical and conceptual paths through the collection. Over the last fifteen years, however, the Museum has become increasingly aware of the importance of interdisciplinary approaches to the presentation of its collection. The division of the galleries into discrete departmental spaces is gradually being balanced by a more synthetic and inclusive reading of the collection that complicates, rather than simplifies, relationships among works of art.

The growth of the Museum's collection has been steady and, at times, dramatic. The first works of art entered the Museum's collection in 1929, the year the Museum was established, and included Aristide Maillol's sculpture *Ile de France*. However, it was not until 1931, after founding trustee Lillie P. Bliss bequeathed to the Museum a superb group of 116 paintings, prints, and drawings, including Paul Cézanne's *The Bather*, *Pines and Rocks*, and *Still Life with Apples*, and Paul Gauguin's *The Moon and the Earth*, that the collection really began to develop. By 1940, the Museum's collection had grown to 2,590 objects, including 519 drawings, 1,466 prints, 436 photographs, 169 paintings, and 1,700 films. Twenty years later, the collection had expanded to over 12,000 objects, and by 1980 it exceeded 52,000. Today, the Museum owns over 6,000 drawings, 50,000 prints and illustrated books, 25,000 photographs, 3,200 paintings and sculptures, 24,000 works of architecture and design, and 20,000 films, videos, and other media works.

Many of the most important works of art in the collection entered the Museum during and immediately after World War II: among them are Pablo Picasso's *Les Demoiselles d'Avignon*, Henri Matisse's *Blue Window*, Vincent van Gogh's *The Starry Night*, and Piet Mondrian's *Broadway Boogie Woogie*. There were many reasons for this, but among the most important were the Nazis' selling of so-called degenerate art from state collections; the economic might of the United States, especially immediately after the end of the war; and the emigration of collectors and artists to the United States and elsewhere, as they sought refuge from the deprivations of the war. Having helped introduce an American audience to avant-garde European art throughout the 1930s, The Museum of Modern Art became a haven for art, artists, and collectors—all victims of Nazi persecution.

Collections, of course, are complex entities that grow and evolve in different ways. They are all the result, however, of discrete decisions made by individuals. In the case of The Museum of Modern Art, these decisions rest with the director and chief curators. In addition, each curatorial department has a working committee, authorized by the Board of Trustees, to act on its behalf in the acquisition process. Since the development of The Museum of Modern Art's collection, like that of most museums, has occurred over time, each generation's choices are woven into the fabric of the collection so that a continuous thread of ideas and interests emerges. The result of this reflects the unfolding pattern of the Museum's history in a highly nuanced collection that is inflected and altered by the particular tastes and ideas of individual directors and curators, and the responses those tastes and ideas engender in their successors, as holes are filled in the collection and areas of overemphasis are modified.

The vast majority of objects in The Museum of Modern Art's collection have been acquired as gifts and bequests, which are often the fruit of relationships nurtured through the years, from generous donors and friends. The Museum's trustees have played a particularly important role in this regard, and the recent bequests of Louise Reinhardt Smith and Florene May Schoenborn, and the gifts of David and Peggy Rockefeller, Philip Johnson, Elaine Dannheisser, Agnes Gund, Ronald S. Lauder, and the Woodner Family are among the most recent examples of a tradition that includes such extraordinary bequests as those of Lillie P. Bliss, William S. Paley, and Gordon Bunshaft. In addition, major gifts from such close friends of the Museum as Sidney and Harriet Janis, Mary Sisler, and Mr. and Mrs. John Hay Whitney, among many others, have also strengthened the collection.

The Museum also purchases works of art, and it occasionally deaccessions an object in order to refine and enhance its collection. Perhaps the most celebrated instance of this was the sale of an Edgar Degas, along with several other works from the Lillie P. Bliss bequest, which enabled the Museum to acquire Picasso's *Les Demoiselles d'Avignon*, one of the most important paintings of the twentieth century and a cornerstone of the Museum's collection. Deaccessioning also permitted the Museum to acquire, in 1989, van Gogh's *Portrait of Joseph Roulin*, as well as, in 1995, Gerhard Richter's celebrated group of fifteen works, *October 18, 1977*, and, in 2003, Jasper Johns's *Diver*, among other important works of art. The principal reason the Museum has the most comprehensive collection of modern art in the world is because from the outset it has accepted only unconditional gifts, with very few exceptions. This has allowed it periodically to reassess the relative importance of any work of art in its collection, but it has come at the price of occasionally seeing works of art go to other institutions (such as the Walter and Louise Arensberg Collection, which was given to the Philadelphia Museum of Art when The Museum of Modern Art was unable to accept the conditions imposed by the donors). Nevertheless, it has also provided The Museum of Modern Art with the ability to reconsider and revise its collection, allowing it to exist in what Alfred Barr would have called a metabolic state of self-renewal. An additional consequence of the Museum's policy concerning gifts is that the institution has been free to integrate works of art into its collection in an unrestricted way that has permitted development of a coherent and relatively unencumbered presentation of its collection, confined only by the limitations of its space.

Given that great collections are inevitably mosaics that shift and change over time, the cumulative result of individual tastes and idiosyncrasies, as well as the vagaries of historical opportunities, it is through the ordering and presentation of their collections that museums encode their ideas and narratives. This is especially true in the case of MoMA, as the collection is the principal means by which it argues for its reading of modern art, and in this sense Mr. Taniguchi's design for the new Museum is radical. Openness—physical as well as intellectual—and a sense of engagement with the full range of the collection lie at the heart of that design, so that while each department maintains separate galleries, there are also spaces that bring together works in different media, and the porosity of the overall layout allows for visual transitions and juxtapositions unpredicted by the traditional narratives of art history. Meanwhile strategically placed windows in the interior architecture allow views from one area to another, again allowing for relationships among the different media. The organization of *Masterworks of Modern Art* provides a similar experience, reproducing works from the full range of the Museum's collection in a finely calibrated layout that reveals the many rich associations inherent in the works of art that make up the Museum's collection.

Modern art began as a great experiment, and it continues to be one today. Much of the early effort of The Museum of Modern Art was given over to trying to make order out of the seemingly confused, and at times baffling, nature of this art. While these efforts helped to explain the complicated relationships among different movements and counter-movements (such as Cubism, Suprematism, Dada, Conceptual art, Minimalism, to name a few), they also, inadvertently, tended to simplify and reconcile competing and contradictory ideas. The positivist assertion of the first decades of the Museum's existence, that modern art forms a single, coherent narrative that can be reflected in the Museum's galleries, needs to be tempered by the recognition that the very ideas of modern and contemporary art imply the possibility of multiple, even contradictory, narratives. To a large degree, of course, the founders of the Museum were aware of the richness of this tradition, and their pioneering efforts initially embraced a broad range of interests, including tribal, naïve, and folk art. But the relatively limited space of the galleries and their linear configuration, compounded by their dramatic growth, inevitably led to a reductivist approach.

Today, contemporary artists challenge us in many of the same ways as artists of the avant-garde of forty years ago (many of whom are now regarded as modern masters) challenged viewers of their day. That we have come to accept the achievements of Picasso and Matisse, Mondrian and Jackson Pollock, does not necessarily mean that their work is either fully understood or that this acceptance is universal. For The Museum of Modern Art, this means that its collection must be a laboratory where the public can explore the relationship between contemporary art and the art of the immediate past, in an ongoing effort to continue to define modern art. By locating objects and people in time as well as space, the Museum is constantly mapping relationships between works of art and their viewers, so that the space of the Museum becomes a site of narration where many individual stories can be developed and realized. This process of experimentation and narration also allows us to create a dialogue between artists (and ideas) of the first years of the twentieth century and those of the century's final years. To do this successfully, the Museum is committed to developing new ways of understanding and presenting its collection. The publication of *Highlights*, whose multidisciplinary approach anticipates the structure of *Masterworks of Modern Art*, was one of the first steps in this process. Another was the Museum's yearlong project of three cycles of exhibitions presented in celebration of the millennium, from fall 1999 through early 2001, which examined its permanent collection in new ways that parallel many of the themes developed in this volume. The opening of the new Museum of Modern Art, in November 2004, with its expanded galleries and new layout, continues this process of exploring the richness and complexity of the Museum's diverse holdings.

This process of reconsidering our understanding of modern art has been realized with the completion of the Museum's new building. It has enabled the Museum to create numerous suites of galleries, allowing for a more layered presentation of the collection. This will both complicate and enrich the story of modern art. *Masterworks of Modern Art* may thus be taken as an initial chapter in that story and as both a record of the Museum's past and a statement in anticipation of an exciting future.

Glenn D. Lowry, Director, The Museum of Modern Art, New York

19th Century

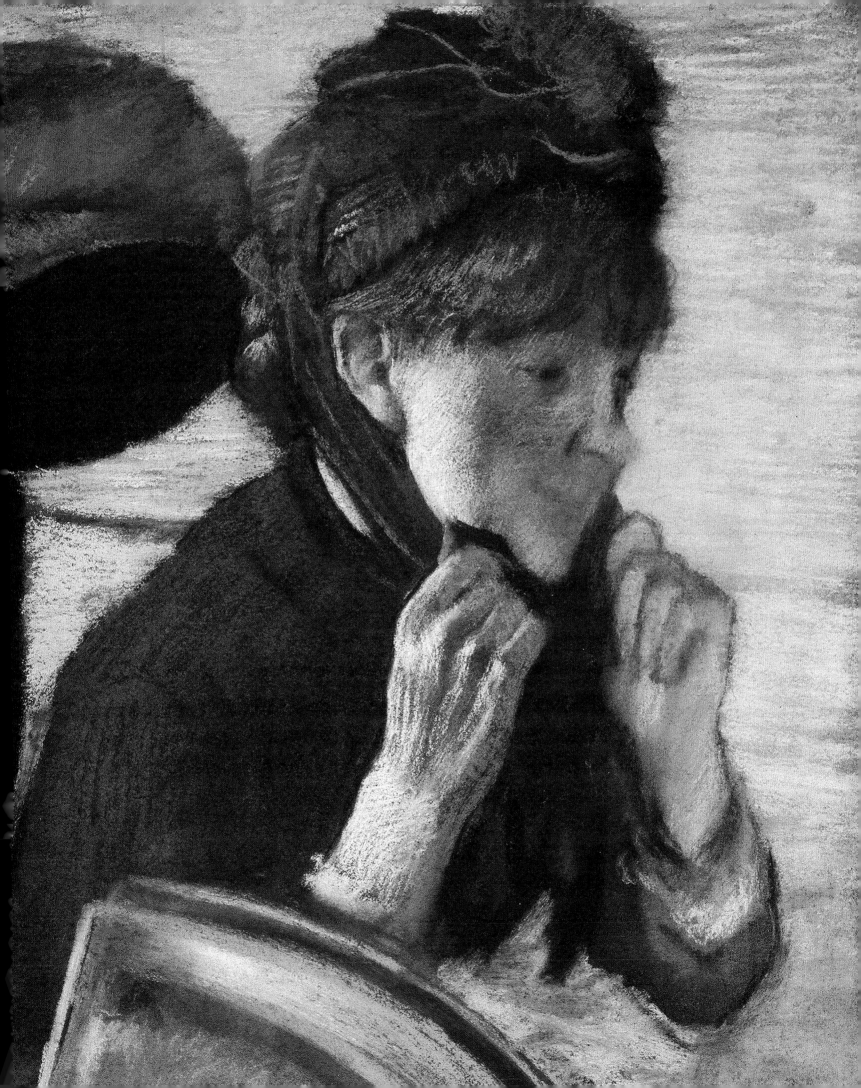

1845

Lace. 1845

Salted paper print, 6½ x 8¾" (16.5 x 22.3 cm)
Gift of Dr. Stefan Stein

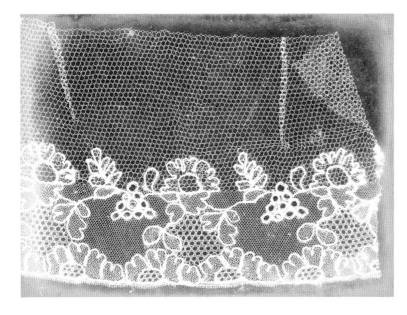

To make this picture, Talbot laid a piece of lace on chemically sensitized paper and allowed the light of the sun gradually to fix its negative image precisely, down to the smallest fold or imperfection. This simple operation had never been possible before photography was invented.

The invention was made public in January 1839, when France announced the daguerreotype as its gift to the world. Talbot, who independently had invented another form of photography several years earlier, then quickly stated his own claim. His process, in which any number of positive paper prints could be made from a single negative, soon triumphed over the daguerreotype process, which produced unique pictures on metal.

Talbot's *Lace* is not merely a copy of unprecedented ease and fidelity. It is also a picture, which transposed the lace from the realm of objects to the realm of pictures, where it has enjoyed a new and unpredictable life.

1880

Claret Pitcher. c. 1880

Glass, silverplate, and ebony, 16⅝ x 9¹⁵/₁₆ x 4" (42.2 x 25.2 x 10.2 cm)
Gift of Mrs. John D. Rockefeller, 3rd

The simple geometry of this elongated claret pitcher is characteristic of Dresser's designs, which stand in stark contrast to the heavily ornamented styles of his time. Dresser had studied Japanese decorative arts, which influenced his own designs and those of his more progressive contemporaries. In this pitcher, the long, vertical ebony handle is almost a direct quotation of the bamboo handles on Japanese vessels. As in many of his designs for metalwork, the fittings on the claret pitcher are made from electroplated metal, a technological innovation that made

silverware available to a growing middle class before the turn of the century. The exposed rivets and joints presage the enthusiasm for the machine aesthetic in industrial design of several decades later.

A trained botanist as well as a designer, Dresser was strongly inspired by the underlying structures of natural forms and by his interest in technological progress. While he shared some of the theories of the English Arts and Crafts movement, which sought to replace the often shoddy design of mass-produced goods with skilled handcraftsmanship, Dresser was completely committed to quality design for machine production, and is one of the world's first industrial designers.

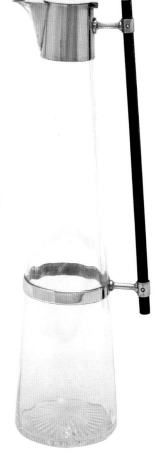

HILAIRE-GERMAIN-EDGAR DEGAS
FRENCH, 1834–1917

At the Milliner's. c. 1882
Pastel on paper, 27⅝ x 27¾" (70.2 x 70.5 cm)
Gift of Mrs. David M. Levy

This cameo of nineteenth-century life maintains its intimacy through Degas's use of pastel, whose chalky texture quiets the scene in multiple veils of color.

Pastel, an important drawing medium at the end of the nineteenth century due in part to a new preoccupation with color, appropriately expresses, through its inherent fragility, the ephemeral encounter between two women of different milieus that lies at the heart of Degas's composition.

Degas often accompanied his female friends to the dressmaker's and the milliner's. Here, one of them, the American artist Mary Cassatt, serves as the model and tries on hats while an attendant waits expectantly behind her. Cassatt's expression of contented self-assurance contrasts sharply with the apprehensive posture of the shopgirl, a figure obscured by cropping and the lack of delineation of her facial features.

In this daring nuanced composition about modern life—the subject is the fleeting encounter rather than the women themselves—Degas heeded the advice of the critic Edmond Duranty, who, in his 1876 pamphlet, *The New Painting*—about the art that came to be known as Impressionism—wrote: "Let us take leave of the stylized human body, which is treated like a vase. What we need is the characteristic modern person in his clothes, in the midst of his social surroundings, at home or out in the street."

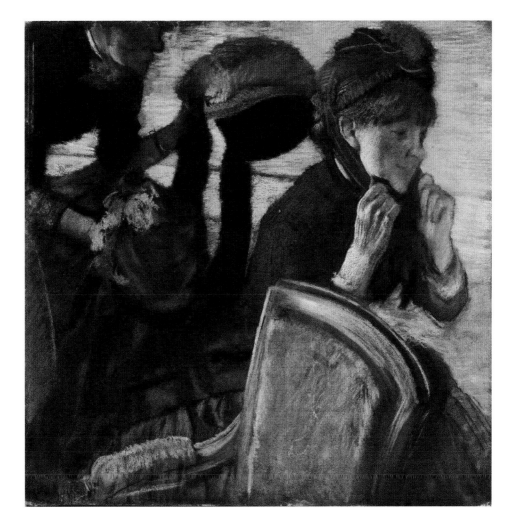

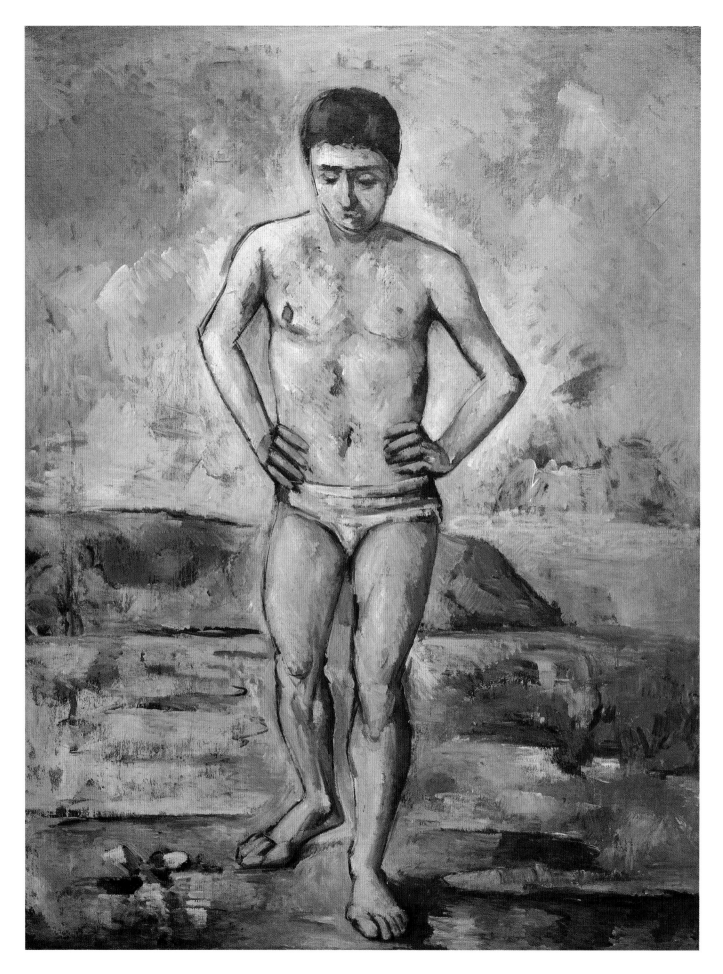

The Bather. c. 1885

Oil on canvas, 50 x 38⅛" (127 x 96.8 cm)
Lillie P. Bliss Collection

The Bather is one of Cézanne's most evocative paintings of the figure, although the unmuscled torso and arms have no heroic pretensions, and the drawing, in traditional, nineteenth-century terms, is awkward and imprecise. The bather's left, forward leg is placed firmly on the ground, but his right leg trails and carries no weight. The right side of his body is pulled higher than the left, the chin curves lopsidedly, and the right arm is elongated and oblique. The landscape is as bare as a desert, but its green, violet, and rose coloration refuses that name. Its dreaming expanse matches the bather's pensiveness. Likewise, the shadows on the body, rather than shifting to black, share the colors of the air, land, and water; and the brushwork throughout is a network of hatchmarks and dapples, restless yet extraordinarily refined. The figure moves toward us but does not meet our gaze.

These disturbances can be characterized as modern: they indicate that while Cézanne had an acute respect for much of traditional art, he did not represent the male nude the way the classical and Renaissance artists had done. He wanted to make an art that was "solid and durable like the art of the museums" but that also reflected a modern sensibility incorporating the new understanding of vision and light developed by the Impressionists. He wanted to make an art of his own time that rivaled the traditions of the past.

Evening, Honfleur. 1886

Oil on canvas, 25¾ x 32" (65.4 x 81.1 cm)
Gift of Mrs. David M. Levy

Seurat spent the summer of 1886 in the resort town of Honfleur, on the northern French coast, a region of turbulent seas and rugged shorelines to which artists had long been attracted. But Seurat's evening scene is hushed and still. Vast sky and tranquil sea bring a sense of spacious light to the picture, yet also have a peculiar visual density. Long lines of cloud echo the breakwaters on the beach—signs of human life and order.

Seurat had used his readings of optical theory to develop a systematic technique, known as pointillism, that involved the creation of form out of small dots of pure color. In the viewer's eye, these dots can both coalesce into shapes and remain separate particles, generating a magical shimmer. A contemporary critic described the light in *Evening, Honfleur* and related works as a "gray dust," as if the transparency of the sky were filled with, or even constituted by, barely visible matter—a sensitive response to the paint's movement between illusion and material substance, as the dots both merge to describe the scene and break into grains of pigment.

Seurat paints a frame around the scene—buffering a transition between the world of the painting and reality, and, at the upper right, the dots on the frame grow lighter, lengthening the rays of the setting sun.

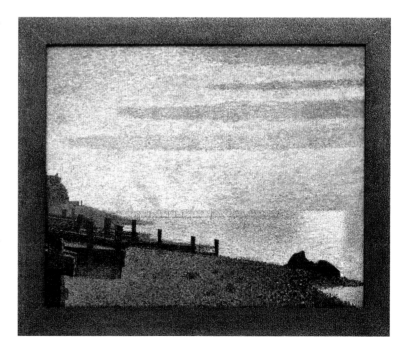

The Starry Night. 1889
Oil on canvas, 29 x 36¼" (73.7 x 92.1 cm)
Acquired through the Lillie P. Bliss Bequest

Van Gogh's night sky is a field of roiling energy. Below the exploding stars, the village is a place of quiet order. Connecting earth and sky is the flamelike cypress, a tree traditionally associated with graveyards and mourning. But death was not ominous for van Gogh. "Looking at the stars always makes me dream," he said, "Why, I ask myself, shouldn't the shining dots of the sky be as accessible as the black dots on the map of France? Just as we take the train to get to Tarascon or Rouen, we take death to reach a star."

The artist wrote of his experience to his brother Theo: "This morning I saw the country from my window a long time before sunrise, with nothing but the morning star, which looked very big." This morning star, or Venus, may be the large white star just left of center in *The Starry Night*. The hamlet, on the other hand, is invented, and the church spire evokes van Gogh's native land, the

Netherlands. The painting, like its daytime companion, *The Olive Trees*, is rooted in imagination and memory. Leaving behind the Impressionist doctrine of truth to nature in favor of restless feeling and intense color, as in this highly charged picture, van Gogh made his work a touchstone for all subsequent Expressionist painting.

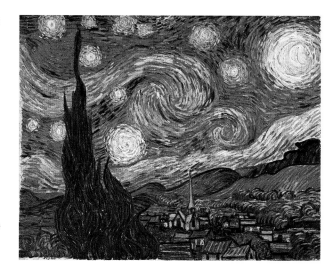

The Olive Trees. 1889
Oil on canvas, 28⅝ x 36" (72.6 x 91.4 cm)
Mrs. John Hay Whitney Bequest

In the blazing heat of this Mediterranean afternoon, nothing rests. Against a ground scored as if by some invisible torrent, intense green olive trees twist and crimp, capped by

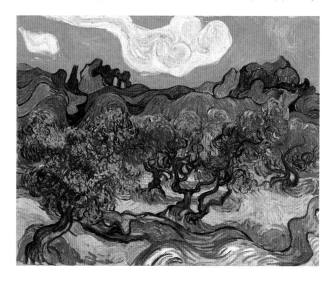

the rolling, dwindling hillocks of the distant Alps, beneath a light-washed sky with a bundled, ectoplasmic cloud.

After van Gogh voluntarily entered the asylum at Saint-Rémy in the south of France in the spring of 1889, he wrote his brother Theo: "I did a landscape with olive trees and also a new study of a starry sky." Later, when the pictures had dried, he sent both of them to Theo in Paris, noting: "The olive trees with the white cloud and the mountains behind, as well as the rise of the moon and the night effect, are exaggerations from the point of view of the general arrangement; the outlines are accentuated as in some old woodcuts."

Van Gogh's letters make it clear that he created this particular intense vista of the southern French landscape as a daylight partner to the visionary nocturne of his more famous canvas, *The Starry Night*. He felt that both pictures showed, in complementary ways, the principles he shared with his fellow painter Paul Gauguin, regarding the freedom of the artist to go beyond "the photographic and silly perfection of some painters" and intensify the experience of color and linear rhythms.

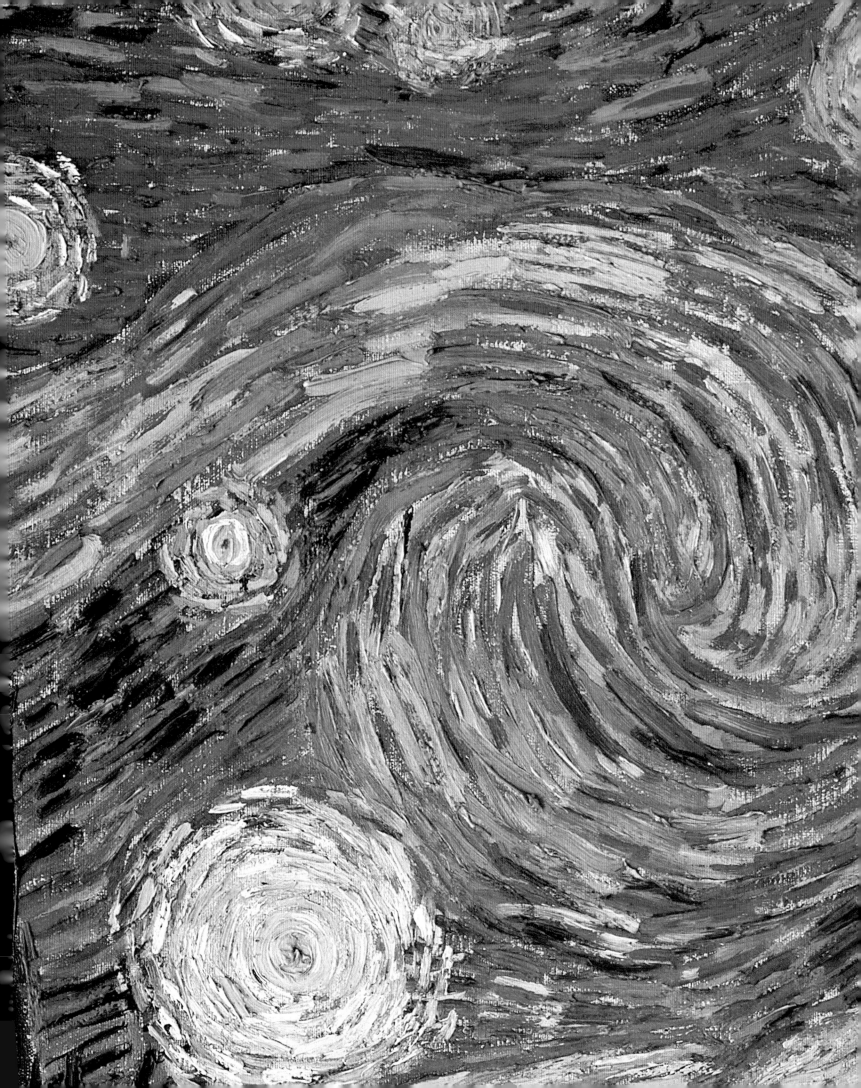

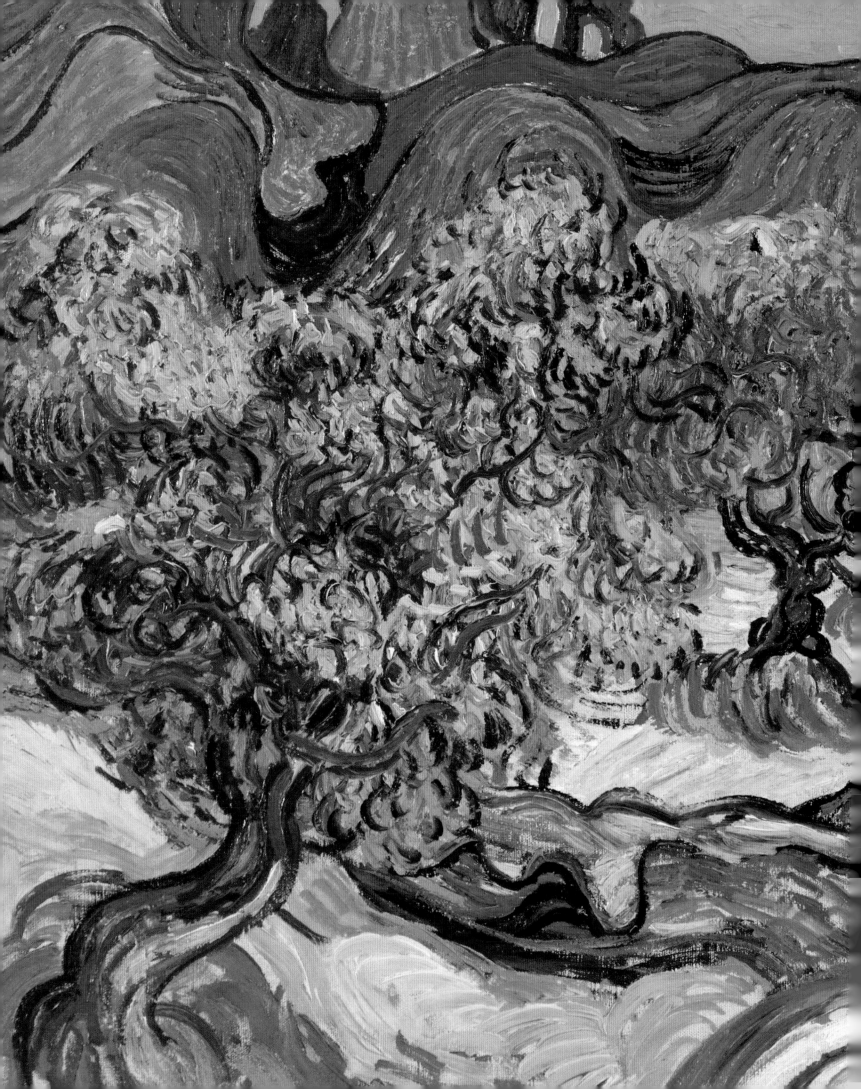

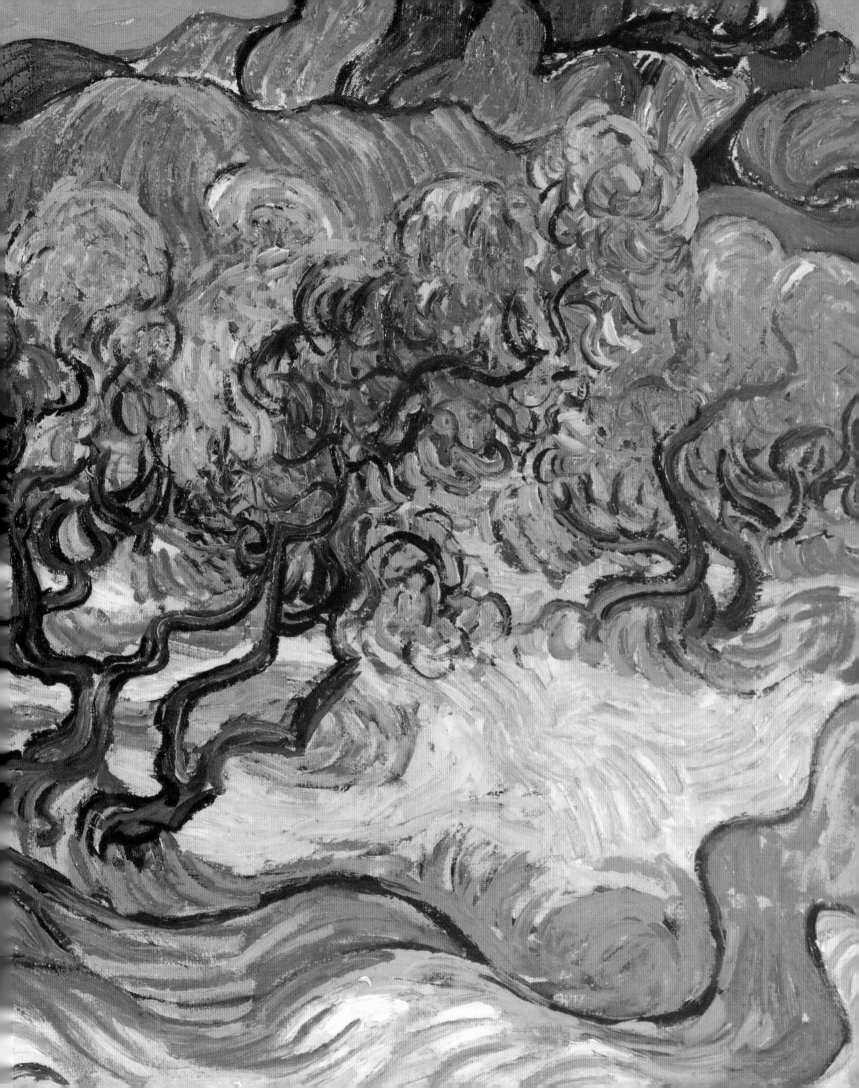

PAUL GAUGUIN FRENCH, 1848–1903

The Seed of the Areoi
(Te aa no areois). 1892
Oil on burlap, 36¼ x 28⅜" (92.1 x 72.1 cm)
The William S. Paley Collection

The Polynesian goddess sits on a blue-and-white cloth. Gauguin's style fuses various non-European sources: ancient Egyptian (in the hieratic pose), Japanese (in the relative absence of shadow and modeling, and in the areas of flat color), and Javanese (in the position of the arms, influenced by a relief in the temple of Borobudur). But there are also signs of the West, specifically through aspects of the pose derived from a work by the French Symbolist painter Pierre Puvis de Chavannes. The color, too, is eclectic: although Gauguin claimed to have found his palette in the Tahitian landscape, the exquisite chromatic chords in *The Seed of the Areoi* owe more to his compositional eye than to the island's visual realities.

In the origin myth of the Areoi, a Polynesian secret society, a male sun god mates with the most beautiful of all women, Vaïraümati, to found a new race. By painting his Tahitian mistress Tehura as Vaïraümati, Gauguin implied a continuity between the island's past and its life during his own stay there. In fact, Tahiti had been profoundly altered by colonialism (the Areoi society itself had disappeared), but Gauguin's anachronistic vision of the place gave him an ideal model for his painting. This vision was particularly powerful for him in its contrast with the West, which, he believed, had fallen into "a state of decay."

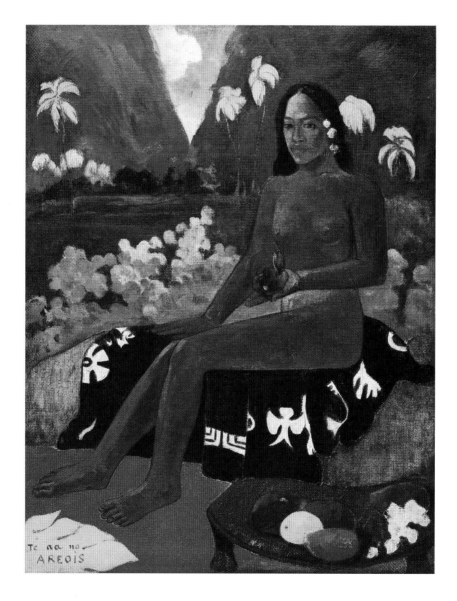

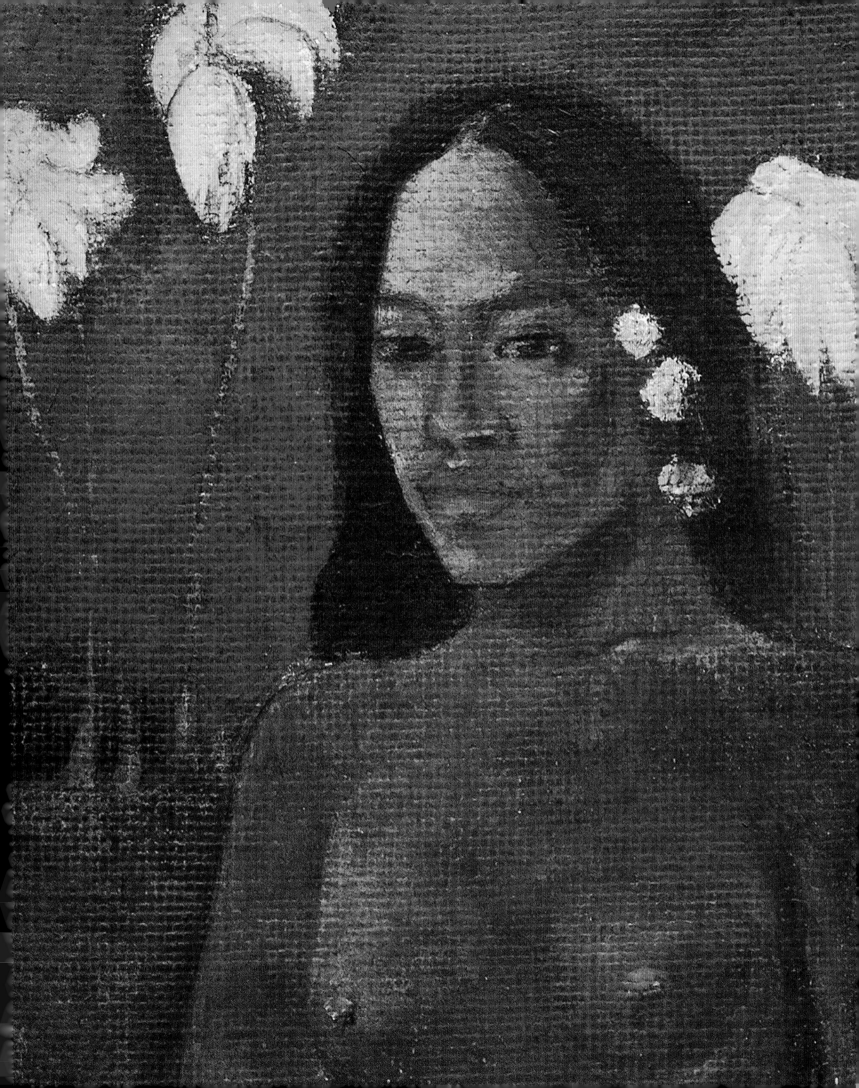

ÉTIENNE-JULES MAREY FRENCH, 1830–1904
or GEORGES DEMENŸ FRENCH, 1850–1917

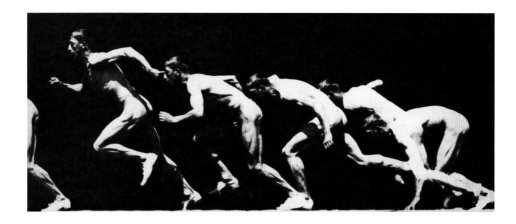

Untitled. c. 1890–1900
Gelatin silver print, 6^1/$_{16}$ x 14^5/$_8$" (15.4 x 37.2 cm)
Gift of Paul F. Walter

Marey, a physiologist, had been studying motion for two decades when the work of the American photographer Eadweard Muybridge led him to try photography in 1881. Unlike Muybridge, who used a battery of cameras to make a sequence of separate frames (like the frames in a movie), Marey recorded the successive phases of motion on single plate. Thus, his studies at once analyze motion and present a virtual image of its course.

Photography has radically enhanced our ability to study the world around us (and the skies beyond) by making visible what once had been too distant, too small, too fast, or otherwise too difficult to see. Many such pictures were made in the service of science, but their impact often has been much broader than their original scientific function. The influence of Marey's pictures on the Futurist painters, such as Giacomo Balla and Gino Severini, who sought to evoke dynamic motion in their work, is only the most familiar example.

Demenÿ worked as Marey's assistant from 1881 to 1893 and then applied Marey's method to the physical training program of the French army. This picture, whose successive exposures were timed to match the strides of the runner, may have been made by him.

HENRI DE TOULOUSE-LAUTREC FRENCH, 1864–1901

Divan Japonais. 1893
Lithographed poster, comp.: 31^5/$_8$ x 23^7/$_8$"
(80.3 x 60.7 cm)
Publisher: Édouard Fournier, Paris
Abby Aldrich Rockefeller Fund

The Divan Japonais, a cabaret in Montmartre, an artists' quarter in Paris, was newly redecorated in 1893 with fashionable Japanese motifs and lanterns. Its owner, Édouard Fournier, commissioned this poster—depicting singers, dancers, and patrons—from Toulouse-Lautrec to attract customers to the opening of his nightclub. In the immediate foreground, Toulouse-Lautrec depicts two of his good friends in the audience: on the right, Édouard Dujardin, an art critic and founder of the literary journal *Revue wagnérienne*, and, at the center, the famous cancan dancer Jane Avril, whose elegant black silhouette dominates the scene. In the background, another well-known entertainer of the period, the singer Yvette Guilbert, performs on stage. Although her head is abruptly cropped in this composition—reflecting the influence of photography and Japanese prints—Guilbert was immediately known to contemporary patrons by the dramatic gesture of her signature long black gloves.

Lithographed posters proliferated during the 1890s due to technical advances in color printing and the relaxation of laws restricting the placement of posters. Dance halls, *café-concerts*, and festive street life invigorated nighttime activities. Toulouse-Lautrec's brilliant posters, made as advertisements, captured the vibrant appeal of the prosperous *Belle Époque*.

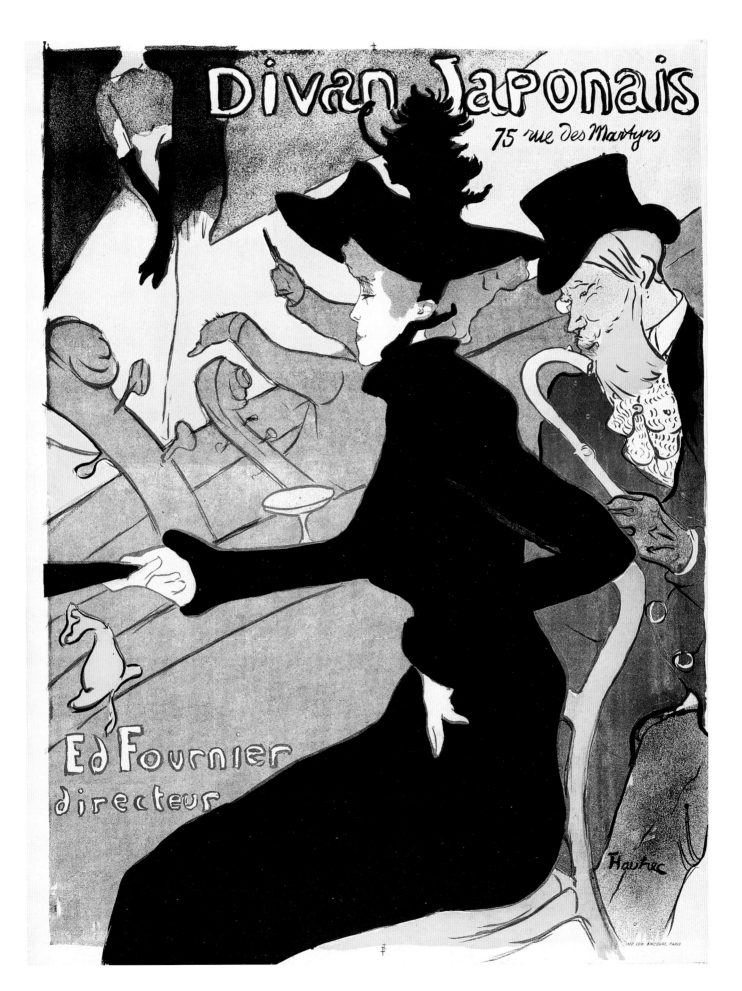

1893

The Storm. 1893

Oil on canvas, 36¹/₈ x 51¹/₂" (91.8 x 130.8 cm)
Gift of Mr. and Mrs. H. Irgens Larsen and
acquired through the Lillie P. Bliss and Abby
Aldrich Rockefeller Funds

Munch painted *The Storm* in
Aasgaardstrand, a small Norwegian seaside
resort where he often stayed. There had
indeed been a violent storm there that
summer, but the painting does not appear to
show it, or even its physical aftermath; the
storm here is an inner one, a psychic
distress. Standing near the water, in an eerie
blue half-light, half-dark Scandinavian
summer night, a young woman clasps her
hands to her head. Other women, standing
apart from her, make the same anguished
gesture—to what end we are not sure.
The circle in which they stand, and the

protagonist's white dress, give to the scene
the feeling of some ancient pagan ritual,
even while the solid house in the
background, its lit windows shining in the
dark, suggests some more regular life from
which these women are excluded—or
perhaps that they find intolerable.

Munch's art suggests a transformation of
personal memories and emotions into a
realm of dream, myth, and enigma. His
exposure to French Symbolist poetry during
a stay in Paris had convinced him of the
necessity for a more subjective art; there
was no need, he said, for more paintings
of "people who read and women who knit."
Associated with the international
development of Symbolism in the 1890s,
he is also recognized as a precursor of
Expressionism.

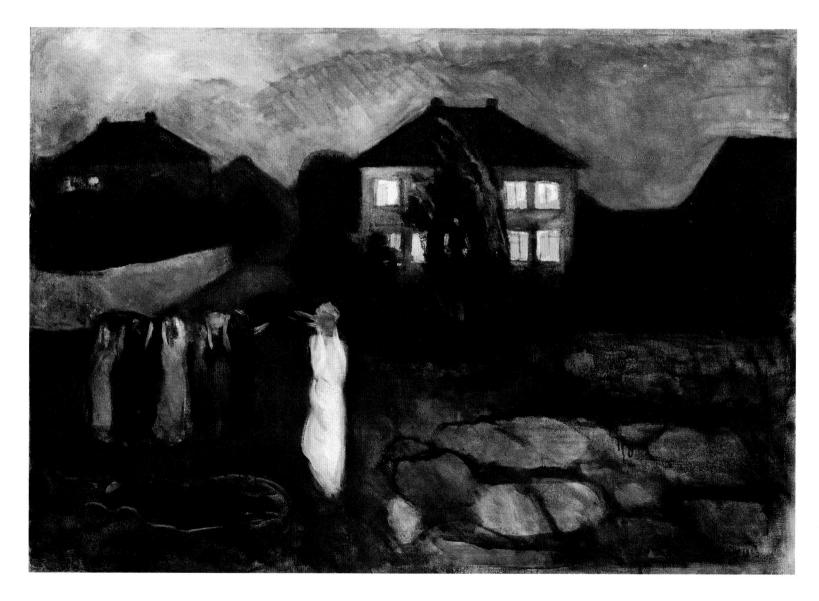

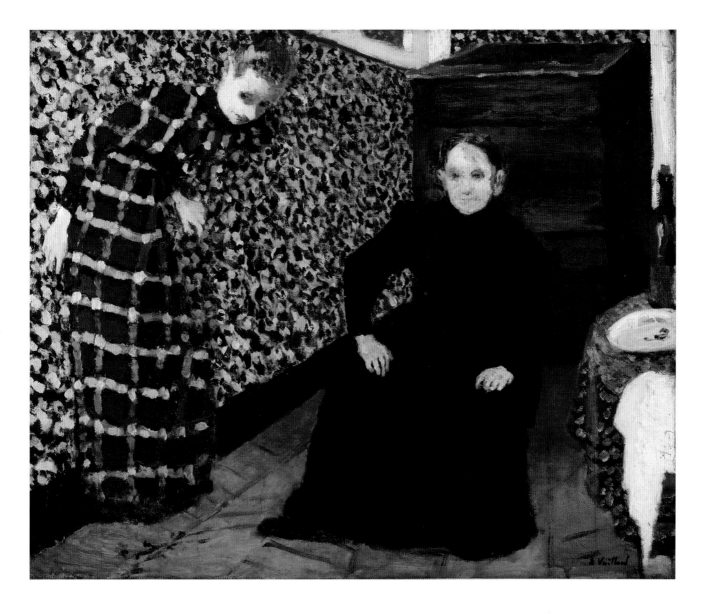

Mother and Sister of the Artist. c. 1893
Oil on canvas, 18¼ x 22¼" (46.3 x 56.5 cm)
Gift of Mrs. Saidie A. May

In this painting, Vuillard's mother and sister are depicted at home. A widow who had supported her family by running her own business, his mother commands a powerful presence. Her pose is solid and stable, her dress is the painting's largest unbroken form, and her face and hands stand out against browns and blacks, and against the extraordinary trapezoid of mottled color that describes the room's wallpaper. Her daughter, by contrast, almost disintegrates into this surface, as if its dots had temporarily organized themselves into the checkered pattern of her dress. Pressing herself awkwardly against the wall, she bends her head and shoulders, apparently greeting a

visitor but also, it seems, forced to bow if she is to fit in the picture's frame.

Intimate in scale, this scene is deceptively casual. Relying on imaginative insight as well as on the direct observation prized by the Impressionists, Vuillard constructs a psychologically suggestive space: the table, the bulky chest of drawers, the overactive wallpaper, and the steeply rising perspective of the floor make a crowded container for the figures, and the claustrophobia this suggests is heightened by slightly leaning angles, an imperfectly centered composition, and the daughter's off-balance posture. The whole space seems apt to fall inward at Mme. Vuillard—a dominating, even oppressive force in the room (and, we suspect, in the family); she is also the gravitational principle that prevents a collapse.

PAUL GAUGUIN FRENCH, 1848–1903

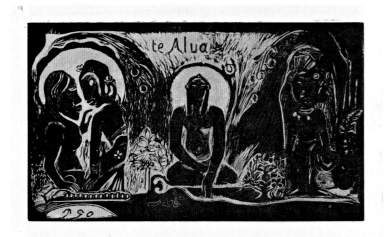

The Gods (Te Atua)
from the series **Noa Noa**. 1893–94
Woodcut, comp.: 8 x 13⁷/₈" (20.5 x 35.2 cm)
Publisher: the artist. Edition: proof before
edition of 35
Gift of Abby Aldrich Rockefeller

The imposing idols seen here reflect the
figural style of Oceanic sculptures that
Gauguin had seen during his travels. To

create these prints, the artist first cut his
composition into a block of hard wood,
delineating the figures with abrupt, gouged
lines. Then he selectively inked and wiped
the block before printing the image on a
sheet of paper. The dark and mysterious
areas of the composition create an aura of
the exotic and the spiritual.

The Gods (Te Atua) is one of ten woodcuts
executed by Gauguin after his return to Paris
from Tahiti in 1893. They were intended as
illustrations to a text that he planned to
publish about his experiences in the South
Seas. With this book, which he titled *Noa
Noa* (the Tahitian word for fragrance), he
hoped to provide a background for the
public's understanding of his new Symbolist
paintings.

Gauguin had left for Tahiti in 1891 to escape
the pressures of modern-day life and to seek
an unspoiled society in tune with nature. There
he painted a number of important canvases
inspired by his Tahitian experiences. He made
his second trip to the South Seas in 1894;
but the *Noa Noa* project was never realized
as the book he had planned. He died in the
Marquesas Islands in 1903.

EDVARD MUNCH NORWEGIAN, 1863–1944

Madonna. 1895–1902
Lithograph and woodcut, comp.: 23³/₄ x 17¹/₂"
(60.5 x 44.5 cm)
Publisher: the artist. Edition: approx. 250
The William B. Jaffe and Evelyn A. J. Hall
Collection

Alluring and inviting, disturbing and
threatening, Munch's *Madonna* is above all
mysterious. This erotic nude appears to float
in a dreamlike space, with swirling strokes of
deep black almost enveloping her. An odd-
looking, small fetuslike figure or just-born infant
hovers at the lower left with crossed skeletal
arms and huge frightened eyes. Forms
resembling sperm pervade the surrounding
border of this print. Little about the Madonna
seems to conform to her holy title, save for a
narrow dark gold band atop her head. This

haunting apparition reflects Munch's alliance
with Symbolist artists and writers.

Woman, in varying roles from mother-
protector to sexual partner to devouring
vampire and harbinger of death, serves as
the chief protagonist in a series of paintings
and corresponding prints about love, anxiety,
and death that Munch grouped together
under enigmatic headings. Madonna was
first executed as a black-and-white
lithograph in 1895. During the next seven
years, Munch hand-colored several
impressions. Finally, the image was revised in
1902, using additional lithographic stones for
color and a woodblock for the textured blue
sky. Self-trained in printmaking, Munch often
used its mediums in experimental ways, such
as the unusual composition of woodcut and
lithography seen here.

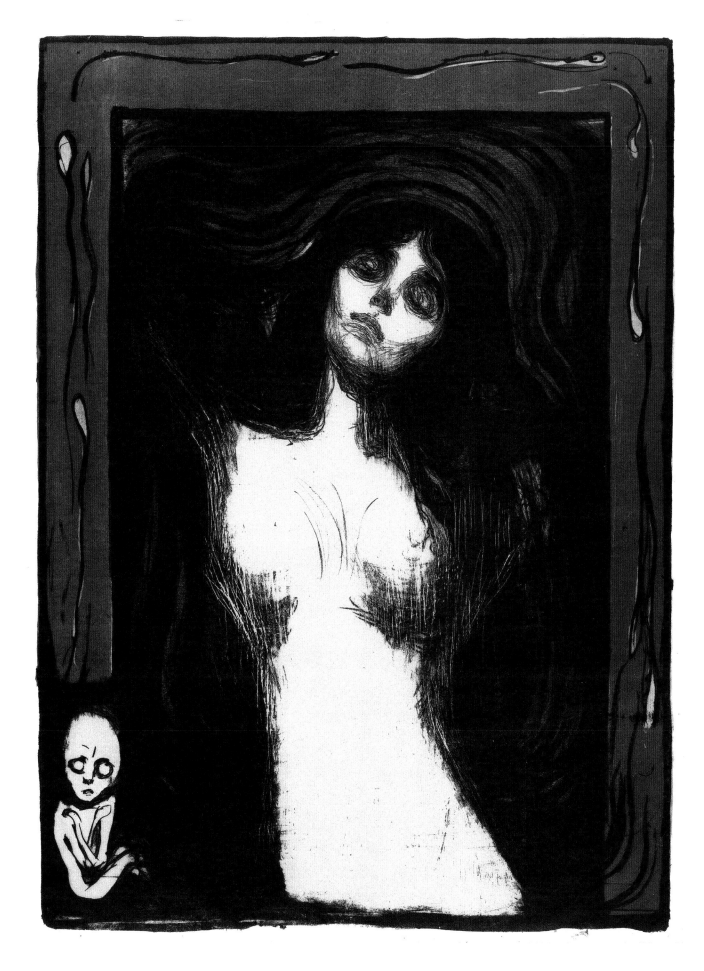

1895

Child's Cradle. c. 1895
Ebonized bentwood, 6' 8¹/₄" x 56¹/₄" x 25⁷/₁₆"
(203.8 x 142.9 x 64.6 cm)
Manufacturer: J. & J. Kohn, Austria
Gift of Barry Friedman

This elaborate bentwood cradle was lined
with thick cushions to create a soft,
sheltered, egg-shaped bed for an infant.
The sinuous and sensual design, with the
elegant, curved forms of the cradle and the
long vertical arm that supported draped
netting, reflects the popular Art Nouveau
style of the time. Such cradles could be
found in stylish, bourgeois homes all over
Europe.

Bentwood designs became ubiquitous as
seating for cafés and gardens and later as
elaborate, upholstered domestic furnishings.
Inexpensive, durable, light, and ideal for
export because components could be
assembled after shipping, pieces such as

J. & J. Kohn's cradle became perfect
symbols of the new industrial age. The
bentwood process had been developed by
the German designer Michael Thonet in the
mid-nineteenth century in order to make
appealing functional furniture efficiently and
economically. In 1867 the manufacturer
J. & J. Kohn became
Thonet's chief
competitor, opening
factories in several
international
locations.

Bentwood furniture was made by
steaming lengths of wood and then
bending them and placing them in
metal molds to dry. The resulting
standardized sections were assembled
with hardware instead of the traditional
hand-carved joints. The idea of
standardized elements revolutionized the
principles of furniture production.

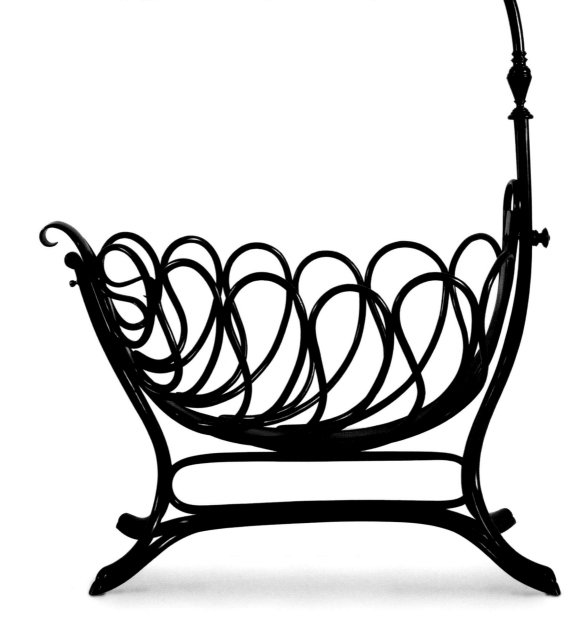

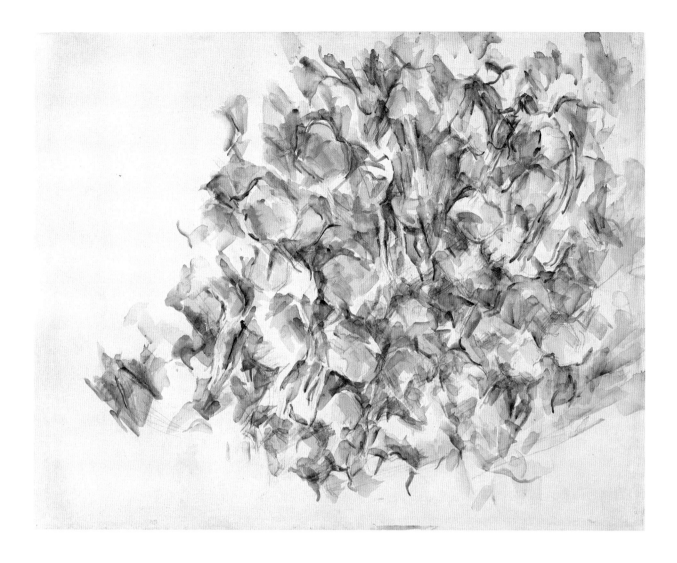

Foliage. 1895–1900
Watercolor and pencil on paper, 17⁵/₈ x 22³/₈"
(44.8 x 56.8 cm)
Lillie P. Bliss Collection

At first glance, this work might strike the
viewer as unfinished, given the blank areas
left on the paper. But Cézanne meant *Foliage*
to be a study in color and line depicting the
rhythms of rustling leaves, which appear to
move across the page. His brushstrokes
deliver deposits of pigment that create the
illusion of light and shadow. Nature is evoked
in the lightness and transparency of the
medium, in the placement of the subject, and
in the inferred movement.

Cézanne's late watercolors, of which this is
a superb example, "are acts of construction
in color." Here he applied discrete unblended
lines and patches of color around lightly
sketched pencil contours and built depth
from color by translating dark-light
gradations into cool-warm ones. In this
mosaic, colored lines and planes and
overlapping shades together fix the depth of
the subject to the surface of the paper—the
white surface that is the final arbiter of
pictorial coherence.

In this way Cézanne redefined modern
drawing according to color "modulation," his
term for that which enabled him not only to
capture the light of southern France, where
he lived and worked, but also to approach
abstraction.

1896

Death Chasing the Flock of Mortals.

1896

Drypoint and etching, plate: 9⁷/₁₆ x 7³/₁₆"
(23.9 x 18.2 cm)
Publisher: the artist
Purchase Fund

A large skeletal flying figure of Death with reptilelike feet brandishes an enormous, menacing scythe over the swarming mob of people jamming the streets below. The figures, most of whom are portrayed only by grimacing masklike faces, flee the oncoming catastrophe. In the building at the right we glimpse a nude woman toasting her companions— a hint of the debauchery, cruelty, and indifference that Ensor perceived in society. Overhead a radiating sun, centered between winged, haloed beings and frightened figures engulfed in flames, suggests heaven, hell, and the Day of Judgment.

Ensor's nightmarish, satiric visions, which reveal a preoccupation with the macabre and with death, were influenced by earlier Flemish art of the fifteenth and sixteenth centuries, specifically that of Hieronymus Bosch and Pieter Bruegel. Ensor's obsession with death and impermanence led him to printmaking. As he stated, "I dread the fragility of painting. I want to survive and I think of solid copper plates, of unalterable inks ... of faithful printing, and I am adopting etching as a means of expression." Indeed, between 1886 and 1905 Ensor was a prolific printmaker, who executed 134 prints.

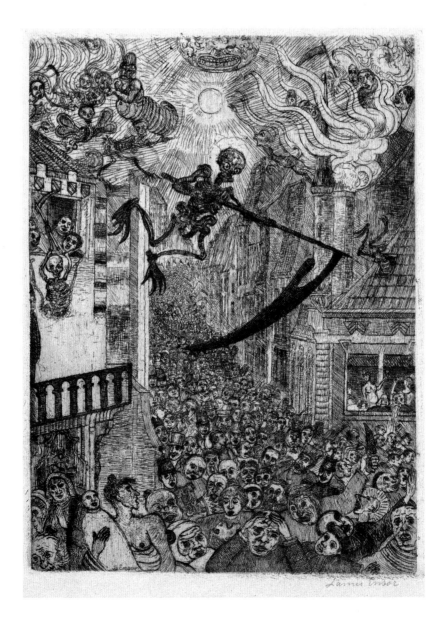

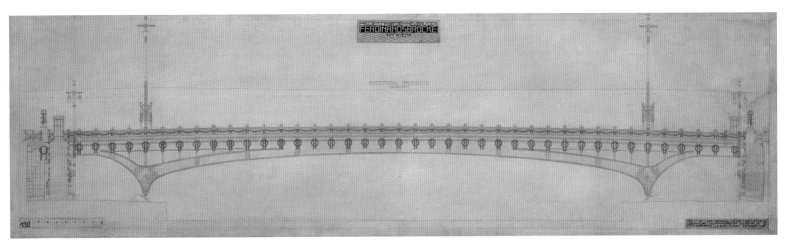

Ferdinandsbrücke, Vienna.
Preliminary version, c. 1896
Elevation: ink on paper with collaged text,
19¹⁄₈ x 66¹⁄₂" (48.6 x 168.9 cm)
Promised gift of Jo Carole and Ronald S. Lauder

In 1895 Otto Wagner, the leading Viennese architect of his time, declared: "The only possible point of departure for our artistic creation is modern life." As shown in this drawing, Wagner's design for the Ferdinandsbrücke, a bridge named in honor of Archduke Francis Ferdinand, is one of his frankest expressions of the techniques of modern engineering. The bridge's steel truss spans the Danube Canal in a low, broad arch. Decorating the naked steel structure are imperial emblems—coats of arms, wreaths, and garlands—particularly appropriate for Vienna, which was the capital of the Austro-Hungarian empire at the turn of the century.

Wagner argued for simplicity and a new "realist" style, which implied that designers should use modern materials and clear methods of construction. He gave shape to his ideas in the many buildings and projects he designed in Vienna, as the city expanded outside its medieval boundaries. Although the Ferdinandsbrücke was not built according to his design, Wagner's prolific output and progressive ideas influenced an entire generation and firmly established him as one of the forefathers of modern architecture.

The Sleeping Gypsy. 1897
Oil on canvas, 51" x 6' 7" (129.5 x 200.7 cm)
Gift of Mrs. Simon Guggenheim

As a musician, the gypsy in this painting is an artist; as a traveler, she has no clear social place. Lost in the self-absorption that is deep, dreaming sleep, she is dangerously vulnerable—yet the lion is calmed and entranced.

The *Sleeping Gypsy* is formally exacting—its contours precise, its color crystalline, its lines, surfaces, and accents carefully rhymed. Rousseau plays delicately with light on the lion's body. A letter of his describes the painting's subject: "A wandering Negress, a mandolin player, lies with her jar beside her (a vase with drinking water), overcome by fatigue in a deep sleep. A lion chances to pass by, picks up her scent yet does not devour her. There is a moonlight effect, very poetic. The scene is set in a completely arid desert. The gypsy is dressed in oriental costume."

A sometime *douanier* (toll collector) for the city of Paris, Rousseau was a self-taught painter, whose work seemed entirely unsophisticated to most of its early viewers. Much in his art, however, found modernist echoes: the flattened shapes and perspectives, the freedom of color and style, the subordination of realistic description to imagination and invention. As a consequence, critics and artists appreciated Rousseau long before the general public did. (See illustration on pages 50-51)

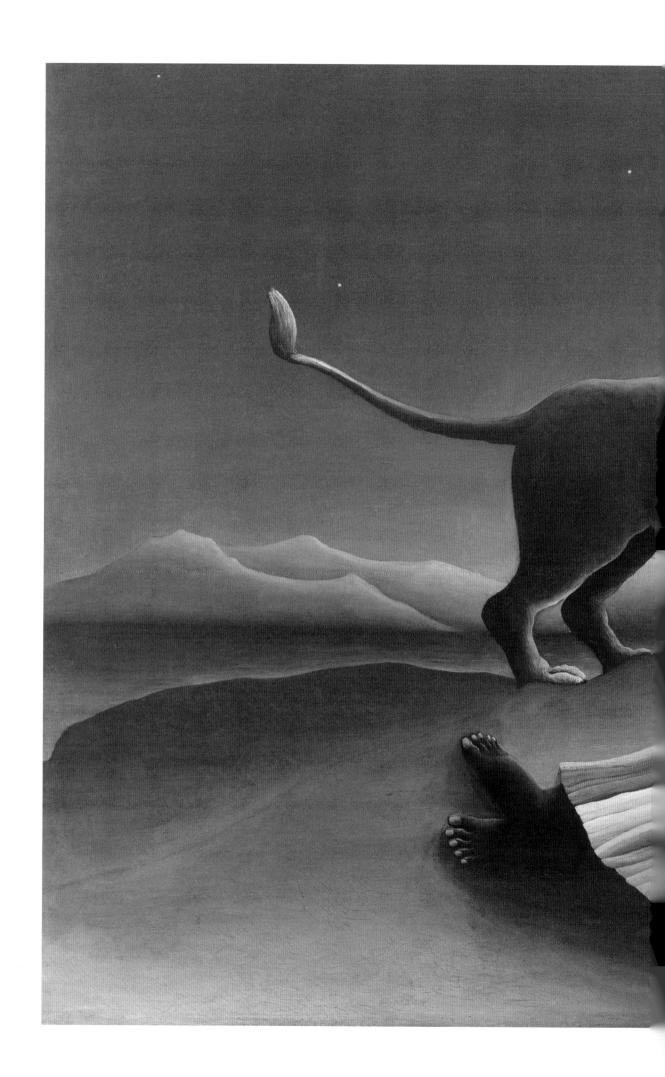

Henri Rousseau,
The Sleeping Gypsy
(see entry on page 49)

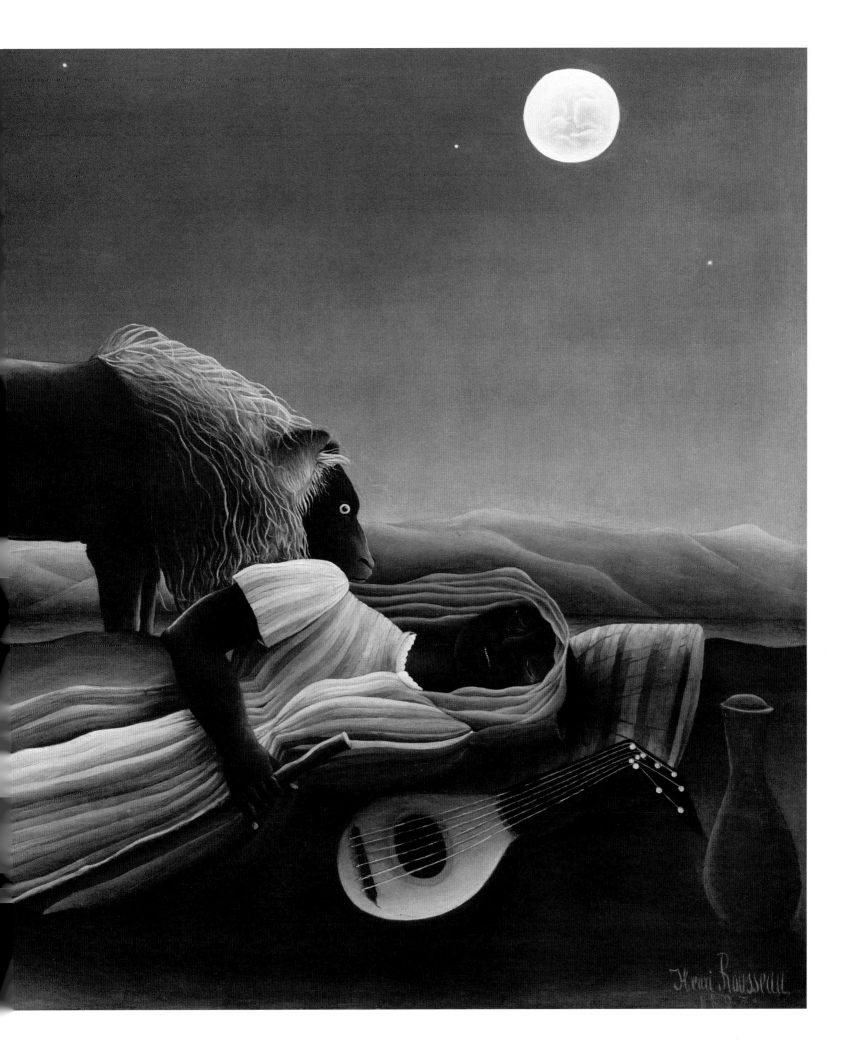

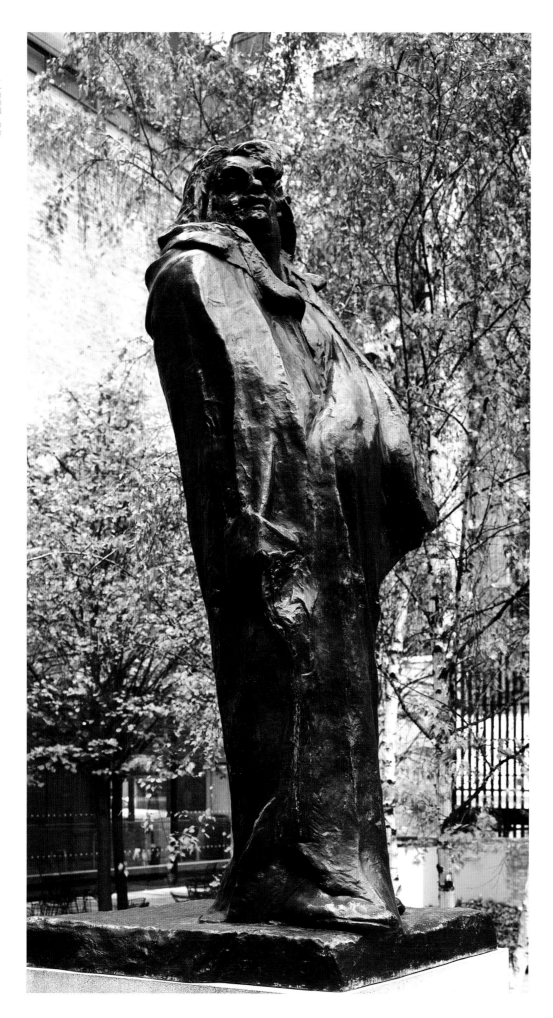

AUGUSTE RODIN
FRENCH, 1840–1917

Monument to Balzac. 1897–98
Bronze (cast 1954), 9' 3" x 48¹/₄" x 41"
(282 x 122.5 x 104.2 cm)
Presented in memory of Curt Valentin
by his friends

Commissioned to honor one of France's
greatest novelists, Rodin spent seven years
preparing for *Monument to Balzac*, studying
the writer's life and work, posing models who
resembled him, and ordering clothes to his
measurements. Ultimately, though, Rodin's
aim was less Honoré de Balzac's physical
likeness than an idea or spirit of the man, and
a sense of his creative vitality: "I think of his
intense labor, of the difficulty of his life, of his
incessant battles and of his great courage. I
would express all that."

Several studies for the work are nudes, but
Rodin finally clothed the figure in a robe
inspired by the dressing gown that Balzac
often wore when writing. (He liked to work at
night.) The effect is to make the figure a
monolith, a single, phallic, upward-thrusting
form crowned by the craggy ridges and
cavities that define the head and face.
Monument to Balzac is a visual metaphor for
the author's energy and genius, yet when the
plaster original was exhibited in Paris in
1898, it was widely attacked. Critics likened it
to a sack of coal, a snowman, a seal, and the
literary society that had commissioned the
work dismissed it as a "crude sketch." Rodin
retired the plaster model to his home in the
Paris suburbs. It was not cast in bronze until
years after his death.

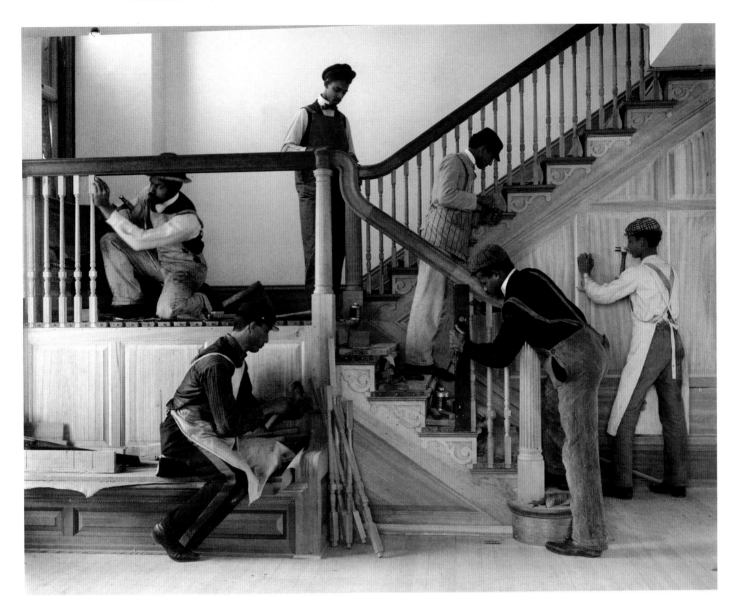

Stairway of Treasurer's Residence: Students at Work. Hampton Institute, Hampton, Virginia. 1899–1900
Platinum print, 7⁹/₁₆ x 9⁹/₁₆" (19.2 x 24.3 cm)
Gift of Lincoln Kirstein

Johnston was a professional photographer, noted for her portraits of Washington politicians and her photographs of coal miners, iron workers, and women workers in the New England textile mills. In 1899 Hampton Institute commissioned her to make photographs at the school for an exhibition about contemporary African American life at the Paris Exposition of 1900. This picture exemplifies Johnston's classical sense of composition and her practice of carefully arranging her subjects. Her complete control over the scene is readily apparent, yet the grace of the men's poses—evenly bathed in natural light—seems to justify her artifice.

Hampton Institute had been established in 1868, three years after the Civil War ended, when the educator and philanthropist Samuel C. Armstrong persuaded the American Missionary Association to fund a school for the vocational training of African Americans. Armstrong admired the "excellent qualities and capacities" of the freed black soldiers who had fought in the War under his command, and he believed that education was essential to them if they were to achieve productive independence.

20th Century

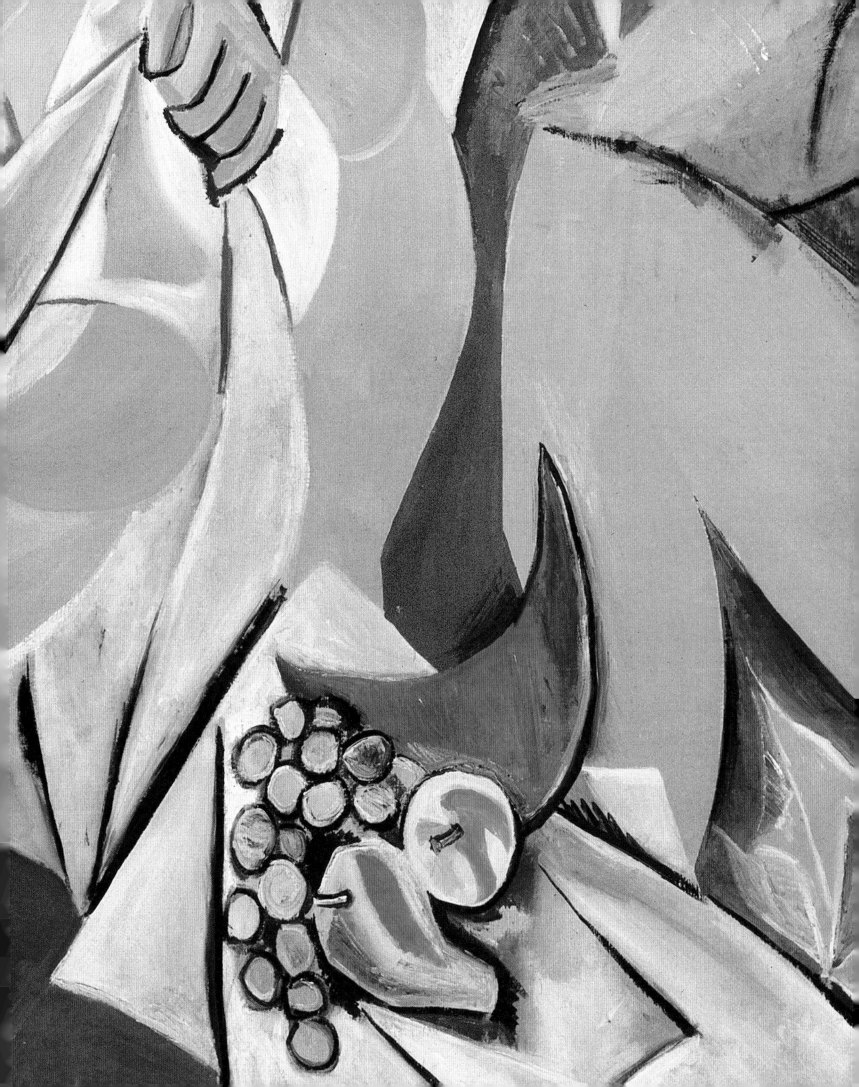

HECTOR GUIMARD
FRENCH, 1867–1942

Entrance Gate to Paris Subway (Métropolitain) Station. c. 1900
Painted cast iron, glazed lava, and glass,
13' 11" x 17' 10" x 32" (424 x 544 x 81 cm)
Gift of Régie Autonome des Transports Parisiens

The emergence of the Art Nouveau style toward the end of the nineteenth century resulted from a search for a new aesthetic that was not based on historical or classical models. The sinuous, organic lines of Guimard's design and the stylized, giant stalks drooping under the weight of what seem to be swollen tropical flowers, but are actually amber glass lamps, make this a quintessentially Art Nouveau piece. His designs for this famous entrance arch and two others were intended to visually enhance the experience of underground travel on the new subway system for Paris.

Paris was not the first city to implement an underground system (London already had one), but the approaching Paris Exposition of 1900 accelerated the need for an efficient and attractive means of mass transportation. Although Guimard never formally entered the competition for the design of the system's entrance gates that had been launched by the Compagnie du Métropolitain in 1898, he won the commission with his avant-garde schemes, all using standardized cast-iron components to facilitate manufacture, transport, and assembly.

While Parisians were at first hesitant in their response to Guimard's use of an unfamiliar vocabulary, his Métro gates, installed throughout the city, effectively brought the Art Nouveau style, formerly associated with the luxury market, into the realm of popular culture.

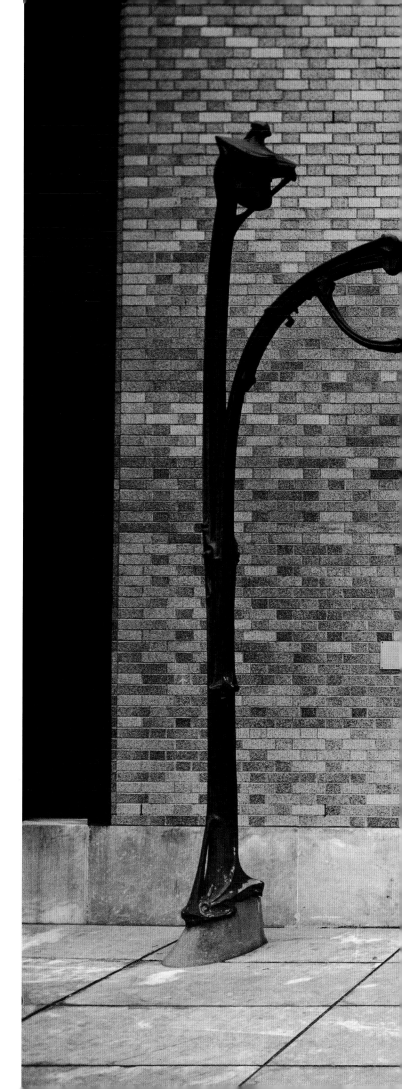

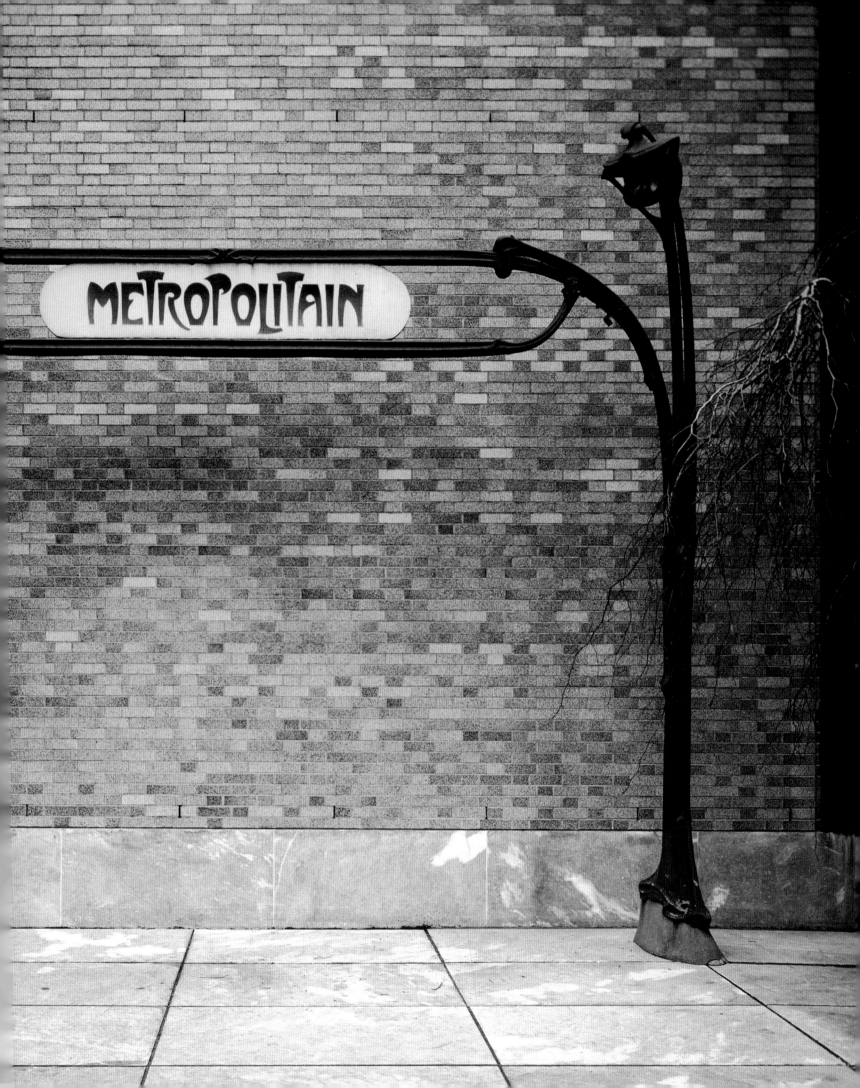

1900

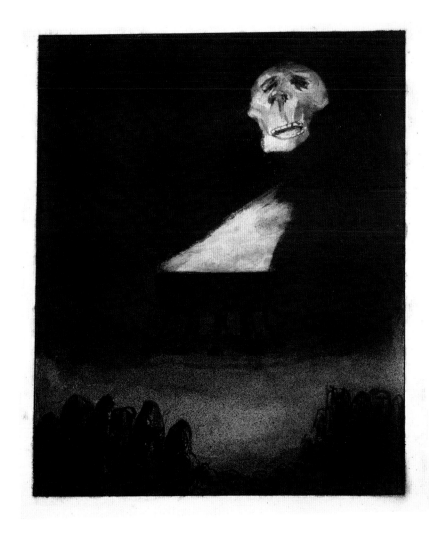

Untitled (The Eternal Flame). c. 1900
Gouache and ink on paper, 13 x 10³/₄"
(32.9 x 27.2 cm)
John S. Newberry Collection

This drawing is related to a later series of
Kubin's works, *The Eternal Flame*, based on
German folktales and myths.

A flaming cauldron placed in the center of
the composition is a recurring motif in the
series. The feeling of horror and mystery of
this image is created through a subtle play of
light and dark that envelops the foreground
figures in an enigmatic veil. Light dramatizes
and brings forth from the shadows both the
flame and the floating skull, thus heightening
the effect of a hallucinatory vision.

Most of Kubin's drawings evoke a fantastic
nightmarish mood, high drama, and mystery.
The eerie, unreal quality characteristic of his
work may possibly be related to his early
apprenticeship to a photographer, since
Kubin's images seem to emerge out of the
darkness, much as negatives develop in a
darkroom.

Although most of Kubin's adult life falls
within the twentieth century, his art—primarily
drawings—belongs to the Austrian
Symbolism of the end of the nineteenth
century. The graphic work of Francisco
Goya, James Ensor, Max Klinger, Odilon
Redon, and particularly Hieronymus Bosch
offered him stylistic inspiration, while his
subject matter was steeped in the
incompatible philosophies of Friedrich
Nietzsche and Arthur Schopenhauer.

The Frugal Repast. 1904

Etching, plate: 18³/₁₆ x 14⁷/₈" (46.2 x 37.8 cm)
Publisher: Ambroise Vollard, Paris.
Edition: proof before edition of 250
Gift of Thomas T. Solley with Mary Ellen Meehan, purchase through the Vincent d'Aquila and Harry Soviak Bequest, and with contributions from Lily Auchincloss, The Associates Fund, The Philip and Lynn Straus Foundation Fund, and John S. Newberry (by exchange)

This gaunt, nearly emaciated couple sit at a bleak table on which only a few scraps of bread and a bit of wine remain. Although the man's elongated fingers tenderly clasp the woman, he, thought to be blind, turns away from her, his anguished face, with lips slightly parted, suggesting grief. Seemingly more resigned, the woman appears lost in thought as she rests her chin on her hand.

This etching was executed early in Picasso's career, when he was a struggling 23-year-old artist and had recently returned from his native Spain to Paris and settled in Montmartre. *The Frugal Repast* reveals the artist's feeling for humanity, especially for the poor and others on the fringes of society. Haunted, lonely people, often itinerant circus workers, populate the artist's compositions during this period.

Although it is only the second etching Picasso made, *The Frugal Repast* demonstrates an astonishing mastery of the medium as the artist deftly captured nuances of light and form purely with line. The soft residue of ink he allowed to remain on the plate's surface creates evocative shadows, which add to the somber mood.

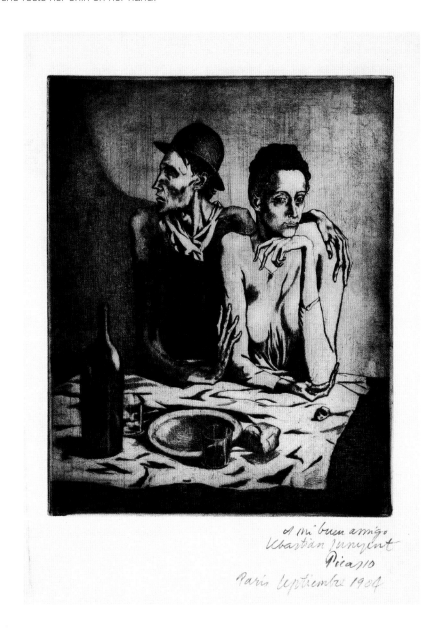

EDWARD STEICHEN AMERICAN, BORN LUXEMBOURG.
1879–1973

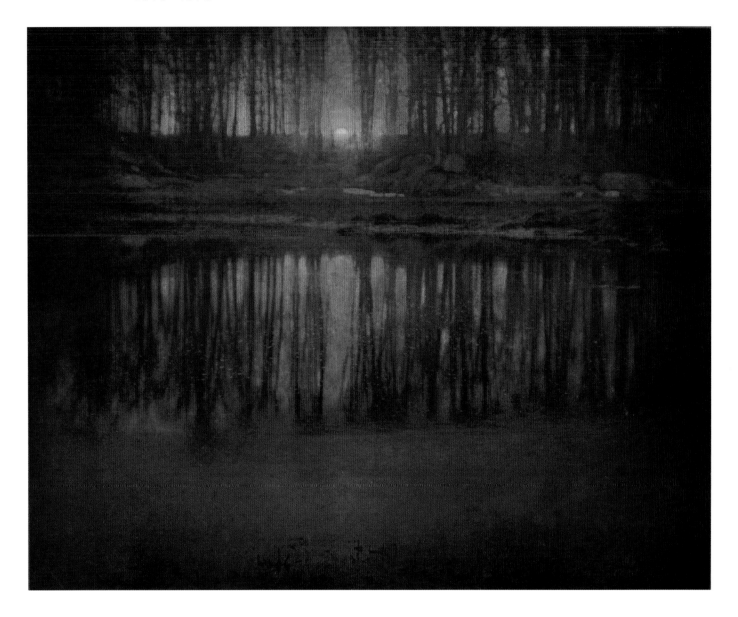

Moonrise, Mamaroneck, New York.
1904
Platinum and ferroprussiate print, 15⁵/₁₆ x 19"
(38.9 x 48.2 cm)
Gift of the artist

The colors in this photograph were not captured in the camera but were concocted later by Steichen in the darkroom, where he also sketched the reeds and grasses in the foreground. These marks of the artist's hand were the young photographer's way of showing that the picture was not an ordinary photograph but a work of art.

Raised in Wisconsin, Steichen made his way in 1900 to New York, where he met the older and more seasoned photographer Alfred Stieglitz, and soon joined him in a vigorous campaign to establish photography as a fine art. Although they failed at first to impress a broad public, they encouraged many talented young photographers to think of themselves as artists and so initiated a rich tradition that flourished for more than half a century.

For Stieglitz and Steichen, pursuing the artistic potential of photography meant rejecting its practical functions in the modern industrialized world. They retreated into an aesthetic world of refinement and comforting values, such as the purity of nature. Pure as it was, however, the nature that they photographed was rarely wild. Mamaroneck surely was more peaceful a century ago than it is today, but it was already a suburb of New York to which Steichen often went to escape from the rigors of city life.

Sitzmaschine Chair with Adjustable Back. c. 1905

Bent beechwood and sycamore panels,
43¹/₂ x 28¹/₄ x 32" (110.5 x 71.8 x 81.3 cm)
Manufacturer: J. & J. Kohn, Austria
Gift of Jo Carole and Ronald S. Lauder

The *Sitzmaschine*, that is, the "machine for sitting," was originally designed by Hoffmann for his Purkersdorf Sanatorium in Vienna. The sanatorium was one of the first important commissions given to the Wiener Werkstätte, a collaborative founded in 1903 by Hoffmann and Koloman Moser espousing many of the English Arts and Crafts movement's tenets of good design and high-quality craftsmanship. It represents one of Hoffmann's earliest experiments in unifying a building and its furnishings as a total work of art.

The *Sitzmaschine* makes clear reference to an adjustable-back English Arts and Crafts chair known as the Morris chair, designed by Philip Webb around 1866. It also stands as an allegorical celebration of the machine. This armchair, with its exposed structure, demonstrates a rational simplification of forms suited to machine production. Yet, at the same time, the grid of squares piercing the rectangular back splat, the bentwood loops that form the armrests and legs, and the rows of knobs on the adjustable back illustrate the fusion of decorative and structural elements typical of the Wiener Werkstätte style. J. & J. Kohn produced and sold this chair in a number of versions, most of which had cushions on the seat and back, until at least 1916. The Kohn firm produced many designs by Hoffmann, forming one of the first successful alliances between a designer and industry in Vienna.

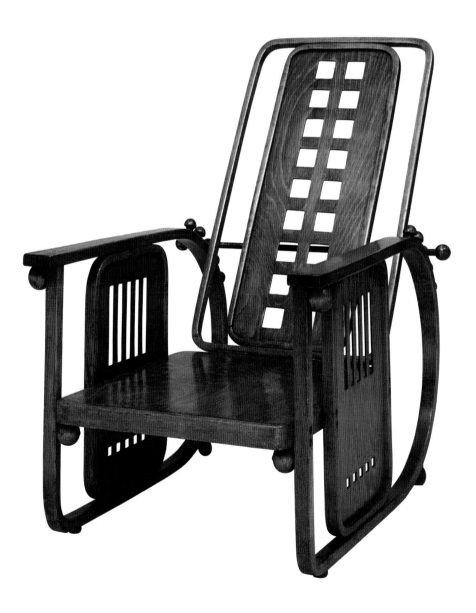

1906

Bridge over the Riou. 1906

Oil on canvas, 32¹/₂ x 40" (82.5 x 101.6 cm)
The William S. Paley Collection

Although *Bridge over the Riou* describes a place in the south of France, its complexly patterned composition suggests a gradual reworking and reshaping rather than a quick and fluid response to what Derain saw there. From the foreground bank, over the riverbed, to the higher ground beyond, the space is compressed and flattened, but the scene can still be identified—the bridge at the lower right, a cabin down in the ravine, the beehive form of a covered well. Houses appear beyond the river, behind the trees.

In 1905 Derain and his peers in the Fauvist group had created a *succès de scandale* through their radical use of color, but they still accepted from Impressionism the idea that a painting should follow nature, and should try to capture the passing moment of contemporary life. By 1906, however, Derain wanted to create images that would "belong to all time" as well as to his own period, and the separate strokes of color seen in his paintings of 1905 are here subsumed into larger colored shapes, some of them outlined in exotic blues or lavenders, or an indian red or pink, say, for a tree trunk. This emotionally high-keyed color relates to the intensity of the light in the south of France, yet belongs less to nature than to art.

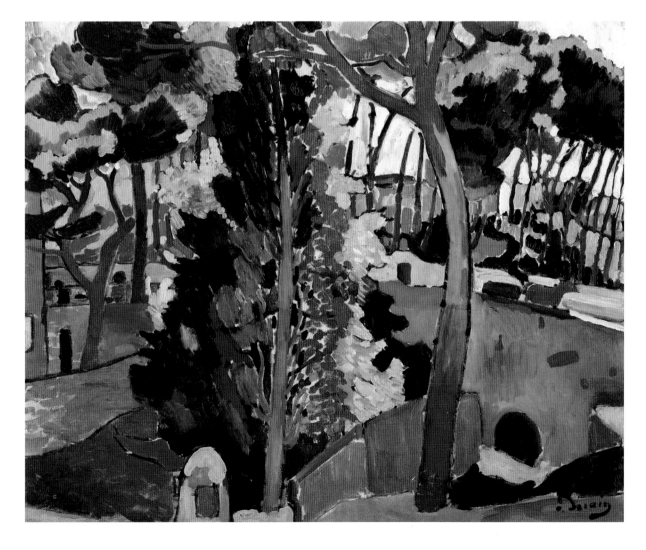

1907

Les Demoiselles d'Avignon. 1907
Oil on canvas, 8' x 7' 8" (243.9 x 233.7 cm)
Acquired through the Lillie P. Bliss Bequest

Les Demoiselles d'Avignon is one of the most important works in the genesis of modern art. The painting depicts five naked prostitutes in a brothel; two of them push aside curtains around the space where the other women strike seductive and erotic poses—but their figures are composed of flat, splintered planes rather than rounded volumes, their eyes are lopsided or staring or asymmetrical, and the two women at the right have threatening masks for heads. The space, too, which should recede, comes forward in jagged shards, like broken glass. In the still life at the bottom, a piece of melon slices the air like a scythe.

The faces of the figures at the right are influenced by African masks, which Picasso assumed had functioned as magical protectors against dangerous spirits: this work, he said later, was his "first exorcism painting." A specific danger he had in mind was life-threatening sexual disease, a source of considerable anxiety in Paris at the time; earlier sketches for the painting more clearly link sexual pleasure to mortality. In its brutal treatment of the body and its clashes of color and style (other sources for this work include ancient Iberian statuary and the work of Paul Cézanne), *Les Demoiselles d'Avignon* marks a radical break from traditional composition and perspective.

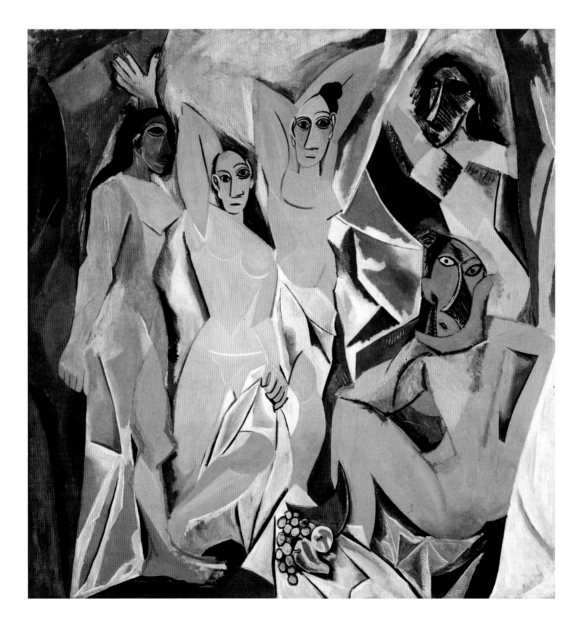

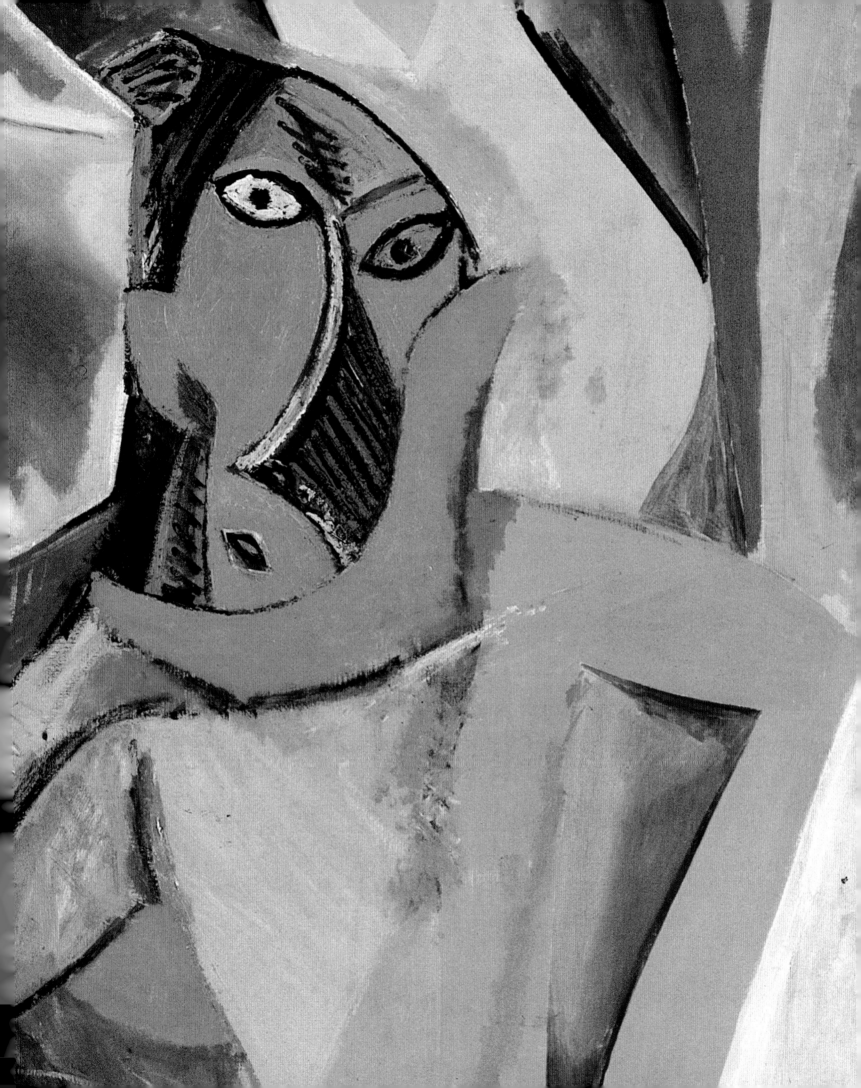

Hope, II. 1907–08

Oil, gold, and platinum on canvas, 43¹/₂ x 43¹/₂"
(110.5 x 110.5 cm)
Mr. and Mrs. Ronald S. Lauder and Helen
Acheson Funds, and Serge Sabarsky

A pregnant woman bows her head and
closes her eyes, as if praying for the safety of
her child. Peeping out from behind her
stomach is a death's head, sign of the
danger she faces. At her feet, three women
with bowed heads raise their hands,
presumably also in prayer—although their
solemnity might also imply mourning, as if
they foresaw the child's fate.

Why, then, the painting's title? Although
Klimt himself called this work *Vision*, he had
called an earlier, related painting of a
pregnant woman *Hope*. By association with

the earlier work, this one has become known
as *Hope, II*. There is, however, a richness
here to balance the women's gravity.

Klimt was among the many artists of his
time who were inspired by sources not only
within Europe but far beyond it. He lived in
Vienna, a crossroads of East and West, and
he drew on such sources as Byzantine art,
Mycenean metalwork, Persian rugs and
miniatures, the mosaics of the Ravenna
churches, and Japanese screens. In this
painting the woman's gold-patterned robe—
drawn flat, as clothes are in Russian icons,
although her skin is rounded and
dimensional—has an extraordinary
decorative beauty. Here, birth, death, and the
sensuality of the living exist side by side
suspended in equilibrium.

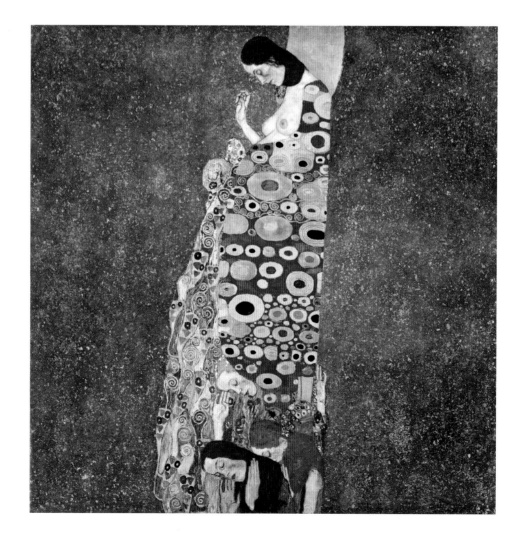

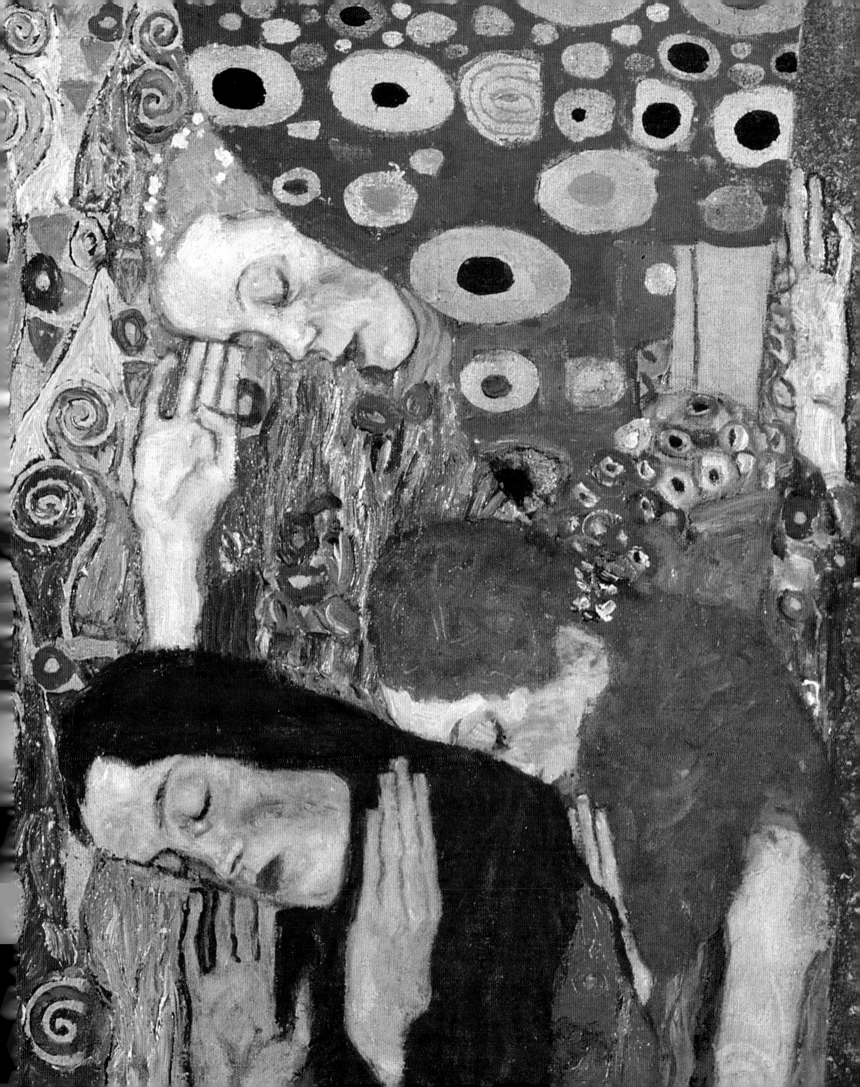

ERNST LUDWIG KIRCHNER

GERMAN, 1880–1938

Street, Dresden. 1908 (dated 1907)
Oil on canvas, 59¹/₄" x 6' 6⁷/₈" (150.5 x 200.4 cm)
Purchase

Street, Dresden is Kirchner's bold, discomfiting attempt to render the jarring experience of modern urban bustle. The scene radiates tension. Its packed pedestrians are locked in a constricting space; the plane of the sidewalk, in an unsettlingly intense pink (part of a palette of shrill and clashing colors), slopes steeply upward, and exit to the rear is blocked by a trolley car. The street—Dresden's fashionable Königstrasse—is crowded, even claustrophobically so, yet everyone seems alone. The women at the right, one clutching her purse, the other her skirt, are holding themselves in, and their faces are expressionless, almost masklike. A little girl is dwarfed by her hat, one in a network of eddying, whorling shapes that entwine and enmesh the human figures.

Developing in parallel with the French Fauves, and influenced by them and by the Norwegian painter Edvard Munch, the German artists of *Die Brücke* explored the expressive possibilities of color, form, and composition in creating images of contemporary life. *Street, Dresden* is a bold expression of the intensity, dissonance, and anxiety of the modern city. Kirchner later wrote, "The more I mixed with people the more I felt my loneliness."

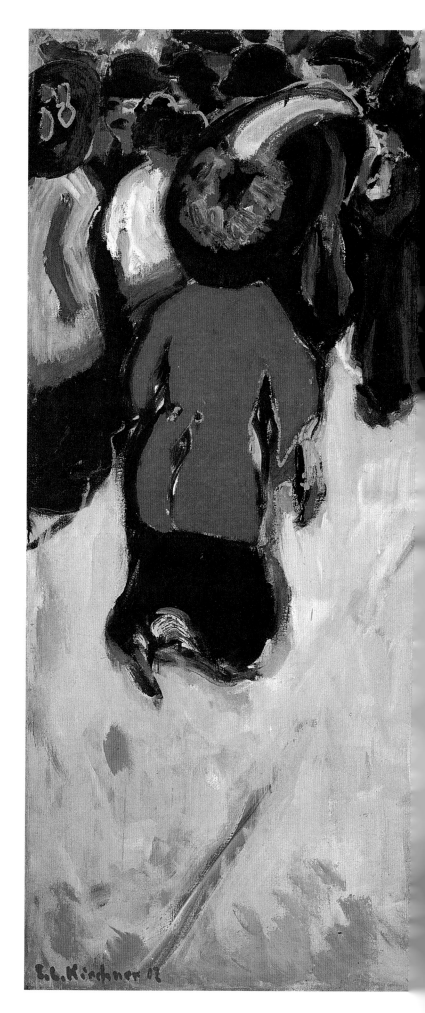

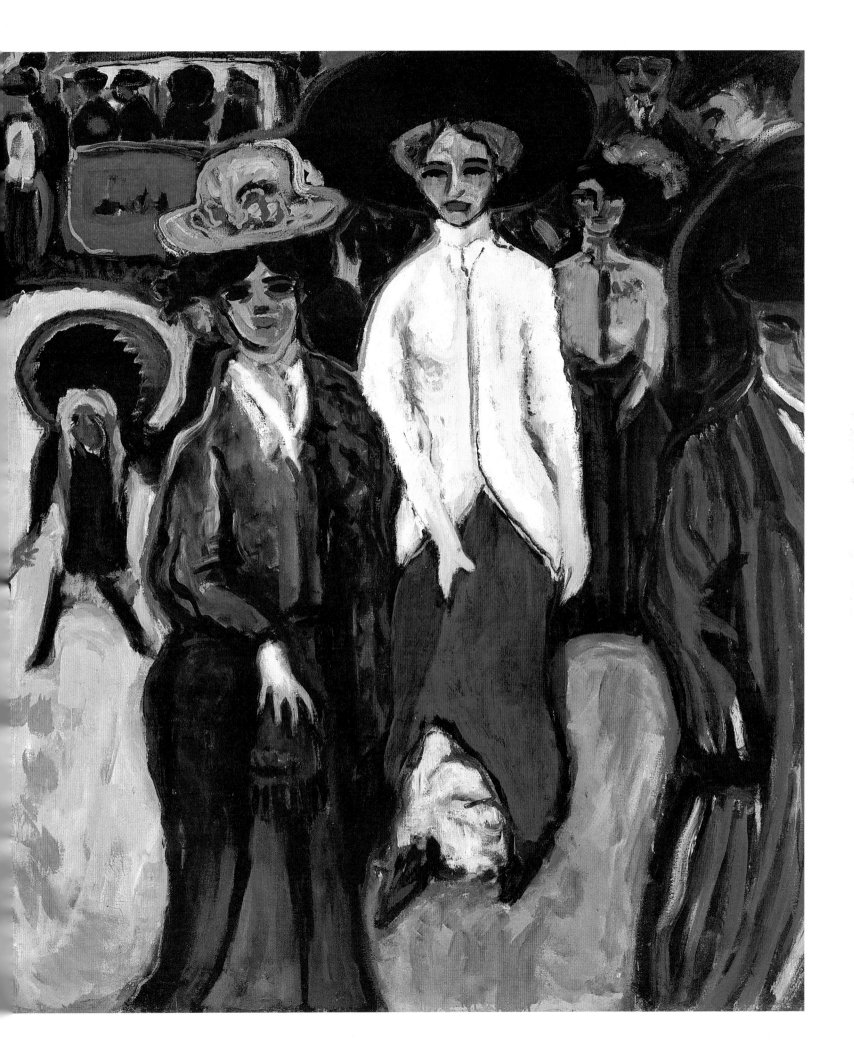

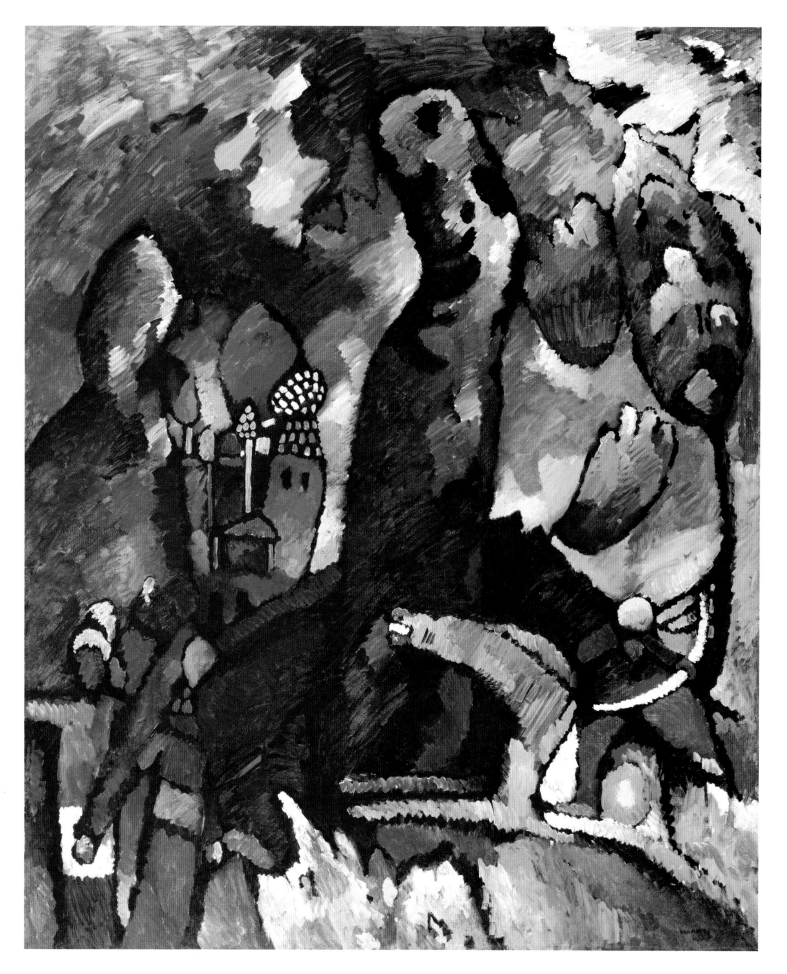

Picture with an Archer. 1909

Oil on canvas, 68⅞ x 57⅜" (175 x 144.6 cm)
Gift and bequest of Mrs. Bertram Smith

The color in *Picture with an Archer* is
vibrantly alive—so much so that the scene is
initially hard to make out. The patchwork
surface seems to be shrugging off the task of
describing a space or form. Kandinsky was
the first modern artist to paint an entirely
abstract composition; at the time of *Picture
with an Archer*, that work was just a few
months away.

Kandinsky took his approach from Paris—
particularly from the Fauves—but used it to
create an Eastern landscape suffused with a
folktale mood. Galloping under the trees of a
wildly radiant countryside, a horseman turns
in his saddle and aims his bow. In the left
foreground stand men in Russian dress;
behind them are a house, a domed tower,
and two bulbous mountainy pinnacles,
cousins of the bent-necked spire in the
picture's center. Russian icons show similar
rocks, which do exist in places in the East,
but even so have a fantastical air. The lone
rider with his archaic weapon, the traditional
costumes and buildings, and the rural setting
intensify the note of fantasy or poetic romance.

There is a nostalgia here for a time or
perhaps for a place: in 1909 Kandinsky was
living in Germany, far from his native Russia.
But in the glowing energy of the painting's
color there is also excitement and promise.

Hans Tietze and Erica Tietze-Conrat.
1909

Oil on canvas, 30⅛ x 53⅝" (76.5 x 136.2 cm)
Abby Aldrich Rockefeller Fund

The Tietzes were socially prominent art
historians, but Kokoschka ignores their
public personas to find a mysterious delicacy
in their private relationship. Erica gazes out
toward us; Hans looks at Erica's hand, and
reaches for it without touching it, so that his
hands and her left arm form an arch that is
broken at its summit by a narrow gap, a
space with a psychic charge. The couple
emerge from a shimmering ground of russets
and dim blues into which their outlines seem
to melt in places. Scratches in the thin oil—
made, according to Erica Tietze-Conrat, with
the artist's fingernails—create a texture of
ghostly half-marks around the figures, a
subtle halo of crackling energy.

Like his Viennese compatriot Egon Schiele,
Kokoschka tried to transcend academic
formulas with an art of emotional and
physical immediacy—an art, in his words,
"to render the vision of people being alive."
Hans Tietze and Erica Tietze-Conrat is one
of his "black portraits," in which he tried to
penetrate his subjects' "closed personalities
so full of tension." (His Vienna was also the
home of Sigmund Freud.)

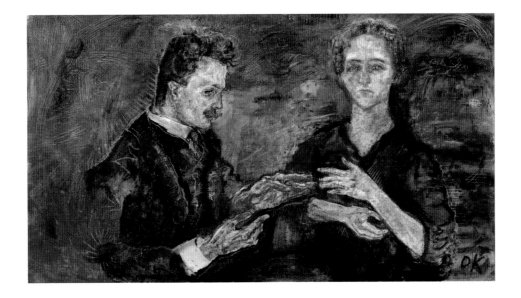

HENRI MATISSE
FRENCH, 1869–1954

Dance (first version). 1909
Oil on canvas, 8' 6¹/₂" x 12' 9¹/₂"
(259.7 x 390.1 cm)
Gift of Nelson A. Rockefeller in honor
of Alfred H. Barr, Jr.

A monumental image of joy and energy,
Dance is also strikingly daring. Matisse made
the painting while preparing a decorative
commission for the Moscow collector Sergei
Shchukin, whose final version of the scene,
Dance (II), was shown in Paris in 1910.
Nearly identical in composition to this work,
its simplifications of the human body were
attacked as inept or willfully crude. Also
noted was the work's radical visual flatness:
the elimination of perspective and
foreshortening that makes nearer and farther
figures the same size, and the sky a plane of
blue. This is true, as well, of the first version.

Here, the figure at the left moves
purposefully; the strength of her body is
emphasized by the sweeping unbroken
contour from her rear foot up to her breast.
The other dancers seem so light they nearly
float. The woman at the far right is barely
sketched in, her foot dissolving in runny paint
as she reels backward. The arm of the
dancer to her left literally stretches as it
reaches toward the leader's hand, where
momentum has broken the circle. The
dancers' speed is barely contained by the
edges of the canvas.

Dance (II) is more intense in color than this
first version, and the dancers' bodies—there
deep red—are more sinewy and energetic. In
whatever canvas they appear, these are no
ordinary dancers, but mythical creatures in a
timeless landscape. Dance, Matisse once
said, meant "life and rhythm."

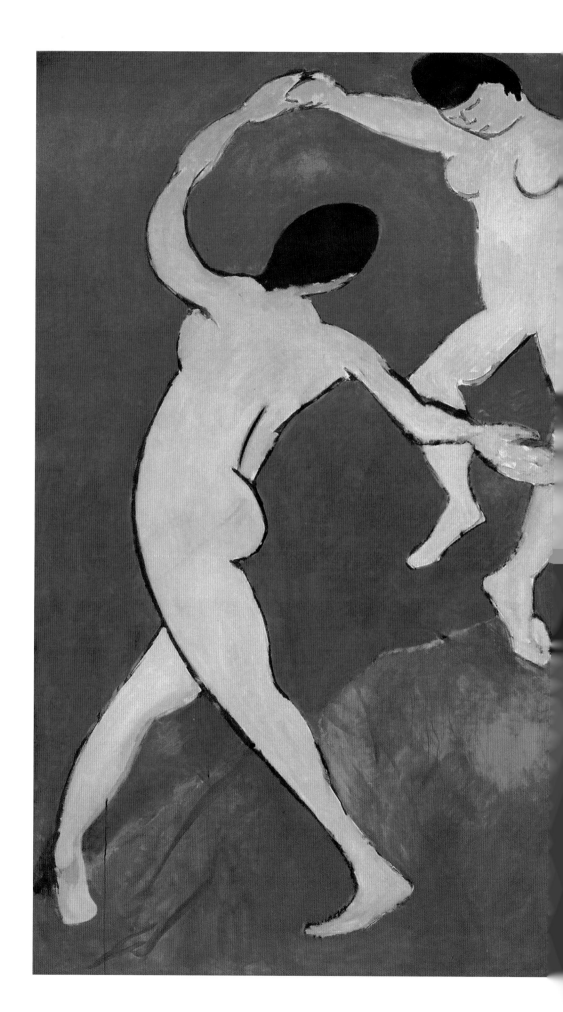

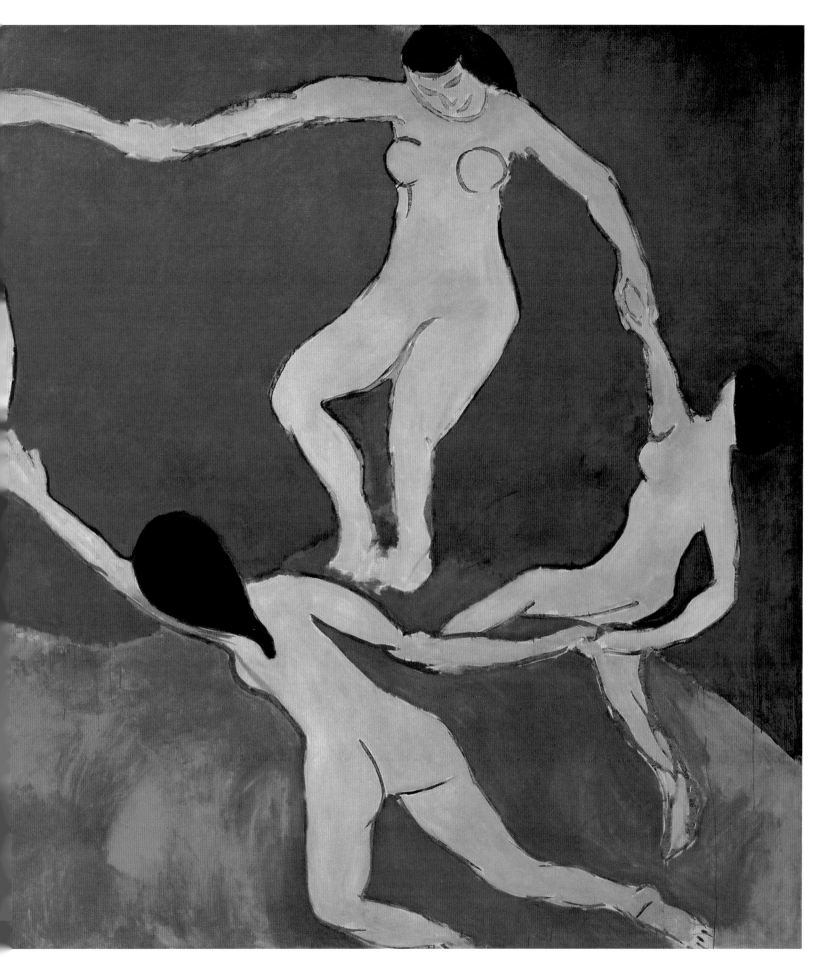

1910

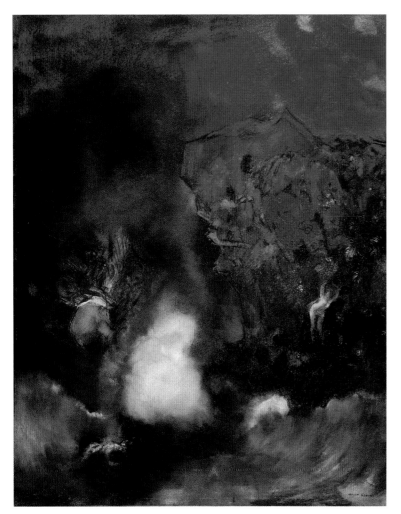

Roger and Angelica. c. 1910
Pastel on paper, 36¹/₂ x 28³/₄" (92.7 x 73 cm)
Lillie P. Bliss Collection

In this evocation of a scene from the sixteenth-century romance *Orlando Furioso*, the knight Roger appears on his fiery steed to save the maiden Angelica from a horrible fate: the dragon, with its evil inner glow, is looming at the lower left. Tendrils of threatening mist curling up from below menace the maiden, while angry storm clouds hover above. The figures themselves are small and sketchily rendered; it is the picture's atmospheric effects, conveyed with light-and-dark contrasts and shots of dazzling color—including those of the imposing crag on which Angelica is stranded—that create the high drama of this tension-ridden scene.

The young Redon is said to have watched the clouds scudding over the flat Bordeaux landscape where he was raised and imagined in them the fantastic beings that he would later conjure up in his paintings, drawings, lithographs, and pastels. *Roger and Angelica*, executed in the last period of his career, when color had bewitched him, exemplifies Redon's consummate ability to imbue his wildly imaginative fantasies with color, light, and shadow, using the mere strokes of a crayon.

Although this work was created in the twentieth century, it reflects the Romanticism of the nineteenth century, in which feeling triumphed over form, and color was the primary vehicle of expression.

1911

Girl with Black Hair. 1911

Watercolor and pencil on buff paper,
22¹/₈ x 14¹/₂" (56.2 x 36.7 cm)
Gift of the Galerie St. Étienne, New York, in memory of Dr. Otto Kallir; promised gift of Jo Carole and Ronald S. Lauder; and purchase

Girl with Black Hair is one of two erotic watercolors of the same subject, both of which are closely related compositionally. Here the young woman, in a half-seated, half-reclining pose, displays her genitalia unashamedly; her partly closed eyes do not confront the artist or the viewer but stare into space with detachment and boredom. Her black skirt, bunched up around her waist, reflects the form of her abundant black hair.

The pose of the girl suggests that the work was executed from a vantage point above the figure. Reportedly, Schiele's favorite mode of working was to observe his models from above (using a stool or ladder) while they reclined on a low couch expressly built by him for this purpose.

Young women in various stages of undressing or nude constituted one of Schiele's favorite subjects. His models were often pubescent girls of working-class background or even young prostitutes, since the artist, having been cut off from any financial support by his family, could not afford to hire professional models. During 1911–12 he executed some of his most provocative depictions of female nudes—often in contorted and unnatural poses: standing, sitting, reclining, or kneeling. Such drawings, exhibiting a bold expressiveness of body language and a masterful handling of the watercolor medium, were in great demand among Schiele's Viennese patrons.

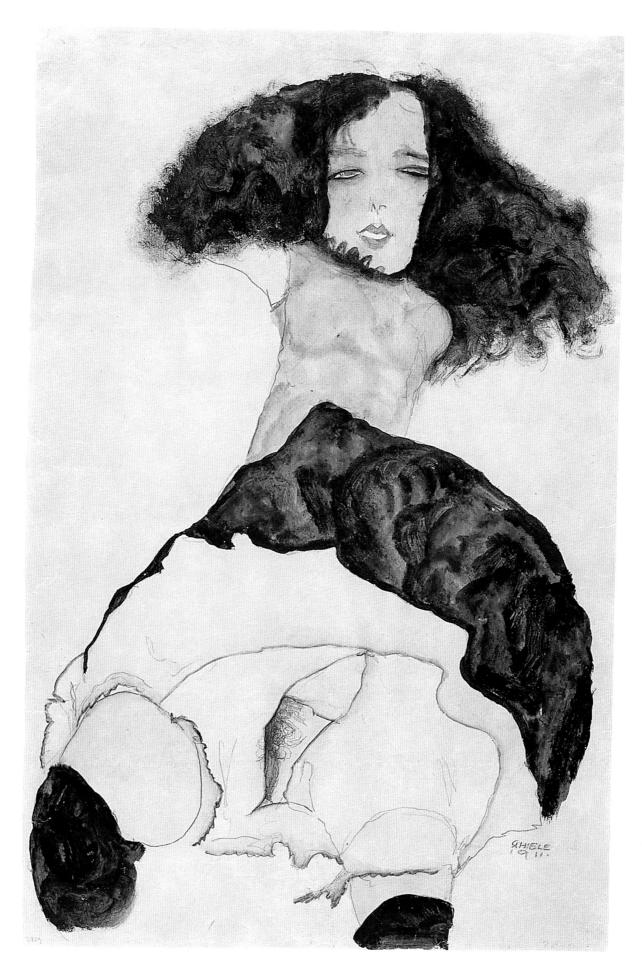

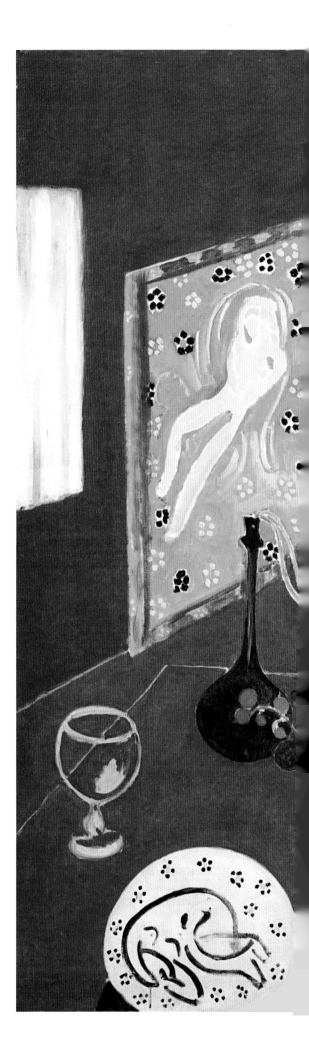

HENRI MATISSE
FRENCH, 1869–1954

The Red Studio. 1911
Oil on canvas, 71¹/₄" x 7' 2¹/₄" (181 x 219.1 cm)
Mrs. Simon Guggenheim Fund

"Modern art," said Matisse, "spreads joy around it by its color, which calms us." In this radiant painting he saturates a room—his own studio—with red. Art and decorative objects are painted solidly, but furniture and architecture are linear diagrams, silhouetted by "gaps" in the red surface. These gaps reveal earlier layers of yellow and blue paint beneath the red; Matisse changed the colors until they felt right to him. (The studio was actually white.)

The studio is an important place for any artist, and this one Matisse had built for himself, encouraged by new patronage in 1909. He shows in it a carefully arranged exhibition of his own works. Angled lines suggest depth, and the blue-green light of the window intensifies the sense of interior space, but the expanse of red flattens the image. Matisse heightens this effect by, for example, omitting the vertical line of the corner of the room.

The entire composition is clustered around the enigmatic axis of the grandfather clock, a flat rectangle whose face has no hands. Time is suspended in this magical space. On the foreground table, an open box of crayons, perhaps a symbolic stand-in for the artist, invites us into the room. But the studio itself, defined by ethereal lines and subtle spatial discontinuities, remains Matisse's private universe.

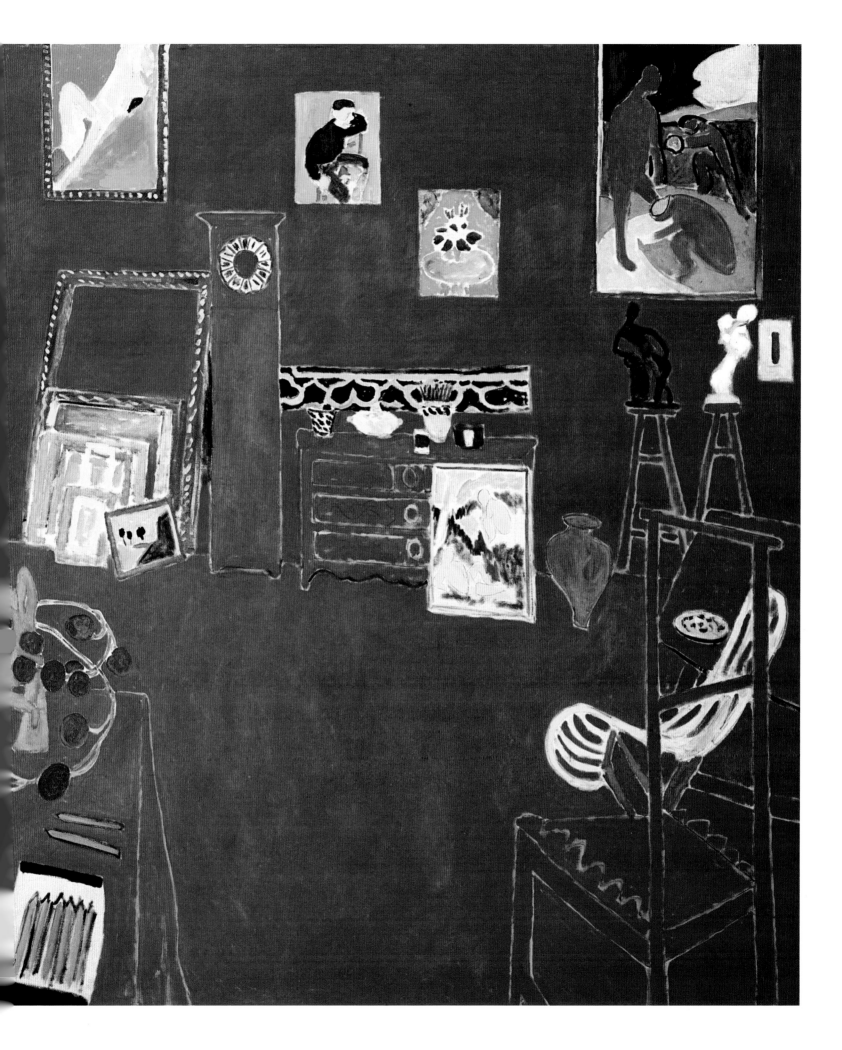

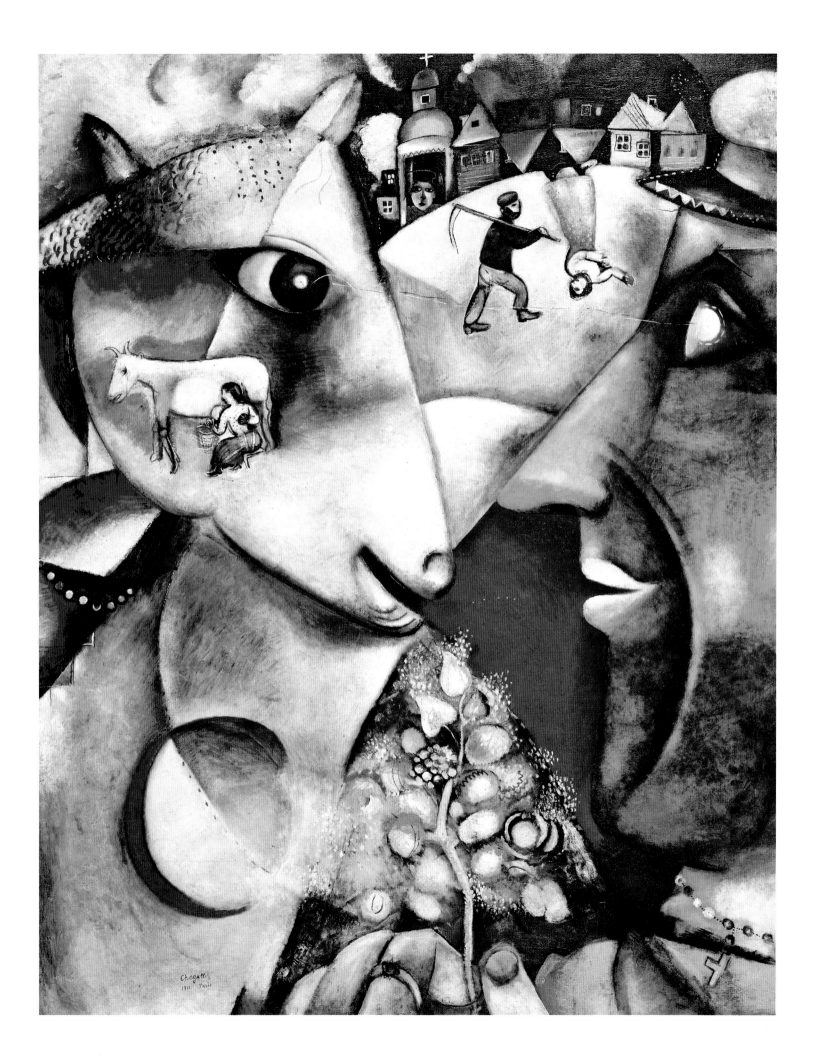

I and the Village. 1911

Oil on canvas, 6' 3⅝" x 59⅝" (192.1 x 151.4 cm)
Mrs. Simon Guggenheim Fund

Painted the year after Chagall came to Paris, *I and the Village* evokes his memories of his native Hasidic community outside Vitebsk. In the village, peasants and animals lived side by side, in a mutual dependence here signified by the line from peasant to cow, connecting their eyes. The peasant's flowering sprig, symbolically a tree of life, is the reward of their partnership. For Hasids, animals were also humanity's link to the universe, and the painting's large circular forms suggest the orbiting sun, moon (in eclipse at the lower left), and earth.

The geometries of *I and the Village* are inspired by the broken planes of Cubism, but Chagall's is a personalized version. As a boy he had loved geometry: "Lines, angles, triangles, squares," he would later recall, "carried me far away to enchanting horizons." Conversely, in Paris he used a disjunctive geometric structure to carry him back home. Where Cubism was mainly an art of urban avant-garde society, *I and the Village* is nostalgic and magical, a rural fairy tale: objects jumble together, scale shifts abruptly, and a woman and two houses, at the painting's top, stand upside-down. "For the Cubists," Chagall said, "a painting was a surface covered with forms in a certain order. For me a painting is a surface covered with representations of things … in which logic and illustration have no importance."

"Ma Jolie." 1911–12

Oil on canvas, 39⅜ x 25¾" (100 x 65.4 cm)
Acquired through the Lillie P. Bliss Bequest

Numerous elusive clues connect *"Ma Jolie"* to reality: a triangular form in the lower center, strung like a guitar or zither; below the strings, four fingers, with an angular elbow to the right; and in the upper half, perhaps a floating smile. Together these elements suggest a woman holding a musical instrument, but the picture hints at reality only to deny it. Planes, lines, spatial cues, shadings, and other traces of painting's language of illusion are abstracted from descriptive uses; the figure almost disappears into a network of flat, straight-edged, semitransparent planes.

Yet *"Ma Jolie,"* an example of high Analytic Cubism, is actually a painting on a very traditional theme—a woman holding a musical instrument. The palette of brown and sepia is reminiscent of the work of Rembrandt, and Picasso emphasizes the handmade nature of the brushstrokes, underlining the artist's human presence. At the bottom of the canvas Picasso also inscribes a treble clef and the words *"Ma Jolie,"* (my pretty one)—both a line from a popular song and a reference to his lover Marcelle Humbert. A kind of stand-in for the woman who can barely be seen, the phrase *"Ma Jolie"* is clear, legible, colloquial, and suggests conventional prettiness—although this was one of the most complex, abstract, and esoteric images of its day.

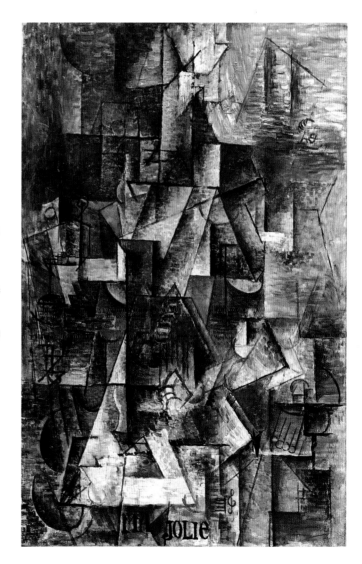

1912

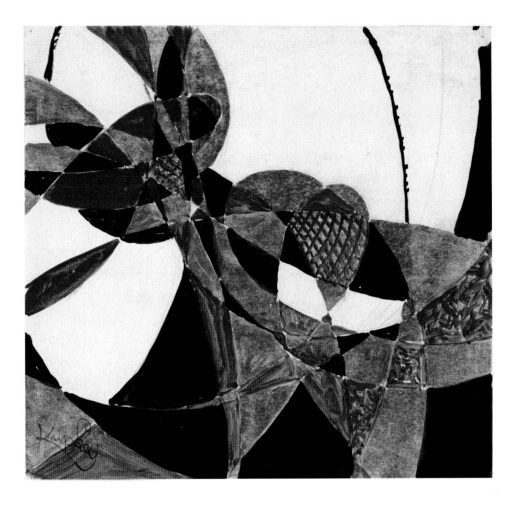

Fugue in Two Colors. 1912

Gouache and ink on paper, 8¹/₂ x 9"
(21.3 x 22.8 cm)
Gift of Mr. and Mrs. František Kupka

This small study for a large painting,
Amorpha, Fugue in Two Colors (1912), is one
of twenty-seven such studies in the collection
of The Museum of Modern Art. It shows a
late interpretation of this theme, the fugue, in
which the irregularly shaped and patterned
panes recall the complexity and translucency
of stained-glass windows. In the final
painting, Kupka simplified the composition
into broader planes of color that constitute a
single monumental arabesque.

The painting was exhibited at the Salon
d'Automne in Paris in 1912, where it
provoked general consternation. Whereas
Kupka's original motifs had been inspired
by nature, his final gouache studies and
the painting itself were totally abstract
and distilled to two colors, red and blue.
These were intended to represent the
interlacing voices of a fugue, in which, as
he himself wrote, "the sounds evolve like
veritable physical entities, intertwine, come
and go."

Born in a small city in eastern Bohemia,
Kupka studied in Prague and Vienna and then
settled permanently in Paris in 1896. By 1912
his painting had evolved to a radically abstract
style, establishing him as one of the earliest
pioneers of abstraction in European painting.

Two Clerestory Windows from Avery Coonley Playhouse, Riverside, Illinois.
1912
Color and clear glass, leaded,
each 18⁵/₁₆ x 34³/₁₆" (46.5 x 86.8 cm)
Joseph H. Heil Fund

To enliven the interior of his Avery Coonley Playhouse, a kindergarten in the suburbs of Chicago for a private client, Frank Lloyd Wright designed stained-glass clerestory windows, which formed a continuous band around the top of the playroom. Each window in the series was composed of lively combinations of simple geometric motifs in bright colors. The windows were inspired by the sights of a parade, and their shapes abstracted from balloons, confetti, and even an American flag.

Wright designed the interior furnishings for almost all of his buildings, thereby creating an organic unity of the whole and its parts. Art glass was integral to the architectural fabric of many of his early works. The arranging of shapes into patterns in the Coonley Playhouse windows relates to the formal strategies Wright adopted in his architecture. His belief in the universality of fundamental geometric forms was as much a response to rational methods of modern machine production as an intuitive understanding that abstract forms carried shared spiritual values. Geometric forms had played a role in Wright's own childhood education through a German system of educational toys, the Froebel blocks, which he later credited as a major influence on his ideas about architecture.

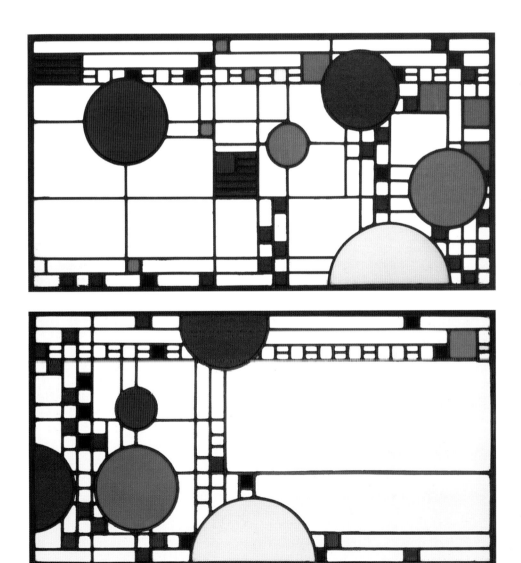

EMIL NOLDE GERMAN, 1867–1956

Prophet. 1912

Woodcut, comp.: 12⁵/₈ x 8³/₄" (32.1 x 22.2 cm)
Publisher: the artist. Edition: 20–30
Given anonymously (by exchange)

This brooding face confronts the viewer with
an immediacy and deep emotion that leave
no doubt about the prophet's spirituality. His
hollow eyes, furrowed brow, sunken cheeks,
and solemn countenance express his
innermost feelings. Three years before Nolde
executed this print, he had experienced a
religious transformation while recovering from
an illness. Following this episode, he began
depicting religious subjects in paintings and
prints, such as the image seen here.

Nolde had joined the German
Expressionist group *Die Brücke* (The Bridge)
in 1906, participating in its exhibitions and in
its exchange of ideas and techniques. He
taught etching to his fellow members, and
they introduced him to woodcuts. During the
1890s, woodcuts had undergone a
resurgence and revamping, when artists
such as Paul Gauguin and Edvard Munch
used them to create bold images that
expressed strong emotional content. In
Prophet, Nolde also exploits the
characteristics inherent to the medium.

Coarsely gouged-out areas, jagged lines,
and the textured grain of the wood effectively
combine in this portrayal of a fervent
believer—a quintessential German
Expressionist print.

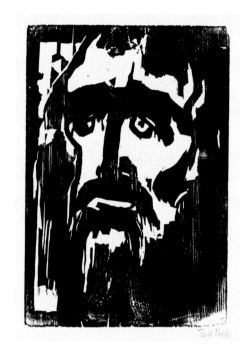

PABLO PICASSO SPANISH, 1881–1973

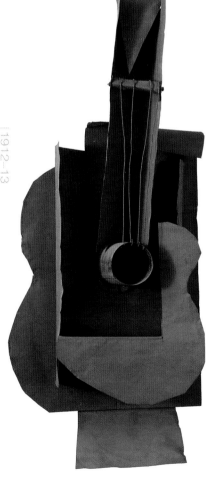

Guitar. 1912–13

Construction of sheet metal
and wire, 30¹/₂ x 13³/₄ x 7⁵/₈"
(77.5 x 35 x 19.3 cm)
Gift of the artist

Before the twentieth century,
sculpture often described the human
form, and was principally an art of
carving and modeling solids. In
Guitar Picasso broke with these age-
old traditions, examining an everyday
object and initiating a new type of
sculptural construction: built up from
sheet metal, *Guitar* has no solid
center but is open to space. A
shallow arrangement of planes to be
viewed from the front, it seems
pictorial as well as sculptural, and
relates to Picasso's Cubist collages of
newspaper clippings and the like.

This points to another departure from
tradition: whereas ambitious sculptors of the
period might work in bronze or marble,
Picasso used sheet metal and wire—
common, everyday materials, like the
newspapers of the collages.

Picasso's guitar sculpture is the same size
and shape as the real thing, but he shatters
its form. If the front of a guitar is a plane
concealing a volume, he cuts that plane
away, opening up the interior as an empty
box. If the sound hole is ordinarily a void, he
gives it substance, turning it into a projecting
cylinder (a device, Picasso said, inspired by
the tubular eyes in an African Grebo mask).
Viewed frontally, the cylinder's open rim
becomes a line drawing of the sound hole.
Here, Picasso has opened up the central
core of sculpture, allowing us to see into
and through it.

Unique Forms of Continuity in Space.
1913
Bronze (cast 1931), 43$^7/_8$ x 34$^7/_8$ x 15$^3/_4$"
(111.2 x 88.5 x 40 cm)
Acquired through the Lillie P. Bliss Bequest

In *Unique Forms of Continuity in Space*, Boccioni puts speed and force into sculptural form. The figure strides forward. Surpassing the limits of the body, its lines ripple outward in curving and streamlined flags, as if molded by the wind of its passing. Boccioni had developed these shapes over two years in paintings, drawings, and sculptures, exacting studies of human musculature. The result is a three-dimensional portrait of a powerful body in action.

In the early twentieth century, the new speed and force of machinery seemed to pour its power into radical social energy. The new technologies and the ideas attached to them would later reveal threatening aspects, but for Futurist artists like Boccioni, they were tremendously exhilarating. Innovative as Boccioni was, he fell short of his own ambition. In 1912, he had attacked the domination of sculpture by "the blind and foolish imitation of formulas inherited from the past," and particularly by "the burdensome weight of Greece." Yet *Unique Forms of Continuity in Space* bears an underlying resemblance to a classical work over 2,000 years old, the *Nike of Samothrace*. There, however, speed is encoded in the flowing stone draperies that wash around, and in the wake of, the figure. Here the body itself is reshaped, as if the new conditions of modernity were producing a new man.

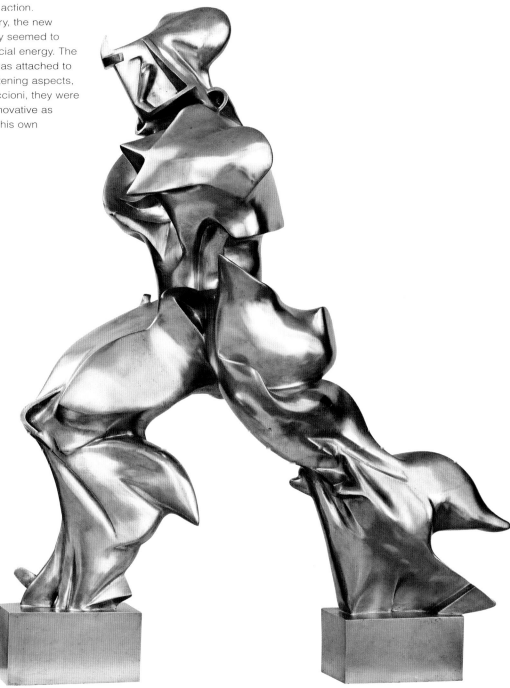

SONIA DELAUNAY-TERK FRENCH, BORN RUSSIA.
1885–1979

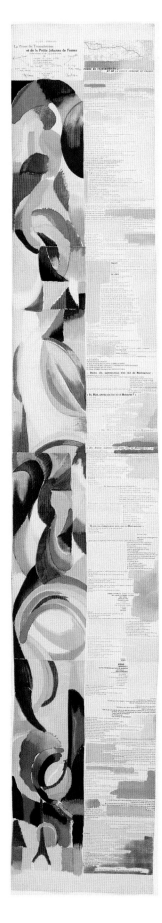

La Prose du Transsibérien
et de la petite Jehanne de France
by Blaise Cendrars. 1913
Illustrated book with pochoir, 6' 9⅝" x 14¼"
(207.4 x 36.2 cm)
Publisher: Éditions des Hommes Nouveaux
(Blaise Cendrars). Edition: 150 announced;
60–100 printed
Purchase

Brilliant swirls of color cascade down the left
side of this elongated composition, ending
with a simplified representation of a red Eiffel
Tower. Juxtaposed on the right, in a parallel
arrangement, are the words of the poet
Cendrars, which end with the text "O Paris."
Colors and words drift in a nonlinear fashion
similar to a stream of consciousness, a state
in which time and location are irrelevant.
Delaunay-Terk's hues and Cendrars's prose
interact on a simultaneous journey,
producing synchronized rhythms of art and
poetry.

The text of *La Prose du Transsibérien et de
la petite Jehanne de France (Prose of the
Trans-Siberian and of little Jeanne of France)*
contains Cendrars's sporadic flashbacks and
flash-forwards to other times and places, and
recounts his railroad journey from Moscow to
the Sea of Japan in 1904. It also includes
recollections of a train ride with his young
French mistress, the "petite Jehanne" of the
title, who repeatedly asked, "Are we very far
from Montmartre?".

Calling their creation "the first simultaneous
book," Delaunay-Terk and Cendrars drew on
the artistic theory of simultaneity, espoused
by the artist's husband, the painter Robert
Delaunay, and modern poets.

1913

**Soleil, lune, simultané 2
(Simultaneous Contrasts:
Sun and Moon)**. 1913 (dated 1912)
Oil on canvas, 53" (134.5 cm) diam.
Mrs. Simon Guggenheim Fund

Delaunay was fascinated by how the interaction of colors produces sensations of depth and movement, without reference to the natural world. In *Simultaneous Contrasts* that movement is the rhythm of the cosmos, for the painting's circular frame is a sign for the universe, and its flux of reds and oranges, greens and blues, is attuned to the sun and the moon, the rotation of day and night. But the star and planet, refracted by light, go undescribed in any literal way. "The breaking up of form by light creates colored planes," Delaunay said. "These colored planes are the structure of the picture, and nature is no longer a subject for description but a pretext." Indeed, he had decided to abandon "images or reality that come to corrupt the order of color."

The poet Guillaume Apollinaire christened Delaunay's style "Orphism," after Orpheus, the musician of Greek legend whose eloquence on the lyre is a mythic archetype for the power of art. The musicality of Delaunay's work lay in color, which he studied closely. In fact, he derived the phrase "Simultaneous Contrasts" from the treatise *On the Law of the Simultaneous Contrast of Colors*, published in 1839 by Michel-Eugène Chevreul. Absorbing Chevreul's scientific analyses, Delaunay has here gone beyond them into a mystical belief in color, its fusion into unity symbolizing the possibility for harmony in the chaos of the modern world.

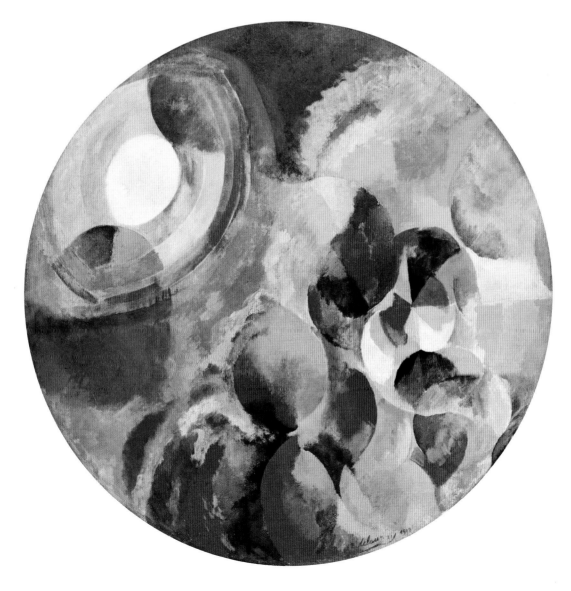

1913

Still Life with Tenora. 1913

Cut-and-pasted papers and newspaper, charcoal, chalk, watercolor, and oil on canvas, 37$^1/_2$ x 47$^3/_8$" (95.2 x 120.3 cm)
Nelson A. Rockefeller Bequest

Still Life with Tenora is a consummate example of Braque's *papier collé* (literally, pasted paper) style. The bold geometric fragments of contrasting types of paper interlaced with the figurative motifs drawn in charcoal evoke the structure of a fugue, in which two distinct melodies intertwine in a rich, sonorous composition, each acting as a foil to the other's reality.

The invention of the *papier collé* in 1912 by Braque and Pablo Picasso introduced a revolution in Western painting, whose repercussions are still being felt today. By pasting fragments of paper (newspaper, wallpaper, and wood-grained paper) onto their still-life compositions, they introduced real materials and textures into an art hitherto based on illusionistic renderings.

The significance of this breakthrough cannot be overestimated because through this technique these artists declared the autonomy of the painted or drawn image, and radically severed it from any attempt at representation. The fragments attached to the picture's surface rarely followed the contours or silhouettes of the drawn motifs (glasses, bottles, or musical instruments), but, paradoxically, contradicted them. Thus, they countered the conventional devices of modeling and depth perspective, and drew attention to the absolute flatness of the two-dimensional plane.

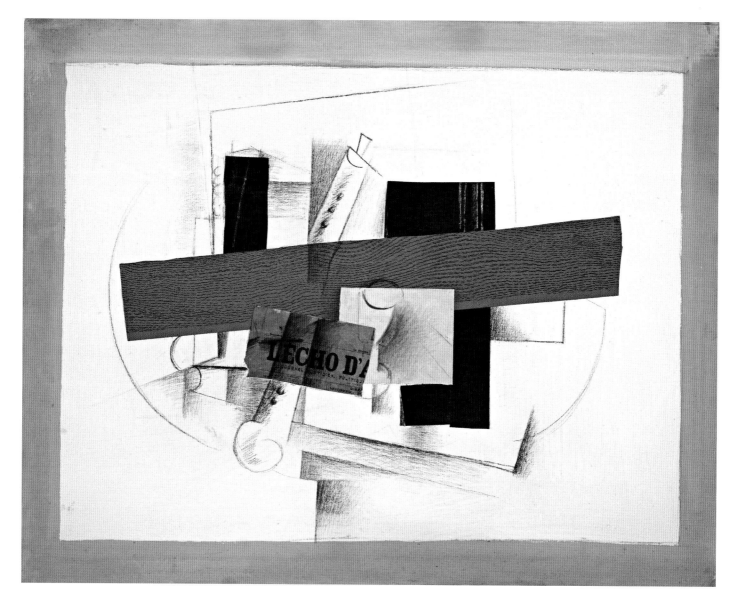

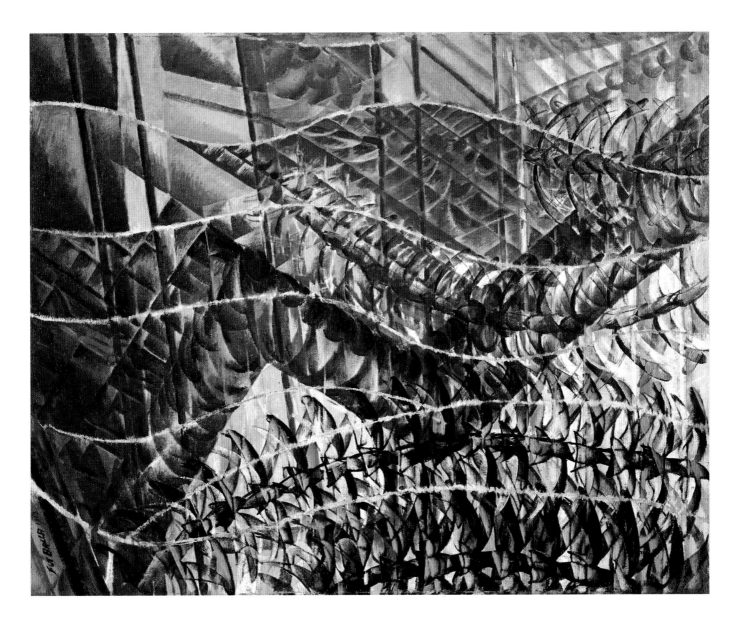

Swifts: Paths of Movement + Dynamic Sequences. 1913

Oil on canvas, 38¹⁄₈ x 47¹⁄₄" (96.8 x 120 cm)
Purchase

"All things move, all things run, all things are rapidly changing," wrote the Futurists, one of them Balla, in 1910. Elaborating on Cubism's experiment in fracturing forms into planes, the Futurists further tried to make painting answer to movement: while the Cubists were concentrating on still lifes and portraits—in other words, were examining stationary bodies—the Futurists were looking at speed. They said: "The gesture which we would reproduce on canvas shall no longer be a fixed *moment* in universal dynamism. It shall simply be the dynamic sensation itself."

The backdrop to this painting is fixed architecture—a window, a drainpipe, a balcony—but the arcs that snake across the foreground are pure rush. The shapes of the swifts (are there four or forty of them?) repeat in stuttering bands, but their substance seems to evaporate: melting into light, the birds are lost in the paths of their own swooping soar. "Dynamic sensation," in Balla's time, was newly susceptible to scientific and visual analysis. Balla knew the photography of Étienne-Jules Marey, which described the movements of animals—including birds—through closely spaced sequences of images; *Swifts* emulates Marey's scientific visual analysis, which, in Balla's time, subjected "dynamic sensation to scrutiny," but adds to it a sense of exhilarated pleasure.

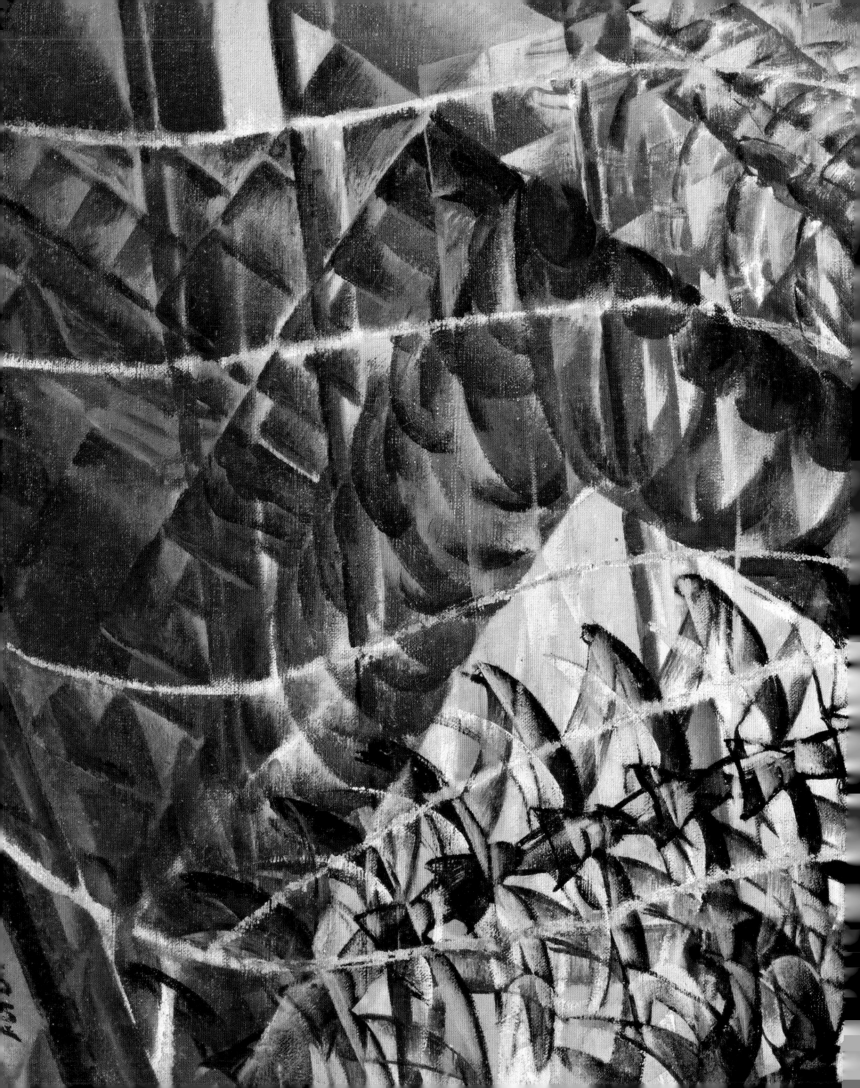

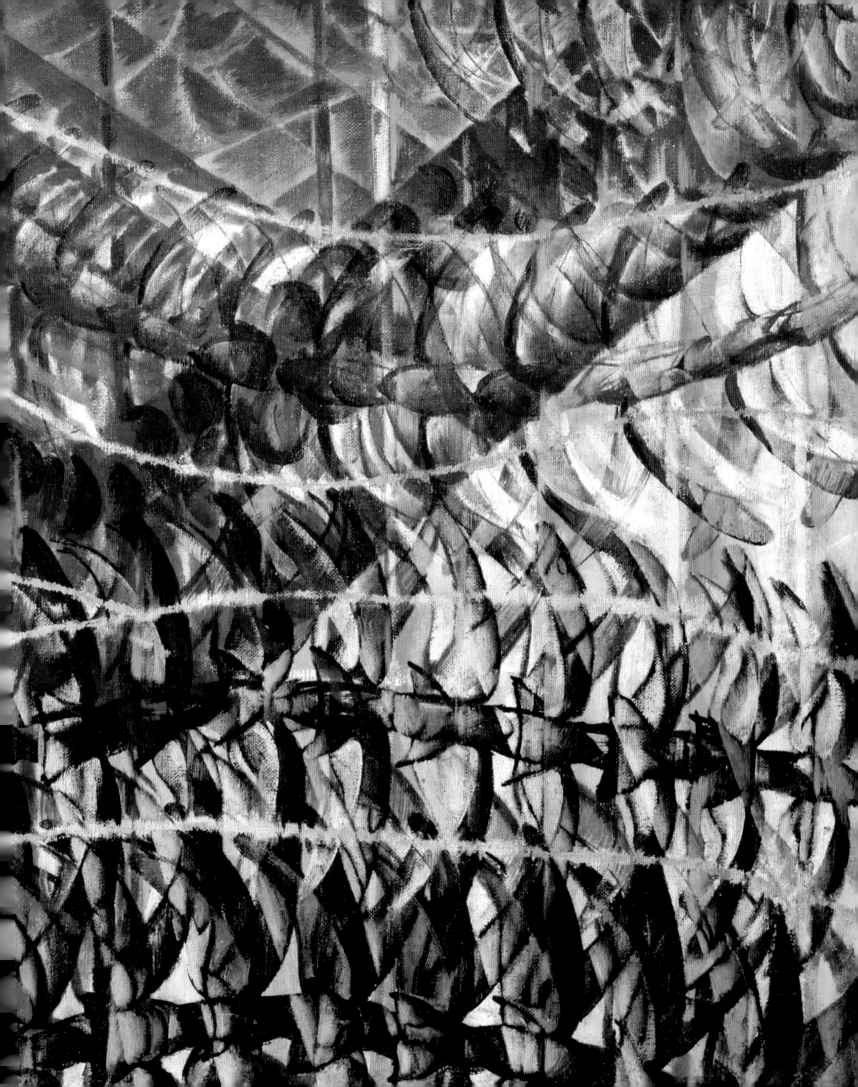

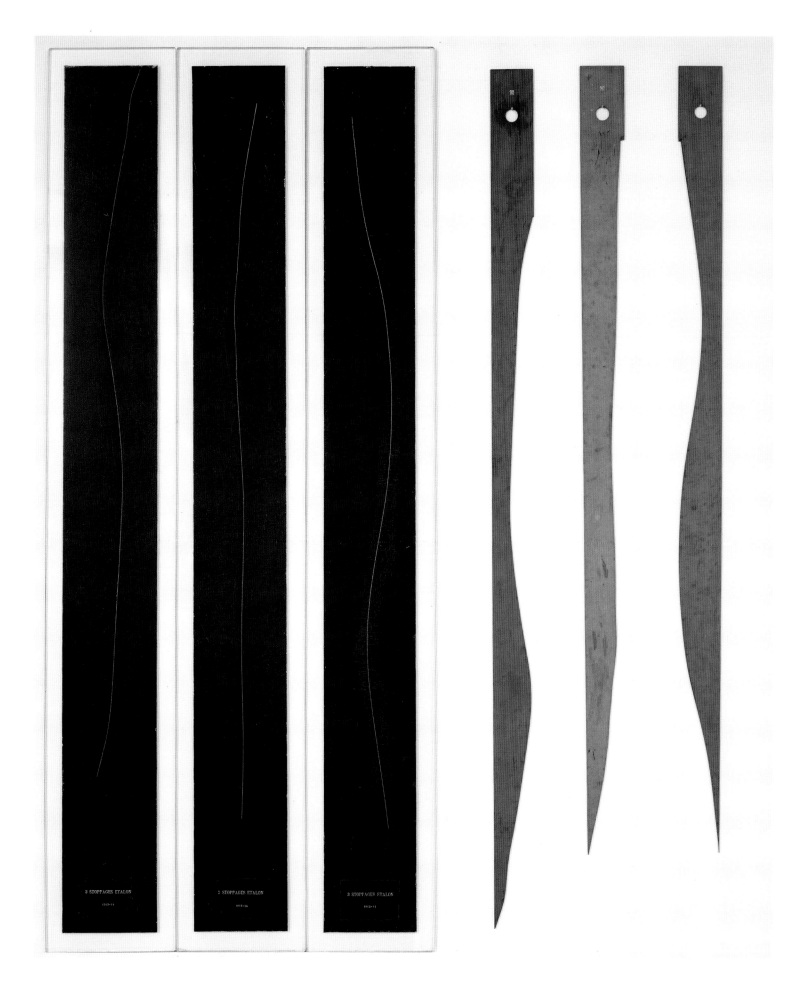

MARCEL DUCHAMP AMERICAN, BORN FRANCE.
1887–1968

3 Standard Stoppages. 1913–14
Assemblage: three threads glued to three painted canvas strips, each 5¹/₄ x 47¹/₄" (13.3 x 120 cm), each mounted on a glass panel, 7¹/₄ x 49³/₈ x ¹/₄" (18.4 x 125.4 x .6 cm); three wood slats, 2¹/₂ x 43 x ¹/₈" (6.2 x 109.2 x .2 cm), 2¹/₂ x 47 x ¹/₈" (6.1 x 119.4 x .2 cm), and 2¹/₂ x 43¹/₄ x ¹/₈" (6.3 x 109.7 x .2 cm), shaped along one edge to match the curves of the threads; the whole fitted into a wood box, 11¹/₈ x 50⁷/₈ x 9" (28.2 x 129.2 x 22.7 cm)
Katherine S. Dreier Bequest

A working note of Duchamp's describes his idea for this enigmatic work: "A straight horizontal thread one meter long falls from a height of one meter onto a horizontal plane twisting as it pleases and creates a new image of the unit of length." Here, three such threads, each fixed to its own canvas with varnish, and each canvas glued to its own glass panel, are enclosed in a box, along with three lengths of wood (draftsman's straightedges) cut into the shapes drawn by the three threads.

Duchamp later said that 3 Standard Stoppages opened the way "to escape from those traditional methods of expression long associated with art," such as what Duchamp called "retinal painting," art designed for the luxuriance of the eye. This required formal intelligence and a skillful hand on the part of the artist. The Stoppages, on the other hand, depended on chance—which, paradoxically, they at the same time fixed and "standardized." (Duchamp used the phrase "canned chance.") Subordinating art both to accident and to something approximating the scientific method (which they simultaneously parodied), 3 Standard Stoppages advanced a conceptual approach, an absurdist strain, and a way of commenting on both art and the broader culture that inspired countless later artists of many different kinds.

MARCEL DUCHAMP AMERICAN, BORN
FRANCE. 1887–1968

Bicycle Wheel. 1951 (third version, after lost original of 1913)
Assemblage: metal wheel, 25¹/₂" (63.8 cm) diam., mounted on painted wood stool, 23³/₄" (60.2 cm) high; overall, 50¹/₂ x 25¹/₂ x 16⁵/₈" (128.3 x 63.8 x 42 cm)
The Sidney and Harriet Janis Collection

Bicycle Wheel is Duchamp's first Readymade, a class of artworks that raised fundamental questions about artmaking and, in fact, about art's very definition. This example is actually an "assisted Readymade": a common object (a bicycle wheel) slightly altered, in this case by being mounted upside-down on another common object (a kitchen stool). Duchamp was not the first to kidnap everyday stuff for art; the Cubists had done so in collages, which, however, required aesthetic judgment in the shaping and placing of materials. The Readymade, on the other hand, implied that the production of art need be no more than a matter of selection—of choosing a preexisting object. In radically subverting earlier assumptions about what the artmaking process entailed, this idea had

enormous influence on later artists, particularly after the broader dissemination of Duchamp's thought in the 1950s and 1960s.

The components of Bicycle Wheel, being mass-produced, are anonymous, identical or similar to countless others. In addition, the fact that this version of the piece is not the original seems inconsequential, at least in terms of visual experience. (Having lost the original Bicycle Wheel, Duchamp simply remade it almost four decades later.) Duchamp claimed to like the work's appearance, "to feel that the wheel turning was very soothing." Even now, Bicycle Wheel retains an absurdist visual surprise. Its greatest power, however, is as a conceptual proposition.

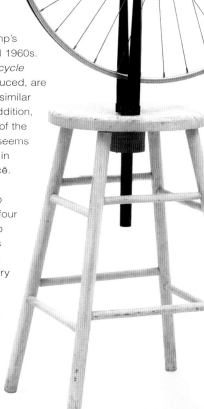

JUAN GRIS (JOSÉ VICTORIANO GONZÁLEZ) SPANISH, 1887–1927

Breakfast. 1914
Cut-and-pasted papers and newspaper, color crayons, charcoal, gouache, and oil on canvas, 31⅞ x 23½" (80.9 x 59.7 cm)
Acquired through the Lillie P. Bliss Bequest

The *papier collé*, invented by Georges Braque and Pablo Picasso in 1912, found a rich and complex expression in the 1914 works of Gris. In conception, his *papiers collés* are closer to paintings than are the sparely drawn compositions of his forerunners; unlike them Gris covers the whole surface with pasted papers and paint. In works such as *Breakfast*, Gris's use of printed papers is more literal than theirs: the wood-grained fragments usually follow some of the contours of a table and are therefore integral to the composition; and his

perspectival cues are relatively legible and precise. His superimposed drawings of domestic objects, fragmented yet softly modeled and most often seen from above, combine to create a more representational pictorial composition than those of Braque and Picasso.

Despite these observations, *Breakfast* is full of troubling contradictions. The striped wallpaper background spills across the table; certain objects (a glass on the left, a bottle in the upper right) appear as ghostly presences; the coffeepot is disjointed; the tobacco packet is painted and drawn in photographically realistic trompe l'oeil, but its label is real. Thus, while aspects of domestic comfort are captured in this image, Gris also raises many subjective and objective questions about how reality is perceived.

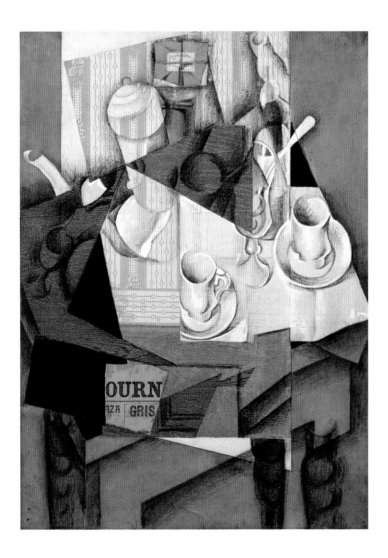

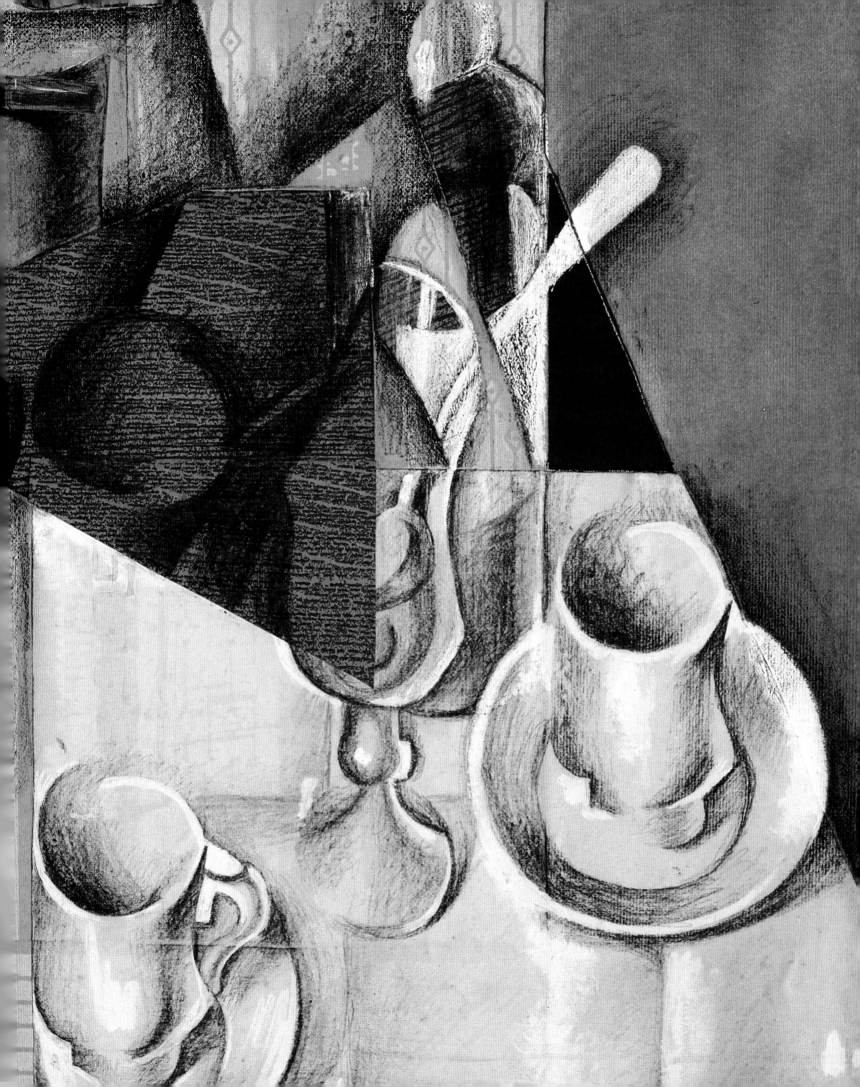

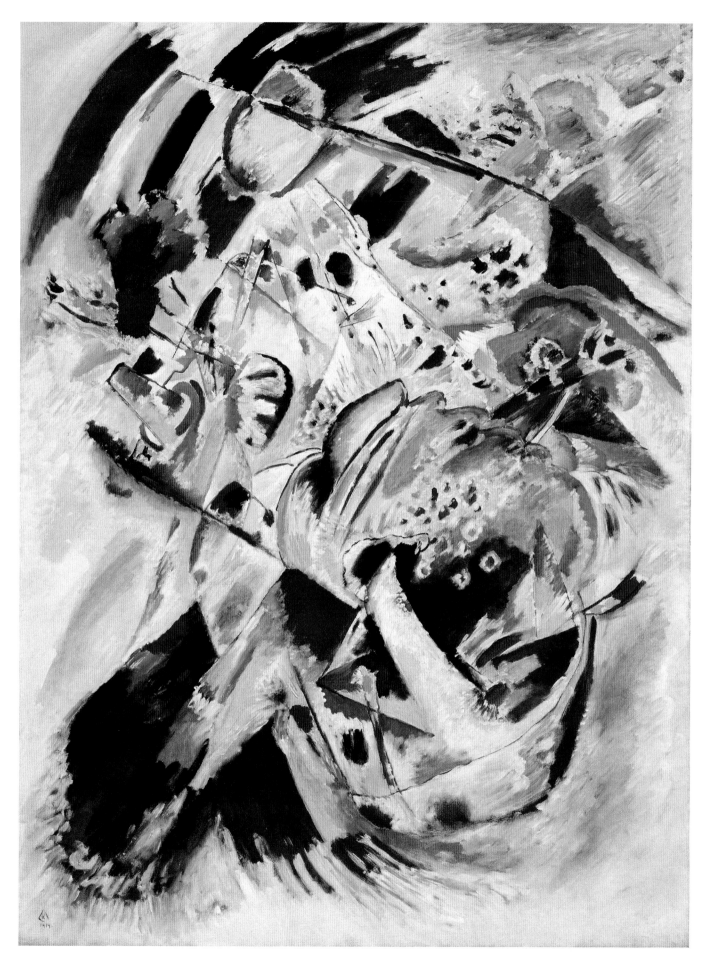

VASILY KANDINSKY FRENCH, BORN RUSSIA.
1866–1944

Panel for Edwin R. Campbell No. 4.
1914
Oil on canvas, 64¼ x 48¼" (163 x 122.5 cm)
Nelson A. Rockefeller Fund (by exchange)

This painting is one of a lush and vibrant suite of four canvases produced at a time when artists in several countries were beginning to explore what Kandinsky, a pioneer of abstract art, called "nonobjective" painting—painting that showed no immediately recognizable objects. Instead, Kandinsky wanted each of his works to be "a graphic representation of a mood." Studies for one of these paintings suggest that he had a landscape in mind when he conceived it, and we might still see in all four works a field, a mountain, or a cloud; but they are much transformed. Similarly, if these works do indeed describe the four seasons, as one scholar has guessed, then their colors and abstract shapes respond to some quality sensed in the year's phases, rather than to any specific scene.

Edwin R. Campbell, who commissioned the series, was an automobile executive, who had the works made to fit the walls in the entrance hall of the New York apartment he shared with his wife, Margery. Unfortunately, the couple separated in 1921, and the paintings separated too, being divided into pairs, and passing through several different collections; they were permanently reunited at The Museum of Modern Art in 1982.

PIET MONDRIAN DUTCH, 1872–1944

Pier and Ocean 5 (Sea and Starry Sky). 1915
Charcoal and gouache on buff paper, 34⅝ x 44" (87.9 x 111.2 cm)
Mrs. Simon Guggenheim Fund
© 2005 Mondrian/Holtzman Trust
c/o HCR International Warrenton Virginia USA

At first glance, this drawing appears to be totally abstract, despite its descriptive title. In fact, the vertical lines at the base of the oval represent a pier that stretches into an ocean of short horizontal and vertical lines above and around it. At times crossing or lying perpendicular to one another, these lines reflect the rhythmic ebb and flow of the sea, and, with the areas of white paint, the reflected starlight overhead.

Mondrian had begun to experiment with abstraction before 1912, when he left for Paris, where for two years he was exposed to Cubism. He returned to the Netherlands with renewed determination to create a purer abstract form at the expense of more illustrative elements. His highly individual version of Cubism simplified it into a vertical-horizontal grid, in which shading was flattened to the surface to form areas of muted color.

In the Pier and Ocean series of 1914–15, color is eliminated, and the grid opens to form a cluster of "plus-and-minus" signs within a Cubist oval. The reduction to vertical and horizontal generalizes the artist's sources in nature into a symbolic structure representing what Mondrian saw as a cosmic dualism between the masculine and spiritual (vertical) and the feminine and material (horizontal). His system of cruciform signs here speaks to flickering light and movement on water and also to a spiritual structure within nature itself—in his words, "a true vision of reality."

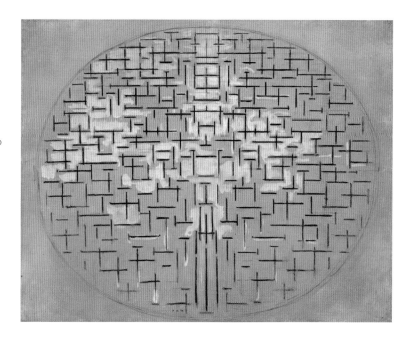

GIORGIO DE CHIRICO ITALIAN, BORN GREECE.
1888–1978

The Song of Love. 1914
Oil on canvas, 28³/₄ x 23³/₈" (73 x 59.1 cm)
Nelson A. Rockefeller Bequest

"M. Giorgio de Chirico has just bought a red rubber glove"—so wrote the French poet Guillaume Apollinaire in July of 1914, noting the purchase because, he went on to say, he knew the glove's appearance in de Chirico's paintings would add to their uncanny power. Implying human presence, as a mold of the hand, yet also inhuman, a clammily limp fragment distinctly unfleshlike in color, the glove in *The Song of Love* has an unsettling authority. Why, too, is this surgical garment pinned to a board or canvas, alongside a plaster head copied from a classical statue, relic of a noble

vanished age? What is the meaning of the green ball? And what is the whole ensemble doing in the outdoor setting insinuated by the building and the passing train?

Unlikely meetings among dissimilar objects were to become a strong theme in modern art (they soon became an explicit goal of the Surrealists), but de Chirico sought more than surprise: in works like this one, for which Apollinaire used the term "metaphysical," he wanted to evoke an enduring level of reality hidden beyond outward appearances. Perhaps this is why he gives us a geometric form (the spherical ball), a schematic building rather than a specific one, and inert and partial images of the human body rather than a living, mortal being.

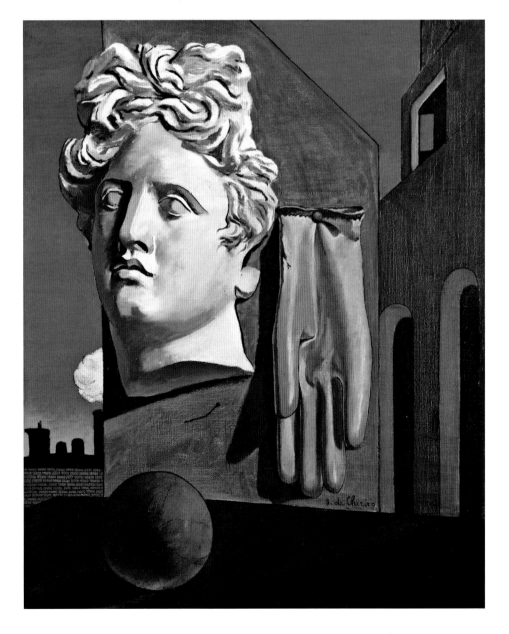

facing page:
Francis Picabia,
*I See Again in Memory
My Dear Udnie*
(see entry on page 98)

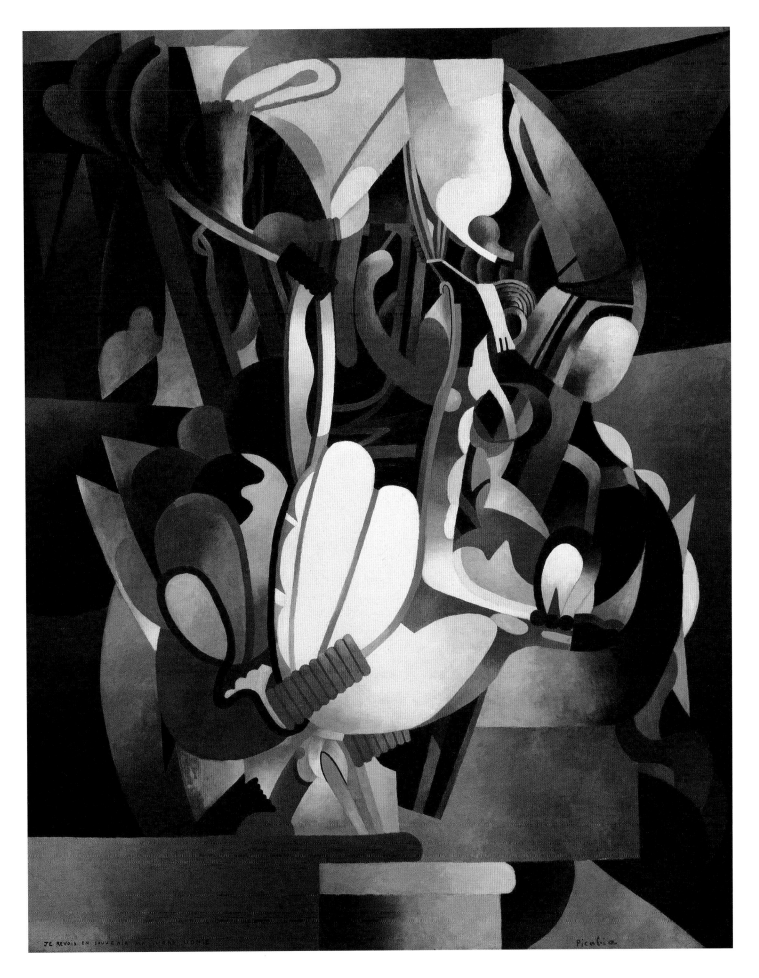

JE REVOIS EN SOUVENIR MA CHERE UDNIE   Picabia

FRANCIS PICABIA FRENCH, 1879–1953

I See Again in Memory My Dear Udnie.
(1914, perhaps begun 1913)
Oil on canvas, 8' 2¹/₂" x 6' 6¹/₄"
(250.2 x 198.8 cm)
Hillman Periodicals Fund

Like the Futurists and like his friend Marcel Duchamp, Picabia recognized the importance of the machine in the dawning technological age. The hard-edged, evenly rounded shapes of *I See Again in Memory My Dear Udnie*, some of them in metallic grays, parallel fusions of the mechanical and the organic in Duchamp's painting, and anticipate more overt references of this kind in Picabia's later work. Perspectival lines at the painting's sides suggest a space around this fragmented body, which seems to stand on a kind of stage. Segmented tubes among the curling forms may have a sexual subtext,

and Picabia himself described his art of this period as trying "to render external an internal state of mind or feeling."

The "Udnie" of this work's title was surely a certain Mlle. Napierskowska, a professional dancer whom Picabia met on the ocean liner that took him to the United States to participate in the famous Armory Show of 1913. Fascinated by Napierskowska's performances (which were suggestive enough to provoke her arrest during her American tour), Picabia began to produce gouaches and watercolors inspired by her even before landing in New York. Over the following year, he extended this imagery in paintings, titling one of them *Udnie (Young American Girl)*—and thus suggesting that the abstract planes of these works relate to the human form.

(See illustration on page 97)

PAUL STRAND AMERICAN, 1890–1976

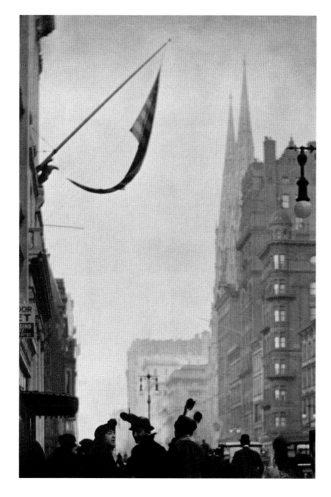

Fifth Avenue, New York. 1915
Platinum print, 12¹/₄ x 8¹/₄" (31.2 x 20.8 cm)
Gift of the artist

The shallow composition, as in a Japanese print, empty at the center and crowded at the edges; the muted tones, as in a print by James MacNeill Whistler; and the elegant shape made by the tethered flag, which rhymes with the spires of the church: these are survivals of photography's aesthetic movement at the turn of the century.

Strand's momentary glimpse of individual pedestrians strolling near a specific church—St. Patrick's Cathedral—on a particular stretch of Fifth Avenue in New York hints of concrete experience and points toward the challenges that the art of photography faced as it emerged from its aesthetic cloister. A woman in the foreground makes eye contact with the photographer. As a result, she is transformed from an element in a decorative frieze into a person with a mind of her own.

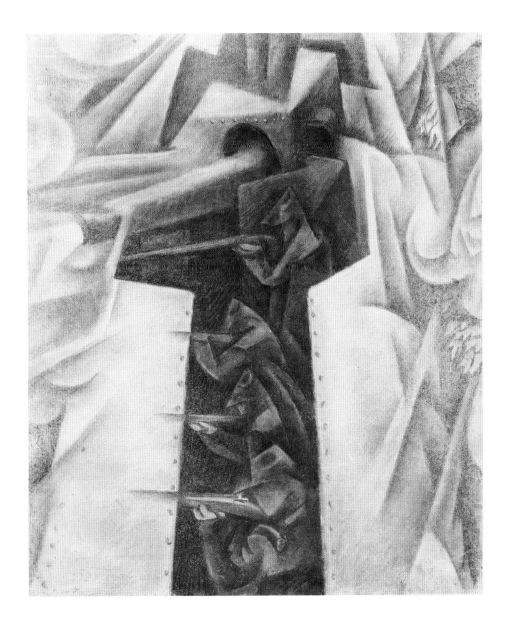

Armored Train in Action. 1915

Charcoal on paper, 22¹/₂ x 18³/₄" (56.9 x 47.5 cm)
Benjamin Scharps and David Scharps Fund

This study for the most famous of the Futurist war paintings, *The Armored Train* (1915), incorporates an unusual aerial perspective in its depiction of a train filled with armed soldiers. Severini enjoyed a unique vantage point—his Paris studio overlooked the Denfert-Rochereau station, from which he was able to observe the constant movement of trains filled with soldiers, supplies, and weaponry. Although Severini remained a noncombatant during World War I, he took the advice of fellow Futurist artist Filippo Tommaso Marinetti to "try to live the war pictorially, studying it in all its marvelous mechanical forms."

The Futurists glorified modern technology, and World War I, the first war of the twentieth century to employ the technological achievements of the industrial age in a program of mass destruction, was for them the most important spectacle of the modern era. Their admiration for speed—made possible by machinery—is represented here by the fractured landscape, which accentuates the train's force and momentum as it cuts through the countryside.

Armored Train in Action foreshadows a fundamental principle of Severini's later art: the "image-idea," in which a single image expresses the essence of an idea. Through a depiction of the plastic realities of war—a train, canon, guns, and soldiers—he provides a pictorial vocabulary necessary to grasp its deeper symbolism.

The Moroccans. 1915–16

Oil on canvas, 71³/₈" x 9' 2" (181.3 x 279.4 cm)
Gift of Mr. and Mrs. Samuel A. Marx

The Moroccans marvelously evokes tropical sun and heat even while its ground is an enveloping black, what Matisse called "a grand black, ... as luminous as the other colors in the painting." Utterly dense, this black evokes a space as tangible as any object, and allows a gravity and measured drama without the illusion of depth once necessary to achieve this kind of grandeur.

The painting, which Matisse described as picturing "the terrace of the little café of the casbah," is divided into three: at the upper left, an architectural section showing a balcony with flowerpot and the dome of a mosque behind; a still life, of four green-leafed yellow melons at the lower left; and a figural scene in which an Arab sits with his back to us. To his right is an arched doorway, and windows above contain vestigial figures. The form to his left is hard to decipher, but has been interpreted as a man's burnoose and circular turban.

During his visit to Morocco in 1912–13, Matisse had been inspired by African light and color. At the same time, he faced the challenge of Cubism, the leading avant-garde art movement of the period, and *The Moroccans* summarizes his memories of Morocco while also combining the intellectual rigor of Cubist syntax with the larger scale and richer palette of his own art.

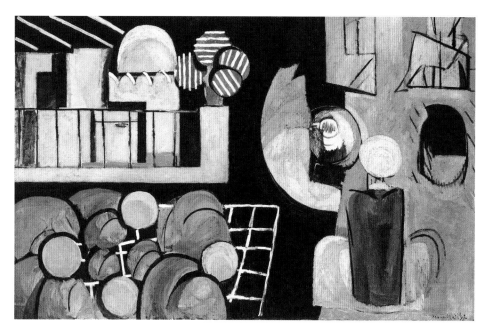

Piano Lesson. 1916

Oil on canvas, 8' ¹/₂" x 6' 11³/₄" (245.1 x 212.7 cm)
Mrs. Simon Guggenheim Fund

The little boy so seriously playing the piano is Matisse's son Pierre. The woman who might be his teacher, apparently watching him from behind, is actually a figure in a painting, Matisse's *Woman on a High Stool (Germaine Raynal)*, which hangs on the wall by the window. Similarly the sensually posed nude at bottom left would be an unlikely class auditor were not this another artwork in Matisse's living room, his own bronze *Decorative Figure*.

Piano Lesson treats two unlike spaces—a view through a window into air and the flat and tangible canvas of *Woman on a High Stool*—as if they were quite equivalent.

Matisse is addressing issues both formal and philosophical. In describing the playing of music he also takes art-making as his subject, and the filigree bar of curves supplied by the music stand and balcony ironwork—a lovely touch amid the painting's interlocking triangles and rectangles—might almost be a visual version of music's curling notes.

Those flat planes of muted color create a system of geometric compartments that link the painting to Cubism, whose radical inventions Matisse had observed over the preceding few years without ever committing himself to the style. Works like this one show him examining Cubist ideas about pictorial structure while also producing an image utterly personal to him.

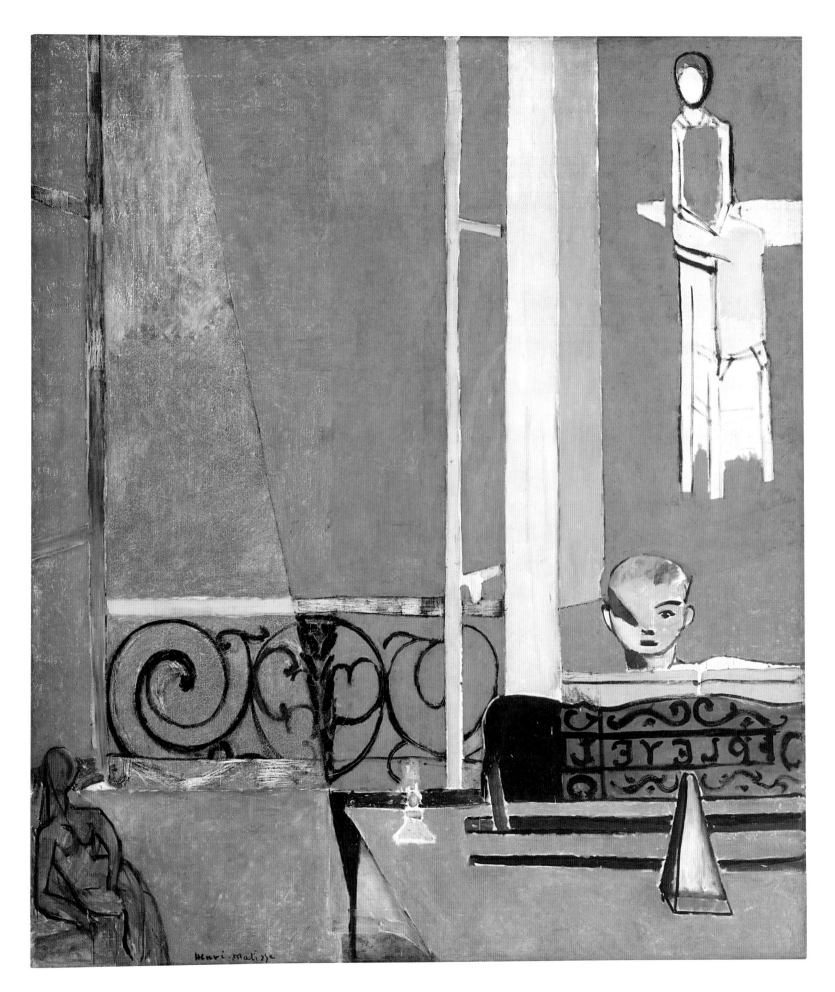

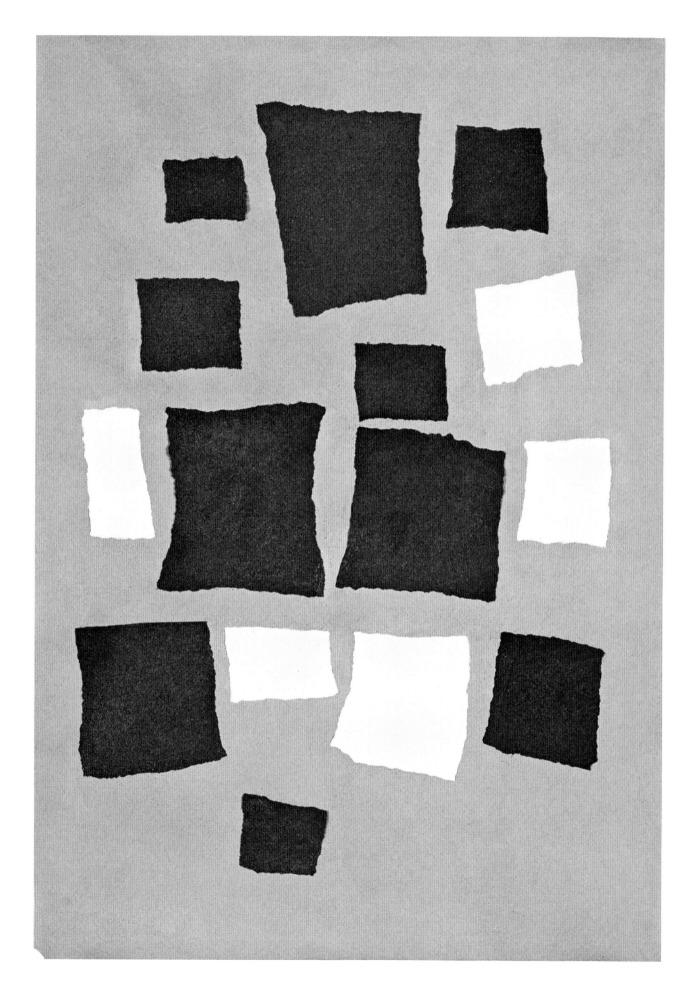

JEAN (HANS) ARP FRENCH, BORN GERMANY (ALSACE). 1887–1966

Collage Arranged According to the Laws of Chance. 1916–17
Torn-and-pasted papers on gray paper,
19¹/₈ x 13⁵/₈" (48.6 x 34.6 cm)
Purchase

This elegantly composed collage of torn-and-pasted paper is a playful, almost syncopated composition in which uneven squares seem to dance within the space. As the title suggests, it was created not by the artist's design, but by chance. In 1915 Arp began to develop a method of making collages by dropping pieces of torn paper on the floor and arranging them on a piece of paper more or less the way they had fallen. He did this in order to create a work that was free of human intervention and closer to nature. The incorporation of chance operations was a way of removing the artist's will from the

creative act, much as his earlier, more severely geometric collages had substituted a paper cutter for scissors, so as to divorce his work from "the life of the hand."

Arp was a founding member of the first Dada group that coalesced in Zurich in 1916 around the Cabaret Voltaire of Hugo Ball, the poet and performer. Dada—its name a nonsensical word chosen at random from the dictionary—was formed to prove the bankruptcy of existing styles of artistic expression rather than to promote a particular style itself. "Dada," wrote Arp, "wished to destroy the hoaxes of reason and to discover an unreasoned order." While this work is far less violent than some of the rhetoric of Dada, Arp's exemplary use of serendipitous composition here perfectly embodies what has been called the heart of Dada practice—the gratuitous act.

HENRI MATISSE FRENCH, 1869–1954

The Back, III. 1916
Bronze, 6' 2¹/₂" x 44" x 6" (189.2 x 111.8 x 15.2 cm)
Edition: 1/10
Mrs. Simon Guggenheim Fund

"Fit your parts into one another and build up your figure as a carpenter does a house. Everything must be constructed—built up of parts that make a unit; a tree like a human body, a human body like a cathedral." So Matisse believed the sculptor should proceed, and the credo can be sensed in this work and throughout the group of four relief sculptures to which it belongs, with its progressive stability and simplicity. Matisse did not conceive The Backs as a series, but occasionally returned to the theme over the years. Even so, these reliefs—his largest sculptures—present a coherent progress, from a relatively detailed naturalism toward a near-abstract monumentality.

This work is the third in the series, and it is more vertical and less sinuous than its precursors. The first work in the series (1909) has a dynamic tension, and an arabesque line flows through it; in the second (1913), the body is more erect, less fluid. The left leg has become a thick pillar; making the figure more solid. The third work leads to the fourth (1931), where Matisse suppresses physical detail, making the contours more fluid, the surface more homogeneous. But if he surrenders expressiveness in the sculpture's parts, he regains it in the symmetrical harmony of the work as a whole.

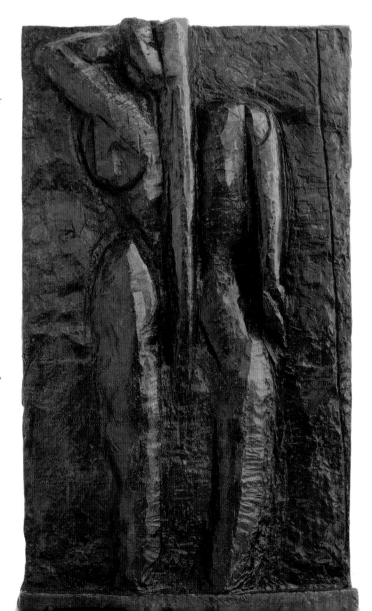

103

LIUBOV SERGEIEVNA POPOVA RUSSIAN, 1889–1924

Painterly Architectonic. 1917

Oil on canvas, 31¹/₂ x 38⁵/₈" (80 x 98 cm)
Philip Johnson Fund

In *Painterly Architectonic*, one of a series of works by this title, Popova arranges areas of white, red, black, gray, and pink to suggest straight-edged planes laid one on top of the other over a white ground, like differently shaped papers in a collage. The space is not completely flat, however, for the rounded lower rim of the gray plane implies that this surface is arching upward against the red triangle. This pressure finds matches in the shapes and placements of the planes, which shun both right angles and vertical or horizontal lines, so that the picture becomes a taut net of slants and diagonals. The composition's orderly spatial recession is energized by these dynamic vectors, along which the viewer's gaze alternately slides and lifts.

Influenced by her long visits to Europe before World War I, Popova helped to introduce the Cubist and Futurist ideas of France and Italy into Russian art. But, no matter how abstract European Cubism and Futurism became, they never completely abandoned recognizable imagery, whereas Popova developed an entirely nonrepresentational idiom based on layered planes of color. The catalyst in this transition was Kazimir Malevich's Suprematism, an art of austere geometric shapes. But where Suprematism was infused with the desire for a spiritual or cosmic space, Popova's concerns were purely pictorial.

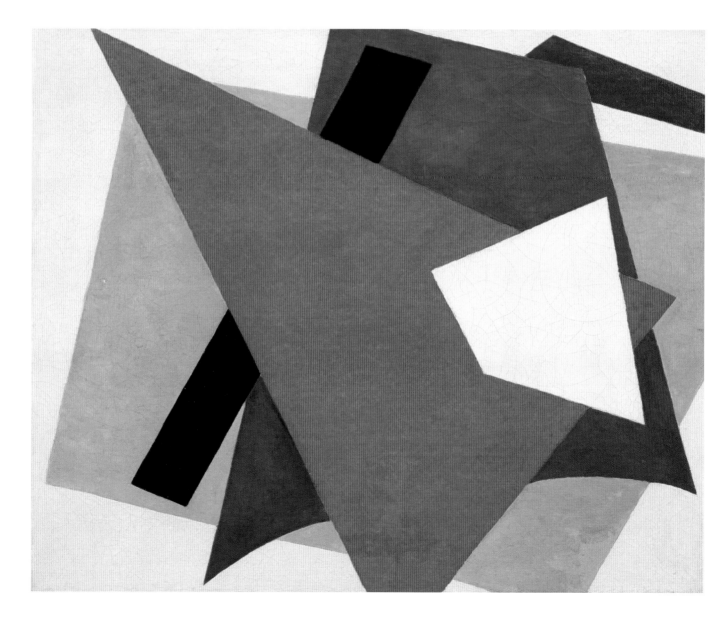

Suprematist Composition: White on White. 1918

Oil on canvas, 31¹/₄ x 31¹/₄" (79.4 x 79.4 cm)

A white square floating weightlessly in a white field, *Suprematist Composition: White on White* was one of the most radical paintings of its day: a geometric abstraction without reference to external reality. Yet the picture is not impersonal: we see the artist's hand in the texture of the paint, and in the subtle variations of the whites. The square is not exactly symmetrical, and its lines, imprecisely ruled, have a breathing quality, generating a feeling not of borders defining a shape but of a space without limits.

After the Revolution, Russian intellectuals hoped that human reason and modern technology would engineer a perfect society.

Malevich was fascinated with technology, and particularly with the airplane, instrument of the human yearning to break the bounds of earth. He studied aerial photography, and wanted *White on White* to create a sense of floating and transcendence. White was for Malevich the color of infinity, and signified a realm of higher feeling.

For Malevich, that realm, a utopian world of pure form, was attainable only through nonobjective art. Indeed, he named his theory of art Suprematism to signify "the supremacy of pure feeling or perception in the pictorial arts"; and pure perception demanded that a picture's forms "have nothing in common with nature." Malevich imagined Suprematism as a universal language that would free viewers from the material world.

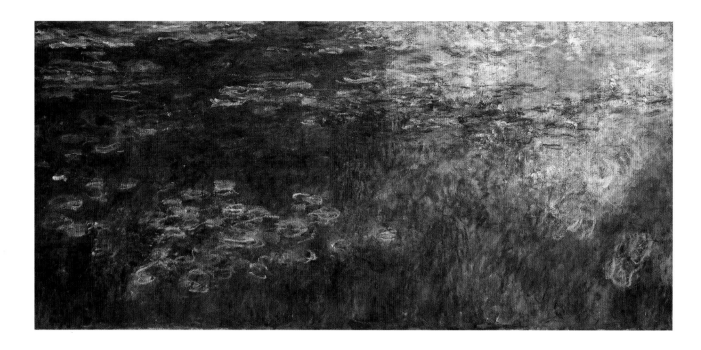

Water Lilies. c. 1920

Oil on canvas, left panel of triptych, each panel
6' 6" x 14' (200 x 425 cm)
Mrs. Simon Guggenheim Fund

Visitors to Monet's Giverny studio in 1918 found "a dozen canvases placed in a circle on the floor ... [creating] a panorama made up of water and lilies, of light and sky. In that infinitude, water and sky have neither beginning nor end." What they had seen was a group of paintings that Monet planned to install abutting each other in an oval, encompassing the viewer in a sensually enveloping space. The aim, he said, was to supply "the illusion of an endless whole, of water without horizon or bank." The *Water Lilies* triptych comes from this series, which describes a scene Monet not only showed in art but shaped in life: the pond in his own garden.

Like his fellow Impressionists, Monet, when young, had attempted a faithfulness to perceived reality, trying to capture the constantly changing quality of natural light and color. The *Water Lilies*, though, seem nearly abstract, for their scale and allover splendor so immerse us in visual experience that spatial cues dissolve: above and below, near and far, water and sky commingle. Perhaps this was the quality that led Monet's visitors to say, "We seem to be present at one of the first hours in the birth of the world." Yet Monet's desire that the installation create "the refuge of a peaceful meditation" seems equally just.

Oval Hanging Construction Number 12.

c. 1920

Plywood, open construction partially painted with aluminum paint, and wire, 24 x 33 x 18½" (61 x 83.7 x 47 cm)
Acquisition made possible through the extraordinary efforts of George and Zinaida Costakis, and through the Nate B. and Frances Spingold, Matthew H. and Erna Futter, and Enid A. Haupt Funds

A series of different-sized ovals that nest and intersect, *Oval Hanging Construction* hangs in space, moving slowly with any current of air. The ovals were measured out on a single flat sheet of plywood, precisely cut, then rotated within each other to make a three-dimensional object resembling a gyroscope. The resulting form suggests a chart of planetary orbits, a cosmic structure. In companion pieces, Rodchenko applied the same principle and method to other basic geometric forms, such as the square, but those works no longer survive.

Rodchenko's interest in mathematical systems reflects the scientific bent of the Russian Constructivists, artists who aspired to create a radically new, radically rational art for the society that came into being with the Russian Revolution. *Hanging Construction* is a stage in Rodchenko's progress away from conventional painting and toward an art taking place in space—ultimately, an art of social involvement. The work has no top, no bottom, no base to rest on. It is virtually weightless, with suspension and movement replacing mass. In short, it was designed to be everything traditional sculpture was not—to reimagine art from ground zero.

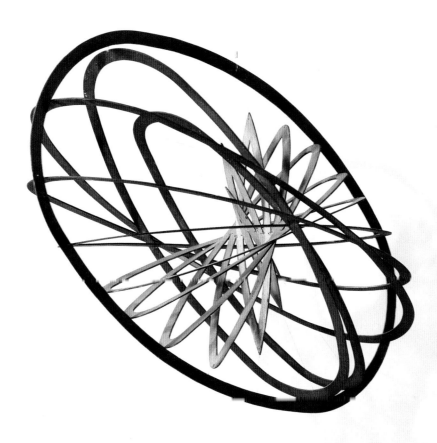

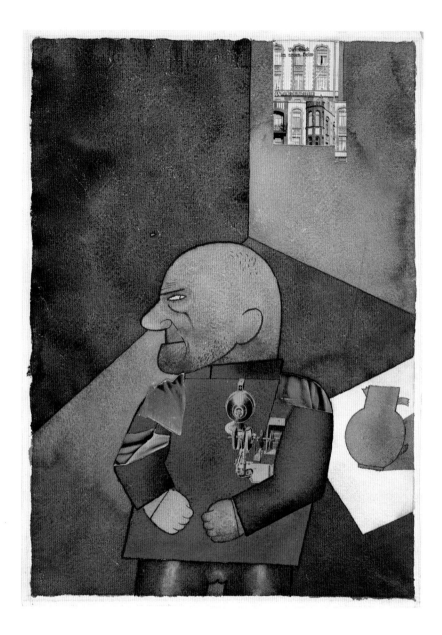

The Engineer Heartfield. 1920

Watercolor, pasted postcards, relief halftone,
and pencil on paper, 16½ x 12" (41.9 x 30.5 cm)
Gift of A. Conger Goodyear

In this work Grosz combines traditional,
delicately hued watercolor with pasted
photomechanical reproductions in an unreal
space, inspired by the work of the Italian
painter Giorgio de Chirico. These pictorial
devices convey the satirical ideology that
Grosz shared with his subject, John
Heartfield, a friend, a fellow Berlin Dada
artist, and a frequent collaborator. Heartfield
is depicted as bald, grim-faced, and with
clenched fists and a machine heart—the
personification of the politically defiant anti-
authoritarian, which was a stance that
infused Heartfield's own art.

His uniform and the drab walls and floor
suggest a prisoner in his cell, and the
segmented view of a building in the distance,
as if glimpsed through a narrow window,
bears the mordant inscription: "Lots of luck in
your new home." The mechanical gears
indicate Heartfield's identity as an engineer
or constructor (*monteur*) of photomontages.
In fact, Heartfield called himself a *monteur-
dada*, rather than an artist, and conceived of
his own assembled works as images
intended only for mass reproduction in
magazines and on book covers and posters.

The Hat Makes the Man. 1920

Gouache, pencil, ink, and cut-and-pasted collotypes on buff paper, 14 x 18" (35.6 x 45.7 cm)
Purchase

Pictures of ordinary hats cut out of a catalogue are stacked one atop the other in constructions that resemble both organic, plantlike forms and anthropomorphic phalluses. With the inscription, "seed-covered stacked-up man seedless waterformer ('edelformer') well-fitting nervous system also tightly fitted nerves! (the hat makes the man) (style is the tailor)," Ernst incorporates verbal humor into this subversive visual pun.

The artist was a major figure of the Dada group, which embraced the concepts of irrationality and obscure meaning. *The Hat Makes the Man* illustrates the use of mechanical reproductions to record Ernst's own hallucinatory, often erotic visions. The origin of this collage is a sculpture made from wood hat molds that Ernst created in 1920 for a Dada exhibition in Cologne. The repetition of the hat, indicative of part of the bourgeois uniform, suggests the Dadaist view of modern man as a conformist puppet. Thus, in true Dada fashion, Ernst combines the contradictory elements of an inanimate object with references to man and to nature; symbols of social conventionality are equated with sexually charged ones.

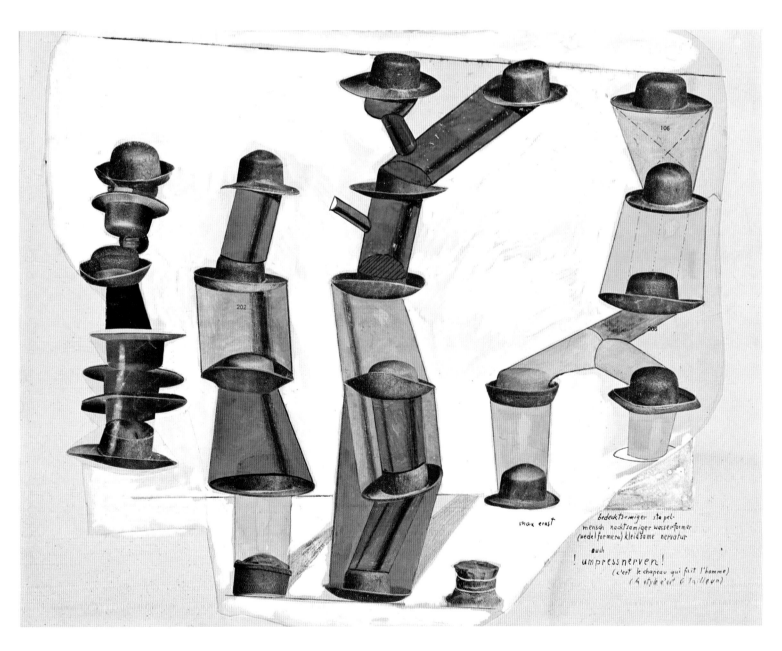

111

FERNAND LÉGER
FRENCH, 1881–1955

Three Women. 1921
Oil on canvas, 6' ¼" x 8' 3" (183.5 x 251.5 cm)
Mrs. Simon Guggenheim Fund

In *Three Women*, Léger translates a common theme in art history—the reclining nude—into a modern idiom, simplifying the female figure into a mass of rounded and somewhat dislocated forms, the skin not soft but firm, even unyielding. The machinelike precision and solidity that Léger gives his women's bodies relate to his faith in modern industry, and to his hope that art and the machine age would together remake the world. The painting's geometric equilibrium, its black bands and panels of white, suggest his awareness of Mondrian, an artist then becoming popular. Another stylistic trait is the return to variants of classicism, which was widespread in French art after the chaos of World War I. Though buffed and polished, the simplified volumes of Léger's figures are, nonetheless, in the tradition of classicists of the previous century.

A group of naked women taking tea, or coffee, together may also recall paintings of harem scenes, for example, by Jean-Auguste-Dominque Ingres, although there the drink might be wine. Updating the repast, Léger also updates the setting—a chic apartment, decorated with fashionable vibrancy. And the women, with their flat-ironed hair hanging to one side, have a Hollywood glamour. The painting is like a beautiful engine, its parts meshing smoothly and in harmony.

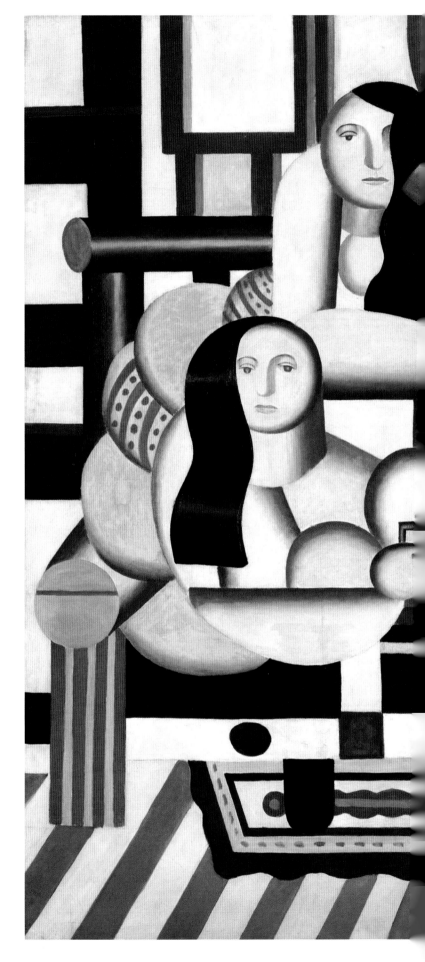

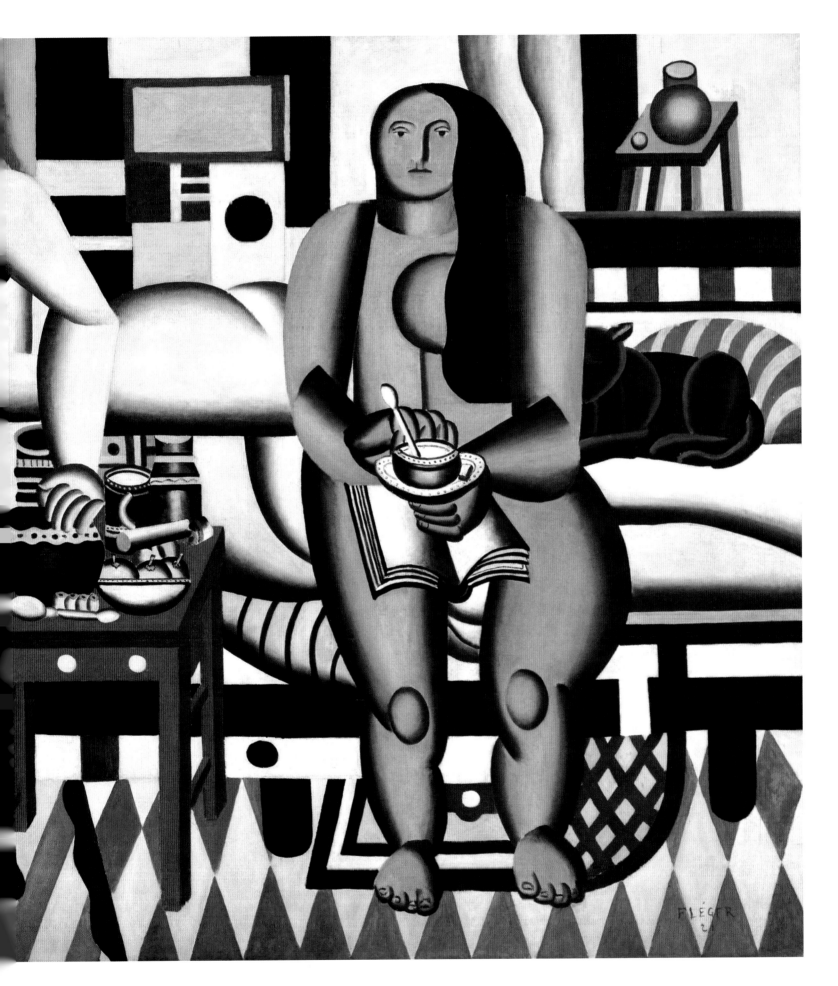

LUDWIG MIES VAN DER ROHE AMERICAN,
BORN GERMANY. 1886-1969

Honeycomb, Friedrichstrasse Skyscraper, Berlin. Competition project, 1921

Perspective, north and east sides: charcoal and pencil on brown paper, mounted on board, 68¼ x 48" (173.4 x 121.9 cm)
Mies van der Rohe Archive. Gift of the architect

This design for a crystal tower was unprecedented in 1921. It was based on the untried idea that a supporting steel skeleton would be able to free the exterior walls from their load-bearing function, allowing a building to have a surface that is more translucent than solid. Mies van der Rohe determined the faceted, prismatic shapes of its three connecting towers by experimenting with light reflections on a glass model. While the design anticipates his later preference for steel and glass, here a highly expressionistic character is more evident than any kind of rationalist intention.

A leader of the revolutionary modern movement in architecture, Mies van der Rohe designed a series of five startlingly innovative projects in the early 1920s, each of which had a profound influence on progressive architects all over the world. This competition entry was one of them. Code-named "Honeycomb," the Friedrichstrasse Skyscraper was distinguished by its daring use of glass, which symbolized the dawning of a new culture, and by an expressive shape that seems to owe nothing to history.

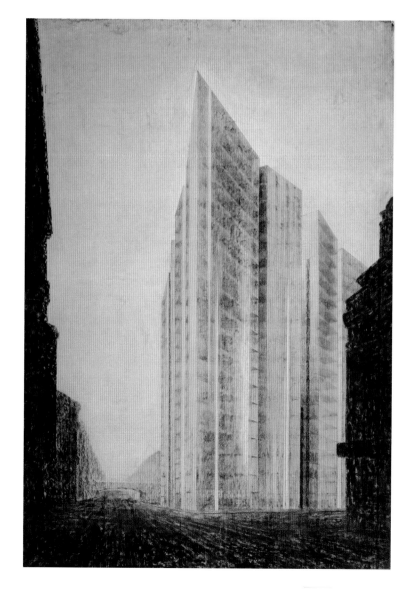

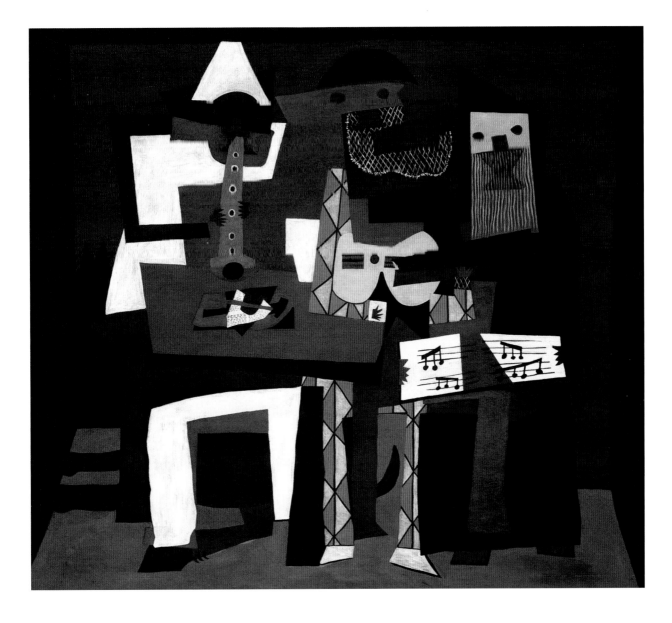

Three Musicians. 1921
Oil on canvas, 6' 7" x 7' 3³/₄" (200.7 x 222.9 cm)
Mrs. Simon Guggenheim Fund

At the left of a bare and boxlike space, a masked Pierrot plays the clarinet. At the right, a singing monk holds sheet music. And in the center, strumming a guitar, is a Harlequin, in Picasso's art a recurring stand-in for the artist himself.

Pierrot and Harlequin are stock characters in the old Italian comic theater known as commedia dell'arte, a familiar theme in Picasso's work. The painting, then, has a whimsical side, epitomized by the near-invisible dog: its head is about halfway up the canvas on the left, one of several subtle browns, and we can also make out front paws, a hind leg, and a jaunty tail popping

up between Harlequin's legs. Overall, though, the work's somber background and large size make the musicians a solemn, even majestic trio.

The intricate, jigsaw-puzzle-like composition sums up the Synthetic Cubist style, the flat planes of unshaded color recalling the cutout and pasted paper forms with which the style began. These overlapping shapes are at their most complex at the center of the picture, which is also where the lightest hues are concentrated, so that an aura of darkness surrounds a brighter center. Along with the frontal poses of the figures, this creates a feeling of gravity and monumentality, and gives *Three Musicians* a mysterious, otherworldly air.

KURT SCHWITTERS BRITISH, BORN GERMANY. 1887–1948

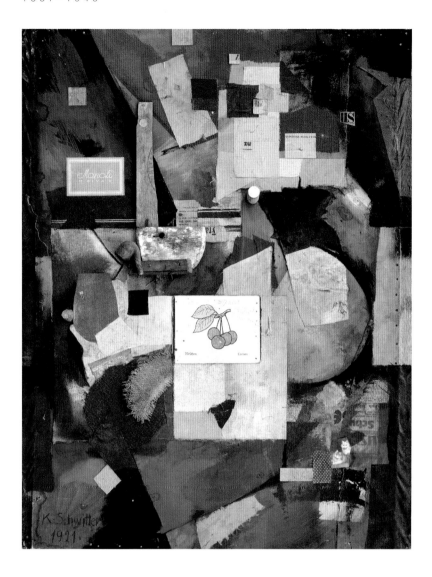

Merz Picture 32A (The Cherry Picture).

1921

Cloth, wood, metal, fabric, cut-and-pasted papers, cork, gouache, oil, and ink on cardboard, 36 1/8 x 27 3/4" (91.8 x 70.5 cm)

Mr. and Mrs. A. Atwater Kent, Jr. Fund

This highly animated picture is dominated by rectangular pieces of paper that cover the surface of the work. Schwitters created the illusion of depth by placing those papers with darker components behind those that are lighter in aspect. The brightest piece of paper, in the center of the composition, shows an eye-catching cluster of red cherries and the printed German and French words for the fruit.

In the winter of 1918–19 Schwitters had collected bits of newspaper, candy wrappers, and other debris, and began making the collages and assemblages for which he is best known today. *The Cherry Picture* belongs to a group of these works he called Merz, a nonsensical word that he made up by cutting a scrap from a newspaper: the second syllable of the German word *Kommerz*, or commerce.

By 1921 Schwitters had been painting seriously for ten years, largely in different naturalistic styles. In doing so, he learned how all art was based on measurement and adjustment and the manipulation of a variable but finite number of pictorial elements. He never forgot these lessons, which form a bridge between his earlier, representational work and the purely formal manipulation of found materials in the *Merz* pictures.

Screen. 1922
Lacquered wood and brass rods,
6' 2¹/₂" x 53¹/₂" x ³/₄" (189.2 x 135.9 x 2 cm)
Hector Guimard Fund

This black lacquered wood screen,
composed of seven horizontal rows of panels
joined by thin vertical brass rods, is not only
a movable wall that serves to demarcate
space but also a sculpture composed of
solids and voids with an underlying Cubist
influence. It is one of the most striking and
elegant creations by Gray, who was one of
the leading designers working in Paris after
World War I. Gray popularized and perfected
the art of lacquered furnishings, and her
preference for its meticulous finish reveals a
predilection for exotic materials, in particular
those used in Japanese decorative arts.

Based on a larger version that Gray
designed in 1922 for the Paris apartment of
Madame Mathieu-Lévy, the owner of an
exclusive millinery shop, the freestanding
block screen can be seen as a bridge
between furniture, architecture, and
sculpture. Gray also became an
accomplished textile designer and architect.
Her first major architectural project, the E-
1027 House in Roquebrune-Cap-Martin,
France, was composed of multifunctional
rooms and furniture, and was much admired
by the Swiss-French architect Le Corbusier.
The flexibility inherent in this project
continued Gray's primary fascination in her
earlier designs: pivoting parts and movable
elements that transform both object and
space.

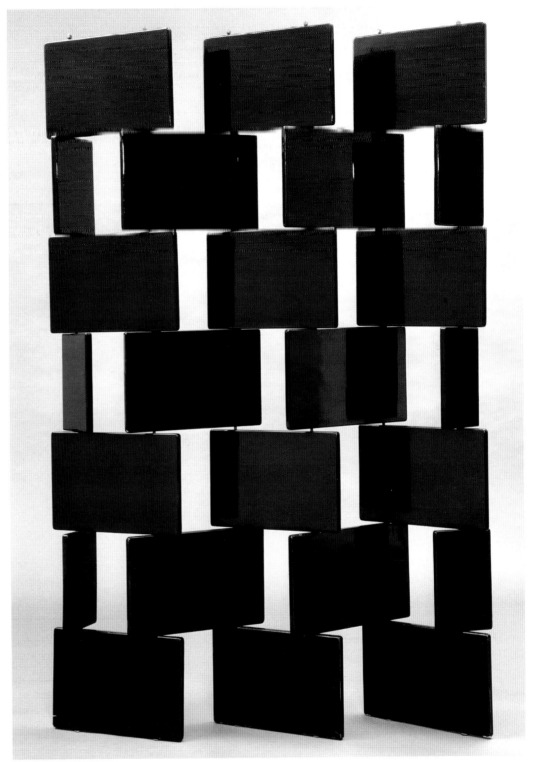

1922

Twittering Machine. 1922

Watercolor and pen and ink on oil transfer
drawing on paper, mounted on cardboard,
25¼ x 19" (63.8 x 48.1 cm)
Purchase

The "twittering" in the title doubtless refers to
the birds, while the "machine" is suggested
by the hand crank. The two elements are,
literally, a fusing of the natural with the
industrial world. Each bird stands with beak
open, poised as if to announce the moment
when the misty cool blue of night gives way
to the pink glow of dawn. The scene evokes
an abbreviated pastoral—but the birds are
shackled to their perch, which is in turn
connected to the hand crank.

Upon closer inspection, however, an
uneasy sensation of looming menace begins
to manifest itself. Composed of a wiry,
nervous line, these creatures bear a
resemblance to birds only in their beaks and
feathered silhouettes; they appear closer to
deformations of nature. The hand crank
conjures up the idea that this "machine" is a
music box, where the birds function as bait
to lure victims to the pit over which the
machine hovers. We can imagine the
fiendish cacophony made by the shrieking
birds, their legs drawn thin and taut as they
strain against the machine to which they are
fused.

Klee's art, with its extraordinary technical
facility and expressive color, draws
comparisons to caricature, children's art, and
the automatic drawing technique of the
Surrealists. In *Twittering Machine*, his affinity
for the contrasting sensibilities of humor and
monstrosity converges with formal elements
to create a work as intriguing in its technical
composition as it is in its multiplicity of
meanings.

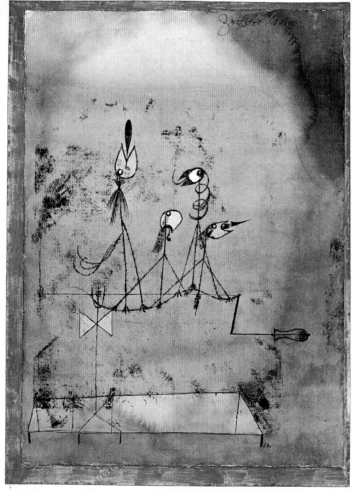

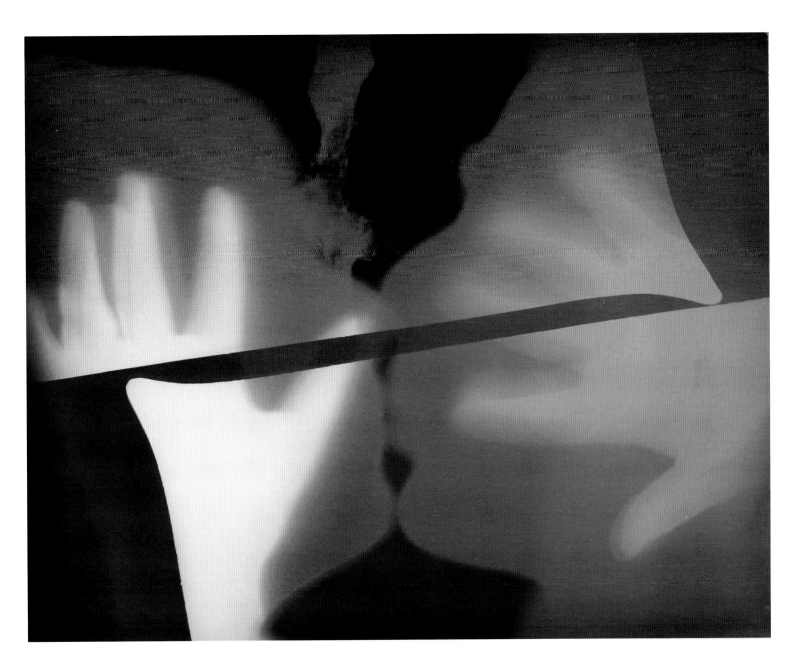

Rayograph. 1922
Gelatin silver print, 9³/₈ x 11³/₄" (23.9 x 30 cm)
Gift of James Thrall Soby

A photogram is a picture made on photographic paper without the aid of a camera. To make this one, Man Ray exposed the paper to light at least three times. Each time a different set of objects acted as a stencil: a pair of hands, a pair of heads kissing, and two darkroom trays, which seem almost to kiss each other with their corner spouts. With each exposure, the paper darkened where it was not masked.

"It is impossible to say which planes of the picture are to be interpreted as existing closer or deeper in space. The picture is a visual invention: an image without a real-life model to which we can compare it," notes curator John Szarkowski. A Surrealist might have said, instead, that it discloses a reality all the more precious because it is otherwise invisible.

Man Ray claimed to have invented the photogram not long after he emigrated from New York to Paris in 1921. Although, in fact, the practice had existed since the earliest days of photography, he was justified in the artistic sense, for in his hands the photogram was not a mechanical copy but an unpredictable pictorial adventure. He called his photograms "rayographs."

1922

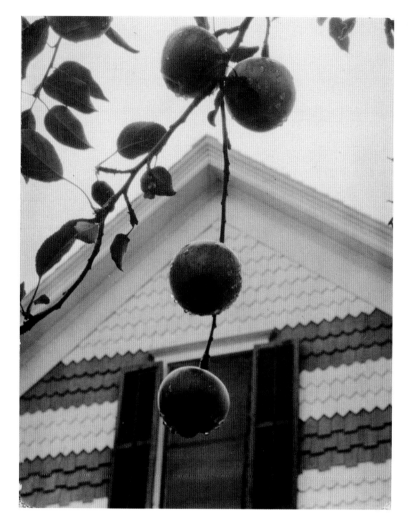

Apples and Gable, Lake George. 1922
Gelatin silver print, 4⅝ x 3⁹/₁₆" (11.6 x 9.1 cm)
Given anonymously

This picture may be read as a symbol—of Eve's temptation in the Garden of Eden, perhaps, or of harmony between nature and mankind. Yet it presents itself as an immediate, sensual experience. You can almost feel yourself reaching up to the apples covered with dew and ripe for the picking.

Stieglitz was fifty-eight years old when he made this photograph at his family's estate on Lake George, New York, where he spent his summers from childhood to old age. At the turn of the century, it had seemed to him that photography, to become an art, must emulate the other arts and so restrain or disguise its earthbound realism. Later, in the 1920s, he helped to prove in his own photographs that engaging the stubborn specificity of his medium was itself a fine art.

FRANK LLOYD WRIGHT AMERICAN, 1867–1959

1923

La Miniatura, Mrs. George Madison Millard House, Pasadena, California.
1923
Perspective: colored pencil and pencil on gampi paper, 20⁹/₁₆ x 19¹¹/₁₆" (52.2 x 50 cm)
Gift of Mr. and Mrs. Walter Hochschild

La Miniatura, the Millard House in Pasadena, is the earliest in a series known as the Textile Block houses, designed by Wright in the 1920s; all are located in southern California. This color rendering depicts the Millard House in its lush surroundings. The house is constructed of a combination of plain-faced and ornamental concrete blocks, which were cast on the site from molds designed by Wright. The square blocks, with perforated,

glass-filled apertures, form a continuous interior and exterior fabric. The relatively small scale of the blocks allows for a design that closely follows the contours of the landscape.

In his autobiography, Wright wrote: "The concrete block? The cheapest (and ugliest) thing in the building world. ... Why not see what could be done with that gutter-rat?" In his Textile Block houses, Wright attempted to introduce a flexible building system, marrying the merits of standardized machine production to the innovative, creative vision of the artist. While the block system was intended to be an efficient, low-cost method of building that incorporated ornament, it proved to be time consuming and more expensive than traditional construction.

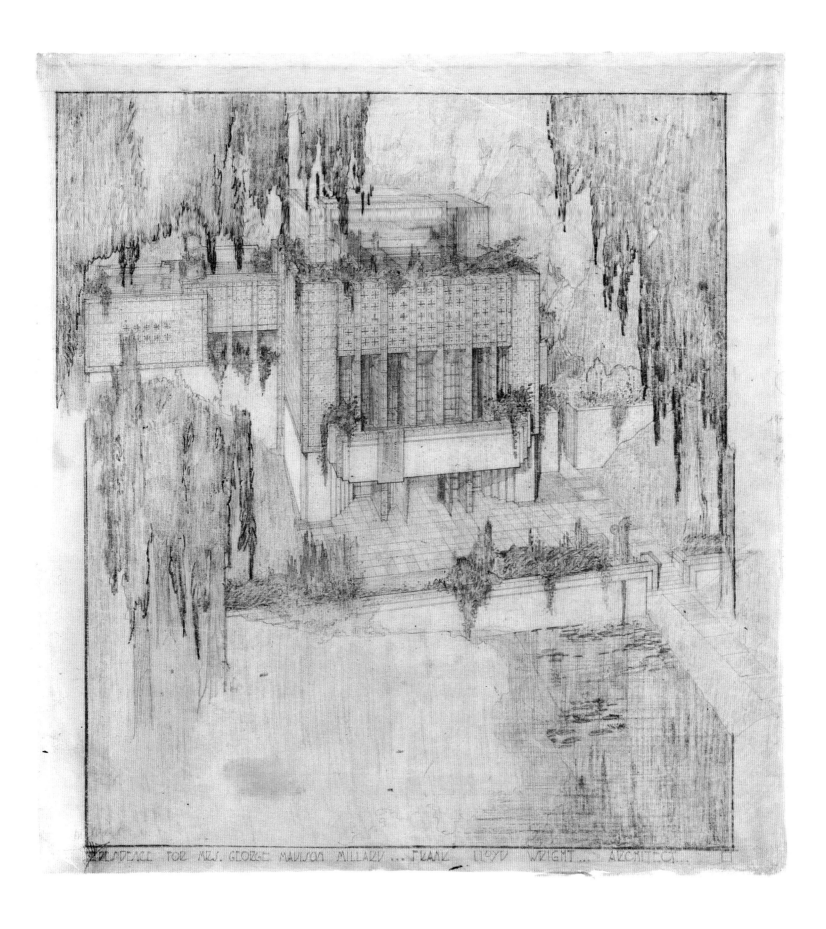

RESIDENCE FOR MRS. GEORGE MADISON MILLARD ... FRANK LLOYD WRIGHT ... ARCHITECT

GERRIT RIETVELD DUTCH, 1888–1964

Red Blue Chair. c. 1923
Painted wood, 34 1/8 x 26 x 33"
(86.7 x 66 x 83.8 cm)
Gift of Philip Johnson

In the Red Blue Chair, Rietveld manipulated rectilinear volumes and examined the interaction of vertical and horizontal planes, much as he did in his architecture. Although the chair was originally designed in 1918, its color scheme of primary colors (red, yellow, blue) plus black—so closely associated with the de Stijl group and its most famous theorist and practitioner Piet Mondrian—was applied to it around 1923. Hoping that much of his furniture would eventually be mass-produced rather than handcrafted, Rietveld aimed for simplicity in construction. The pieces of wood that comprise the Red Blue Chair are in the standard lumber sizes readily available at the time.

Rietveld believed there was a greater goal for the furniture designer than just physical comfort: the well-being and comfort of the spirit. Rietveld and his colleagues in the de Stijl art and architecture movement sought to create a utopia based on a harmonic human-made order, which they believed could renew Europe after the devastating turmoil of World War I. New forms, in their view, were essential to this rebuilding.

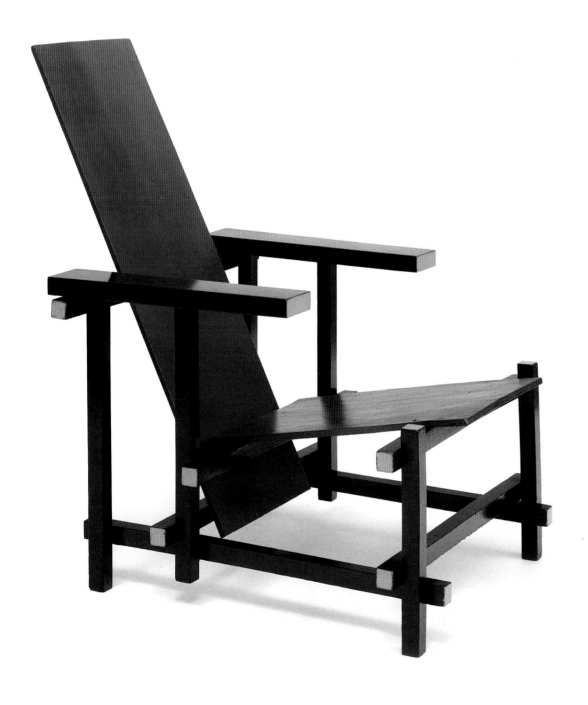

THEO VAN DOESBURG DUTCH, 1883–1931
CORNELIS VAN EESTEREN DUTCH, 1897–1988

Contra-Construction Project. 1923
Project for a private house: axonometric drawing, gouache on paper, 22½ x 22½" (57.2 x 57.2 cm)
Edgar Kaufmann, Jr. Fund

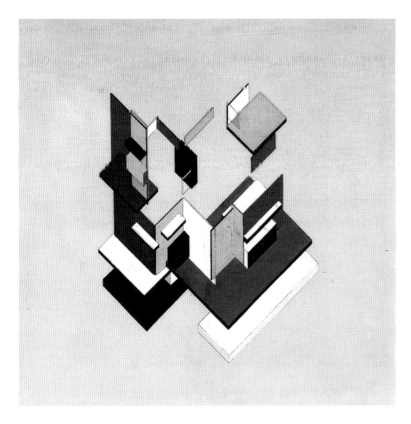

Van Doesburg, a painter, writer, editor, and architect, was a founder and driving force behind the de Stijl movement, which was centered in the Netherlands in the late teens and early 1920s. Cornelis van Eesteren, an architect, joined the group in 1922. Artists and others contributing to van Doesburg's periodical, *De Stijl*, attempted to create a new harmonic order in the aftermath of World War I. They attempted to construct a utopian solidarity between art and life under the influence of Piet Mondrian's early theories of Neo-Plasticism, which proposed that the essence of the imagined and seen world could be conveyed only through a logical system of abstraction based on the line, square, and rectangle and the primary colors plus black and white.

According to van Doesburg, architecture had to be approached in an entirely new way, which would ultimately give rise to a universal aggregate of easel painting, sculpture, and architecture. As suggested by this axonometric drawing, one of a group rendered but never built, architecture, enlivened by flat colors, was to be economical and dynamic, with planar elements balanced asymmetrically around an open core. Such structures would allow the modern individual to achieve harmony with his or her surroundings.

WILHELM WAGENFELD GERMAN, 1900–1990
CARL J. JUCKER SWISS, 1902–1997

Table Lamp. 1923–24
Glass and chrome-plated metal, 18 x 8" (45.7 x 20.3 cm) diam. at base
Manufacturer: Metallwerkstätte, Staatliches Bauhaus, Germany
Gift of Philip Johnson

This object, known as the "Bauhaus lamp," embodies an essential idea—form follows function—advanced by the influential Bauhaus school, founded in 1919 by the architect Walter Gropius, which taught a modern synthesis of both fine and applied arts. Through the employment of simple geometric shapes—circular base, cylindrical shaft, and spherical shade—Wagenfeld and Jucker achieved "both maximum simplicity and, in terms of time and materials, greatest economy." The lamp's working parts are visible; the opaque glass shade, a type formerly used only for industrial lighting, helps to diffuse the light.

The lamp was produced in the Bauhaus metal workshop after its reorganization under the direction of the artist László Moholy-Nagy in 1923. The workshop promoted the use of new materials and favored mass production under a collaborative, rather than individual, approach.

Initial attempts at marketing the lamp in 1924 were unsuccessful, primarily because most of its parts were still hand assembled at the Bauhaus. Today, the lamp is widely produced by Techno-lumen of Bremen, Germany, and is generally perceived as an icon of modern industrial design.

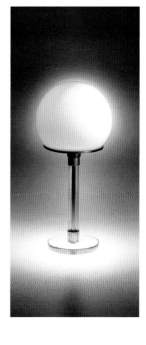

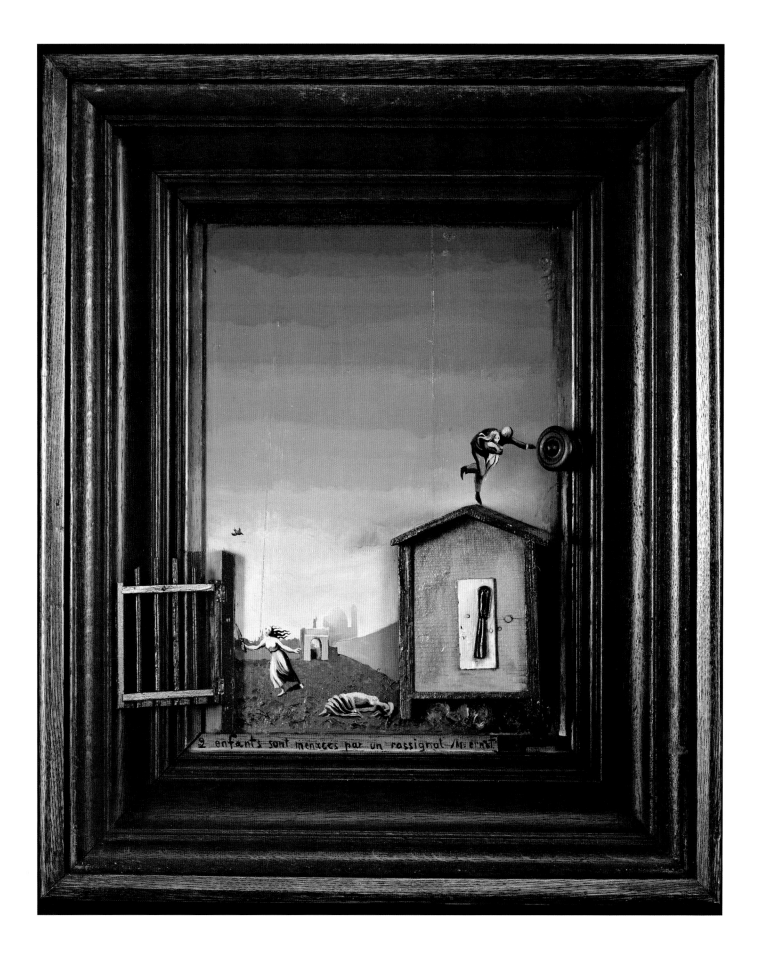

Two Children Are Threatened by a Nightingale. 1924

Oil on wood with wood construction,
27¹/₂ x 22¹/₂ x 4¹/₂" (69.8 x 57.1 x 11.4 cm)
Purchase

In *Two Children Are Threatened by a Nightingale,* a girl, frightened by the bird's flight (birds appear often in Ernst's work), brandishes a knife, another faints away. A man carrying a baby balances on the roof of a hut, which, like the work's gate (which makes sense in the picture) and knob (which does not), is a three-dimensional supplement to the canvas. This combination of unlike elements, flat and volumetric, extends the collage technique, which Ernst cherished for its "systematic displacement." "He who speaks of collage," the artist believed, "speaks of the irrational." But even if the

scene were entirely a painted illusion, it would have a hallucinatory unreality, and indeed Ernst linked his work of this period to childhood memories and dreams.

Ernst was one of many artists who emerged from service in World War I deeply alienated from the conventional values of his European world. In truth, his alienation predated the war; he would later describe himself when young as avoiding "any studies which might degenerate into bread winning," preferring "those considered futile by his professors—predominantly painting. Other futile pursuits: reading seditious philosophers and unorthodox poetry." The war years, however, focused Ernst's revolt and put him in contact with kindred spirits in the Dada movement. He later became a leader in the emergence of Surrealism.

EUGÈNE ATGET FRENCH, 1857–1927

Store, avenue des Gobelins. 1925

Albumen silver print, 8¹/₈ x 6⁵/₁₆" (20.6 x 16 cm)
Abbott-Levy Collection. Partial gift of Shirley
C. Burden

For more than three decades, Atget photographed Paris—its ancient streets and monuments and finely wrought details, its corners and hovels and modern commerce, and its outlying parks. He was not an artist in the conventional sense but a specialized craftsman, who supplied pictorial records of French culture to artists, antiquarians, and librarians. That, at least, is how he earned his living. Shortly before his death, however, other photographers began to recognize that Atget's work is art in everything but name: full of wit, invention, beauty, wisdom, and the disciplined cultivation of original perceptions.

This picture of the front of a men's clothing store belongs to a series of photographs of store windows that Atget made in the highly creative last years of his life. He easily could have minimized the reflection in the window, in which we see part of the Gobelins complex, where tapestries had been made for nearly three centuries. Instead, he welcomed it. Indelibly melding two images into one, the photograph simultaneously evokes France's modern fashions and one of her most noble artistic traditions.

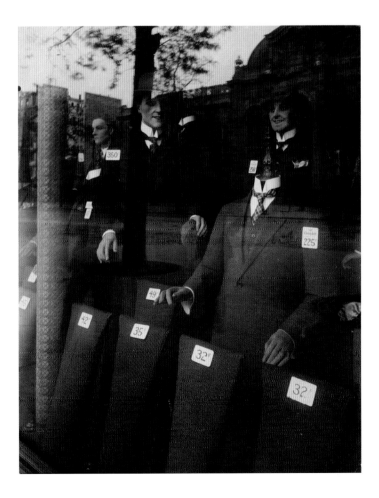

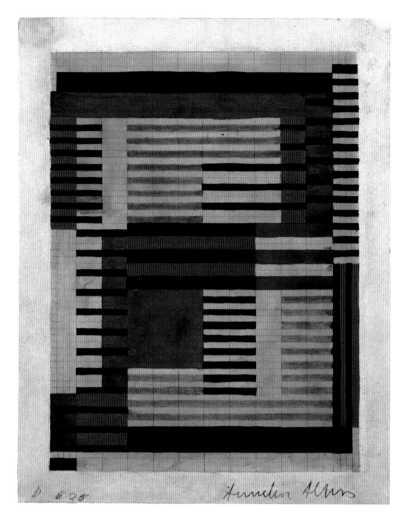

Design for Smyrna Rug. 1925

Watercolor, gouache, and pencil on paper,
8 1/8 x 6 9/16" (20.6 x 16.7 cm)
Gift of the designer

Albers was one of the most esteemed students of the weaving workshop at the Bauhaus, which she attended from 1920 to 1922 before teaching there herself until 1929. She often began her weaving projects with design sketches, such as this drawing for a rug. In this study, she explored the theme of horizontal-vertical construction using color, shape, proportion, and rhythm. The design reveals her admiration for the work of the painter Paul Klee, who also taught at the Bauhaus.

Of the weaving workshop she later observed: "Technique was acquired as it was needed and as a foundation for future attempts. Unburdened by any practical considerations, this play with materials produced amazing results, textiles striking in their novelty, their fullness of color and texture, and possessing often a quite barbaric beauty."

Albers used textiles as her primary artistic medium for almost forty years, experimenting directly with innovative materials and creating prototypes for industrial production. She became as acclaimed for her activities as a teacher and writer on design and weaving as for her textile designs. Albers continued to explore relationships of color and line most markedly after 1963, when her interest shifted to printmaking.

The Birth of the World. 1925

Oil on canvas, 8' 2 3/4" x 6' 6 3/4" (250.8 x 200 cm)
Acquired through an anonymous fund, the Mr. and Mrs. Joseph Slifka and Armand G. Erpf Funds, and by gift of the artist

According to the first Surrealist manifesto of 1924, "the real functioning of the mind" could be expressed by a "pure psychic automatism," "the absence of any control exercised by reason." Miró was influenced by Surrealist ideas, and said, "Rather than setting out to paint something, I begin painting and as I paint, the picture begins to assert itself. ... The first stage is free, unconscious." But, he added, "The second stage is carefully calculated."

The Birth of the World reflects just this combination of chance and plan. Miró primed the canvas unevenly, so that paint would here sit on the surface, there soak into it. His methods of applying paint allowed varying degrees of control—pouring, brushing, flinging, spreading with a rag. The biomorphic and geometric elements, meanwhile, he drew deliberately, working them out in a preparatory drawing.

Miró's works in this vein suggest something both familiar and unidentifiable, yet even at his most ethereal, Miró never loses touch with the real world: we see a bird, or a kite; a shooting star, a balloon on a string, or a spermatozoa; a character with a white head. *The Birth of the World* is the first of many Surrealist works that deal metaphorically with artistic creation through an image of the creation of a universe. In Miró's words, it describes "a sort of genesis."

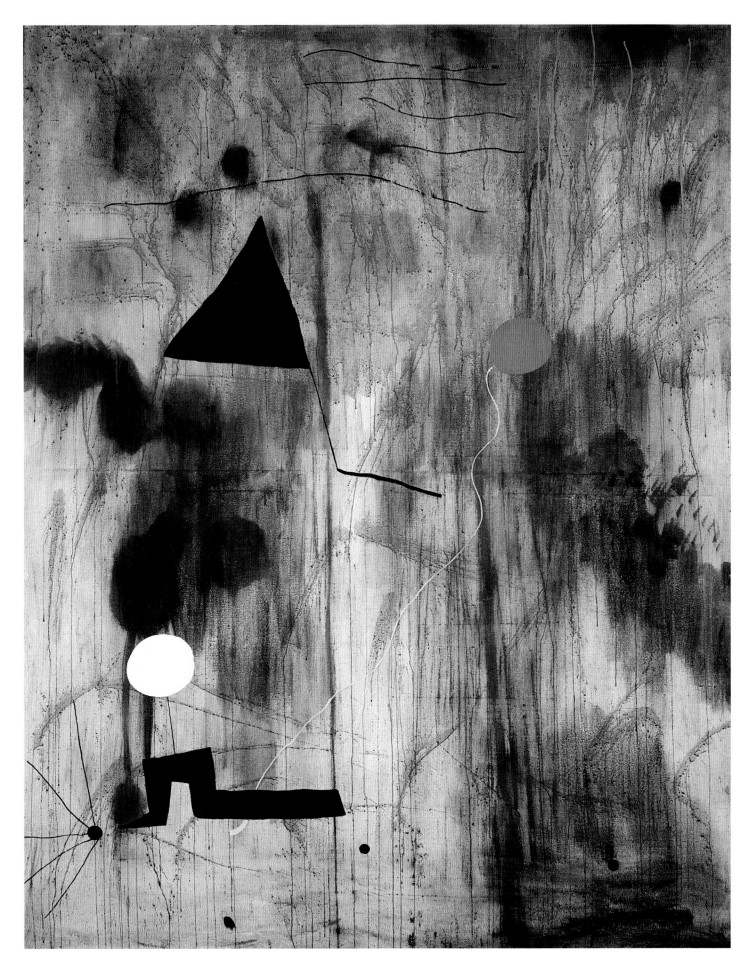

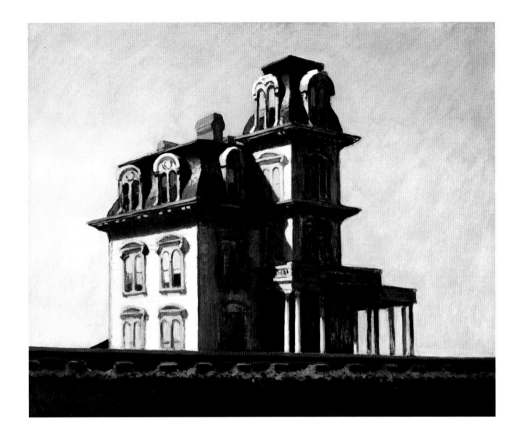

House by the Railroad. 1925
Oil on canvas, 24 x 29" (61 x 73.7 cm)
Given anonymously

Past and present meet in Hopper's picture: the railroad, symbol of modern industry, slices through a rural America embodied by a forlorn Victorian mansion. This once grand home stands tall but blank, isolated against the sky, and its verandah, designed for the leisurely contemplation of nature, now looks out on the steel tracks that cut across the foreground, obscuring both the horizon and the house's foundations in the earth. There is no human presence, but the window shades—some closed, others half open— suggest that the house may not be abandoned. Adding to the mystery and drama is the light flooding in from the left, reflecting an almost blinding white off part of the house but hiding the rest in deep shadow.

As a stubborn realist painter in a century of aesthetic innovation, Hopper had something in common with the building in *House by the Railroad*, old-fashioned in a changing world. But the color and the construction of Hopper's painting are precise and perduring, and his brand of realism has a haunting emotional quality. He finds the pathos in the slightly fussy grandiosity of this aging architecture, which, unlike the railroad tracks, isn't going anywhere.

Dr. Mayer-Hermann, 1926

Oil and tempera on wood, 58³/₁ x 39"
(149.2 x 99.1 cm)
Gift of Philip Johnson

When Dix painted this picture of Wilhelm Mayer-Hermann, a prominent Berlin doctor, he was a favorite portraitist of Germany's cultural bohemia and its patrons. Yet his eye could be coolly unflattering. Dix had fought in World War I, a crucial formative experience. "It is necessary to see people in this unchained condition in order to know something about man," he said, and he came out of the war wanting "to depict things as they really are." Having experimented earlier with Expressionist and other modern styles, in 1920 he abandoned them for an approach and technique modeled on fifteenth- and sixteenth-century German art. In the process he was identified with what became known as the Neue Sachlichkeit (New Objectivity) movement, which advocated an unsentimental realism in the treatment of modern life.

Dix may portray the doctor exactly, but the pose and the setting seem chosen to stress his rotundity. Everything is round: the face, the bags under the eyes, the double chin, the shoulders, the position of the arms, the tummy. A round lamp is affixed to the doctor's forehead, and the circular x-ray machine behind him reflects the room as rounded. Also behind him are a round clock face and a round electrical socket. However precise the depiction, it verges on satire.

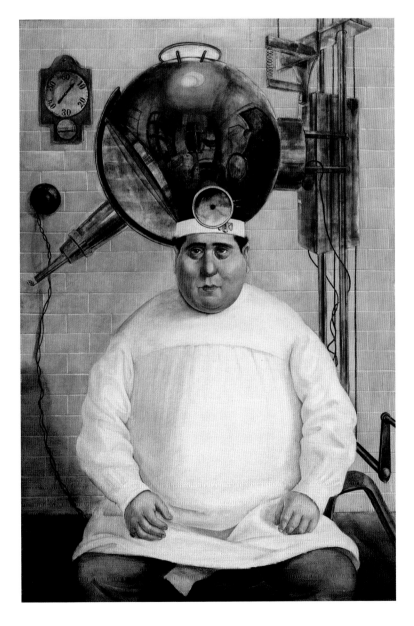

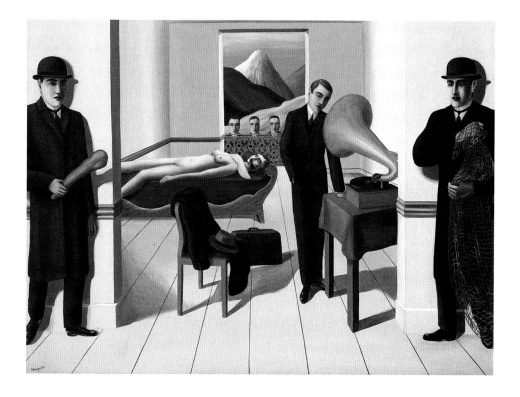

The Menaced Assassin. 1926

Oil on canvas, 59¼ x 6' 4⅞" (150.4 x 195.2 cm)
Kay Sage Tanguy Fund

A woman's naked body, blood trickling from her mouth, lies on a couch. The well-dressed man who is presumably her killer—the assassin of the painting's title—stands ready to leave, his coat and hat on a chair and his bag adjoining, but he is delayed by the sound of music: languidly relaxed, he listens to a gramophone. Meanwhile two men (agents of the law?), oddly alike, wait in the foyer to ambush him, armed with club and net. And behind him three more men, triplets to the others' twins, watch from over the balcony, witnesses outside the action's frame—like reflections of the painting's viewers, peering in from the other direction.

Magritte's Belgian brand of Surrealism deals in clear visions with unclear meanings. Unlike the fantastic dreamscapes of Paris Surrealists such as Salvador Dalí, his settings are strangely normal, and his protagonists are bourgeois gentlemen in ties and bowler hats. Yet he specialized in permanent irresolution, in mysteries without a key. *The Menaced Assassin* must be rooted in detective novels and movies, which fascinated Magritte, but its studied frozen quality, the impassivity of its actors, puts it in another dimension from the dime thriller.

Disturbingly, the gaze of the three men at the back meets the viewers' own. The murderer himself is menaced; the viewers themselves are viewed.

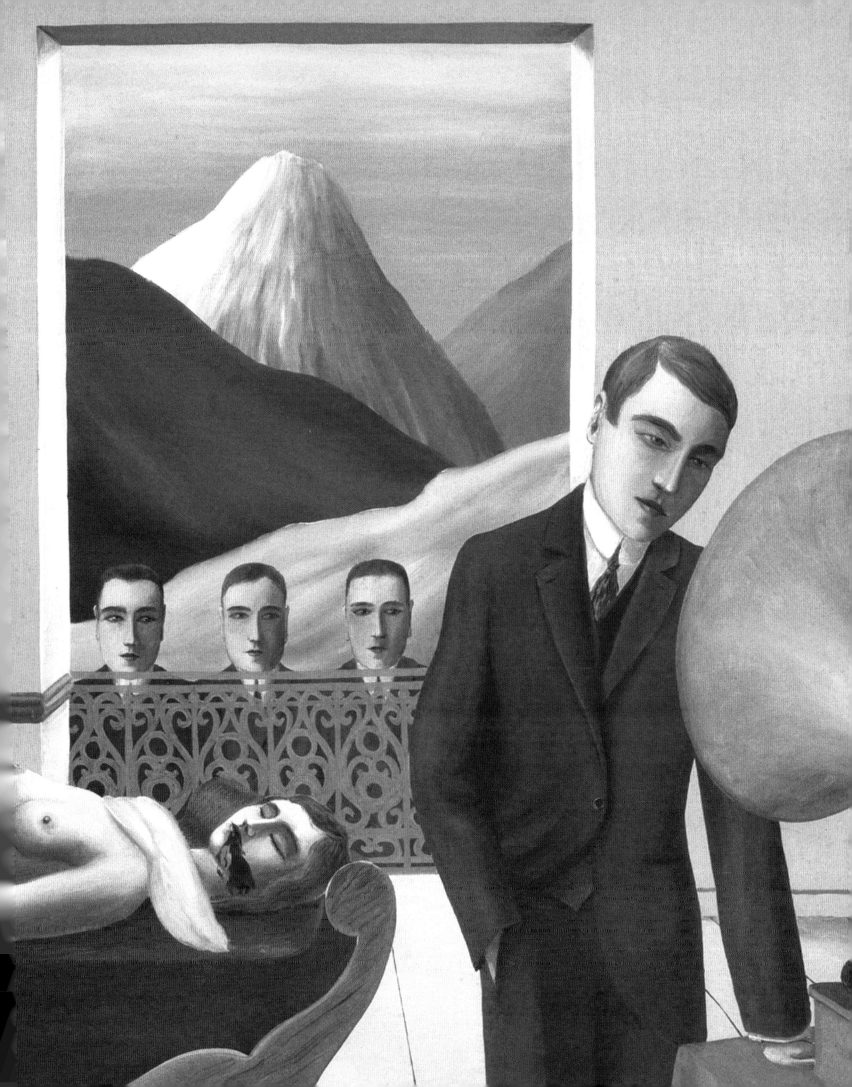

Mexico, D.F. 1925

Platinum print, 9⁹/₁₆ x 7³/₁₆" (24.3 x 18.3 cm)
Gift of the artist

It would be difficult to imagine a more austere nude. Framed in isolation against a dark, empty ground, the body has become a simple, symmetrical shape. This is as close as photography has come to achieving an image of ideal form, uncomplicated by earthly experience. And yet we see right away that it is a human body with volume and weight: an undeniably physical presence.

Weston's work of the 1920s, especially his nudes and photographs of vegetables and shells and other organic forms, set a new and demanding standard for modern photography. Nothing was left to chance in his pictures, no detail distracted from the power and clarity of the whole. At the same time, the photographs were unmistakably direct descriptions of particular things. The enormous influence of Weston's aesthetic rested on his ability to discover the abstract ideal within the perfectly real.

The title refers to Mexico, Distrito Federal—Mexico City—where Weston was living when he made the picture.

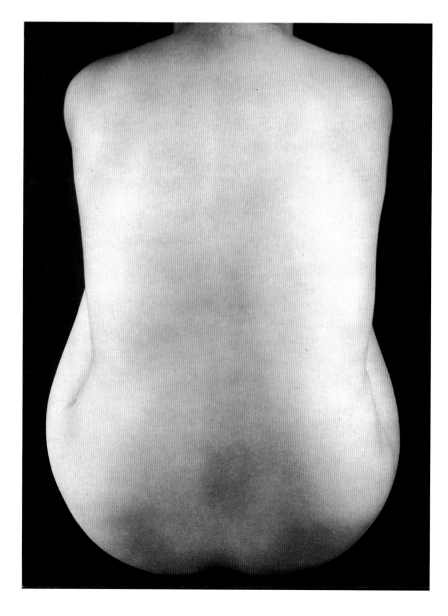

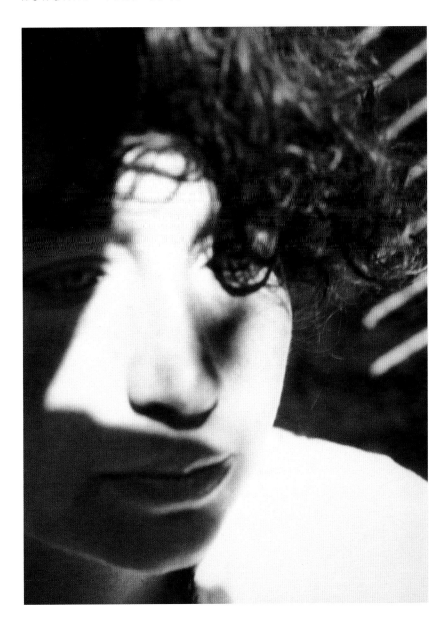

Head. c. 1926

Gelatin silver print, 14⁹/₁₆ x 10⁵/₈" (37 x 27 cm)
Given anonymously

The term *abstraction*, as it is generally applied to photography, is misleading. Completely indecipherable photographs are quite rare and usually quite boring. More common and more interesting are pictures such as this one, in which an unfamiliar configuration of form competes for our attention with what we are inclined to call the subject—in this case, the woman's face. That competition is the true subject of the picture.

Moholy-Nagy taught at the Bauhaus in Germany between 1920 and 1933. He began his career as a painter, but in the mid 1920s he came to regard photography as the universal visual language of the modern era because it was mechanical and impersonal and, therefore, objective—no matter how unexpected the results might be. Perhaps it was precisely the unpredictability of photography that he loved, because it unveiled fresh experiences.

In 1925 he published a picture book titled *Painting, Photography, Film*, which illustrated the many ways in which photography challenged old habits of seeing—by showing very distant or very small things, for example, or by looking up or down. The great majority of the illustrations were the work of scientists, journalists, amateurs, and illustrators—not of artists. The message was clear: photography had revolutionized modern vision without the aid of art.

133

1926

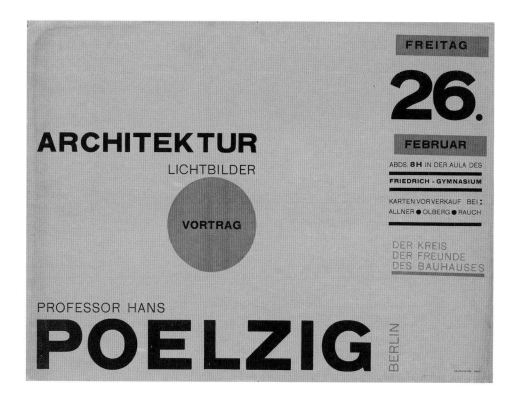

Architecture Slide Lecture, Professor Hans Poelzig (Architektur Lichtbilder Vortrag Professor Hans Poelzig). 1926
Poster: letterpress, 19⅛ x 25⅝" (48.6 x 65.1 cm)
Gift of Philip Johnson

This poster announcing a slide talk to be given by a guest lecturer, Hans Poelzig, an architect and professor, exemplifies what came to be known as the "new typography" of the 1920s: a strict use of sans-serif type, a single type treatment (here the exclusive use of uppercase letters), an underlying grid for the layout, and an asymmetrical composition. This revolutionary arrangement of type afforded a greater rationalism in the organization and communication of information.

As director of the new printing workshop established at the Bauhaus in 1925, Bayer had sought to overturn the typography styles prevailing in the early part of the twentieth century, in particular the overly decorative typefaces of the Art Nouveau and Gothic lettering commonly used in Germany. Building on what he had learned as a Bauhaus student under László Moholy-Nagy, Bayer promoted a new form of typography, a logical and universal means of graphic expression aimed, above all, at clarity. Bayer hoped to do what he called "a thorough alphabetical house-cleaning" in all publications issued by the Bauhaus. He and other devotees of the new style discarded the art of illustration, which they found subjective, in favor of unadorned typography, photography, and the modern technique of collage.

Wassily Chair. 1927–28

Chrome-plated tubular steel and canvas,
28 1/8 x 30 1/4 x 27 3/4" (71.4 x 76.8 x 70.5 cm)
Manufacturer: attributed to Standard Möbel,
Germany
Gift of Herbert Bayer

While teaching at the Bauhaus, Breuer often rode a bicycle, a pastime that led him to what is perhaps the single most important innovation in furniture design in the twentieth century: the use of tubular steel. The tubular steel of his bicycle's handlebars was strong and lightweight, and lent itself to mass production. Breuer reasoned that if it could be bent into handlebars, it could be bent into furniture forms.

The model for this chair is the traditional overstuffed club chair; yet all that remains is its mere outline, an elegant composition traced in gleaming steel. The canvas seat, back, and arms seem to float in space. The body of the sitter does not touch the steel framework. Breuer spoke of the chair as "my most extreme work ... the least artistic, the most logical, the least 'cozy' and the most mechanical." What he might have added is that it was also his most influential work. An earlier version of this chair was designed by Breuer in 1925, and within a year, designers everywhere were experimenting with tubular steel, which would take furniture into a radically new direction. The chair became known as the "Wassily" after the painter Kandinsky, Breuer's friend and fellow Bauhaus instructor, who praised the design when it was first produced.

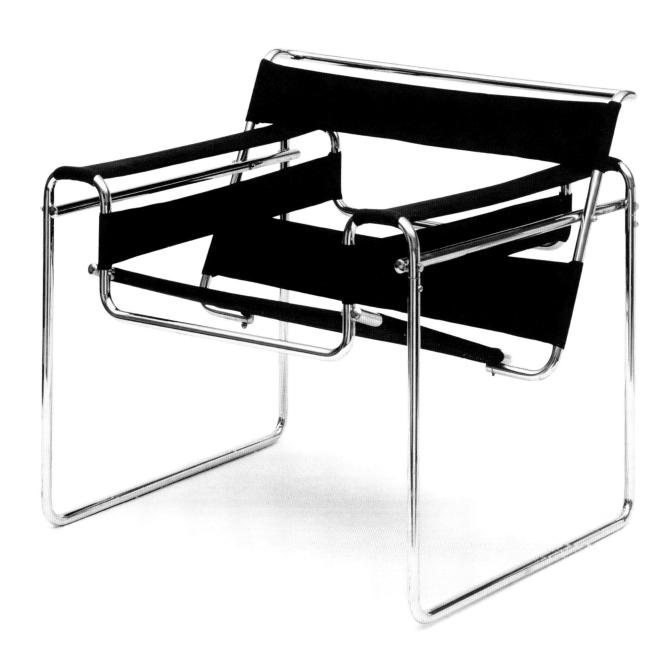

AUGUST SANDER GERMAN, 1876–1964

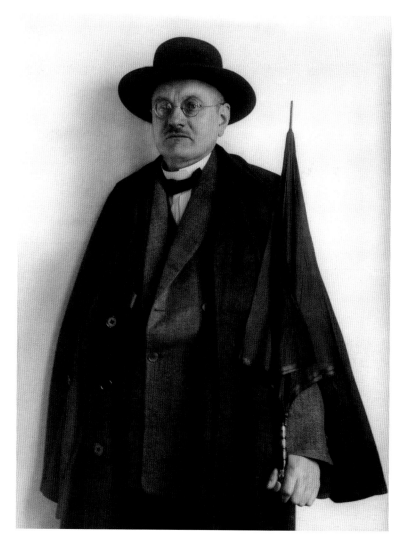

Member of Parliament and First Deputy of the Democratic Party (Johannes Scheerer). 1928

Gelatin silver print, 11⅝ x 8¾" (29.6 x 22.3 cm)
Gift of the artist

Photographic works have often taken the form of an extended series of photographs presented in a book or album. Among the most ambitious projects in the history of photography was Sander's brilliant, unfinished *People of the Twentieth Century*, a systematic survey of German society comprising portraits of representative types from all walks of life.

Here, the politician's cape sweeps upward in an unbroken line that extends to the tip of his umbrella—an appropriate attribute of a representative of the people—which he holds with proper German rectitude.

In 1929 Sander published a book of sixty photographs. Accompanying the book was an invitation to subscribe to the eventual publication of the entire body of portraits, which the photographer claimed to have made "without prejudice for or against any party, alignment, class, society." In 1934, the year after the Nazis came to power, they seized the book and destroyed its plates in 1936.

ALEKSANDR RODCHENKO RUSSIAN, 1891–1956

Assembling for a Demonstration.
1928–30
Gelatin silver print, 19½ x 13⅞" (49.5 x 35.3 cm)
Mr. and Mrs. John Spencer Fund

Photographs made from above or below or at odd angles are all around us today—in magazine and television ads, for example—but for Rodchenko and his contemporaries they were a fresh discovery. To Rodchenko they represented freedom and modernity because they invited people to see and think about familiar things in new ways. This

courtyard certainly was familiar to Rodchenko; he made the picture from the balcony of his own Moscow apartment.

The photograph strikes a perfect balance between plunging depth and a flat pattern—two darker forms enclosing a lighter one—and between this simple pattern and the many irregular details that enliven it. Rodchenko's control over the image is suggested by his particular point of view: to keep the balcony below him from intruding its dark form into the lighter courtyard, he was obliged to lean rather precariously over the railing of his own balcony.

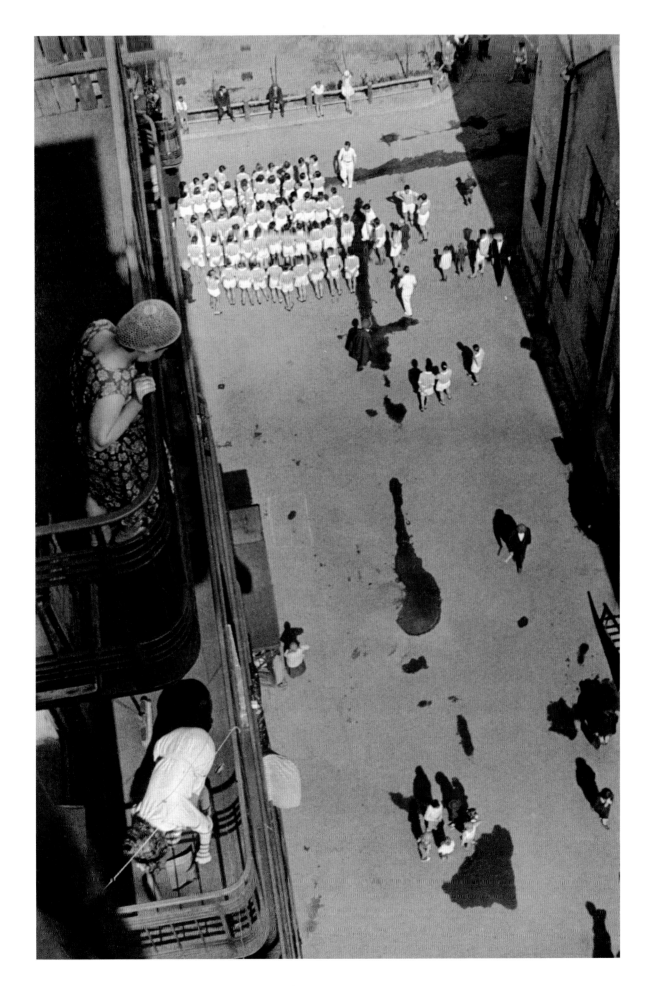

137

1928

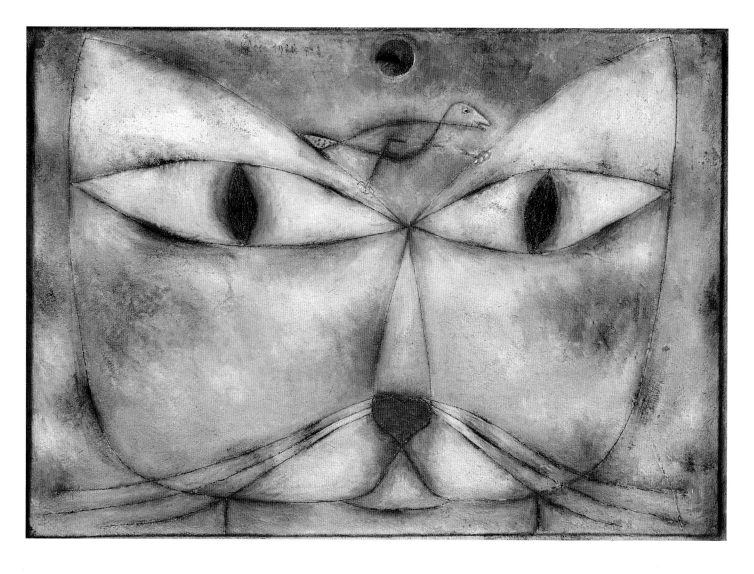

Cat and Bird. 1928

Oil and ink on gessoed canvas, mounted on
wood, 15 x 21" (38.1 x 53.2 cm)
Sidney and Harriet Janis Collection Fund and gift
of Suzy Prudden and Joan H. Meijer in memory
of F. H. Hirschland

Klee was one of the many modernist artists
who wanted to practice what he called "the
pure cultivation of the means" of painting—in
other words, to use line, shape, and color for
their own sake rather than to describe
something visible. That priority freed him to
create images dealing less with perception
than with thought, so that the bird in this
picture seems to fly not in front of the cat's
forehead but inside it—the bird is literally on
the cat's mind. Stressing this point by making

the cat all head, Klee concentrates on
thought, fantasy, appetite, the hungers of the
brain. One of his aims as an artist, he said,
was to "make secret visions visible."

The cat is watchful, frighteningly so, but it
is also calm, and Klee's palette too is calm,
in a narrow range from tawny to rose with
zones of bluish green. This and the
suggestion of a child's drawing lighten the
air. Believing that children were close to the
sources of creativity, Klee was fascinated by
their art, and evokes it here through simple
lines and shapes: ovals for the cat's eyes
and pupils (and, more loosely, for the bird's
body), triangles for its ears and nose. And
the tip of that nose is a red heart, a sign of
the cat's desire.

138

Lake George Window. 1929

Oil on canvas, 40 x 30" (101.6 x 76.2 cm)
Acquired through the Richard D. Brixey Bequest

Lake George Window shows a detail of the farmhouse on Lake George, in northern New York State, where O'Keeffe and her husband, the photographer Alfred Stieglitz, spent many summers. The window's structure, flanking shutters, and ornamental pediment can all be recognized in many of Stieglitz's photographs of the house, but O'Keeffe
simultaneously an essence of Americana and a near abstraction. Viewing the window straight on and close up, she evens and flattens its forms; framing it tightly to show only narrow bands of the wall around it, she almost erases its context. The composition becomes a geometric arrangement of rectangles, broken by the decorative curves and triangle of the pediment.

The clean straight lines and right angles of *Lake George Window* reflect a Precisionist side of O'Keeffe's work, which elsewhere entails a sensual response to organic shapes and a luxurious delicacy of color. But the austerity of the painting's flat planes and limited palette disguises a conceptual puzzle: the shutters announce a window but apparently hold a door as well, with
pane—the green rectangle—above. These features seem to offer a pun on transparency, while the green links the "interior" to the clapboard siding. O'Keeffe could see a universe of color in a petal; through this clear glass, though, she finds a dense opacity.

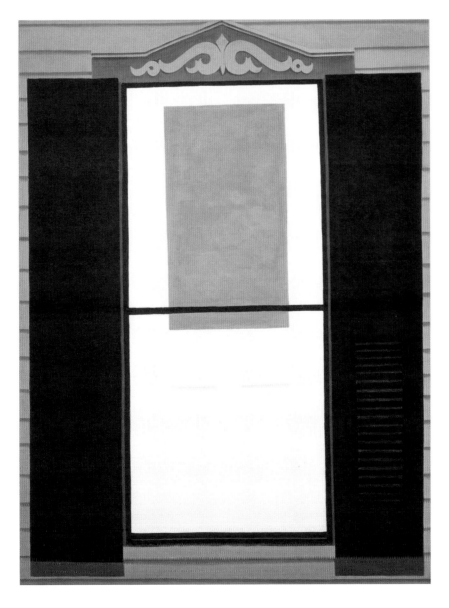

EL LISSITZKY (LAZAR MARKOVICH LISSITZKY)
RUSSIAN, 1890–1941

U.S.S.R. Russian Exhibition (USSR Russische Ausstellung). 1929
Poster: gravure, 49 x 35¼" (124.5 x 89.5 cm)
Jan Tschichold Collection. Gift of Philip Johnson

This propaganda poster, publicizing an exhibition in Switzerland about the Soviet Union, shows El Lissitzky's characteristic application of the photomontage technique, part of the new visual vocabulary employed in the graphic arts, replacing the objective art of illustration with collage. The two idealized portraits show young Soviets peering happily into Russia's bright future. Their androgyny and joined faces suggest the equal roles young men and women were to play in building the new Soviet society.

Visual artists in the Soviet Union rejected the fine arts in favor of the functional arts after the Bolshevik Revolution of 1917. It was believed that while painting and sculpture would have little utility in the burgeoning socialist regime, design could help advance the goals of the Revolution. Graphic design became the medium of choice for promoting specific political agendas.

El Lissitzky traveled more frequently than many of his Russian colleagues and thus was an important link between developments at the German Bauhaus, the Dutch de Stijl movement, and the Russian Constructivism of the 1920s and 1930s. His use of montage, straightforward typography, and dynamic compositions greatly influenced the evolution of modern graphic design.

LUDWIG MIES VAN DER ROHE AMERICAN,
BORN GERMANY, 1886–1969

Barcelona Chair. 1929
Stainless steel bars and leather upholstery,
31 x 29⅜ x 30" (78.7 x 74.6 x 76.2 cm)
Manufacturer: Knoll International, USA
Gift of the manufacturer

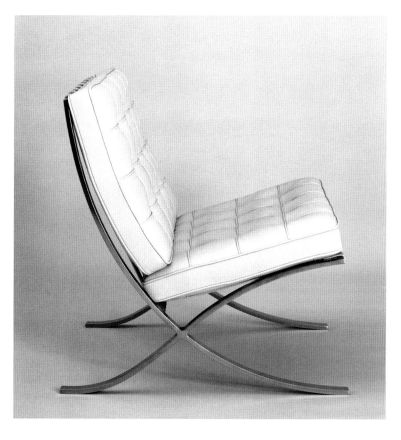

The Barcelona Chair achieves the serenity of line and the refinement of proportions and materials characteristic of Mies van der Rohe's highly disciplined architecture. It is supported on each side by two chrome-plated, flat steel bars. Seen from the side, the single curve of the bar forming the chair's back and front legs crosses the S-curve of the bar forming the seat and back legs, making an intersection of the two. This simple shape derives from a long history of precedents, from ancient Egyptian folding stools to nineteenth-century neoclassical seating. The cantilevered seat and the back of the original chairs were upholstered in white kid leather with welt and button details.

Mies van der Rohe designed this chair for his German Pavilion at the Barcelona Exposition of 1929. The Pavilion was the site of the inaugural ceremony for the German exhibits at the exposition, and the Spanish king was to preside. It had to be an "important chair, a very elegant chair," according to the architect. "The government was to receive a king. ... The chair had to be ... monumental. In those circumstances, you just couldn't use a kitchen chair."

Although only two Barcelona chairs were made for the German Pavilion, the design was put into production and became so popular that, with the exception of one sixteen-year period, it has been manufactured since 1929.

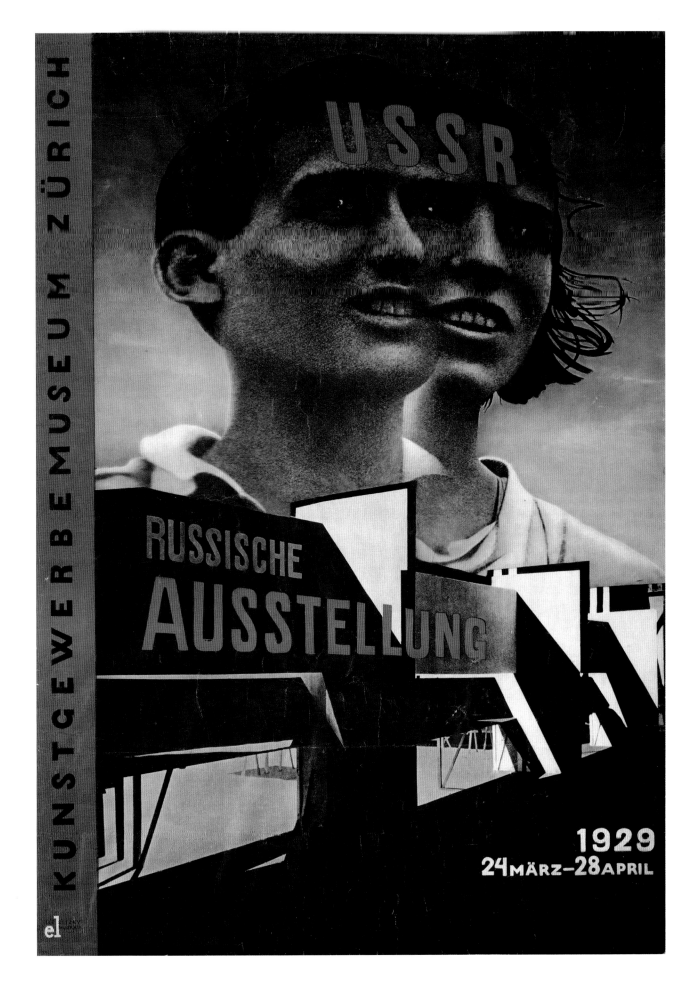

LE CORBUSIER (CHARLES-ÉDOUARD JEANNERET)
FRENCH, BORN SWITZERLAND. 1887–1965
WITH **PIERRE JEANNERET** SWISS, 1896–1967

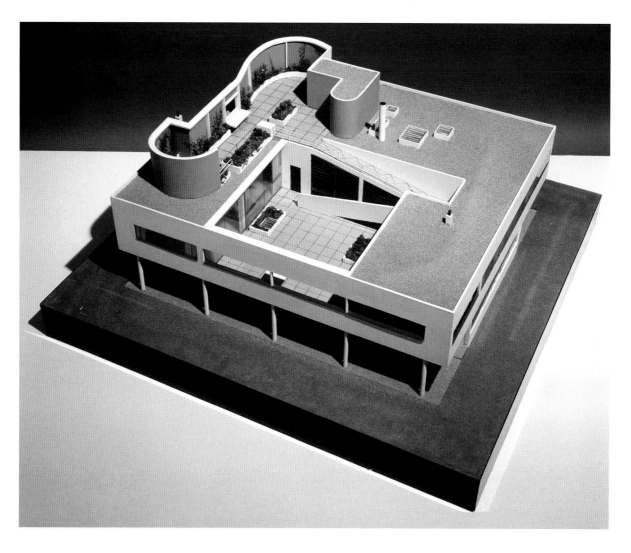

Villa Savoye, Poissy-sur-Seine, France. 1929–31

Model: wood, aluminum, and plastic,
14¹/₂ x 31¹/₂ x 34" (36.8 x 80 x 86.4 cm)
Modelmaker: Theodore Conrad (1932)
Purchase

The Villa Savoye, a weekend house outside Paris, is perhaps the finest example of Le Corbusier's early work. Le Corbusier, along with his cousin Pierre, planned the entire composition as a sequence of spatial effects. Arriving by automobile, the visitor drives underneath the house, circling around to the main entrance. From the entrance hall, he or she ascends the spiral stairs or the ramp to the main-level living area. The ramp continues from the central terrace to the upper-level sun deck. Sheltered by brightly colored wind screens, it is a perfect vantage point for savoring sunlight, fresh air, and nature.

In his famous book of 1923, *Vers une architecture (Towards a New Architecture)*, arguably the most influential architecture book of the twentieth century, Le Corbusier declared houses to be "machines for living in." Villa Savoye, a white rectilinear volume on a flat landscape, celebrates Le Corbusier's belief that ideal, universal forms, although rooted in the classical tradition, were appropriate to architecture for the machine age. The design incorporates Le Corbusier's "five points of architecture," which he believed to be indispensable elements: *pilotis* (reinforced-concrete columns), the free plan, the free facade, horizontal bands of windows, and the roof garden.

This model was included in The Museum of Modern Art's first architecture exhibition, in 1932, which documented the various trends that came to be known as the International Style.

Paimio Chair. 1931–32
Bent plywood, bent laminated birch, and solid
birch, 26 x 24 x 34¹/₂" (66 x 61 x 87.6 cm)
Manufacturer: Oy Huonekalu-ja
Rakennustyötehdas Ab, Finland
Gift of Edgar Kaufmann, Jr.

Admired as much for its sculptural presence
as for its comfort, the Paimio Chair is a tour
de force in bentwood that seems to test the
limits of plywood manufacturing. The chair's
framework consists of two continuous loops of
laminated wood, forming arms, legs, and
floor runners, between which rides the seat—
a thin sheet of plywood tightly bent at both
top and bottom into sinuous scrolls, giving it
greater resiliency. Inspired by Marcel
Breuer's tubular-steel Wassily Chair of

1927–28, Aalto chose, instead, native birch
for its natural feel and insulating properties,
and developed a more organic form.

The Paimio Chair, the best-known piece of
furniture designed by Aalto, is named for the
town in southwestern Finland for which Aalto
designed a tuberculosis sanatorium and all
its furnishings. Used in the patients' lounge,
the angle of the back of this armchair was
intended to help sitters breathe more easily.

Aalto's bentwood furniture had a great
influence on the American designers Charles
and Ray Eames and the Finnish-born Eero
Saarinen. In 1935 the Artek company was
established in Finland to mass-produce and
distribute wood furniture designed by Aalto
and his wife, Aino. Most of their designs
remain in production.

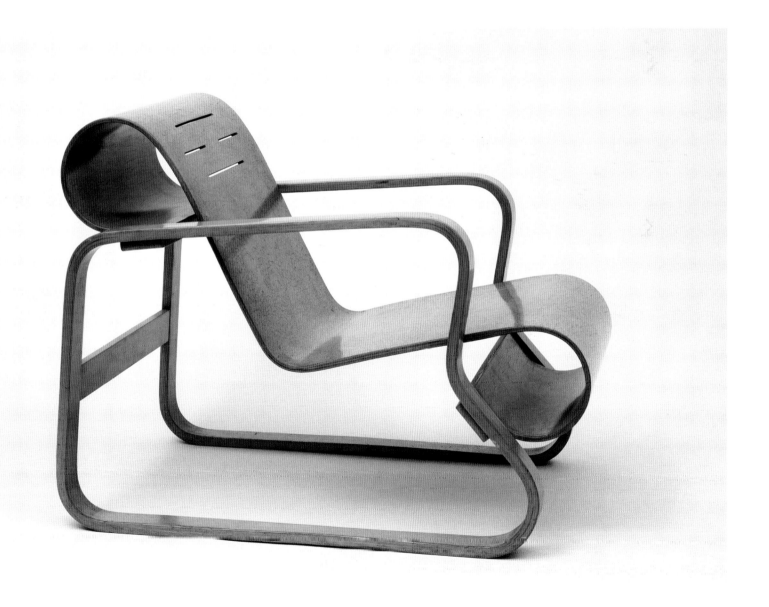

HANNAH HÖCH GERMAN, 1889–1978

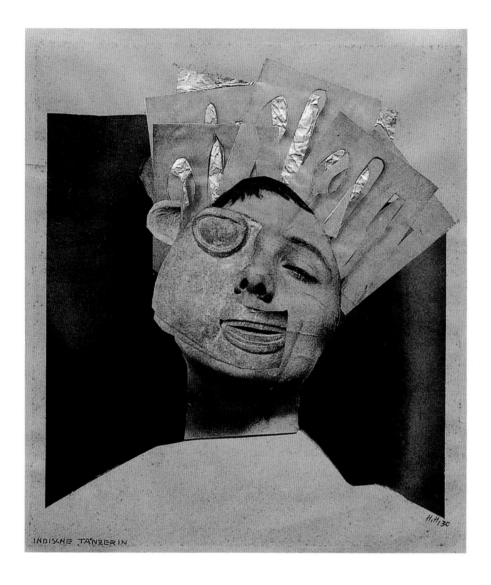

Indian Dancer (From an Ethnographic Museum). 1930

Cut-and-pasted gravure, relief halftone, and
silver-and-gold-embossed foil on buff paper,
10¹/₈ x 8⁷/₈" (25.7 x 22.4 cm)
Frances Keech Fund

In this collage Höch obliquely makes
reference to Joan of Arc, the androgynous
heroine who went to battle dressed as a
man, was later charged with heresy, burned
at the stake, and subsequently regarded as
a martyr. The mask covering the mouth and
one eye may be read as an effort to restrain
the figure, while the cutlery on the crown
emphasizes the domestic role that women
usually play. The paper framing the truncated
head simulates the museological presentation
of an object. In this compellingly strange
image, it is the modern woman rather than a
colonized artifact that is on display.

The woman in the photograph affixed to
this work is the actress Renée (Maria)
Falconetti portraying the title role in Carl
Theodor Dreyer's 1928 film *The Passion of
Joan of Arc*. Over the mournful face, Höch
pasted a fragmented photograph of an
African wood dance mask and, on top, a
paper-and-foil headdress ornamented with
cutouts of knives and spoons. This work
belongs to a series of photomontages
called *From an Ethnographic Museum*
(1924–34), most of which juxtapose images
of women and magazine reproductions of
tribal art. Höch cited a visit to an
ethnographic museum as an influence in
the conception of this series; however, she
used ethnographic material mostly as a point
of departure in order to comment on the
status of women in contemporary German
society.

Fish. 1930
Gray marble, 21 x 71 x 5¹/₂" (53.3 x 180.3 x 14 cm),
on three-part pedestal of marble 5¹/₈" (13 cm)
high, and two limestone cylinders 13" (33 cm)
high and 11" (27.9 cm) high x 32¹/₈" (81.5 cm)
diam. at widest point
Acquired through the Lillie P. Bliss Bequest

Less an image of a fish than an embodiment
of the idea of one, *Fish* conjures the animal's
liquid course by simplifying details like fin
and scale, tail and head, into smooth
streamline. ("Simplicity," Brancusi believed,
"is not an end in art, but we usually arrive at
simplicity as we approach the true sense of
things.") The material too contributes: a blue-
gray marble veined with flecks of flowing
white, its surface intimates both movement
through water and moving water itself.

Brancusi was fascinated by animals, and
believed in the primacy of animal
consciousness. In reducing animals to
elemental shapes, he felt he was
approaching the essence of nature. Also, like
a number of European artists of his period,
he was excited by art from outside the
classical tradition so influential in Western
aesthetics. The art of Africa, Native America,
and the Pacific, and also the art of prehistory
(including Cycladic sculpture, a particular
influence on Brancusi), took imaginative
liberties with human and animal bodies,
alternately exaggerating, attenuating, and
eliminating their features. These examples
liberated Brancusi and others in their
treatment of form. By the time he made *Fish*,
in fact, Brancusi seems almost to have left
form behind altogether, for something more
incorporeal: what he described as the fish's
"speed, its floating, flashing body seen
through the water ... the flash of its spirit."

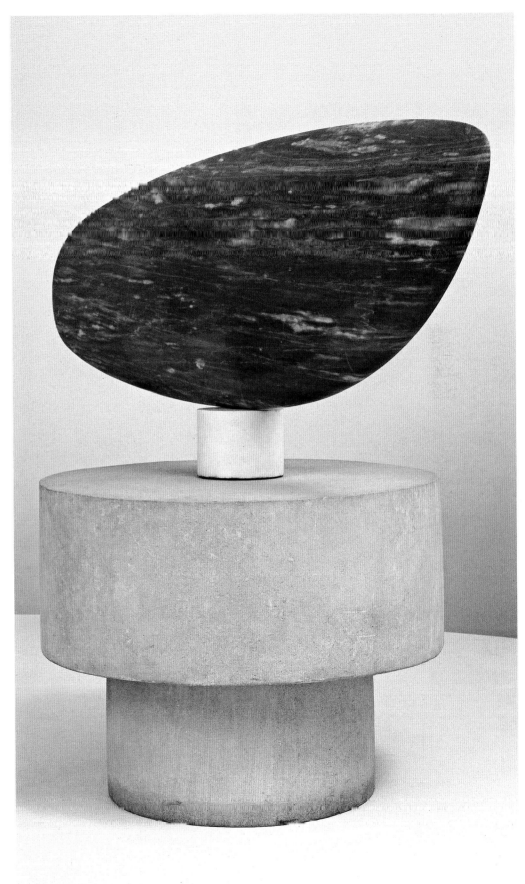

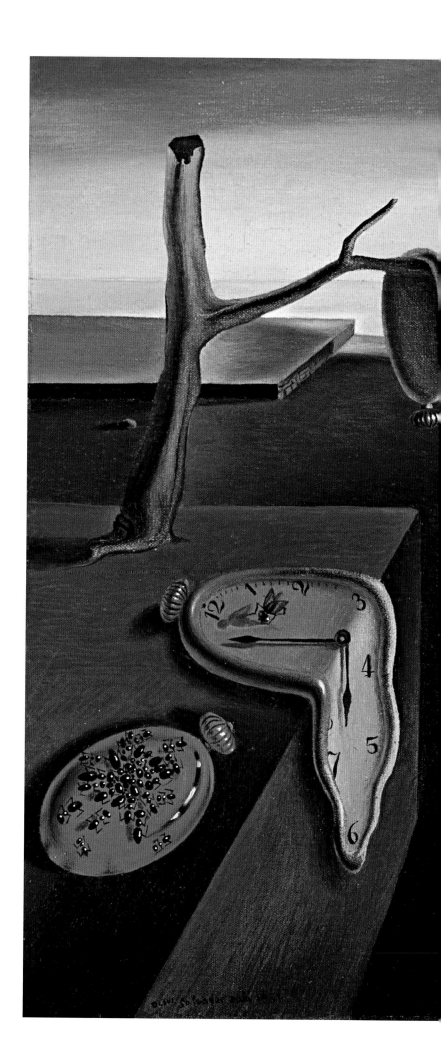

SALVADOR DALÍ
SPANISH, 1904–1989

1931

The Persistence of Memory. 1931
Oil on canvas, 9¹/₂ x 13" (24.1 x 33 cm)
Given anonymously

The Persistence of Memory is aptly named,
for the scene is indelibly memorable. Hard
objects become inexplicably limp in this
bleak and infinite dreamscape, while metal
attracts ants like rotting flesh. Mastering what
he called "the usual paralyzing tricks of eye-
fooling," Dalí painted with what he called "the
most imperialist fury of precision," but only,
he said, "to systematize confusion and thus
to help discredit completely the world of
reality." It is the classical Surrealist ambition,
yet some literal reality is included too: the
distant golden cliffs are the coast of
Catalonia, Dalí's home.

   Those limp watches are as soft as overripe
cheese—indeed "the camembert of time," in
Dalí's phrase. Here time must lose all
meaning. Permanence goes with it: ants, a
common theme in Dalí's work, represent
decay, particularly when they attack a gold
watch, and become grotesquely organic. The
monstrous fleshy creature draped across the
painting's center is at once alien and familiar:
an approximation of Dalí's own face in profile,
its long eyelashes seem disturbingly
insectlike or even sexual, as does what may
or may not be a tongue oozing from its nose
like a fat snail.

   The year before this picture was painted,
Dalí formulated his "paranoiac-critical
method," cultivating self-induced psychotic
hallucinations in order to create art. "The
difference between a madman and me," he
said, "is that I am not mad."

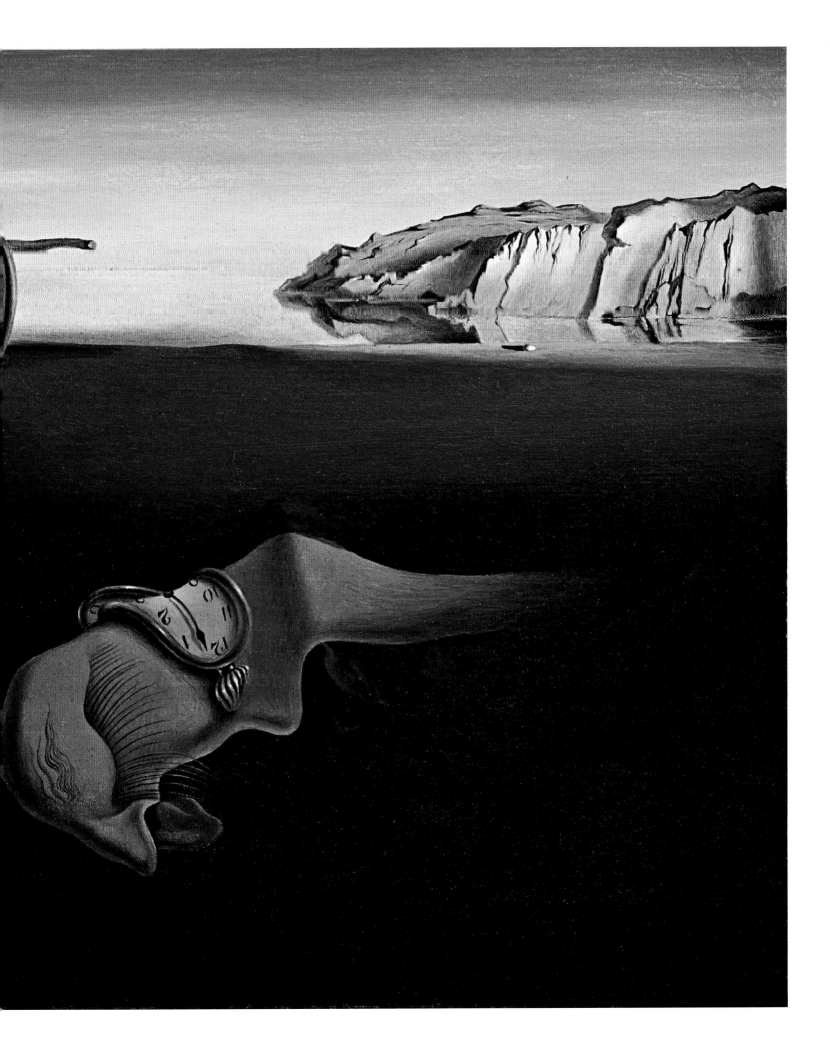

GASTON LACHAISE AMERICAN, BORN FRANCE.
1882–1935

Standing Woman. 1932
Bronze, 7' 4" x 41¹/₈" x 19¹/₈"
(223.6 x 104.3 x 48.4 cm)
Mrs. Simon Guggenheim Fund

"At twenty, in Paris," Lachaise wrote in 1928, "I met a young American person who immediately became the primary inspiration which awakened my vision and the leading influence that has directed my forces." The young American in question, Isabel Nagle, would eventually become Lachaise's wife, and *Standing Woman* and other works are certainly inspired by her. In Isabel, Lachaise seems to have seen greater forces and principles of human life: "You are," he once told her, "the Goddess I am searching to express in all things."

Like many twentieth-century sculptors,

Lachaise wanted to escape the classical tradition, and some of his smaller, more private works distend and exaggerate parts of the female body in ways that recall the swollen forms of Paleolithic fertility figures. The unshakable calm and dignity of *Standing Woman* are closer to classical art, but Lachaise stretches classical proportion with muscular rounding and augmented mass and height. For all their weight, the figure's breasts and hips, arms and thighs balance evenly around her slender waist. Her easy pose, commanding uprightness, and direct gaze give her a regal force. *Standing Woman* embodies Lachaise's stated ambition for his art: to express "the glorification of the human being, of the human body, of the human spirit, with all that there is of daring, of magnificence, of significance."

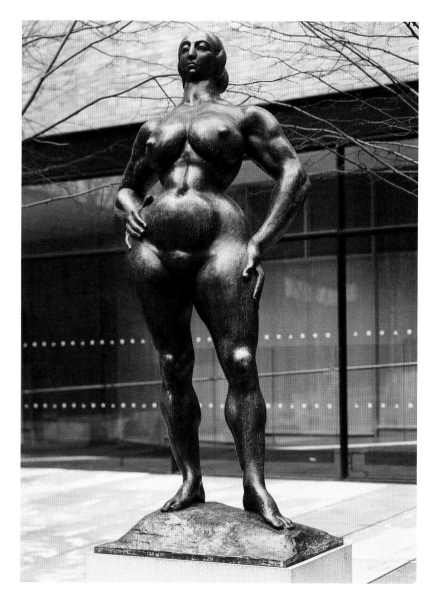

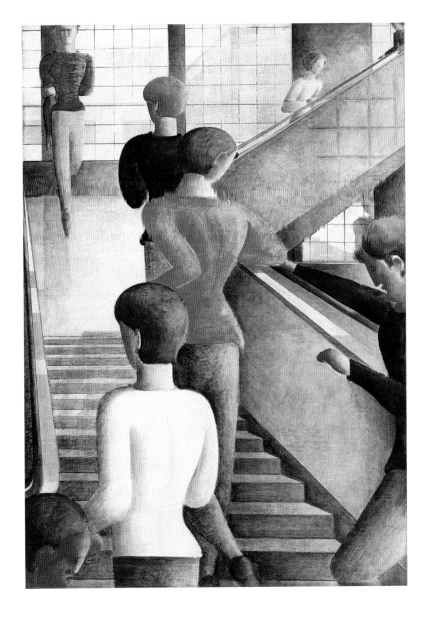

Bauhaus Stairway. 1932
Oil on canvas, 63⁷⁄₈ x 45" (162.3 x 114.3 cm)
Gift of Philip Johnson

Visiting Stuttgart in the spring of 1933, Alfred H. Barr, Jr., the founding director of The Museum of Modern Art, discovered that an exhibition by Schlemmer had closed after a brutal and intimidating review in a Nazi paper. Barr responded by cabling Philip Johnson, already a frequent donor to The Museum of Modern Art, to ask him to acquire *Bauhaus Stairway* as an eventual gift. Barr acted, he later wrote, "partly to spite the Nazis just after they had closed [Schlemmer's] exhibition."

Schlemmer painted *Bauhaus Stairway* three years after leaving his teaching post at the Bauhaus, the famous school of modern art, architecture, and design. The work's gridded structure celebrates Bauhaus design principles, and its upward movement, including the man *en pointe* at top left (Schlemmer had worked in dance), evokes the school's former optimism. Encouraging our involvement in this mood are the figures facing the same way we do, some of them partly cut off by the frame, as if they were in our space. Their simplified, almost modular shapes giving them an Everyman quality, they step up into the picture and then on up the stair.

Schlemmer's several staircase scenes of the early 1930s may reflect a desire to transcend a threatening period in German history. He exhibited this particular work soon after hearing that the Nazis had shut down the Bauhaus.

PIERRE BONNARD FRENCH, 1867–1947

Nude in Bathroom. 1932
Oil on canvas, 47⅝ x 46½" (121 x 118.1 cm)
Florene May Schoenborn Bequest

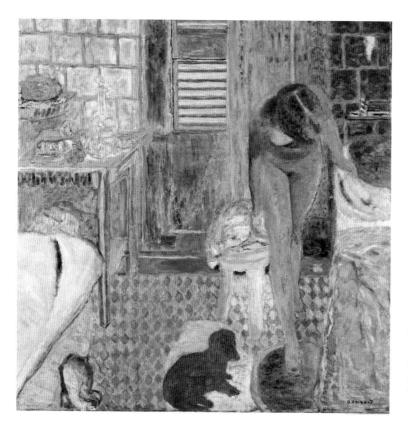

The scene is the bathroom of Bonnard's own home—Le Bosquet, his house near Cannes—and the woman naked at her toilette is the artist's wife, Marthe. The choice of both space and figure, then, is intensely personal, and the work maintains a sense of privacy and even of confinement. Although Marthe appears in many of Bonnard's paintings, seldom is her face fully visible: here she bows her head low. The window is shuttered, sealing off the outside world. A painting in which the whites of bath and stool are brighter and more vibrant than the barred panel of daylight suggests claustrophobia as well as intimacy, even though Bonnard's extraordinary painted color implies the richness of the domestic and interior life.

Bonnard's composition is asymmetrical, darker on the right than on the left, and its human subject is off-center and out of focus. His technique and use of color emerge from Impressionism, but advance the independence of paint quality and surface from form. Indeed the work's intensity as a field of color may outweigh its descriptiveness: overlapping planes, indistinct patterns, balanced areas of coolness and warmth, and close-valued hues create a blurring of edges and textures, a shimmer. Behind the curving foreground forms, systematic grids of rectangles and lozenges create a structure of eminent logic.

PABLO PICASSO SPANISH, 1881–1973

Girl Before a Mirror. 1932
Oil on canvas, 64 x 51¼" (162.3 x 130.2 cm)
Gift of Mrs. Simon Guggenheim

Girl Before a Mirror shows Picasso's young mistress Marie-Thérèse Walter, one of his favorite subjects in the early 1930s. Her white-haloed profile, rendered in a smooth lavender pink, appears serene. But it merges with a more roughly painted, frontal view of her face—a crescent, like the moon, yet intensely yellow, like the sun, and "made up" with a gilding of rouge, lipstick, and green eye-shadow. Perhaps the painting suggests both Walter's day-self and her night-self, both her tranquillity and her vitality, but also the transition from an innocent girl to a worldly woman aware of her own sexuality.

It is also a complex variant on the traditional Vanity—the image of a woman confronting her mortality in a mirror, which reflects her as a death's head. On the right, the mirror reflection suggests a supernatural x-ray of the girl's soul, her future, her fate. Her face is darkened, her eyes are round and hollow, and her intensely feminine body is twisted and contorted. She seems older and more anxious. The girl reaches out to the reflection, as if trying to unite her different "selves." The diamond-patterned wallpaper recalls the costume of the Harlequin, the comic character from the commedia dell'arte with whom Picasso often identified himself—here a silent witness to the girl's psychic and physical transformations.

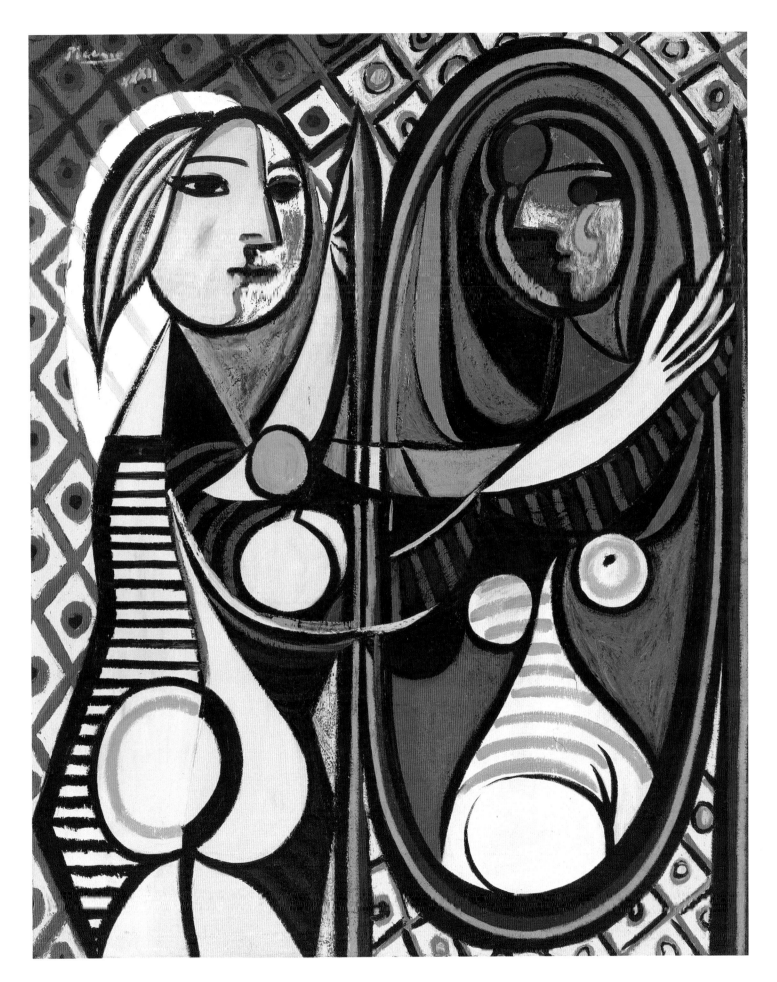

1932–33

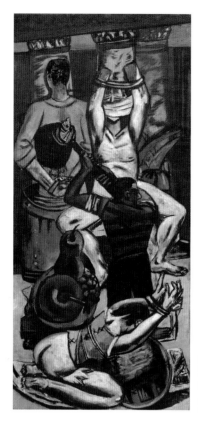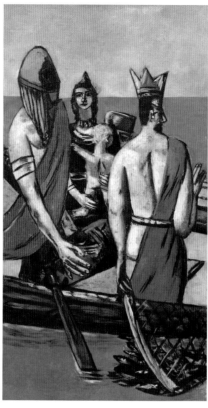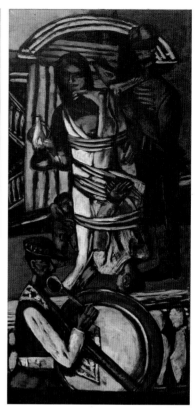

Departure. 1932–33

Oil on canvas; triptych, center panel,
7' ³/₄" x 45³/₈" (215.3 x 115.2 cm), side panels,
each 7' ³/₄" x 39¹/₄" (215.3 x 99.7 cm)
Given anonymously (by exchange)

In the right panel of *Departure*, Beckmann
once said, "You can see yourself trying to
find your way in the darkness, lighting the
hall and staircase with a miserable lamp,
dragging along tied to you, as part of
yourself, the corpse of your memories." The
triptych is full of personal meaning, and also
of mysteries. The often-appearing fish, for
example, are ancient symbols of redemption,
but may also connote sexuality. Perhaps the
woman under torture gazes prophetically into
a crystal ball—but what she seems to see is
the daily paper. Men's faces are hidden:

averted in the side panels, masked in the
center. Is it the same couple whose fate each
image tracks?

Beckmann's accounts of *Departure* are
fragmentary, and, in any case, he believed
that "if people cannot understand it of their
own accord, ... there is no sense in showing
it." But the work, however elusive in its
details, is clear overall: painted at a dark
time in Germany (that of Hitler's rise to
power), it tells of harsh burdens and sadistic
brutalities through which the human spirit,
regally crowned, may somehow sail in
serenity. Beckmann called the center panel
"The Homecoming," and said of it, "The
Queen carries the greatest treasure—
Freedom—as her child in her lap. Freedom is
the one thing that matters—it is the
departure, the new start."

The Palace at 4 a.m. 1932–33
Construction in wood, glass, wire, and string,
25 x 28¼ x 15¾" (63.5 x 71.8 x 40 cm)
Purchase

An empty architecture of wood scaffolding,
The Palace at 4 a.m. undoes conventional
ideas of sculptural mass. Even early on,
Giacometti once wrote, he had struggled to
describe a "sharpness" that he saw in reality,
"a kind of skeleton in space"; human bodies,
he added, were never for me a compact
mass but like a transparent skeleton time."
Here he extends that vision to render a
building as a haunting stage set.

Haunting and haunted, for the palace is
lived in: isolated forms and figures inhabit its
spaces. The enigma of their connection
charges the air that is the sculpture's
principal medium. Giacometti was a
Surrealist when he made the *Palace*, and it
has the requisite eerie mood. It was his
practice, he said, to execute "sculptures that
presented themselves to my mind entirely
accomplished. I limited myself to
reproducing them ... without asking myself
what they could mean."

Yet Giacometti did relate *The Palace at 4
a.m.* to a period he had spent with a woman
who enchanted him, and with whom he had

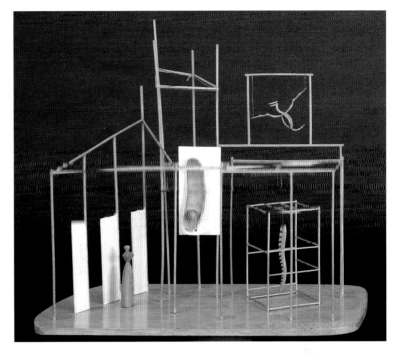

built "a fantastic palace at night, ... a very
fragile palace of matchsticks." He did not
know why he had included the spinal column
or the skeletal bird, though he associated
both with her. As for "the red object in front of
the board; I identify it with myself."

TULLIO D'ALBISOLA (TULLIO SPARTACO MAZZOTTI)
ITALIAN, 1899–1971

Parole in libertà futuriste, tattili-termiche olfattive by Filippo
Tommaso Marinetti. 1932–34
Illustrated book with 26 lithographs on metal,
page: 9³⁄₁₆ x 8¹¹⁄₁₆" (23.3 x 22 cm)
Publisher: Edizioni Futuriste di Poesia, Rome.
Edition: approx. 25
Gift of The Associates of the Department of Prints
and Illustrated Books and of Elaine Lustig Cohen
in memory of Arthur A. Cohen

This extraordinary book, with its cover and
bound pages made completely of metal,
heralds technological achievement in the
service of art. Marinetti, the Futurist artist,
poet-author, and force behind this project,
consulted with workers in a can factory in
Savona, Italy, which had printed a poem on a
sheet of tin in 1931.

The making of this book, however, posed
special difficulties in devising a spine that
allowed the heavy pages to turn freely. The
solution was the cylindrical mechanism seen
at the left edge of the cover. The layout of the

book was designed by Marinetti and
d'Albisola, a sculptor and ceramist who
executed the lithographs, combining
typography with crisp geometric shapes. As
seen on this cover, the artist created
dynamic compositions, using sleek modern
typefaces in boldly distorted sizes.

The Futurists promoted
free verse and poetry based
on sound rather than
meaning, expanding their
reach to the visual and
performing arts. They
exalted the machine, with its
seemingly limitless
possibilities for the future, as
a symbol of the modern
age. *Parole in libertà
futuriste* represents a
remarkable collaboration of
artist, artisan, technician,
and machine, which resulted
in the first mechanical book.

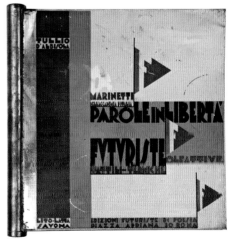

1933

The Daughter of the Dancers
(La Hija de los Danzantes), 1933
Gelatin silver print, 9¼ x 6¹¹/₁₆" (23.5 x 17 cm)
Purchase

In this picture, as in many of Álvarez Bravo's
photographs, our experience begins with the
theme of looking: we must wonder what it is
that the girl sees, or what she seeks. It has
been suggested that her awkwardly placed
feet, with one foot atop the other as she
stands on her toes, evokes the figures in
Mexican reliefs and carvings made before
the Spanish conquest, and that the girl,
dressed in traditional Mexican costume, may

be interpreted as representing a Mexico
searching for its past through the window in
the well-worn wall. Clearly, the picture was
staged, and we know that the photographer
has intentionally provoked our curiosity.

Photography has an inherent power to
create mystery because it only describes
aspects of things and never tells the whole
story. In the hands of a skillful photographer,
this capacity to intrigue can become the
foundation of an aesthetic, a way of working.
Throughout his seventy-five-year career, the
Mexican photographer Álvarez Bravo
consistently made deeply human
photographs rife with enigma.

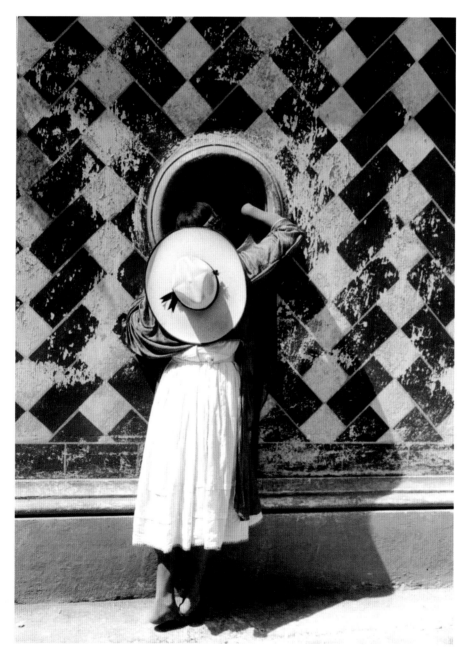

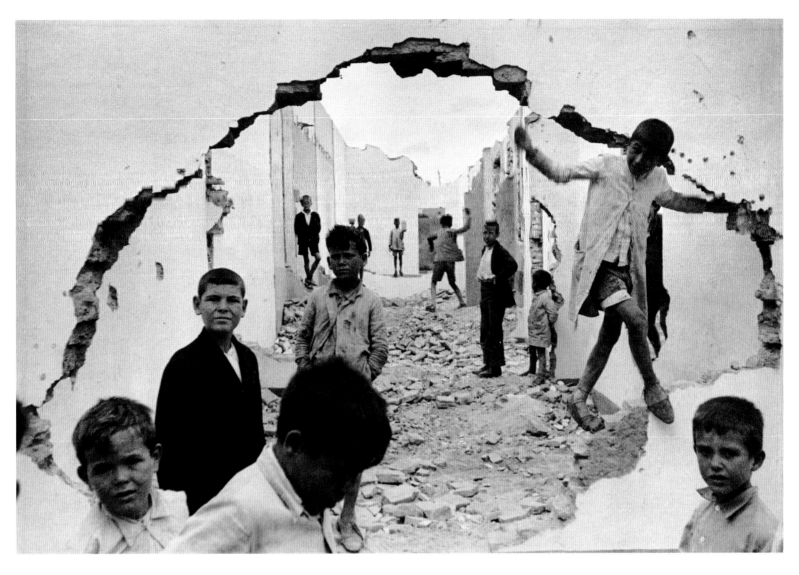

Seville. 1933
Gelatin silver print, 9³/₁₆ x 13⁹/₁₆" (23.4 x 34.5 cm)
Gift of the artist

This picture describes a group of children both as living individuals and as shapes deployed against the jagged forms of the crumbling walls, and its vitality arises from the reciprocal relationship between these two ways of looking at the world. In fact, only two of the boys are in motion, but the vitality of graphic pattern infuses the whole picture with the antic energy of youth. Cartier-Bresson coined a term for the instant at which the interplay of human meaning and photographic form can yield such a surprise. He called it "the decisive moment."

Later, as a photojournalist after World War II, Cartier-Bresson earned the envy of his peers for his ability to seem invisible—to capture an event without disturbing it by his presence. In many of his early photographs, however, his subjects were aware of and even performed for him, as the boy at the upper right does here. It is as if the unpredictable theater of the street had been choreographed for the photographer alone.

This photograph has sometimes been misinterpreted as a document of the Spanish Civil War, but it was made three years before that war began. However, its social dimension—the photographer's identification with the poor and disenfranchised—is quite real.

BRASSAÏ (GYULA HALÁSZ) FRENCH, BORN
TRANSYLVANIA. 1899–1984

Kiki Singing in a Montparnasse Cabaret. 1933

Gelatin silver print, 15⅝ x 11¾" (39.7 x 29.8 cm)
David H. McAlpin Fund

Kiki was celebrated among avant-garde
artists, who haunted the bars and cabarets of
Montparnasse, her Paris neighborhood, in
the 1920s. She is pictured here in the full
glow of her own professional persona, as an
authentic descendant of the ribald heroines
of the fifteenth-century poet François Villon.
The accordionist, who gazes at her with awe
and affection, is unidentified.

Brassaï's photographs are the last great
expression of a tradition of picturing Parisian
popular culture that included such masters
as Edgar Degas and Henri de Toulouse-
Lautrec. By the time this picture was made,
that tradition had become tinged with
nostalgia for the past, and was soon to be
obliterated by the engines of modernity and
the business of tourism.

Brassaï's blunt, no-nonsense pictures,
such as this one, in which the subject is often
fixed by the unapologetic scrutiny of a flash,
soon became, and remain, a model of
photography's fierce curiosity and proof of
the mystery of unvarnished photographic
fact—a foundation of what came to be called
the documentary tradition.

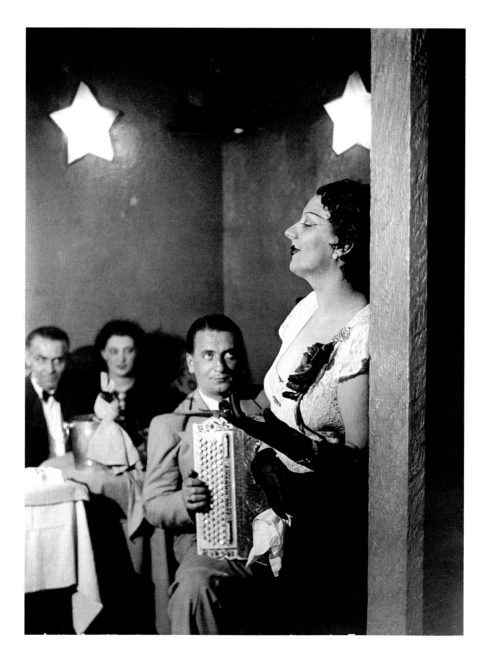

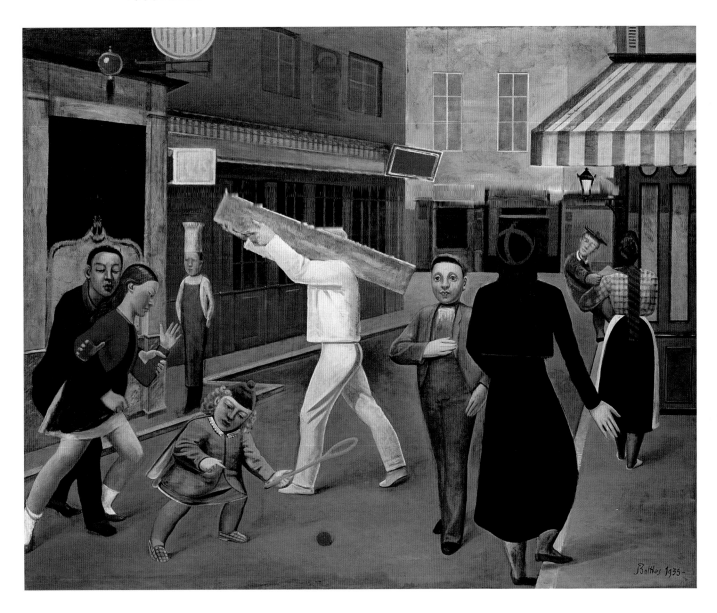

The Street. 1933
Oil on canvas, 6' 4³/₄ x 7' 10¹/₂" (195 x 240 cm)
James Thrall Soby Bequest

Though set in a real place—the rue Bourbon-le-Château, Paris—*The Street* has the intensity of a dream. The figures in this strange frozen dance are precisely placed in a shallow, friezelike line, yet except for the struggling couple on the left, they don't interact at all. The toque-wearing chef isn't even human—he is a pavement sign for a restaurant—but he stands no more stiffly than the other characters, who, stylized and solid, seem less to walk than to pose.

Part of the work's tension comes from the diversity in the traditions it fuses. Its receding architectural perspective emulates Renaissance geometry, for Balthus much admired Quattrocento artists, particularly Piero della Francesca. But another, quite different influence links him to his Surrealist peers: long after painting *The Street*, he would still say that he had never stopped seeing things as he saw them in childhood. He well knew children's books such as Lewis Carroll's "Alice" stories, with their illustrations by John Tenniel, and, indeed, the girl caught in the tussle has been said to be Alice herself; the youth in the center resembles Tweedledum or Tweedledee; and the man with the plank could be Carroll's carpenter, without his walrus companion—though his simultaneous resemblance to a figure in Piero's *Discovery and Proving of the True Cross*, at Arezzo (c. 1455) suggests a different symbolic register.

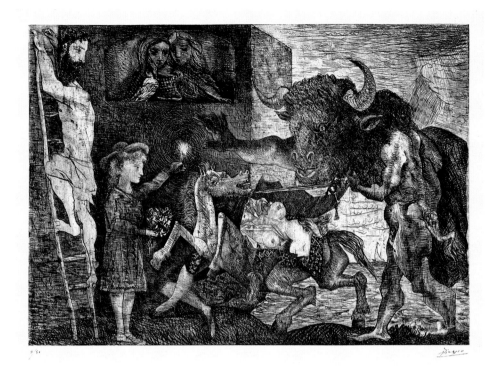

Minotauromachy. 1935

Etching and engraving, plate: 19¹/₂ x 27³/₈"
(49.6 x 69.6 cm)
Publisher: the artist. Edition: approx. 55
Abby Aldrich Rockefeller Fund

This provocative scene, full of symbolic content, is difficult but not impossible to interpret. Several actions take place in a narrow, confined space. The main protagonists—a young girl with a candle and a bouquet of flowers, and a huge Minotaur, a mythological creature with a human body and a bull's head—appear frozen in their confrontation. Between them a wounded female bullfighter is flung across a lacerated horse that snarls with teeth bared. Above, two girls with doves, symbols of peace, peer out from a window, while a bearded man appears on a ladder at the left. A tiny sailboat can be glimpsed on the far horizon.

Executed when Picasso's personal life was in turmoil and he had ceased to paint, *Minotauromachy* presents a deeply private mythology. Not only was his marriage to Olga Khokhlova troubled at the time, but he was also ambivalent about the pregnancy of his young mistress, Marie-Thérèse Walter, whose facial features are similar to those of the female figures. The paradoxical Minotaur, the bull-man, was a frequent theme for the artist during this time.

This disturbing and violent representation is also prophetic of the Spanish Civil War, which began in 1936, a year after this print was executed. *Minotauromachy* served as a visual source for Guernica, Picasso's famous mural of 1937 about that conflict, which contains some of the same imagery that is seen here.

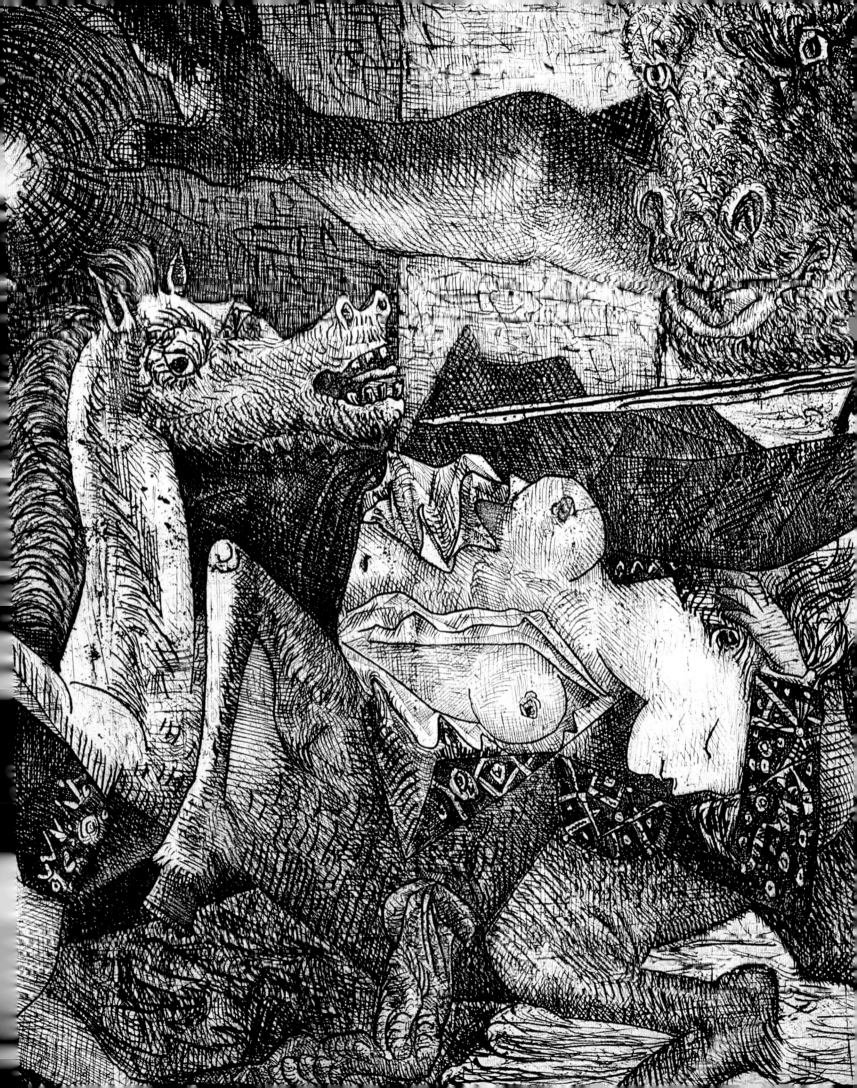

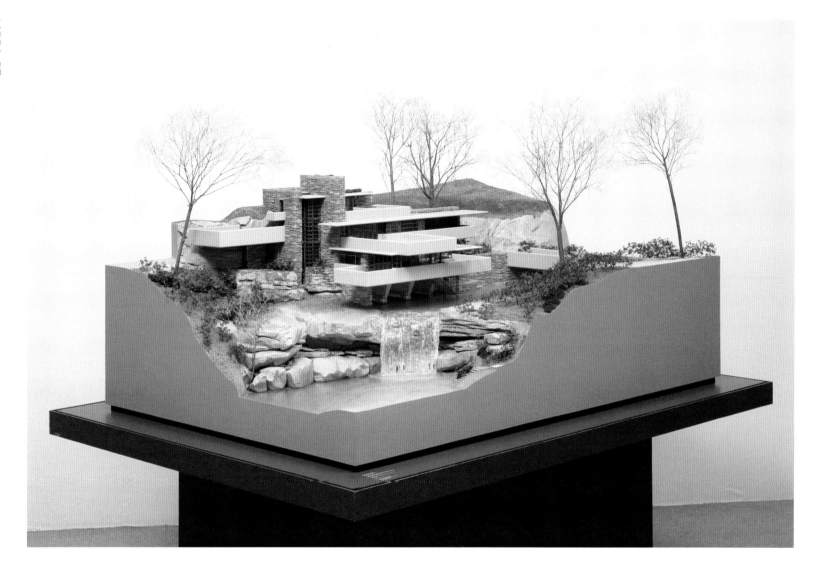

Fallingwater, Edgar J. Kaufmann House, Mill Run, Pennsylvania. 1934–37

Model: acrylic, wood, metal, expanded polystyrene, and paint, 40¹/₂ x 71¹/₂ x 47⁵/₈" (102.8 x 181.6 x 121 cm)
Modelmakers: Paul Bonfilio with Joseph Zelvin, Larry List, and Edith Randel (1984)
Best Products Company Architecture Fund

From the moment Fallingwater was built, critics recognized this private retreat for Edgar J. Kaufmann, a Pittsburgh department store magnate, as a masterpiece of modern architecture. It is one of Wright's boldest creations, integrating architecture and nature. Situated atop a waterfall in a wooded ravine in western Pennsylvania, the house is anchored to a large boulder, which serves in the interior as the central hearth and the symbolic core of domestic life. From here the house extends vertically and horizontally in rhythmic patterns out into the landscape. Made of rough-cut stone from a nearby quarry, the walls and chimney complement the natural strata of the site.

As shown in The Museum of Modern Art's model, sleek cantilevered balconies of reinforced concrete, made possible by modern engineering, seem to float effortlessly, if precariously, over the water. Their shape echoes the stepped rock ledges in the stream. An outdoor staircase suspended from below the living room leads to the plunge pool below.

Fallingwater embodies Wright's deeply held values about the underlying unity of humans and nature, which is reflected in his selection of building materials. As a great work of art, Fallingwater transcends its function as a house to meet a client's needs and symbolizes an American democratic ideal: to be able to live a free life in nature.

1936

Gibraltar. 1936

Construction of lignum vitae, walnut, steel rods,
and painted wood, 51⁷/₈ x 24¹/₄ x 11³/₈"
(131.7 x 61.3 x 28.7 cm)
Gift of the artist

Although *Gibraltar* is abstract, the connection
is easily made between its base—a weighty
lump of lignum vitae (a tropical hardwood)—
and the Mediterranean rock that gives the
work its name. This mass of wood is rough
and solid, and seemingly unshaped. More
delicate, and more clearly marked by human
artifice, are the work's sloping plane of
walnut, its painted wood ball, and its two
steel rods balancing a crescent and a
sphere, respectively. *Gibraltar* recalls the
biomorphic forms in Surrealist art, particularly
that of Joan Miró, a strong influence on
Calder. But there is also a poetic whimsy that
is Calder's alone.

The sculpture is contradictory in its
qualities. The rods are thin and linear, and
express an upward, airborne drive and
eccentric balance; the lignum vitae is heavy,
earth-hugging, solid. The surfaces, too, show
various materials being variously treated,
implying methods from machine-making to
hand-polishing to leaving well enough alone.
These disjunctions have a good-humored wit,
which does not disguise the work's grace.
Calder once said that "the underlying sense
of form" in his work was "the system of the
Universe," and *Gibraltar*, with its sun, moon,
and heavy earth, is a solar system in
miniature—a system revealed as a fine-tuned
balance of opposites.

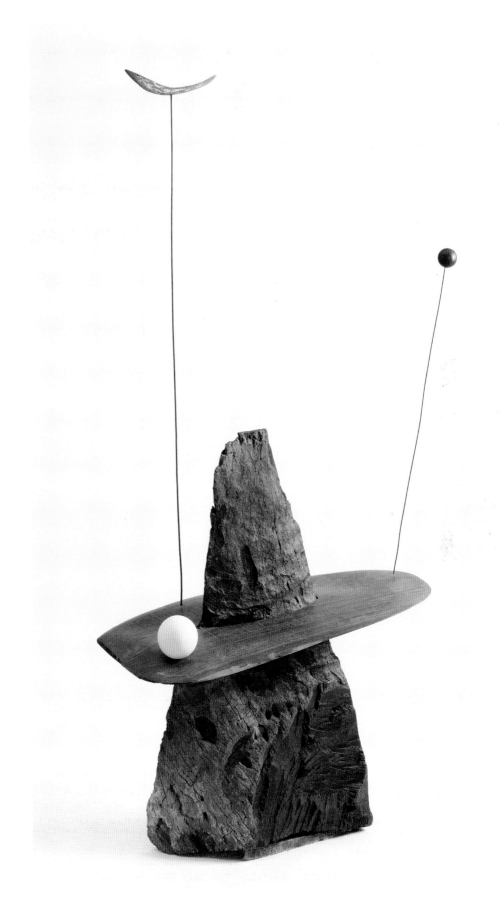

1936

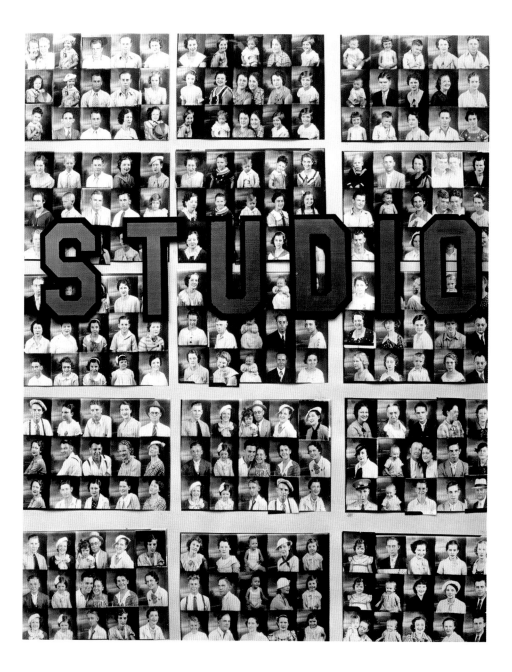

Penny Picture Display, Savannah, Georgia. 1936
Gelatin silver print, 8⅝ x 6¹⁵/₁₆" (21.9 x 17.6 cm)
Gift of Willard Van Dyke

In the Savannah photographer's window there are fifteen blocks of fifteen pictures each, for a total of 225 portraits, less the ones hidden by the letters. Most of the sitters appear at least twice, but altogether there are more than one hundred different men, women, and children: a community.

Evans explored the United States of the 1930s—its people, its architecture, its cultural symbols (including photographs)—with the disinterested eye of an archaeologist studying an ancient civilization. *Penny Picture Display* might be interpreted as a celebration of democracy or as a condemnation of conformity. Evans takes no side.

The photograph is very much a modern picture—crisp, planar, and resolutely self-contained. But instead of reconfirming a timeless ideal, as artistically ambitious American photographers before Evans generally had aimed to do, it engages a contemporary particular, rooted in history. And it announces Evans's allegiance to the plainspoken vernacular of ordinary photographers, such as the Savannah portraitist who made the pictures in the window.

Object (Le Déjeuner en fourrure). 1936
Fur-covered cup, saucer, and spoon; cup 4³/₈"
(10.9 cm) diam.; saucer, 9³/₈" (23.7 cm) diam.;
spoon 8" (20.2 cm) long; overall height 2⁷/₈"
(7.3 cm)
Purchase

Oppenheim's fur-lined teacup is perhaps the single most notorious Surrealist object. Its subtle perversity was inspired by a conversation between Oppenheim, Pablo Picasso, and the photographer Dora Maar at a Paris café: admiring Oppenheim's fur-trimmed bracelets, Picasso remarked that one could cover just about anything with fur. "Even this cup and saucer," Oppenheim replied.

In the 1930s, many Surrealist artists were arranging found objects in bizarre combinations that challenged reason and summoned unconscious and poetic associations. *Object*—titled *Le Déjeuner en fourrure* (*The lunch in fur*) by the Surrealist leader André Breton—is a cup and saucer that was purchased at a Paris department store and lined with the pelt of a Chinese gazelle. The work takes advantage of differences in the varieties of sensual pleasure: fur may delight the touch but it repels the tongue. And a cup and spoon, of course, are made to be put in the mouth.

A small concave object covered with fur, *Object* may also have a sexual connotation and politics: working in a male-dominated art world, perhaps Oppenheim was mocking the prevailing "masculinity" of sculpture, which conventionally adopts a hard substance and vertical orientation that can be seen as almost absurdly self-referential.

Chic, wry, and simultaneously attractive and disturbing, *Object* is shrewdly and quietly aggressive.

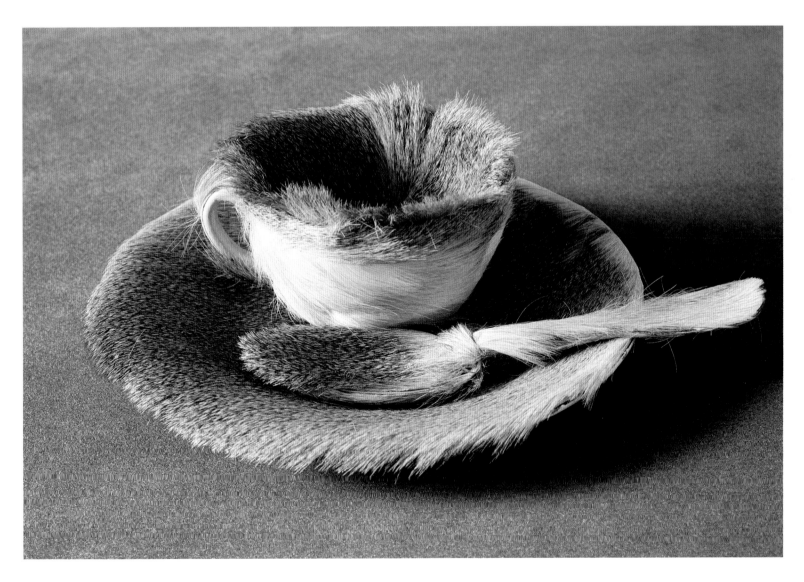

Woman Combing Her Hair. 1936

Wrought iron, 52 x 23^1/$_2$ x 24^5/$_8$"
(132.1 x 59.7 x 62.4 cm)
Mrs. Simon Guggenheim Fund

"To draw in space": that, for González, was the exciting possibility in the art of his time. A painter and draftsman as well as a sculptor, González realized that by cutting, rolling, and bending metal, or fusing found metal pieces into an assemblage, he could draw images not on paper but in air, his instrument not a pencil but a welding torch. He often worked in iron, a tough, unyielding material utterly lacking in the fine sinuosity of the precious metals. The stiff spine, shallow curves, and spiky, spearlike lines and points of *Woman Combing Her Hair* seem integral to the medium itself, but the work tempers its austerity with a subtle eroticism.

González himself associated iron with weaponry and with engineering, but wanted to direct it elsewhere. "It is high time," he wrote, "that this metal cease to be a murderer and the simple instrument of an overly mechanical science. Today, the door is opened wide to this material to be ... forged and hammered by the peaceful hands of artists." Decorative ironwork is a Spanish tradition, and González learned it as a young man, but considered it only a craft until, in 1928, he began to advise Pablo Picasso on making iron sculpture—an experience that inspired him to become a sculptor himself.

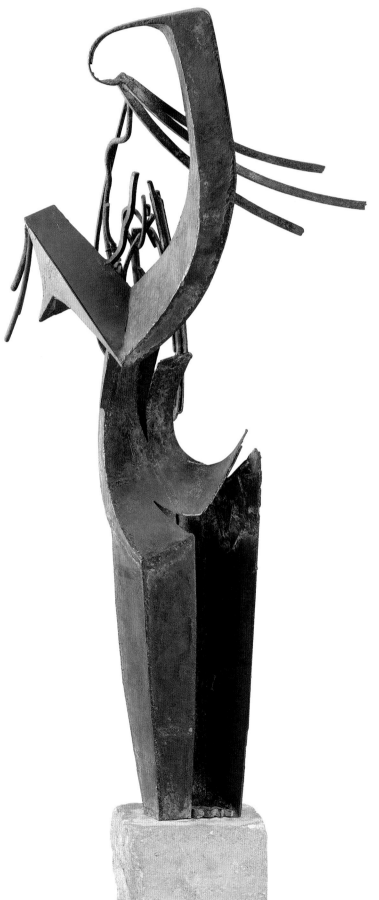

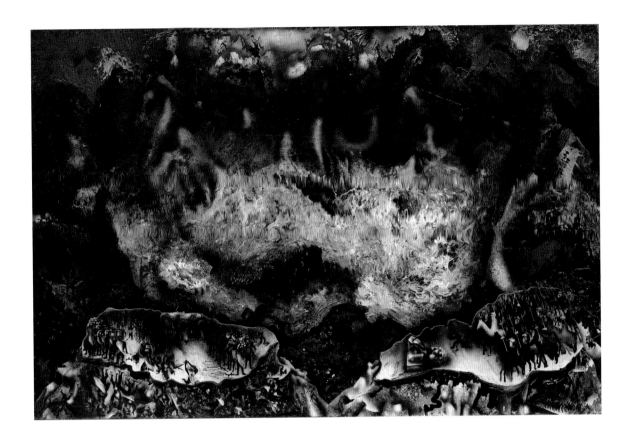

Collective Suicide. 1936

Enamel on wood with applied sections,
49" x 6' (124.5 x 182.9 cm)
Gift of Dr. Gregory Zilboorg

Collective Suicide is an apocalyptic vision
of the Spanish conquest of Mexico, when
many of the indigenous inhabitants killed
themselves rather than submit to slavery.
Siqueiros shows armored Spanish troops
advancing on horseback, a bowed captive
staggering before them in chains. The
broken statue of a god demonstrates the
ruin of the indigenous culture. Chichimec
indians, separated from their tormentors by
a churning pit, slaughter their own children,
hang themselves, stab themselves with
spears, or hurl themselves from cliffs.
Mountainous forms create a backdrop
crowned with swirling peaks, like fire
or blood.

Siqueiros, one of the Mexican mural
painters of the 1920s and 1930s, advocated
what he called "a monumental, heroic, and
public art." An activist and propagandist for
social reform, he was politically minded even
in his choices of materials and formats:
rejecting what he called "bourgeois easel
art," he used commercial and industrial
paints and methods. *Collective Suicide* is
one of his relatively few easel paintings, but
here, too, he used spray guns and stencils
for the figures, and strategically let the
paints—commercial enamels—flow together
on the canvas. *Collective Suicide* is both a
memorial to the doomed pre-Hispanic
cultures of the Americas and a rallying cry
against contemporary totalitarian regimes.

1938

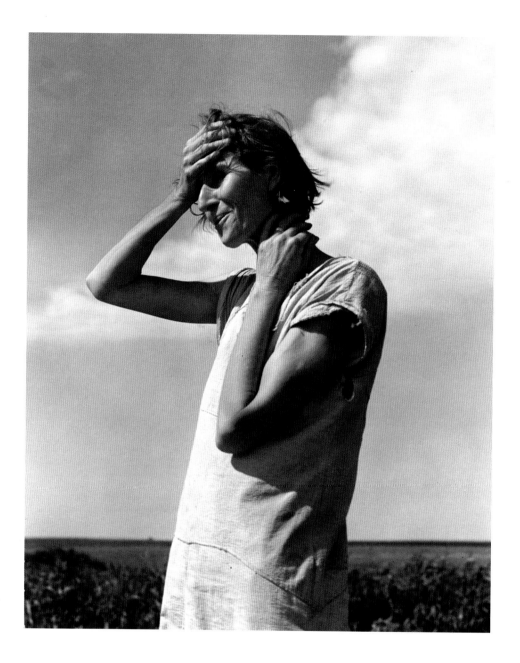

Woman of the High Plains, Texas Panhandle. 1938

Gelatin silver print, 12³/₈ x 10" (31.5 x 25.4 cm)
Purchase

Seen from slightly below, the woman in this photograph has become a monumental figure, set against the open sky and the unforgiving earth. Her gesture is full of suffering but tells us nothing specific about her life or travails. Yet the sunlight falls on the palpable flesh of a person and on the worn cloth of her shift.

The picture exemplifies Lange's exceptional talent for making the leap from concrete fact to arching symbol without leaving reality behind. She made it for the Farm Security Administration, a government agency whose photographic unit was charged with documenting the plight of the rural poor in the 1930s. Her work created a lasting image of the Great Depression. It also deepened the link between the descriptive style of documentary photography and the ideal of social engagement, becoming a touchstone for photographers who felt that their work should not only record social conditions but try to persuade people to improve them.

The River. 1938–43

Lead (cast 1948), 53³/₄" x 7' 6" x 66" (136.5 x
228.6 x 167.7 cm), on lead base designed by the
artist, 9³/₄ x 67 x 27³/₄" (24.8 x 170.1 x 70.4 cm)
Mrs. Simon Guggenheim Fund

The daring instability and torsion of *The River*
are rare in Maillol's sculpture. Instead of
trying to emulate the dynamism of twentieth-
century life, as did so many artists of his
time, Maillol usually sought an art of serenity
and stillness, of classical nobility and
simplicity. As late as 1937, in fact, he
remarked, "For my taste, there should be as
little movement as possible in sculpture." Yet
within a year or so afterward he had

conceived *The River*, a work in which the
movement is almost reckless.

Commissioned to create a monument to a
notable pacifist, the French writer Henri
Barbusse, Maillol conceived the sculpture as
a work on the theme of war: a woman
stabbed in the back, and falling. When the
commission fell through, he transformed the
idea into *The River*. In a departure from the
usual conventions of monumental sculpture,
the figure lies low to the ground and rests
apparently precariously on the pedestal
even hanging below its edge. Twisting and
turning, her raised arms suggesting the
pressure of some powerful current, this
woman is the personification of moving water.

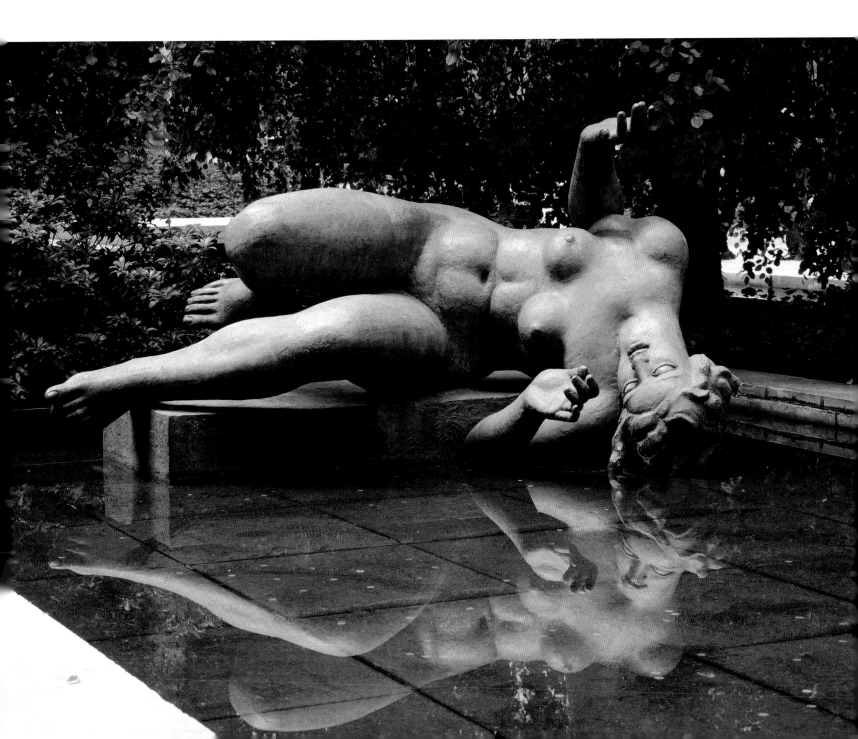

Autumn, Yosemite Valley. 1939
Gelatin silver print, 7¼ x 9½" (18.4 x 24.1 cm)
Gift of Albert M. Bender

From the late 1920s through the 1960s, Adams made hundreds of photographs of Yosemite Valley, and he often aimed to evoke its vastness and sublime grandeur. Many of his pictures, however, are quite intimate. In this view, for example, the cliffs do not seem to loom above us. Instead, along with the trees and the reflections in the water, the face of the cliff belongs to a gossamer tissue of glittering detail, animated by light.

Adams's devotion to wild nature made him a figurehead for conservationists, and his mastery of technique made him a hero to many who were unable to distinguish between the art and craft of photography. But all that came much later. When he made this picture, Adams was still practically unknown. His love of nature was a matter of private feeling, not political conviction; and his attention to craft was not a matter of slavish adherence to formulas and rules. It was made necessary by his art, in which the most ephemeral fluctuation of weather or light could be a major event.

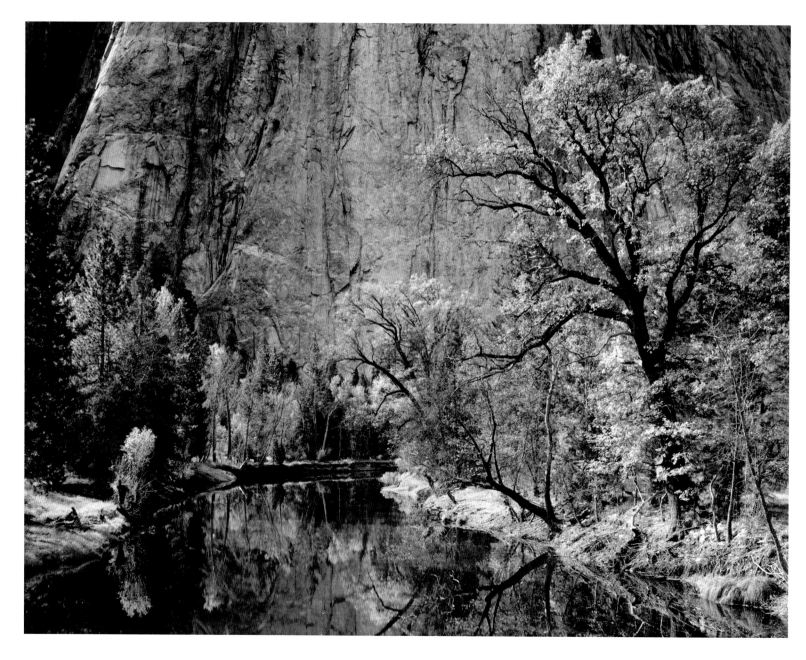

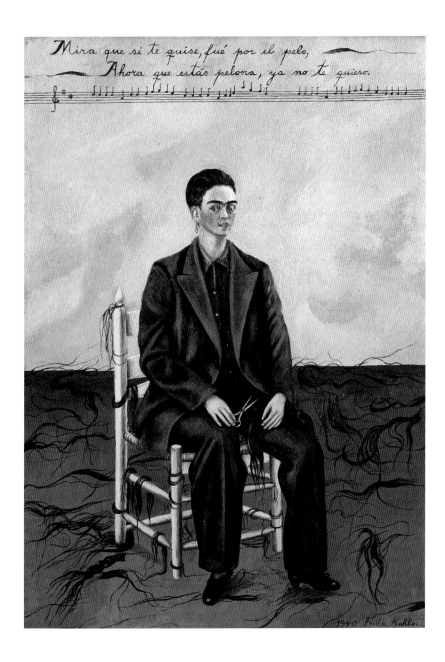

Self-Portrait with Cropped Hair. 1940

Oil on canvas, 15³/₄ x 11" (40 x 27.9 cm)
Gift of Edgar Kaufmann, Jr.

Kahlo painted *Self-Portrait with Cropped Hair* shortly after she divorced her unfaithful husband, the artist Diego Rivera. As a painter of many self-portraits, she had often shown herself wearing a Mexican woman's traditional dresses and flowing hair, now, in renunciation of Rivera, she painted herself short-haired and in a man's shirt, shoes, and oversized suit (presumably her former husband's).

Kahlo knew adventurous European and American art, and her own work was embraced by the Surrealists, whose leader, André Breton, described it as "a ribbon around a bomb." But her stylistic inspirations were chiefly Mexican, especially nineteenth-century religious painting, and she would say, "I do not know if my paintings are Surrealist or not, but I do know that they are the most frank expression of myself." The queasily animate locks of fresh-cut hair in this painting must also be linked to her feelings of estrangement from Rivera (whom she remarried the following year), and they also have the dreamlike quality of Surrealism. For, into the work she has written the lyric of a Mexican song: "Look, if I loved you it was because of your hair. Now that you are without hair, I don't love you anymore."

Taglioni's Jewel Casket. 1940
Wood box containing glass ice cubes, jewelry, etc., 4³/₄ x 11⁷/₈ x 8¹/₄" (12 x 30.2 x 21 cm)
Gift of James Thrall Soby

The art form that Cornell made his own was the box, its contents carefully arranged to evoke a mood or narrative. These works may recall toys the artist had played with as a child, but they must also trace back to devices in Surrealist art (which Cornell knew well) and, earlier, in paintings by Giorgio de Chirico. In *Taglioni's Jewel Casket*, small glass cubes lie in a wood box. Beneath them, and under blue glass, necklaces, sand, crystal, and rhinestones rest on a mirrored surface. This romantic scene of ice and jewels relates to an event in the life of the legendary nineteenth-century ballerina Marie Taglioni.

A label in the box's lid tells the story: "On a moonlight night in the winter of 1835 the carriage of Marie Taglioni was halted by a Russian highwayman, and that enchanting creature commanded to dance for this audience of one upon a panther's skin spread over the snow beneath the stars. From this actuality arose the legend that to keep alive the memory of this adventure so precious to her, Taglioni formed the habit of placing a piece of artificial ice in her jewel casket or dressing table where, melting among the sparkling stones, there was evoked a hint of the atmosphere of the starlit heavens over the ice-covered landscape."

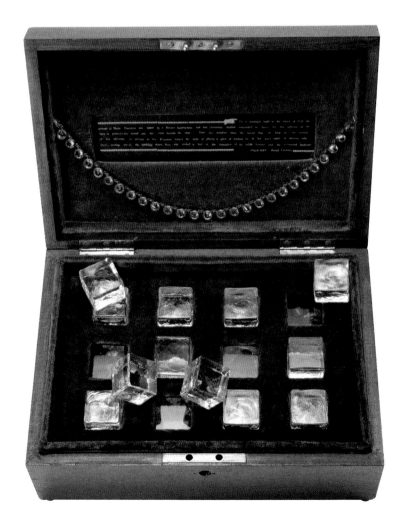

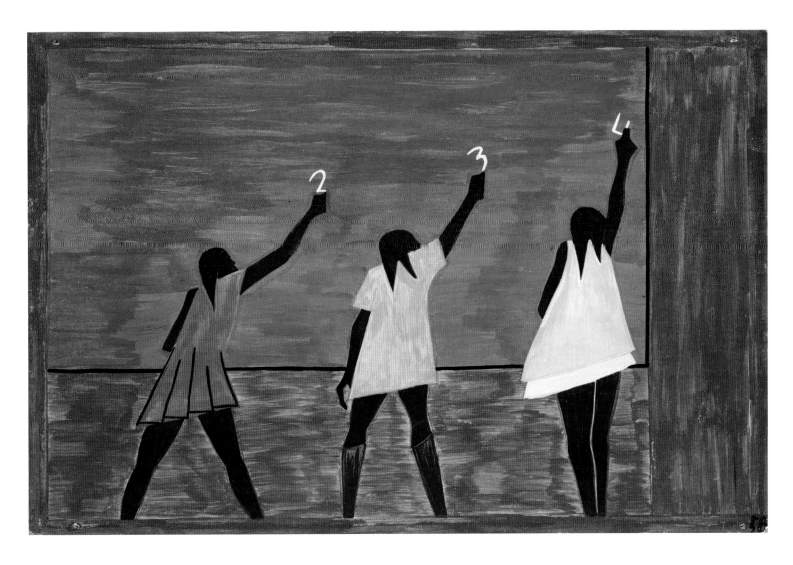

The Migration Series. 1940–41

Number 58, from a series of 60 works (30 in the Museum): tempera on gesso on composition board, 12 x 18" (30.5 x 45.7 cm)
Gift of Mrs. David M. Levy

During the first half of the twentieth century, as the expanding modern industries in America's northern cities demanded ever more workers, great numbers of African Americans saw in these jobs a chance to escape the poverty and discrimination of the rural South. Between 1916 and 1930 alone, over a million people moved north. Lawrence's own parents made this journey, and he grew up hearing stories about it; as a young artist living in Harlem, the heart of New York City's African American community, he recognized it as an epic theme. Originally known as *The Migration of the Negro*, but renamed by the artist in 1993, this distinguished cycle of images chronicles a great exodus and arrival.

Visually, the cycle moves between panels of great incident and panels of near abstraction and emptiness. Using exaggerated perspectives, rhythmic constructions, astringent colors, and angular figures, Lawrence bent decorative forms to the task of history, and made social realism consonant with modern art. Yet he never lost touch with the task of telling a complex story clearly and accessibly. Leaving hardships behind in the South, African Americans received a mixed reception in the North; along with the possibility of jobs, the vote, and education, the new life also brought unhealthy living conditions, race riots, and other trials all documented in Lawrence's cycle, along with his community's heroic perseverance in facing them. Each part of the story carries a legend by the artist; for the image shown here, the legend reads: "In the North the Negro had better educational facilities."

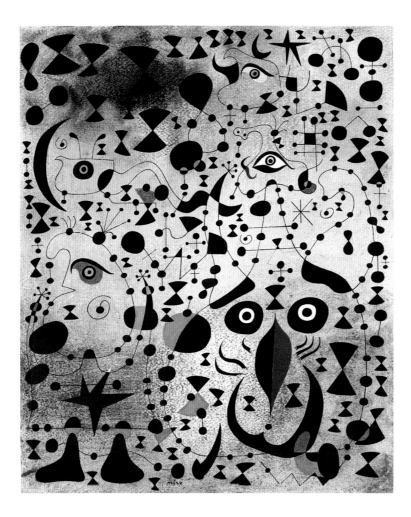

The Beautiful Bird Revealing the Unknown to a Pair of Lovers. 1941
Gouache, pencil, and oil wash on paper, 18 x 15"
(46 x 38 cm)
Acquired through the Lillie P. Bliss Bequest

This is one of a celebrated group of twenty-four drawings, collectively referred to as the Constellation series, which was executed during a period of personal crisis for Miró triggered by the Spanish Civil War and World War II. Trapped in France from 1936 to 1940, the artist embarked on these obsessively meticulous works on paper in an attempt to commune with nature and escape the tragedies of current events. Despite their modest formats, they represented the most important works of his career up to that time, a fact he quickly realized.

The first eleven works in the series were executed in Normandy between December 1939 and May 1940. Although the motifs throughout correspond to Miró's classic repertory, in the earlier works the washed grounds are more saturated, the motifs larger, and the compositions looser than in those that would follow. In the later thirteen works, executed in Palma de Mallorca in 1940–41, of which *The Beautiful Bird Revealing the Unknown to a Pair of Lovers* is exemplary, the grounds are almost opalescent, and the familiar motifs are smaller and tightly woven into a continuous linear web. In its elusive poetry yet rigorous control, this work not only embodies Miró's artistic personality, but it also mirrors the luminous tracks of constellations in a clear night sky.

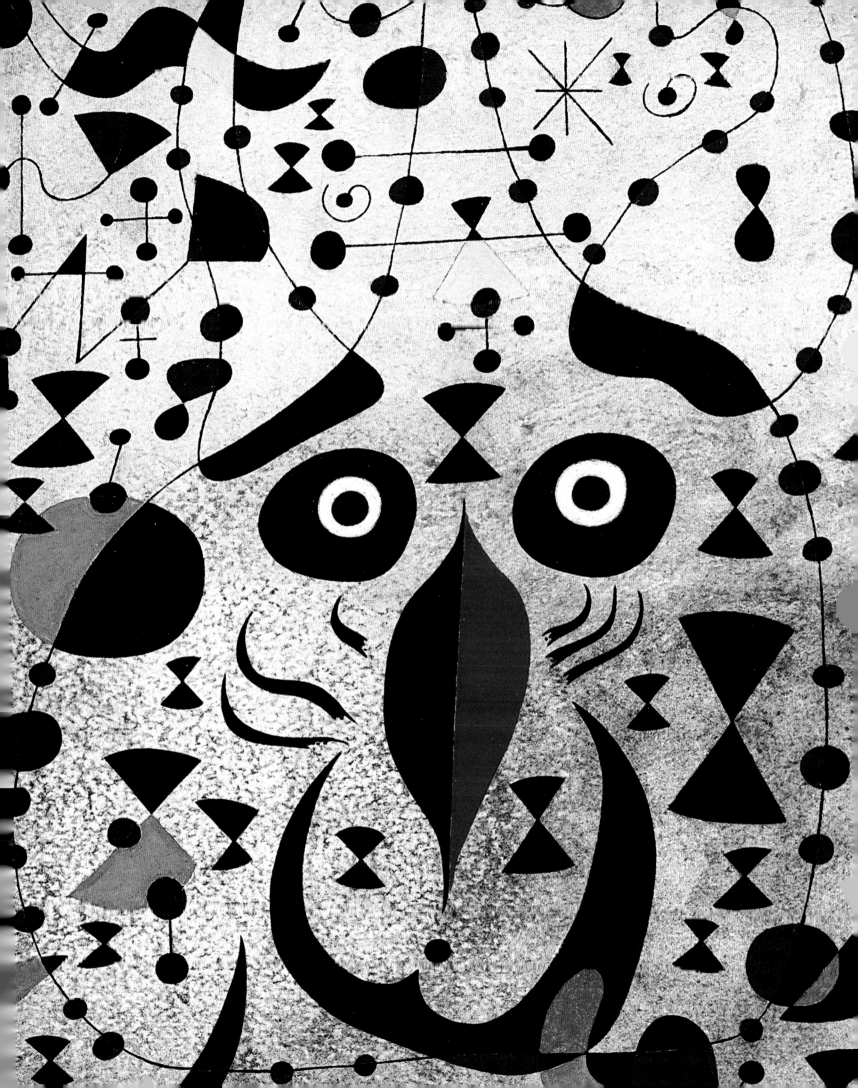

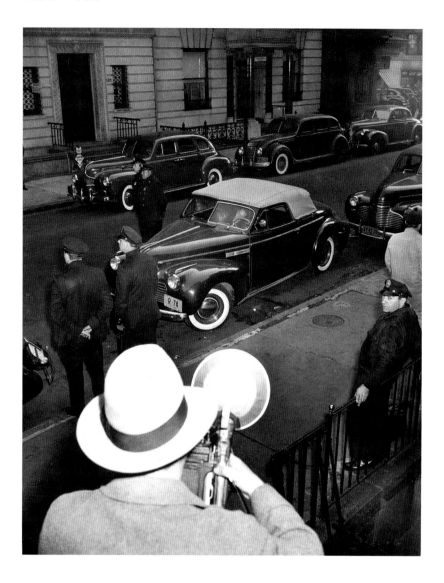

Harry Maxwell Shot in a Car. 1941
Gelatin silver print, 13¹⁵/₁₆ x 10¹/₂" (35.4 x 26.6 cm)
Gift of the artist

Weegee, a news photographer, borrowed his professional name from the ouija board as a way of advertising his uncanny ability to show up in the right place at the right time. On this occasion, however, it appears that he was not the first to arrive at the scene. Instead of a grisly close-up of the corpse, he gives us a generous view of the aftermath of the crime: the cops have seen it all before and pass the time in bored distraction while the photographers work.

Photographs began to appear in newspapers around the turn of the century, and the heyday of newspaper photography did not get under way until the 1920s. But it did not take long thereafter to establish the staples of the trade: winners and losers, heroes and villains, catastrophes and celebrations—timeless dramas reinvigorated on a daily basis by the specificity of photographic fact. The genre was at its most pure in the tabloid papers, which dispensed with the facade of journalistic reserve in their headlong pursuit of sensation. Nevertheless, as the writer Luc Sante notes: "In Weegee's hands, this cynicism is so extreme it almost becomes a kind of innocence."

Broadway Boogie Woogie. 1942–43
Oil on canvas, 50 x 50" (127 x 127 cm)
Given anonymously
© 2005 Mondrian/Holtzman Trust
c/o HCR International Warrenton Virginia USA

Mondrian arrived in New York in 1940, one of
the many European artists who moved to the
United States to escape World War II. He fell
in love with the city immediately. He also fell
in love with boogie-woogie music, to which
he was introduced on his first evening in New
York, and he soon began, as he said, to put
a little boogie-woogie into his paintings.

Mondrian's aesthetic doctrine of Neo-
Plasticism restricted the painter's means to
the most basic kinds of line—that is, to
straight horizontals and verticals—and to a
similarly limited color range, the primary triad
of red, yellow, and blue plus white, black,
and the grays between. But *Broadway
Boogie Woogie* omits black and breaks
Mondrian's once uniform bars of color into
multicolored segments. Bouncing against
each other, these tiny, blinking blocks of
color create a vital and pulsing rhythm, an
optical vibration that jumps from intersection
to intersection like the streets of New York. At
the same time, the picture is carefully
calibrated, its colors interspersed with gray
and white blocks in an extraordinary
balancing act.

Mondrian's love of boogie-woogie must
have come partly because he saw its goals
as analogous to his own: "destruction of
melody which is the destruction of natural
appearance; and construction through the
continuous opposition of pure means—
dynamic rhythm."

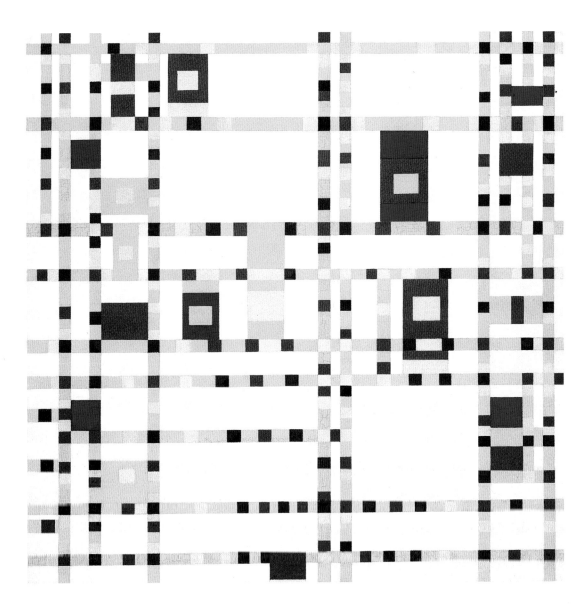

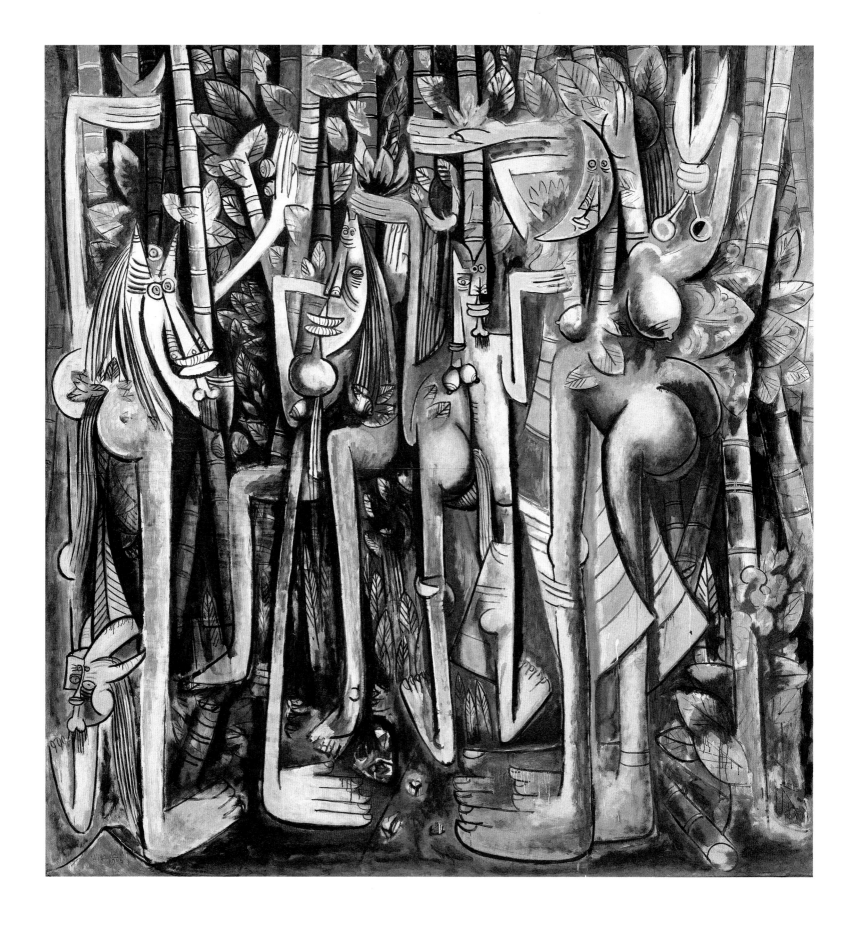

176

The Jungle. 1943

Gouache on paper, mounted on canvas,
7' 10¹/₄" x 7' 6¹/₂" (239.4 x 229.9 cm)
Inter-American Fund

In this monumental and thematically complex gouache, masked figures simultaneously appear and disappear amid the thick foliage of sugarcane and bamboo. The multiperspectival rendering of these figures mirrors Cubist vocabulary, while the fantastical moonlit scene around these monstrous beings—half man, half animal—emerging out of a primeval jungle evokes the realm of the Surrealists. In his desire to express the spirit of Afro-Cuban culture, in particular that of the uprooted Africans "who brought their primitive culture, their magical religion, with its mystical side in close correspondence with nature," Lam reinforces the Surrealist aspect of this work.

Born in Cuba, Lam spent eighteen years in Europe (1923–41), which deeply affected his artistic vision. While there, he befriended Pablo Picasso and also established himself as an integral member of the Surrealist movement. The artistic and cultural traditions of Lam's homeland and Europe converged when he returned to Cuba and renewed his familiarity with its light, vegetation, and culture. In *The Jungle* the presence of the woman horse, who in Afro-Cuban mysticism refers to a spirit in communication with the natural world, mirrors Lam's own confrontational mingling with the so-called primitive interests expressed in advanced European painting. His work is an example of this confluence of two cultures.

JACKSON POLLOCK AMERICAN, 1912–1956

The She-Wolf. 1943

Oil, gouache, and plaster on canvas, 41⁷/₈ x 67"
(106.4 x 170.2 cm)
Purchase

When Pollock painted *The She-Wolf* he had not yet arrived at his so-called "drip" style, one of the great inventions of Abstract Expressionism. The canvas's traces of multicolored washes and spatters show that a free-form abstraction and an unfettered play of materials were already parts of his process; but in this work and others his focus is a compound of mythology and an iconography of the unconscious. (He was influenced here both by Surrealism and his own Jungian analysis.) Perhaps Pollock's she-wolf is the legendary foster-mother to Romulus and Remus, the founders of ancient Rome. But he himself refused to identify her, saying, "*She Wolf* came into existence because I had to paint it. Any attempt on my part to say something about it, to attempt explanation of the inexplicable, could only destroy it."

Drawn in heavy black and white lines, the wolf advances leftward. Her body is overlaid with abstract lines and patches, a thick, unreadable calligraphy that spreads throughout the canvas. These hieroglyphic intimations, along with the somber palette and the conjuring of myth, reflect the climate of a period shadowed by war. Intended to approach ultimate human mysteries, they were to be simultaneously meaningful and unknowable.

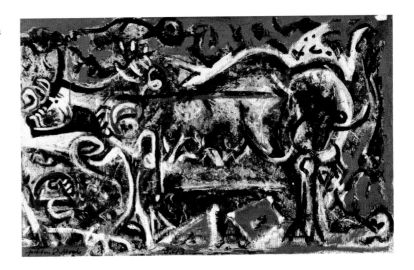

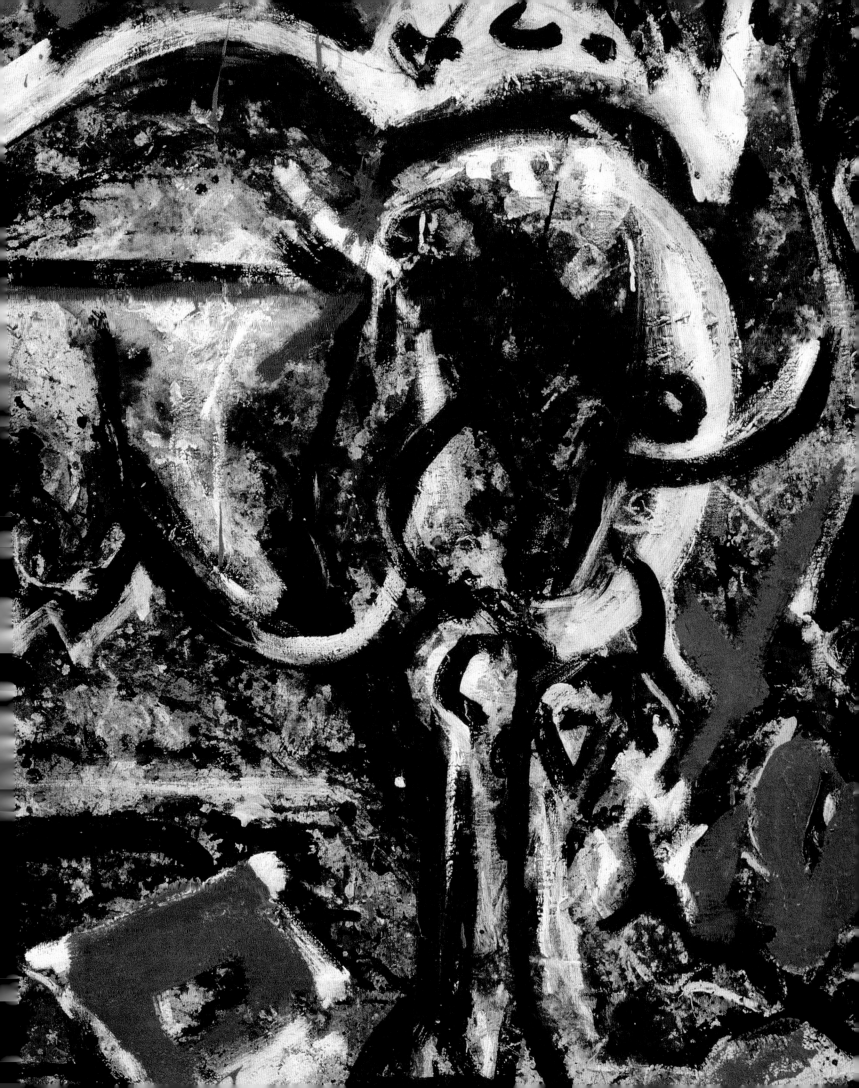

HENRI MATISSE FRENCH, 1869–1954

The Knife Thrower from **Jazz**
by Henri Matisse. 1943–47
Illustrated book with 20 pochoirs, page:
16¹/₂ x 12¹¹/₁₆" (42 x 32.2 cm)
Publisher: Tériade Éditeur, Paris. Edition: 270
The Louis E. Stern Collection

The energetic, vivid fuchsia form shown here
at the left represents a knife thrower, while
the static, pale blue form with upraised arms
at the right suggests his female partner in the
popular circus act. Shapes resembling
leaves float across the composition,
providing a dreamlike atmosphere for this
aesthetic vision. "These images, with their
lively and violent tones, derive from
crystallizations of memories of circuses,
folktales, and voyages." So wrote Matisse in
the poetic text accompanying his
compositions for *Jazz*, his extraordinary
artist's book. *The Knife Thrower* is one of
twenty images in this volume, which are
interleaved with pages on which his own
handwritten words are printed.

Late in his career, after being bedridden
following surgery in 1941, Matisse turned to
making collages from painted papers. Using
scissors, he cut curved shapes, which he
then arranged in animated compositions. The
adventurous publisher Tériade encouraged
Matisse to create a book from these dazzling
creations. The artist chose the printing
technique of pochoir, which is notable for its
ability to achieve saturated areas of flat
brilliant colors by a process of applying
gouache inks through stencils.

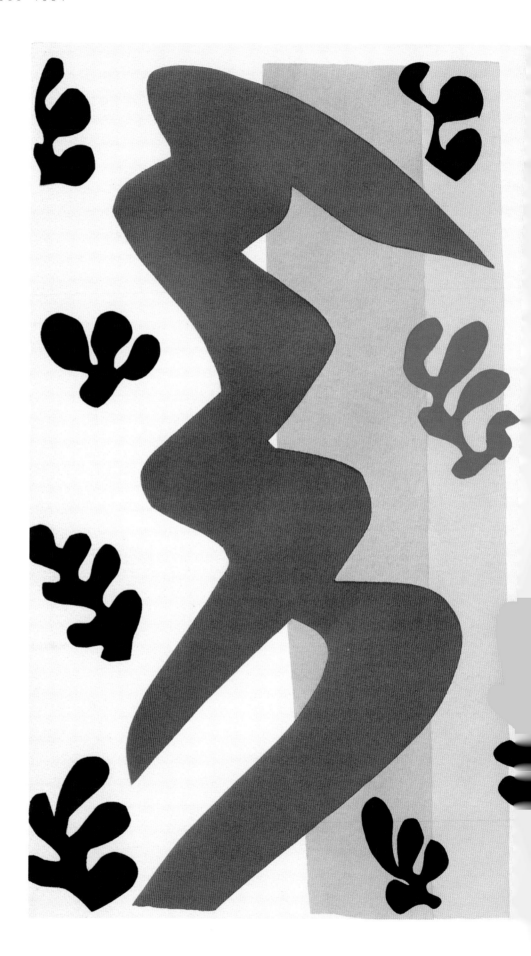

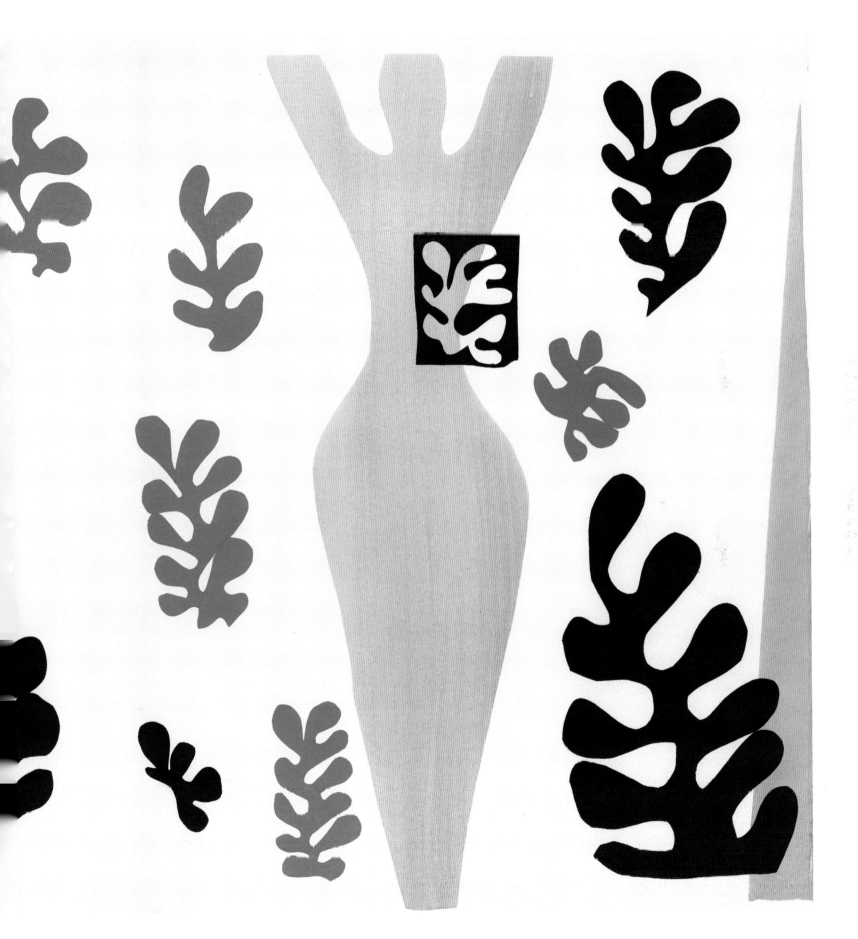

181

MATTA (ROBERTO SEBASTIÁN ANTONIO MATTA ECHAURREN)
CHILEAN, 1911–2002

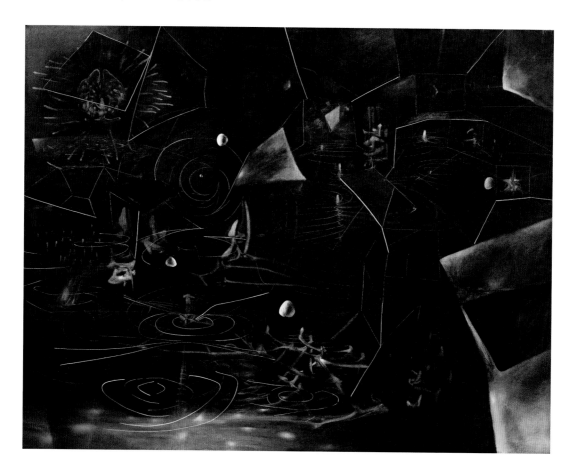

The Vertigo of Eros. 1944
Oil on canvas, 6' 5" x 8' 3" (195.6 x 251.5 cm)
Given anonymously

Matta's paintings do not describe the world we see when we open our eyes. Nor are these the dream or fantasy scenes of his fellow Surrealists Salvador Dalí and René Magritte, which include commonplace objects from waking life; the forms in Matta's works suggest many things but can be firmly identified with none. In the late 1930s and early 1940s Matta had produced works he called "inscapes," imaginary landscapes that he imagined as projections of psychological states. *The Vertigo of Eros* evokes an infinite space that suggests both the depths of the psyche and the vastness of the universe.

A galaxy of shapes suggesting liquid, fire, roots, and sexual parts floats in a dusky continuum of light. It is as if Matta's forms reached back beyond the level of the dream to the central source of life, proposing an iconography of consciousness before it has hatched into the recognizable coordinates of everyday experience. There is a sense of suspension in space, and indeed the work's title relates to Freud's location of human consciousness as caught between Eros, the life force, and Thanatos, the death wish. Constantly challenged by Thanatos, Eros produces vertigo. The human problem, then, is to achieve physical and spiritual equilibrium.

In French, the work's title is a pun, *Le Vertige d'Eros* doubling as *Le Vert Tige des roses* (the green stem of the roses).

Apparition. 1945

Soft ground etching, plate: 20¹/₈ x 15¹/₄"
(51.1 x 38.7 cm)
Publisher: the artist. Edition: 15
The Associates Fund

The mysterious *Apparition* is composed of a dense patchwork of tone and texture. Compartmentalized figures and cryptic signs, icons, and symbols occupy flat, rectilinear areas stacked above one another, with the narrow four-tiered shaft to the right of center suggesting totems. Eyes appear on almost every form; a pair dominates center stage and other, more enigmatic, single eyes occur frequently. Not one apparition but multiple manifestations magically reveal themselves at the same moment as we enter a new realm, peopled with fantastical inventions of the artist's subconscious.

This work belongs to a unique type of picture, divided into grids, that Gottlieb called the "pictograph." Taking myth as a subject appropriate to the violence of the time in which they were conceived—the turbulent years of World War II—and finding a sense of primeval spirituality in the arts of Native Americans and other tribal cultures, Gottlieb created these highly evocative compositions spontaneously, letting a visual "stream of consciousness" direct his artistic imagination. In *Apparition* the velvety qualities of the soft ground etching technique produce a blurred, dreamlike atmosphere, creating one of Gottlieb's most haunting pictographs.

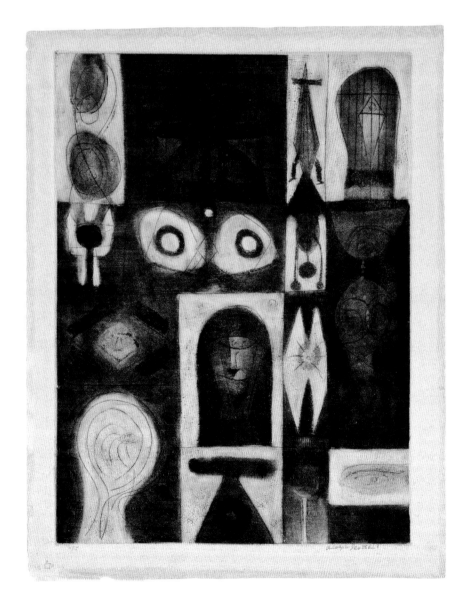

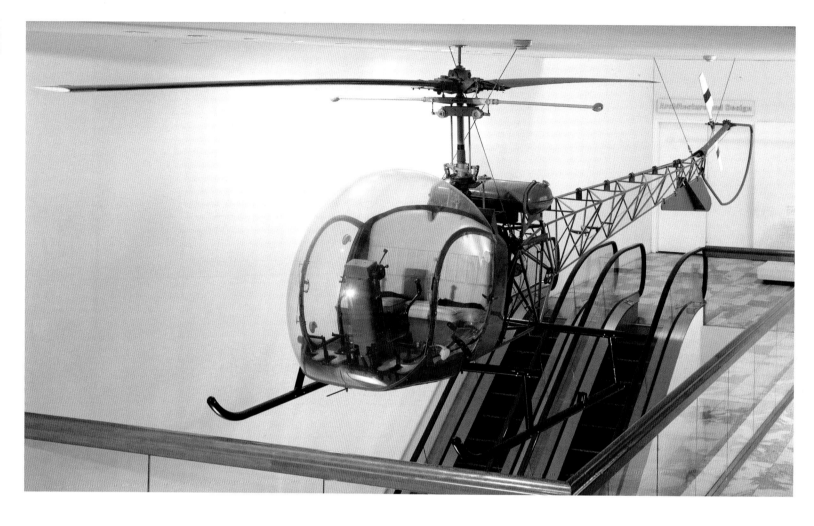

Bell-47D1 Helicopter. 1945

Aluminum, steel, and acrylic, 9' 2³/₄" x 9' 11" x
41' 8³/₄" (281.3 x 302 x 1271.9 cm)
Manufacturer: Bell Helicopter Inc., USA
Marshall Cogan Purchase Fund

More than three thousand Bell-47D1
helicopters were made in the United States
and sold in forty countries between 1946 and
1973, when production ceased. While the
Bell-47D1 is a straightforward utilitarian craft,
its designer, Young, who was also a poet and
a painter, consciously juxtaposed its
transparent plastic bubble with the open
structure of its tail boom to create an object
whose delicate beauty is inseparable from its
efficiency. That the plastic bubble is made in
one piece rather than in sections joined by
metal seams sets the Bell-47D1 apart from
other helicopters. The result is a cleaner,
more unified appearance.

The bubble also lends an insectlike
appearance to the hovering craft, which
generated its nickname, the "bug-eyed
helicopter." It seems fitting, then, that one of
the principal uses of the Bell-47D1 has been
for pest control in crop dusting and spraying.
It has also been used for traffic surveillance
and for the delivery of mail and cargo to
remote areas. During the Korean War, it
served as an aerial ambulance.

Awarded the world's first commercial
helicopter license by the Civil Aeronautics
Administration (now the FAA), the Bell-47D1
weighs 1,380 pounds. Its maximum speed is
92 miles per hour and its maximum range
194 miles. It can hover like a dragonfly at
altitudes up to 10,000 feet.

Low Side Chair (model LCM). 1946

Molded walnut veneered plywood, chrome-
plated steel rods, and rubber shock mounts,
27³/₈ x 22¹/₄ x 25³/₈" (69.5 x 56.3 x 64.5 cm)
Manufacturer: Herman Miller Inc., USA
Gift of the manufacturer

The LCM (Lounge Chair Metal) was
conceived by Eames, who, with his wife and
professional partner, Ray, formed one of the
most influential design teams of the twentieth
century. First produced in 1946, the LCM and
its companion, the DCM (Dining Chair Metal),
met with great commercial success and have
become icons of modern design. The LCM's
molded-plywood seat and back sit on a
chrome-plated steel frame, with rubber shock
mounts in between. That the back and seat

are separate pieces simplified production,
while also providing visual interest.

Together with Eero Saarinen, Eames had
first experimented with bent plywood for a
group of prize-winning designs they
submitted to the 1940 competition "Organic
Design in Home Furnishings," organized by
The Museum of Modern Art. These, however,
proved difficult to manufacture, and most
were upholstered for comfort. Intent on
producing high-quality objects at economical
manufacturing costs, the Eameses devoted
the better part of the next five years to
refining the technique of molding plywood to
create thin shells with compound curves. The
chair was initially manufactured by the Evans
Products Company; in 1949 Herman Miller
Inc. bought the rights to produce it.

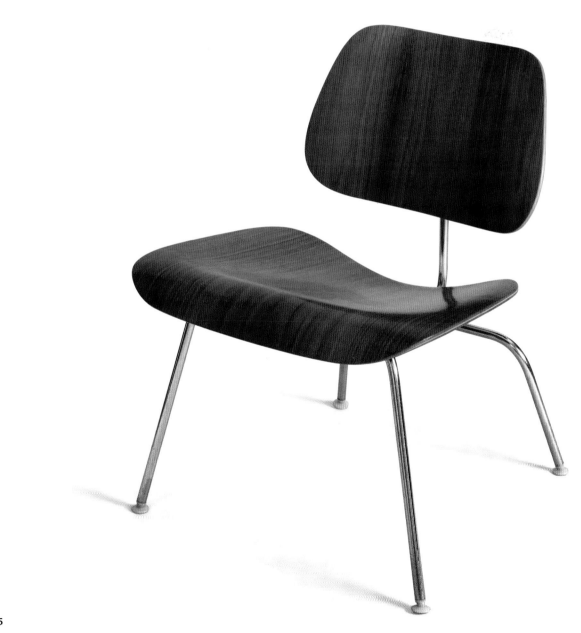

LUDWIG MIES VAN DER ROHE AMERICAN,
BORN GERMANY. 1886–1969

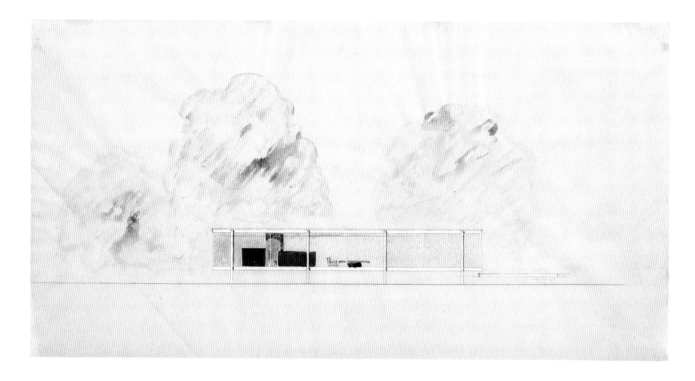

Farnsworth House, Plano, Illinois.

1946–51

Preliminary version, north elevation, 1946: pencil
and watercolor on tracing paper, 13 x 25"
(33 x 63.5 cm)
Mies van der Rohe Archive. Gift of the architect

The weekend house for Dr. Edith Farnsworth
represented by this rendering is one of Mies
van der Rohe's clearest expressions of his
ideas about the relationship between
architecture and landscape. The
transcendent quality he achieved in his
architecture is epitomized by the reductive
purity and structural clarity of this steel and
glass structure. The space of the house is
defined by its roof and floor planes, the
whole supported by eight steel columns. All
the steel elements are painted white. The
architect claimed: "We should strive to bring
Nature, houses, and people together into a
higher unity. When one looks at Nature
through the glass walls of the Farnsworth
House it takes on a deeper significance than
when one stands outside. More of Nature is
thus expressed— it becomes part of a
greater whole."

Set in a meadow overlooking the Fox River,
which is prone to flooding, the house is
elevated above the ground. Aesthetically, this
contributes to the effect of weightlessness,
reinforced by the cantilevered roof and floor
planes and by the asymmetrical placement
of the two travertine terraces that imply an
infinite extension into space. Mies van der
Rohe's transformation of a classical pavilion
into a completely modern, abstract idiom—
based on a carefully studied sense of
proportion and structural logic—is a sublime
testament to his apocryphal statement: "less
is more."

186

Joë Bousquet in Bed from **More Beautiful Than They Think: Portraits**.
1947
Oil emulsion in water on canvas, 57⅝ x 44⅞"
(146.3 x 114 cm)
Mrs. Simon Guggenheim Fund

Joë Bousquet was a poet who had been paralyzed in World War I, and lived, bedridden, for over thirty years in Narbonne, in the south of France. Dubuffet shows him lying in bed. Beside him on the covers lie two of his books (*La Connaissance du soir* and *Traduit du silence*), a newspaper, two letters addressed to him, and a package of Gauloises cigarettes.

The newspaperlike brochure for Dubuffet's October 1947 show in Paris included the announcement, "People are more beautiful than they think they are. Long live their true faces. ... Portraits with a resemblance extracted, with resemblance cooked and conserved in the memory, with a resemblance exploded in the memory of Mr. Jean Dubuffet, painter." At a time when few modern artists were producing portraits, the perpetually rebellious Dubuffet depicted the intellectuals who were his friends, but he made no effort at descriptive or psychological exactness. Inspired by the art of children, the insane, and the unschooled (all of which he collected under the name *l'art brut*), he made crude, caricatural images, roughly scratched into a thick impasto. Repelled by the conformity of modern life, he hoped that this crudeness would make his work more authentic.

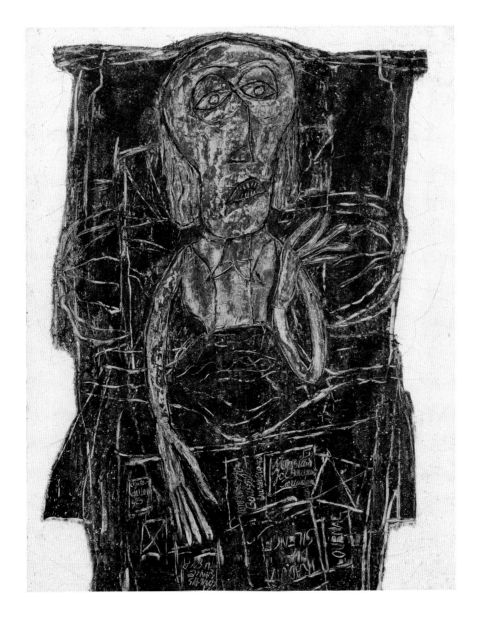

1947

Man Pointing, 1947

Bronze, 70½ x 40¾ x 16⅜" (179 x 103.4 x 41.5 cm),
at base 12 x 13¼" (30.5 x 33.7 cm)
Edition: 1/6
Gift of Mrs. John D. Rockefeller, 3rd

Frail yet erect, a man gestures with his left
arm and points with his right. We have no
idea what he points to, or why. Anonymous
and alone, he is also almost a skeleton. For
the Existentialist philosopher Jean-Paul
Sartre, in fact, Giacometti's sculpture was
"always halfway between nothingness and
being."

Such sculptures were full of meaning to
Sartre, who said of them, "At first glance we
seem to be up against the fleshless martyrs
of Buchenwald. But a moment later we have
a quite different conception: these fine and
slender natures rise up to heaven. We seem
to have come across a group of
Ascensions."

In the years leading up to World War II,
Giacometti abandoned his earlier Surrealism.
Dissatisfied with the resource of imagination,
he returned to the resource of vision,
focusing on the human figure and working
from live models. Under his eyes, however,
these models seem virtually to have
dissolved. Working in clay (the preparation to
casting in bronze), Giacometti scraped away
the body's musculature, so that the flesh
seems eaten off by a terrible surrounding
emptiness, or to register the air around it as
a hostile pressure. Recording the touch of
the artist's fingers, the surface of *Man
Pointing* is as rough as if charred or
corroded. At the same time, the figure
dominates its space, even from a distance.

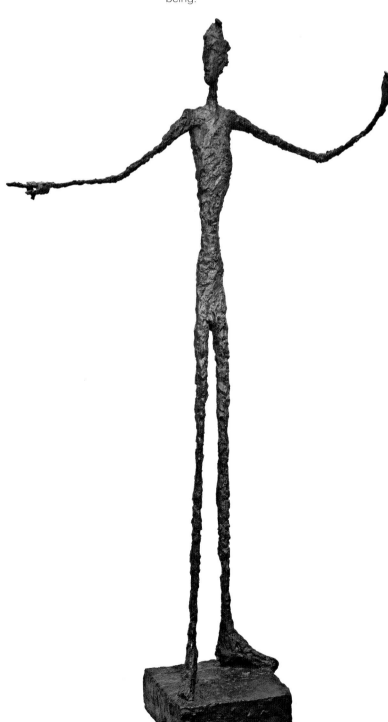

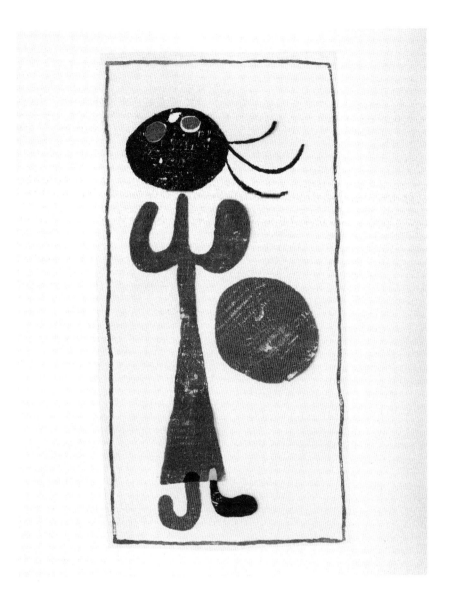

À toute épreuve by Paul Éluard. 1947–58
Illustrated book with 79 woodcuts including
collagraph and collage, page: 12^9/$_{16}$ x 9^{13}/$_{16}$"
(32 x 25 cm)
Publisher: Gérald Cramer, Geneva. Edition: 130
The Louis E. Stern Collection

On facing pages, two fantastical beings of
Miró's imagination engage the viewer with
dramatic gestures and bright colors. The
whimsical abstract form on the right appears
to reach out to the female figure at the left
with the assertion, "Je n'ai jamais changé" ("I
have never changed"). These words repeat
the last line from a poem on the previous
page.

À toute épreuve, a monumental project
executed over more than a decade, consists
of a series of lyrical poems that Éluard had
written in the late 1920s, at the time that his

wife, Gala, abandoned him for Salvador Dalí.
This book about love and the Catalan region
of Spain was a collaborative effort involving
the artist Miró, the poet Éluard, and the Swiss
publisher Cramer. All three had a hand in the
imaginative layouts—which interlock text and
images—and the choice of paper and
typeface.

Miró's woodcuts and collagraphs
demonstrate the inventiveness of his
printmaking. Instead of cutting into a block of
wood to create the compositions, Miró
arranged his designs composed of "found"
scraps of wood—on pieces of plywood. He
also bent metal wires into linear elements
and then glued these components to a
plywood backing before printing. The results
are some of the most exuberant graphic
images ever created.

ARSHILE GORKY (VOSDANIG MANOOG ADOIAN)
AMERICAN, BORN ARMENIA. 1904–1948

Summation. 1947
Pencil, pastel, and charcoal on buff paper
mounted on composition board, 6' 7⁵/₈" x 8' 5³/₄"
(202.1 x 258.2 cm)
Nina and Gordon Bunshaft Fund

The sheer grandness of *Summation*, its alloy
of precision and imposing scale, associates
it with the classical masters of the past. Quite
unclassical, though, is the drawing's nervous,
extraordinarily sensuous bonding of sexual or
visceral images and references to animals
and plants. "This is a world," Gorky said of
Summation, but it is a world ambiguously
placed—a nature felt in the flesh. Some of its
creatures have orifices, joints, and limbs,
while others seem to *be* such body parts, or
else internal organs. They blossom or flop,

poke or rub or tickle each other, pile up or
scurry off in a flock, defying identification
even while their forms are definite and clear.

Surrealist automatism had freed Gorky's
line, reinforcing its mobility. It is this mobility
that allows the line to form what the Surrealist
leader André Breton called "hybrids"—units
with multiple metaphoric meanings. Separate
yet related, clusters of incident form a
structure both episodic and unified: the work
is conceived not as a whole made up of
parts but of parts that together make up a
whole. We easily read (if not quite decipher)
the various motifs, and by recognizing the
formal and familial analogies among them,
and the soft continuity of the shading around
them, we also read them as one single, richly
detailed image.

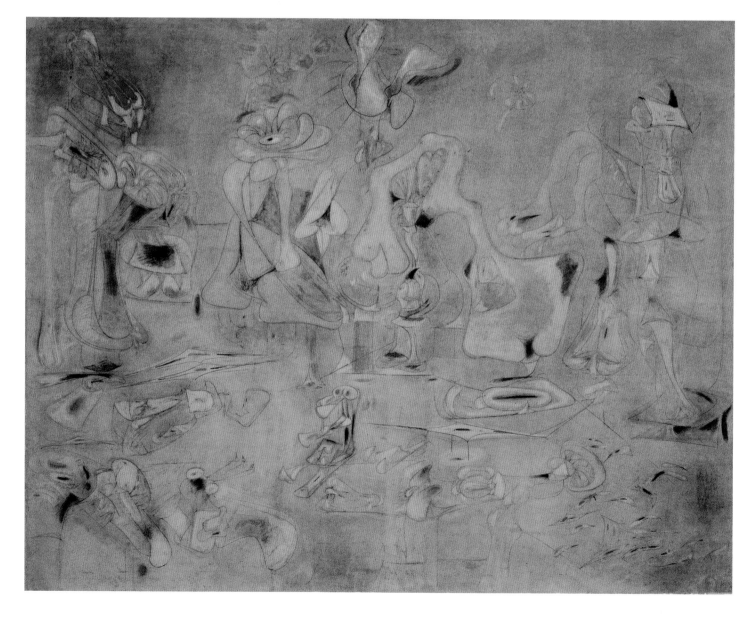

Untitled from **"Country Doctor."** 1948
Gelatin silver print, 13³/₈ x 10³/₁₆" (33.9 x 25.9 cm)
Purchase

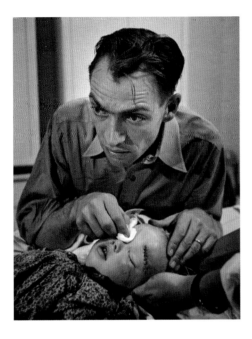

In the photograph Dr. Ernest Ceriani attends Lea Marie Wheatley, two and a half years old, who has been kicked in the head by a horse. The photographer had been sent to remote Kremmling, Colorado, to shoot a photo-essay on Ceriani, whom the editors of *Life* magazine had selected as a typical country doctor. Smith's "Country Doctor," comprising twenty-eight pictures plus text, appeared in *Life* on September 20, 1948.

Picture magazines such as *Life*, founded in 1936, gave photographers the opportunity to address millions of readers. However, this opportunity obliged the photographer to work with editors and writers as part of a team, and it imposed the formula of the photo-essay, in which weaker pictures might be chosen over stronger ones because they did a better job of moving the story along.

No one struggled harder or with more success than Smith to make this system of journalism responsive to his personal convictions and artistic standards, and "Country Doctor" is among his most persuasive essays. His best individual pictures, such as this one, are more persuasive still.

Painting. 1948
Enamel and oil on canvas, 42⁵/₈ x 56¹/₈"
(108.3 x 142.5 cm)
Purchase

Painting is a scene of tensile energy. Black forms fluidly outlined in white interlock and overlap, slip under or into each other. Their springing curves evoke the human body, and also perhaps letters of the alphabet, supplying familiarity without legibility. The palette is simplified but the handling is various: paint may drip or bleed, black may be solid or run to gray, white may be pulled thin across black or may suggest a width between black shapes. Figure and ground confuse in this shallow space, yet the painting conveys less ambiguity than enormous certainty.

Painting is one of a group of black-and-white abstractions that de Kooning produced in the late 1940s. He had painted abstractly before, but had also addressed the human figure, and, in fact, continued to do so in other pictures from the same period as this one; abstraction and figuration are not mutually exclusive in de Kooning's art, but

feed into each other, not only in similarities among forms in outwardly abstract and outwardly figurative paintings, but often within the same image. "Even abstract shapes must have a likeness," the artist believed, and many viewers have seen the forms of breasts, limbs, and buttocks in the black-and-white works. The critic Thomas Hess, discussing these and other abstractions of de Kooning's, remarked, "He also includes orgies."

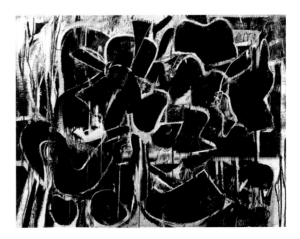

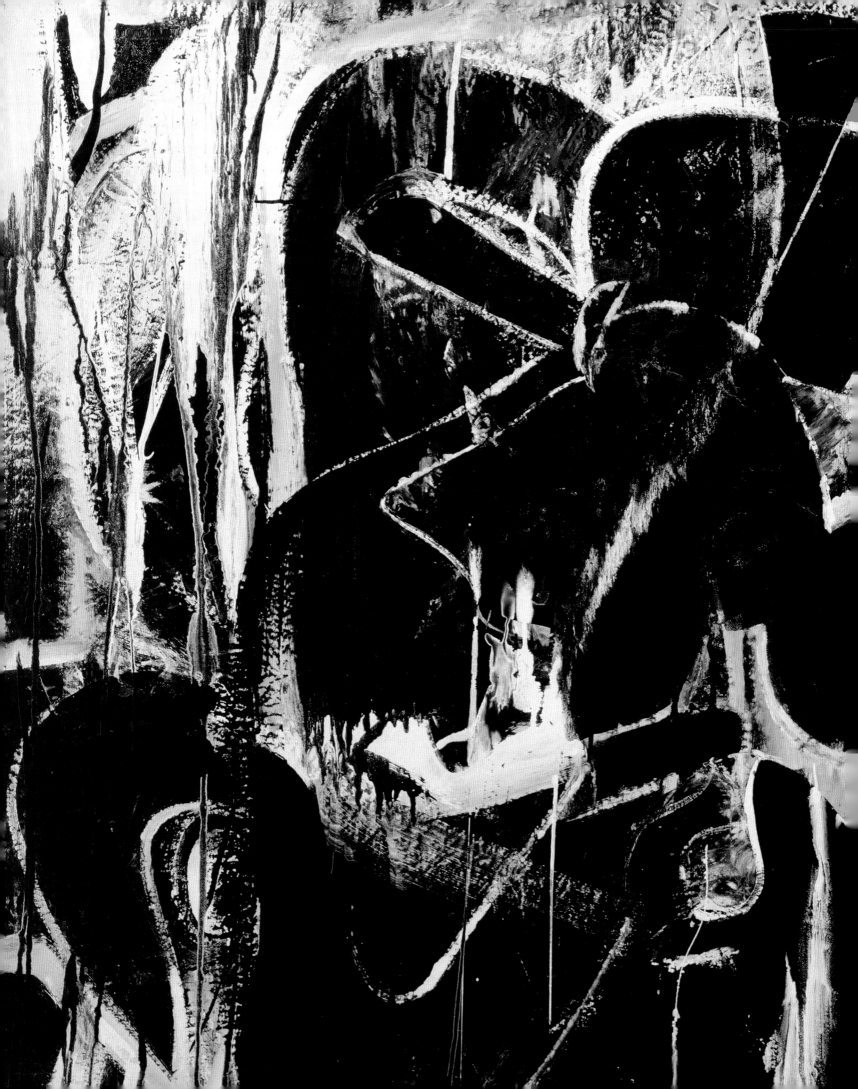

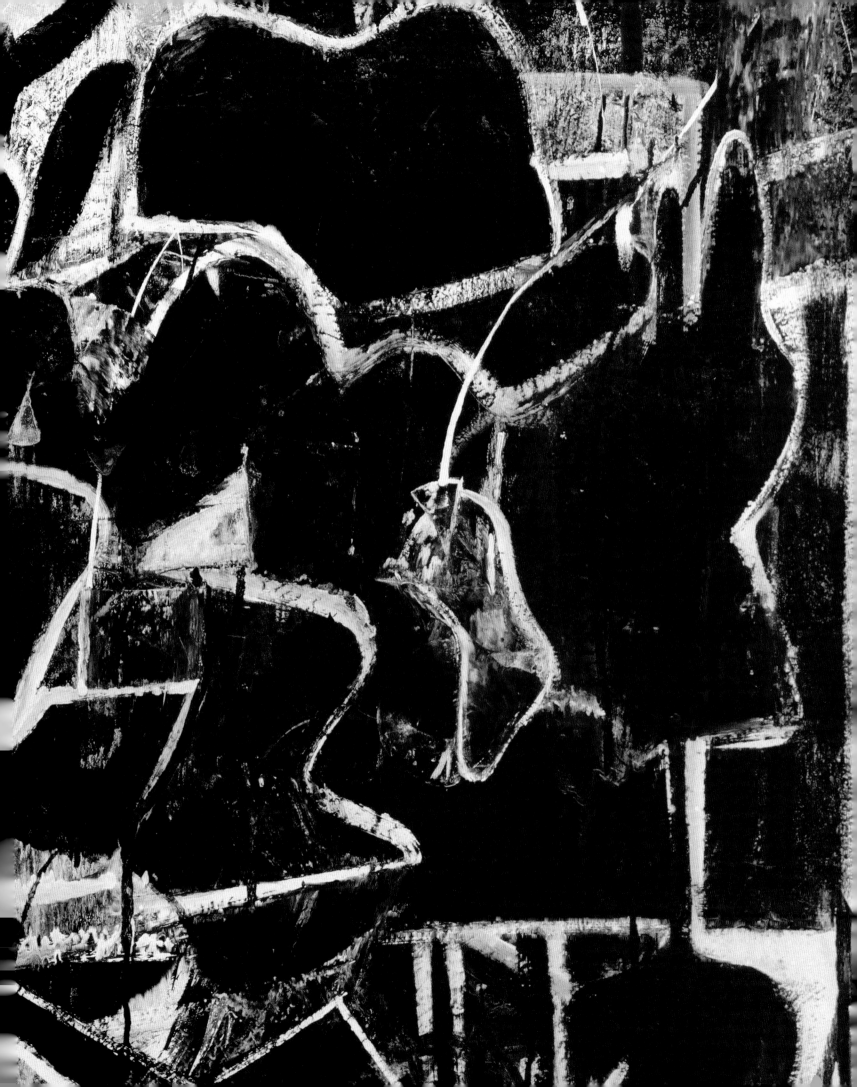

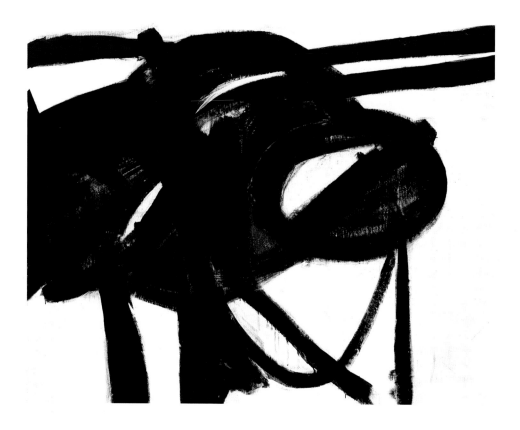

Chief. 1950
Oil on canvas, 58³/₈" x 6' 1¹/₂" (148.3 x 186.7 cm)
Gift of Mr. and Mrs. David M. Solinger

True to an alternate name for Abstract
Expressionism, "action painting," Kline's
pictures often suggest broad, confident,
quickly executed gestures reflecting the
artist's spontaneous impulses. Yet Kline
seldom worked that way. In the late 1940s,
chancing to project some of his many
drawings on the wall, he found that their
lines, when magnified, gained abstraction
and sweeping force. This discovery inspired
all of his subsequent painting; in fact many
canvases reproduce a drawing on a much
larger scale, fusing the improvised and the
deliberate, the miniature and the monumental.

"Chief" was the name of a locomotive Kline
remembered from his childhood, when he
had loved the railway. Many viewers see
machinery in Kline's images, and there are
lines in *Chief* that imply speed and power as
they rush off the edge of the canvas, swelling
tautly as they go. But Kline claimed to paint
"not what I see but the feelings aroused in
me by that looking," and *Chief* is abstract, an
uneven framework of horizontals and
verticals broken by loops and curves. The
cipherlike quality of Kline's configurations,
and his use of black and white, have
provoked comparisons with Japanese
calligraphy, but Kline did not see himself as
painting black signs on a white ground;
"I paint the white as well as the black," he
said, "and the white is just as important."

facing page:
Mark Rothko,
*Magenta, Black, Green
on Orange*
(see entry on page 196)

195

Magenta, Black, Green on Orange.
1949

Oil on canvas, 7' 1³/₈" x 65" (216.5 x 164.8 cm)
Bequest of Mrs. Mark Rothko through
The Mark Rothko Foundation, Inc.

Magenta, Black, Green on Orange follows a compositional structure that Rothko explored for twenty-three years beginning in 1947. Narrowly separated, rectangular blocks of color hover in a column against a colored ground. Their edges are soft and irregular, so that when Rothko uses closely related tones, the rectangles sometimes seem barely to coalesce out of the ground, concentrations of its substance. The green bar in *Magenta, Black, Green on Orange*, on the other hand, appears to vibrate against the orange around it, creating an optical flicker. In fact the canvas is full of gentle movement, as blocks emerge and recede, and surfaces breathe. Just as edges tend to fade and blur, colors are never completely flat, and the faint unevenness in their intensity, besides hinting at the artist's process in layering wash on wash, mobilizes an ambiguity, a shifting between solidity and impalpable depth.

The sense of boundlessness in Rothko's paintings has been related to the aesthetics of the sublime, an implicit or explicit concern of a number of his fellow painters in the New York School. In fact, the remarkable color in his paintings was for him only a means to a larger end: "I'm interested only in expressing basic human emotions—tragedy, ecstasy, doom," he said. "If you ... are moved only by ... color relationships, then you miss the point." (See illustration on page 195)

One (Number 31, 1950). 1950
Oil and enamel on unprimed canvas,
8' 10" x 17' 5⁵/₈" (269.5 x 530.8 cm)
Sidney and Harriet Janis Collection Fund
(by exchange)

One is a masterpiece of the "drip," or pouring, technique, the radical method that Pollock contributed to Abstract Expressionism. Moving around an expanse of canvas laid on the floor, Pollock would fling and pour ropes of paint across the surface. *One* is among the largest of his works that bear evidence of these dynamic gestures. The canvas pulses with energy: strings and skeins of enamel, some matte, some glossy, weave and run, an intricate web of tans, blues, and grays lashed through with black and white. The way the paint lies on the canvas can suggest speed and force, and the image as a whole is dense and lush—yet its details have a lacelike filigree, a delicacy, a lyricism.

The Surrealists' embrace of accident as a way to bypass the conscious mind sparked Pollock's experiments with the chance effects of gravity and momentum on falling paint. Yet although works like *One* have neither a single point of focus nor any obvious repetition or pattern, they sustain a sense of underlying order. This and the physicality of Pollock's method have led to comparisons of his process with choreography, as if the works were the traces of a dance. Some see in paintings like *One* the nervous intensity of the modern city, others the primal rhythms of nature.

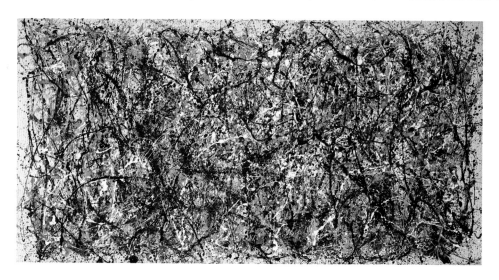

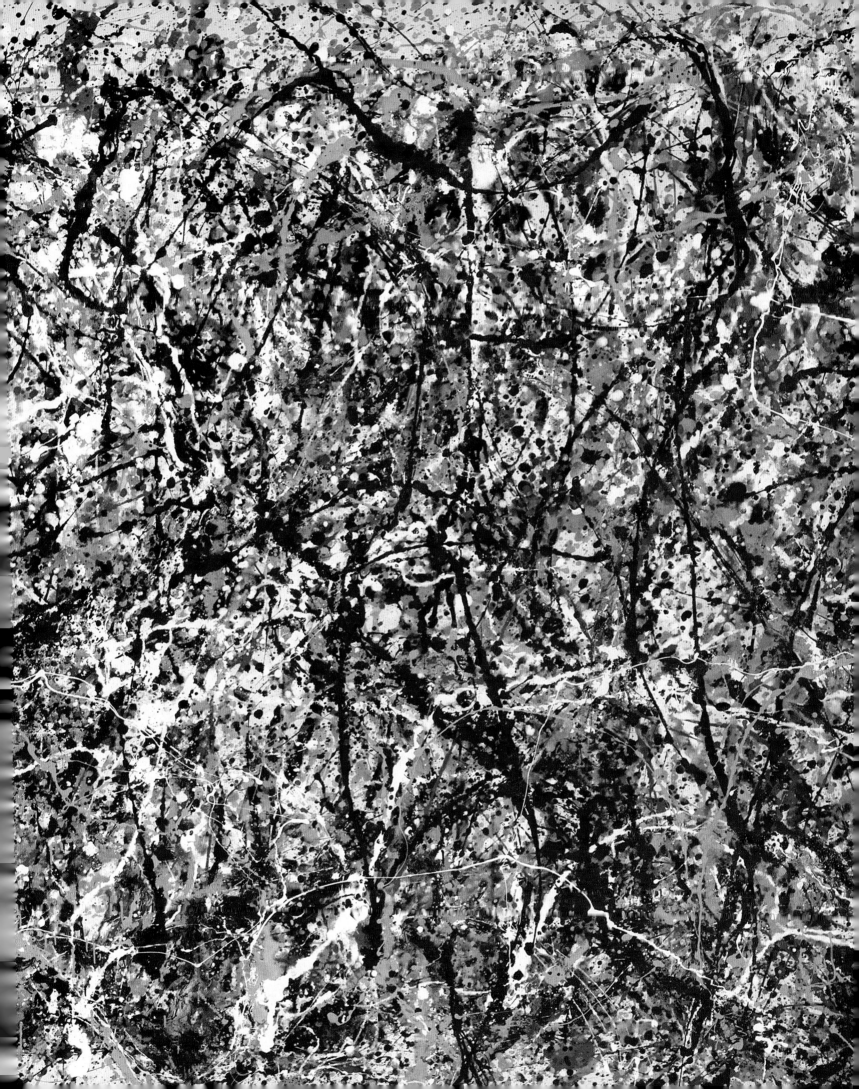

Vir Heroicus Sublimis. 1950–51
Oil on canvas, 7' 11³/₈" x 17' 9¹/₄"
(242.2 x 541.7 cm)
Gift of Mr. and Mrs. Ben Heller

Newman may appear to concentrate on shape and color, but he insisted that his canvases were charged with symbolic meaning. Like Piet Mondrian and Kazimir Malevich before him, he believed in the spiritual content of abstract art. The very title of this painting—in English, "Man, heroic and sublime"—points to aspirations of transcendence.

Abstract Expressionism is often called "action painting," but Newman was one of the several Abstract Expressionists who eliminated signs of the action of the painter's hand, preferring to work with broad, even expanses of deep color. *Vir Heroicus*

Sublimis is large enough so that when the viewer stands close to it, as Newman intended, it creates an engulfing environment—a vast red field, broken by five thin vertical stripes. Newman admired Alberto Giacometti's bone-thin sculptures of the human figure, and his stripes, or "zips," as he called them, may be seen as symbolizing figures against a void. Here they vary in width, color, and firmness of edge: the white zip at center left, for example, looks almost like the gap between separate planes, while the maroon zip to its right seems to recede slightly into the red. These subtly differentiated verticals create a division of the canvas that is surprisingly complex, and asymmetrical; right in the middle of the picture, however, they set off a perfect square.

1951

Australia. 1951

Painted steel, 6' 7¹/₂" x 8' 11⁷/₈" x 16¹/₈"
(202 x 274 x 41 cm); at base, 14 x 14"
(35.6 x 35.6 cm)
Gift of William Rubin

In *Australia* Smith uses thin rods and plates
of steel, simultaneously delicate and strong,
to draw in space. Sculpture has traditionally
gained power from solidity and mass, but
Australia is linear, a skeleton. The
Constructivists were the first to explore this
kind of penetration of sculpture by empty
space. Smith learned about it from
photographs of the welded sculpture of
Pablo Picasso: he had begun his career as a
painter, but he knew how to weld (he had
worked as a riveter in the automobile

industry) and Picasso's works liberated him
to start working in steel.

Like a painting or drawing, *Australia* must
be seen frontally if its form is to be grasped.
It has been identified as an abstraction of a
kangaroo, and its lines have that animal's
leaping vitality; but it is an essay in tension,
balance, and shape more than it is any kind
of representation. In calling the work
Australia, Smith may have had in mind the
passages on that country in James Joyce's
novel *Finnegans Wake*. He may also have
been thinking of the magazine illustration of
aboriginal Australian cave drawings that the
critic Clement Greenberg sent him in
September of 1950, with the note, "The one
of the warrior reminds me particularly of
some of your sculpture."

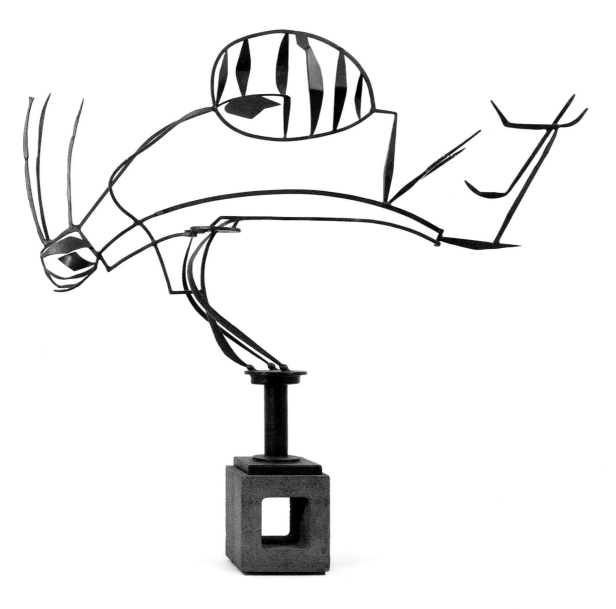

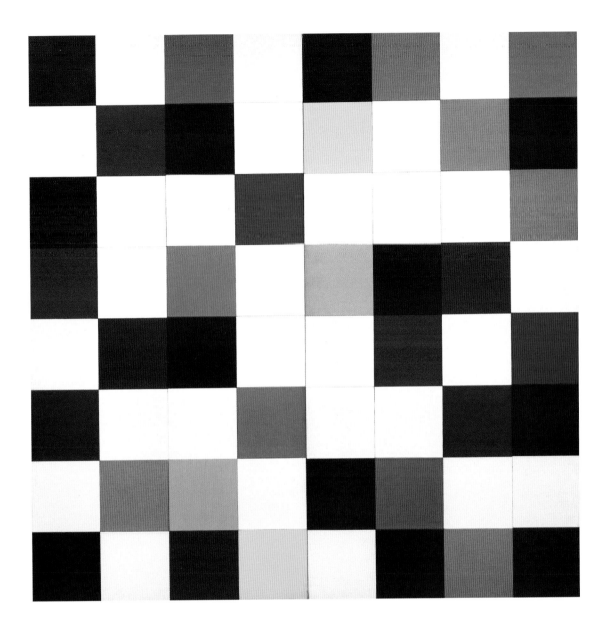

Colors for a Large Wall. 1951
Oil on canvas, mounted on sixty-four wood
panels; overall, 7' 10¼" x 7' 10½"
(239.3 x 239.9 cm)
Gift of the artist

"I have never been interested in painterliness,"
Kelly has said, using painterliness to mean "a
very personal handwriting, putting marks on
a canvas." There is no personal handwriting,
nor even any marks as such, in *Colors for a
Large Wall*, which comprises sixty-four
abutting canvases, each the same size (a
fraction under a foot square) and each
painted a single color. Not even the colors
themselves, or their position in relation to
each other, could be called personal; Kelly
derived them by chance; their sequence is
arbitrary. Believing that "the work of an

ordinary bricklayer is more valid than the
artwork of all but a very few artists," he fused
methodical procedure and a kind of
apollonian detachment into a compositional
principle.

As a serial, modular accumulation of
objects simultaneously separate and alike,
Colors for a Large Wall anticipated the
Minimalism of the 1960s, but it is unlike
Minimalism in the systematic randomness of
its arrangement, which is founded on
chance. Produced at the height of Abstract
Expressionism (but quite independently of it,
since Kelly had left New York for Paris), the
work also has that art's mural scale, and
Kelly thought deeply about the relationship of
painting to architecture; but few Abstract
Expressionists could have said, as he has, "I
want to eliminate the 'I made this' from my work."

WILLEM DE KOONING AMERICAN, BORN THE NETHERLANDS, 1904–1997

Woman, I. 1950–52

Oil on canvas, 6' 3⁷⁄₈" x 58" (192.7 x 147.3 cm)
Purchase

Woman, I is the first in a series of de Kooning works on the theme of Woman. The group is influenced by images ranging from Paleolithic fertility fetishes to American billboards, and the attributes of this particular figure seem to range from the vengeful power of the goddess to the hollow seductiveness of the calendar pinup. Reversing traditional female representations, which he summarized as "the idol, the Venus, the nude," de Kooning paints a woman with gigantic eyes, massive breasts, and a toothy grin. Her body is outlined in thick and thin black lines, which continue in loops and streaks and drips, taking on an independent life of their own. Abrupt, angular strokes of orange, blue, yellow, and green pile up in multiple directions as layers of color are applied, scraped away, and restored.

When de Kooning painted *Woman, I*, artists and critics championing abstraction had declared the human figure obsolete in painting. Instead of abandoning the figure, however, de Kooning readdressed this age-old subject through the sweeping brushwork of Abstract Expressionism, the prevailing contemporary style. Does the woman partake of the brushwork's energy to confront us aggressively? Or is she herself under attack, nearly obliterated by the welter of violent marks? Perhaps something of both; and, in either case, she remains powerful and intimidating.

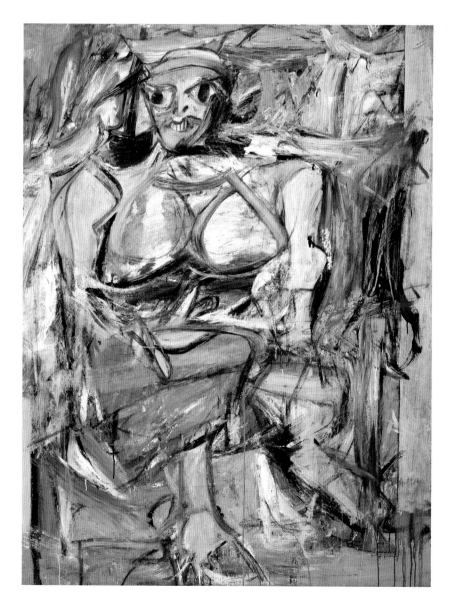

1952

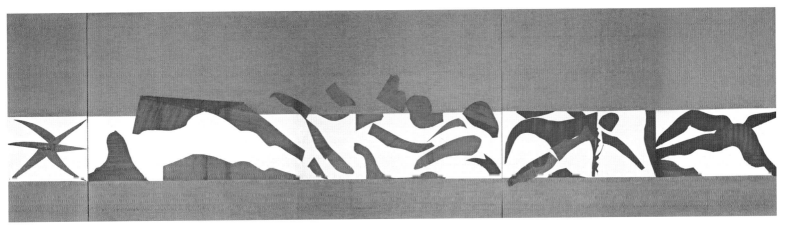

The Swimming Pool. 1952

Nine-panel mural in two parts: gouache on paper, cut-and-pasted, on white painted paper, mounted on burlap, a–e: 7' 6⅝" x 27' 9½" (230.1 x 847.8 cm); f–i: 7' 6⅝" x 26' 1½" (230.1 x 796.1 cm)
Mrs. Bernard F. Gimbel Fund

Commenting on *The Swimming Pool*, his largest cutout, Matisse said, "I have always adored the sea, and now that I can no longer go for a swim, I have surrounded myself with it." Indeed, this nearly fifty-four-foot-long frieze of blue bathers silhouetted against a white rectangular band was designed to adorn the walls of Matisse's dining room at the Hôtel Régina in Nice. At the time of its creation, the artist was restricted to his bed or to a wheelchair, and he conjured this lyrical depiction of the natural world for his personal enjoyment.

Read from right to left, beginning and ending with a representation of a starfish, the contours of the diving or swimming forms eventually dissolve until the blue shapes define the splashing water and the negative white space represents the abstract figures. In a dynamic interplay with the background support, each bather flows rhythmically into the next, sometimes breaking free of the horizontal band in a graceful arabesque. Matisse combines contrasting viewing angles—from above looking down into the water or sideways as if from in the water—so that the different postures of the figures themselves determine the composition as a whole. With this spirited yet serene aquatic imagery, the artist brings to brilliant culmination his career-long desire to create an idealized environment.

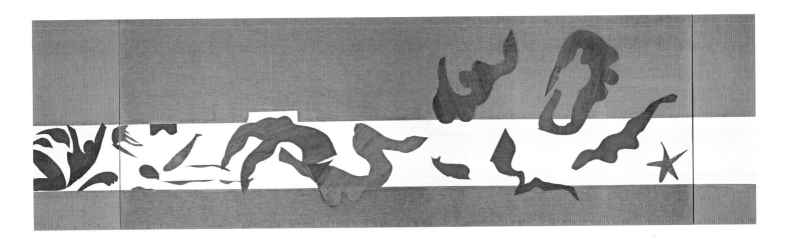

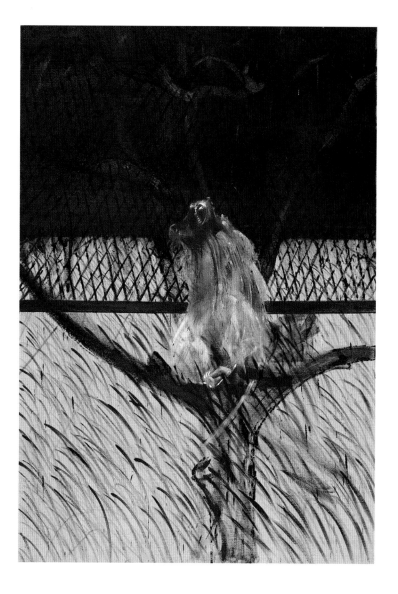

Study of a Baboon. 1953

Oil on canvas, 6' 6¹/₈" x 54¹/₈" (198.3 x 137.3 cm)
James Thrall Soby Bequest

By his own account, Bacon completed his first mature painting in 1944, during World War II. Appropriately to the time, he addressed themes not just of suffering but of torment, and drew from a combination of mythological and Christian sources to articulate themes of violent revenge. The mood endured throughout his work, and certainly informed the somber *Study of a Baboon.*

Bacon often derived his images from photographs—from newsprint and film stills and, notably, a reproduction of a Diego Velázquez painting—and he copied this baboon from one of his favorite books, Marius Maxwell's *Stalking Big Game with a Camera in Equatorial Africa*, published in 1925. The photographs are chiefly of large wild animals such as the elephant and the rhinoceros, but among the plates is a startling reproduction of baboons in acacia trees. The baboon at the right is perched on a forked tree trunk much like that in Bacon's work. Bacon had traveled often in Africa and was reportedly fascinated to see monkeys and apes of various kinds caged in the parks, while outside others roamed in freedom. *Study of a Baboon* pointedly incarnates this ambivalence. The baboon is half imprisoned, half free. The vigorously painted bars of the cage force the baboon uncomfortably close to the viewer. Its body is partly transparent and ghostly, but its sinister open maw and glinting white fangs mark a very real presence. Bacon pens the viewer into the enclosure with the ferocious creature, suggesting a close correlation between the two beings.

Bed. 1955

Combine painting: oil and pencil on pillow, quilt, and sheet on wood supports, 6' 3¼" x 31½" x 8" (191.1 x 80 x 20.3 cm)
Gift of Leo Castelli in honor of Alfred H. Barr, Jr.

Bed is one of Rauschenberg's first Combines, his own term for his technique of attaching cast-off items, such as rubber tires or old furniture, to a traditional support. In this case he framed a well-worn pillow, sheet, and quilt, scribbled them with pencil, and splashed them with paint, in a style derived from Abstract Expressionism. In mocking the seriousness of that ambitious art, Rauschenberg predicted an attitude more widespread among later generations of artists—the Pop artists, for example, who also appreciated Rauschenberg's relish for everyday objects.

Legend has it that the bedclothes in *Bed* are Rauschenberg's own, pressed into use when he lacked the money to buy a canvas. Since the artist himself probably slept under this very sheet and quilt, *Bed* is as personal as a self-portrait, or more so—a quality consistent with Rauschenberg's statement, "Painting relates to both art and life. ... (I try to act in that gap between the two)." Although the materials here come from a bed, and are arranged like one, Rauschenberg has hung them on the wall, like a work of art. So the bed loses its function, but not its associations with sleep, dreams, illness, sex—the most intimate moments in life. Critics have also projected onto the fluid-drenched fabric connotations of violence and morbidity.

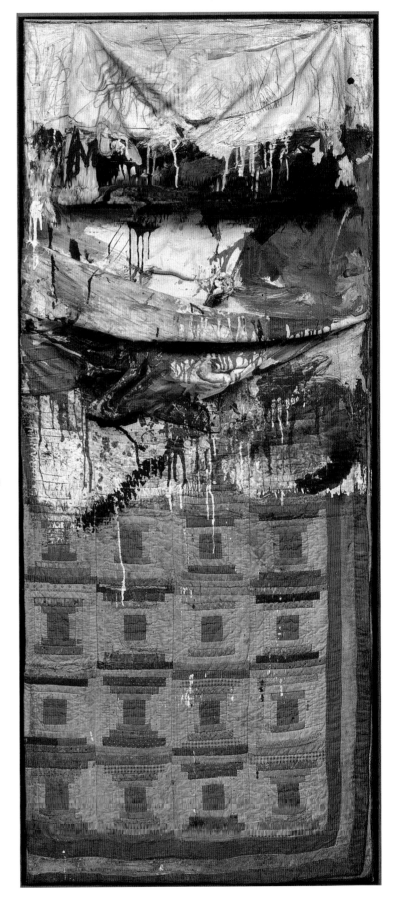

1955

1954–55

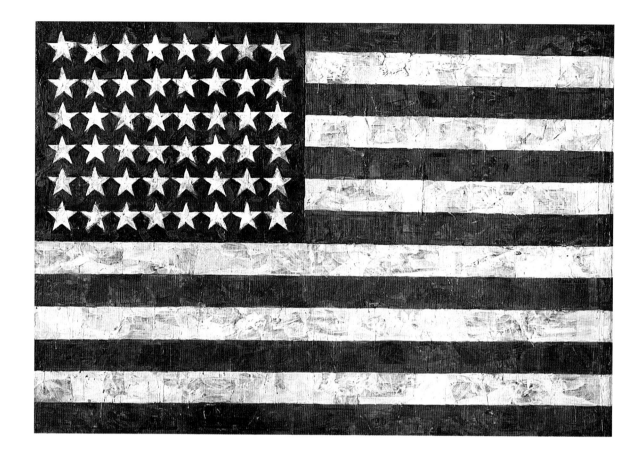

Flag. 1954–55 (dated on reverse 1954)
Encaustic, oil, and collage on fabric, mounted on plywood, 42¼ x 60⅝" (107.3 x 153.8 cm)
Gift of Philip Johnson in honor of Alfred H. Barr, Jr.

When Johns made *Flag*, the dominant American art was Abstract Expressionism, which enthroned the bold, spontaneous use of gesture and color to evoke emotional response. Johns, though, had begun to paint common, instantly recognizable symbols—flags, targets, numbers, letters. Breaking with the idea of the canvas as a field for abstract personal expression, he painted "things the mind already knows." Using the flag, Johns said, "took care of a great deal for me because I didn't have to design it." That gave him "room to work on other levels"—to focus his attention on the making of the painting.

The color, for example, is applied not to canvas but to strips of newspaper—a material almost too ordinary to notice. Come close to the painting, though, and those scraps of newsprint are as hard to ignore as they are to read. Also, instead of working with oil paint, Johns chose encaustic, a mixture of pigment and molten wax that has left a surface of lumps and smears; so that even though you recognize the image in a second, close up it becomes textured and elaborate. It is at once impersonal, or public, and personal; abstract and representational; easily grasped and demanding of close attention.

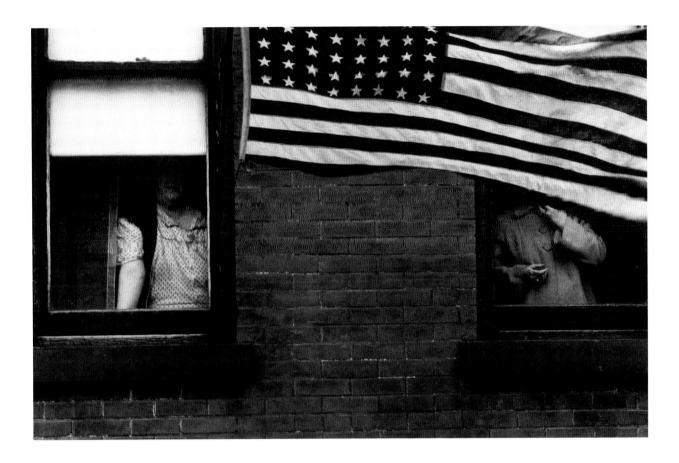

Parade, Hoboken, New Jersey. 1955
Gelatin silver print, 8$^1/_8$ x 12$^{15}/_{16}$" (20.6 x 31.2 cm)
Purchase

In this picture two citizens observe a parade, and a flag is on display to celebrate the patriotic occasion. The mood is dark, however, and the faces of the people are obscured, one of them by the flag itself.

The photograph is from Frank's book *The Americans*, first published in France in 1958 and in the United States the following year. In the years before museums and galleries took widespread notice of photography—that is, before the 1970s—books conceived and edited by the photographer played a leading role in bringing advanced photography to public notice. *The Americans*, one of the touchstones of this genre, helped to establish the artistic significance of what photographers call "a body of work"—a series of pictures unified by the author's sensibility and outlook rather than by a particular theme or by an assignment from a magazine editor.

In fact, the nominal subject of *The Americans* is so broad that it scarcely serves as an organizing principle. The book's coherence rests instead on Frank's talent for transforming fragments of observation into articulate symbols, all of them tinged by his caustic and forlorn vision of his adoptive country. The pictures are knit together, as well, by recurring icons of national identity, notably the flag, which appears and reappears on the scene like the sinister protagonist of a tragedy.

Tulip Armchair. 1955–56

Fiberglass-reinforced polyester shell, cast aluminum base with fused plastic finish, and upholstered cushion, 31$\frac{1}{2}$ x 25$\frac{3}{4}$ x 23"
(80 x 65.4 x 58.4 cm)
Manufacturer: Knoll International, USA
Gift of the manufacturer

The Tulip Armchair, which resembles the flower but also a stemmed wineglass, is part of Saarinen's last furniture series. This one-legged chair was meant to alleviate one of Saarinen's great concerns: clutter. Describing his intentions to simplify and clarify structure, he said: "The undercarriage of chairs and tables in a typical interior makes an ugly, confusing, unrestful world. I wanted to clear up the slum of legs. I wanted to make the chair all one thing again." Saarinen designed each piece in the Tulip series of furniture with a single pedestal leg, creating a unified environment of chairs, tables, and stools.

The Tulip chair also marks the culmination of Saarinen's efforts to create a chair molded from a single material, which furthered his design concept of "one piece, one material." But, while the elegant Tulip chair looks as if it is made of all one material, the sculptural fiberglass shell seat is actually supported on an aluminum stem with a fused plastic finish.

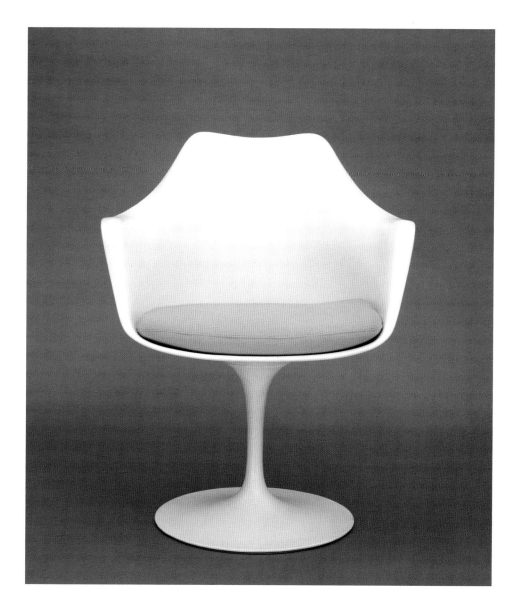

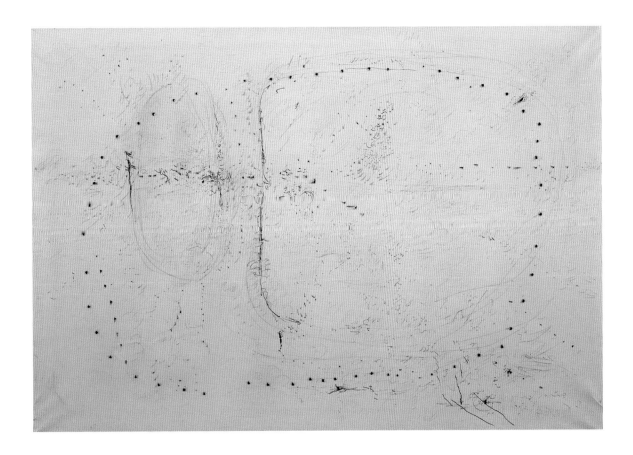

Spatial Concept. 1957

Pen and ink on paper, mounted on canvas,
with punctures and scrapes, 55" x 6' 6⁷/₈"
(139.3 x 200.3 cm)
Gift of Morton G. Neumann

The strongest visual device in *Spatial Concept* is a wide, irregular oval of rough holes, their broken rims poking outward as if some force in the hidden dark behind the picture plane were struggling to break through. Scratches of black ink, most of them short and bristlelike, scatter in flurries across the surface: the lighter lines and whorls are abrasions scored in the thick paper, ridged scars that compensate for their relative faintness with their violence. Fontana's Spatial Concepts—the first of which dates from 1949—have a physical concreteness in tune with the anti-idealist mood of postwar Europe.

Fontana felt that scientific advances demanded parallel innovations in art, which, he declared, should reach out into its surroundings—should exist not in two dimensions but in space. Sculpture, being three-dimensional, did this necessarily, as did the kind of environmental installation that Fontana explored early on (the form has since become a whole genre of art). Painting, though, would demand radical surgery: the rupturing of the picture's flatness.

The canvas or paper support is a literal foundation of painting, the stage on which all of the picture's events must play themselves out. To puncture this plane, or to slash it with a knife, is a daring, even shocking act for a painter. *Spatial Concept* clearly conveys the considerable psychological nerve Fontana's gesture took.

209

1957

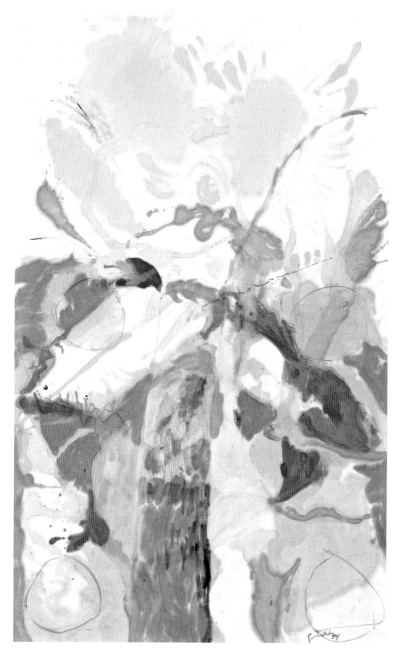

Jacob's Ladder. 1957

Oil on unprimed canvas, 9' 5³/₈" x 69⁷/₈"
(287.9 x 177.5 cm)
Gift of Hyman N. Glickstein

The delicately colored *Jacob's Ladder* shows compositional echoes ranging back to Cubism and the early abstractions of Vasily Kandinsky, but as a young New York artist in the 1950s, Frankenthaler was most influenced by the Abstract Expressionists. Like Jackson Pollock, she explored working on canvases laid on the floor (rather than mounted on an easel or wall), a technique opening new possibilities in the handling of paint, and therefore in visual appearances. Letting paint fall onto canvas emphasized its physicality, and the physicality of the support too. Frankenthaler also admired the scale of Pollock's work, and she took from him, she said, her "concern with line, fluid line, calligraphy, and ... experiments with line not as line but as shape."

Frankenthaler departed from Pollock's practice in the way she used areas of color and in her distinctive thinning of paint so that it soaked into her unprimed canvases. Because the image is so plainly embedded in the cloth, its presence as flat pigmented canvas tends to overrule any illusionistic reading of it—a priority in the painting of the time. Nor should the work's title suggest any preplanned illustrational intention. "The picture developed (bit by bit while I was working on it) into shapes symbolic of an exuberant figure and ladder," Frankenthaler said, "therefore *Jacob's Ladder*."

Alfred Newton Richards Medical Research Building, University of Pennsylvania, Philadelphia. 1957–61

Model: basswood, 13¹/₂ x 14³/₄ x 22³/₄"
(34.2 x 37.5 x 57.8 cm)
Gift of the architect

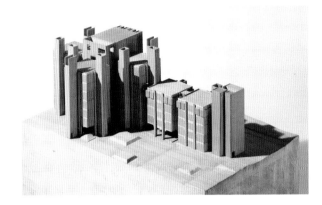

The design of the Richards Medical Research Building, as shown in this model, was a reaction against the prevalent idea in modern architecture that a single envelope of space should encompass all parts of a building. The distinction between what Kahn called "served" and "servant" spaces underlies the highly articulated massing and overall structure of the Richards Medical Research Building. Kahn explained that he conceived its design "in recognition of the realizations that science laboratories are studios and that the air to breathe should be away from the air to throw away." By placing the "servant" spaces—stairs, elevators, and air-handling towers—on the periphery, Kahn was also able to provide the "served" spaces—the laboratories—maximum flexibility by means of their uninterrupted floor areas. While Kahn developed a practical response to programmatic needs, he made aesthetic choices as well: the towers echo the lively silhouette of the neighboring turn-of-the-century dormitories.

The model shows the innovative structural system of precast, post-tensioned concrete that Kahn designed with structural engineer August Komendant. The clear division between the concrete structural members (the trusses and cantilevered beams) and the brick-and-glass infill is a further indication of the hierarchical order underlying Kahn's work.

Vanna Venturi House, Chestnut Hill, Pennsylvania. 1959–64

Model, Scheme VI (final): cardboard and paper, 7³/₄ x 20¹/₂ x 6³/₄" (19.7 x 52 x 17.1 cm)
Gift of Venturi, Rauch and Scott Brown, Inc.

The design represented by this modest, cardboard study model of a house for the architect's mother is deceptively simple. The front facade of Venturi's design, for example, has the elements of a conventional house: large gable, chimney, front door, and windows. Yet throughout the building, the adept juxtaposition of big and little elements and the intentional distortion of symmetry establish a richness of meaning and perceptual ambiguity that make the Vanna Venturi residence one of the most important houses of the second half of the twentieth century.

The design for the house coincided in 1961–62 with Venturi's writing of *Complexity and Contradiction in Architecture* (published by The Museum of Modern Art in 1966). This brilliant architectural critique, supported by numerous illustrations of historical buildings, sought to overturn the limitations and reductive simplicity of orthodox modern architecture. Describing his own mannerist inclusive sensibility as "both-and," as opposed to "either-or," he wrote: "If the source of the both-and phenomenon is contradiction, its basis is hierarchy, which yields several levels of meanings among elements with varying values. It can include elements that are both good and awkward, big and little, closed and open, continuous and articulated, round and square, structural and spatial. An architecture which includes varying levels of meaning breeds ambiguity and tension." The Vanna Venturi House is one of the earliest demonstrations of the architect's highly influential ideas.

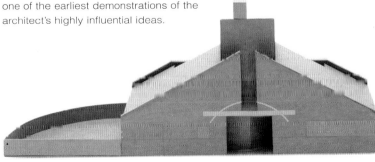

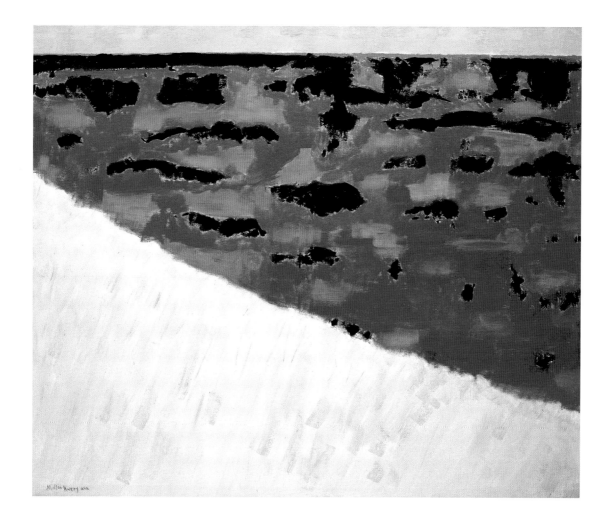

Sea Grasses and Blue Sea. 1958

Oil on canvas, 60¹/₈" x 6' ³/₈" (152.7 x 183.7 cm)
Gift of friends of the artist

Avery painted scenes of nature throughout his career, but he preferred simple forms to realistic details, and his palette is distinctively personal. The results come close to abstraction. In *Sea Grasses and Blue Sea* (based on Avery's memories of Provincetown, Massachusetts), the sky is a straight and narrow blue band at the painting's upper rim. The rest of the canvas is divided into two trapezoids of almost equal size and shape. The lower of these, the sea grass, is pale and lightly streaked, and echoes the tonality of the sky; above it is a wedge of a predominantly darker, saturated blue, with patches both of a lighter blue and, more sharply, of deep black. Magically, the overall effect is of waves flecked with white foam.

That black is paradoxical: as Matisse remarked of the black in one of his own paintings, it is used as "a color of light and not as a color of darkness." In various ways, in fact, Avery is closer to Henri Matisse than to the styles that prevailed in America during his lifetime—in his love of clarified form and flat color, for example, and in the sense of rich serenity that permeates his art.

Towards Disappearance, II. 1958

Oil on canvas. 9' 1/2" x 10' 5⁷/₈"
(275.6 x 319.7 cm)
Blanchette Rockefeller Fund. Purchased from
Robert Elkon Gallery, New York

Towards Disappearance, II is a cloud of
blues, yellows, and reds, and of red's
variants in oranges and pinks. In earlier
works, Francis had used a structure of
interlocking cells or globules, close in size
and shape; traces of this structure remain,
but more-ragged formations and drips
suggest a less orderly energy. Restraining
clusters of black collect in the upper part of
the canvas, but their weight only heightens
the force of the exuberant primaries, which
seem to loft them by bubbling up from below.
After the mid-1950s, Francis increasingly
enjoyed creating contrast through areas of
white. Pressing in from the sides, and
glimmering in the crevices among the
patches of pigment, the white in *Towards
Disappearance, II* only makes the colors
brighter.

Studying painting in California in the late
1940s, Francis had seen exhibitions of
Abstract Expressionism, and had absorbed
the ideas of the New York School. His next
stop, though, was not New York but Paris,
where he lived through much of the 1950s;
he admired Pierre Bonnard and Henri
Matisse, and was particularly influenced by
the iridescent atmospheres of Claude
Monet's Water Lilies series. In consequence,
Francis is often seen as inheriting the potent
love of color in French art. As he himself
said, "Color is the real substance for me, the
real underlying thing which drawing and line
are not."

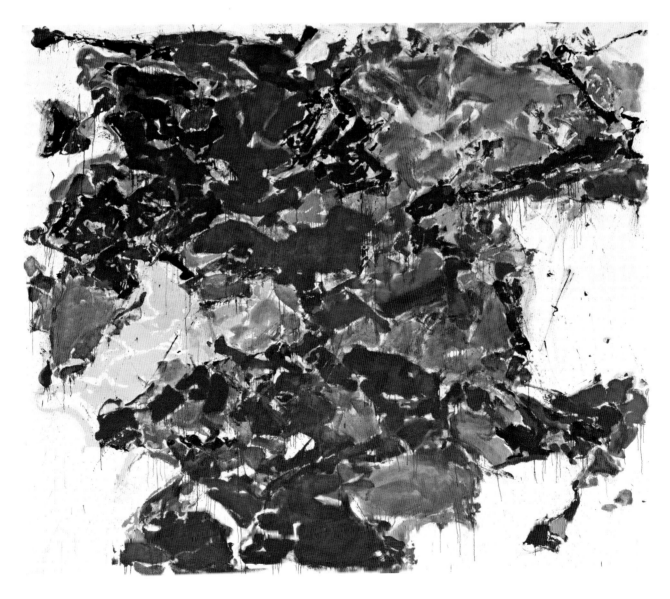

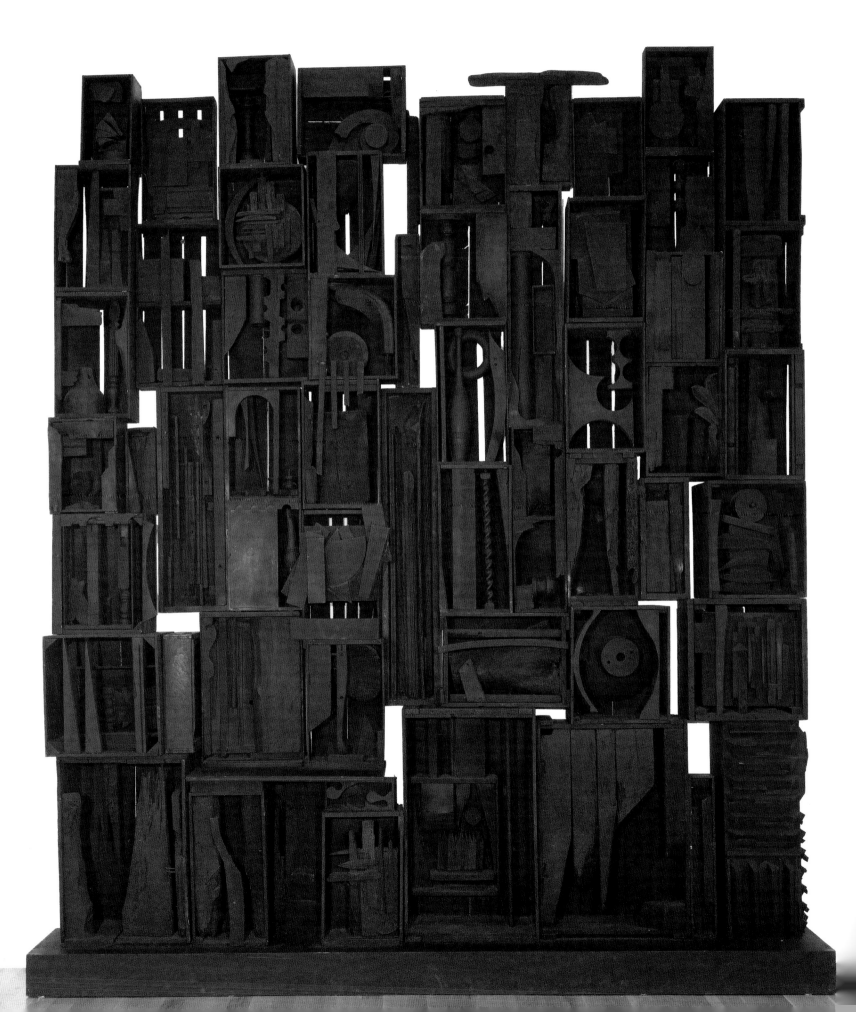

LOUISE NEVELSON AMERICAN, BORN UKRAINE.
1899–1988

Sky Cathedral. 1958
Assemblage: wood construction painted black,
11' 3¹/₂" x 10' ¹/₄" x 18" (343.9 x 305.4 x 45.7 cm)
Gift of Mr. and Mrs. Ben Mildwoff

As a rectangular plane to be viewed from the front, *Sky Cathedral* has the pictorial quality of a painting—perhaps one of the preceding decade's Abstract Expressionist canvases, which share its mural scale. But this sculpture in relief commands a layered depth. Its intricacy lies in both the method of its construction—it is made of shallow open boxes fitted together in a jigsawlike stack—and those boxes' contents, the salvaged wood bits and pieces with which Nevelson filled many of her works. These include moldings, dowels, spindles, chair parts, architectural ornaments, and scroll-sawed fragments. Nevelson makes this material into a high wall variegated by a play of flatness and recession, straight lines and curves, overlaps and vacancies, that has been likened to the faceting of Cubism and has an absorbing visual complexity.

A Surrealist artist might have shared Nevelson's relish for curious bric-à-brac, but might also have arranged such a collection in jarring and disorienting juxtapositions. Nevelson, by contrast, paints every object and box the same dully glowing black, unifying them visually while also obscuring their original identities. The social archaeology suggested by the objects' individual histories and functions, then, is muted but not erased; it is as if we were looking at the wall of a library, in which all of the books had been translated into another language.

ROBERT RAUSCHENBERG AMERICAN, BORN 1925

Canto XXXI: The Central Pit of Malebolge, The Giants: Illustration for Dante's Inferno. 1959–60
Solvent transfer, pencil, gouache, and color pencil on paper, 14³/₈ x 11³/₈" (36.6 x 29 cm)
Given anonymously

In eighteen months, Rauschenberg created thirty-four illustrations for Dante's *Inferno*, using the technique of transfer drawing. Each illustration, one for each canto, is intended to be read vertically from upper left to lower right as an episodic narrative with sequential events flowing into one another. Characters in the allegory are represented by photographs—culled from the mass media—of athletes, politicians, and astronauts, among others. In this image, Dante and his guide, Virgil, approach the eighth circle of Hell. Dante appears in the upper left-hand corner as a man wrapped in a towel. The guardians of Hell, described in the poem as formidable giants, are shown at the lower right as Olympic athletes standing on a podium. The oversized chain link indicates the giants' power; it also refers to their being chained for their sins. Below, the tiny figures of the two poets are lowered into the pit. By using recognizable imagery to relate the classic text of a quest for divine truth, Rauschenberg integrates the high and the low, the real and the illusory, the past and the present.

In creating his illustrations, the artist clipped reproductions from magazines, coated them with chemical solvent, and placed them face down on the drawing surface. The reverse sides of the clippings were rubbed over with a pen, transferring the images onto the paper. Finally, an overlay of transparent washes of gouache and pencil marks was added to allude to different moods or emotional states.

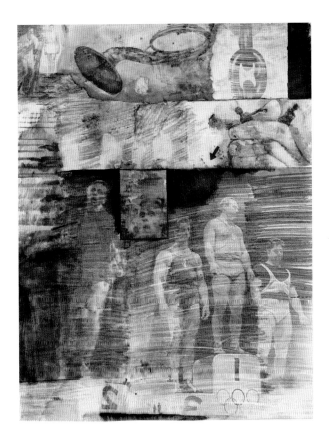

FRANK STELLA
AMERICAN, BORN 1936

The Marriage of Reason and Squalor, II.
1959

Enamel on canvas, 7' 6³/₄" x 11' ³/₄"
(230.5 x 337.2 cm)
Larry Aldrich Foundation Fund

In each half of *The Marriage of Reason and Squalor, II*, stripes outline stripes in an inverted U-shape, a regular, self-generating pattern. Filling the canvas according to a methodical program, Stella suggests an idea of the artist as laborer or worker. (He also uses commercial paint—black enamel—and a house-painter's brush.) The systematic quality of Stella's Black Paintings decisively departed from the ideas of inspired action associated with Abstract Expressionism, the art of the preceding generation, and anticipated the machine-made Minimal art of the 1960s. But many of them, like this one, are subtly personal: Stella worked freehand, and irregularities in the lines of the stripes reveal the slight waverings of his brush. His enamel, too, suggests a bow to the Abstract Expressionist Jackson Pollock, who had also used that paint.

Stella's use of stripes was motivated by the work of Jasper Johns, particularly Johns's paintings of flags. "The thing that struck me most," Stella has said, "was the way he stuck to the motif ... the idea of stripes—rhythm and interval—the idea of repetition." But Stella went farther than Johns in "sticking to the motif," removing the flag and leaving only the stripes. "My painting," he said, "is based on the fact that only what can be seen there is there... What you see is what you see."

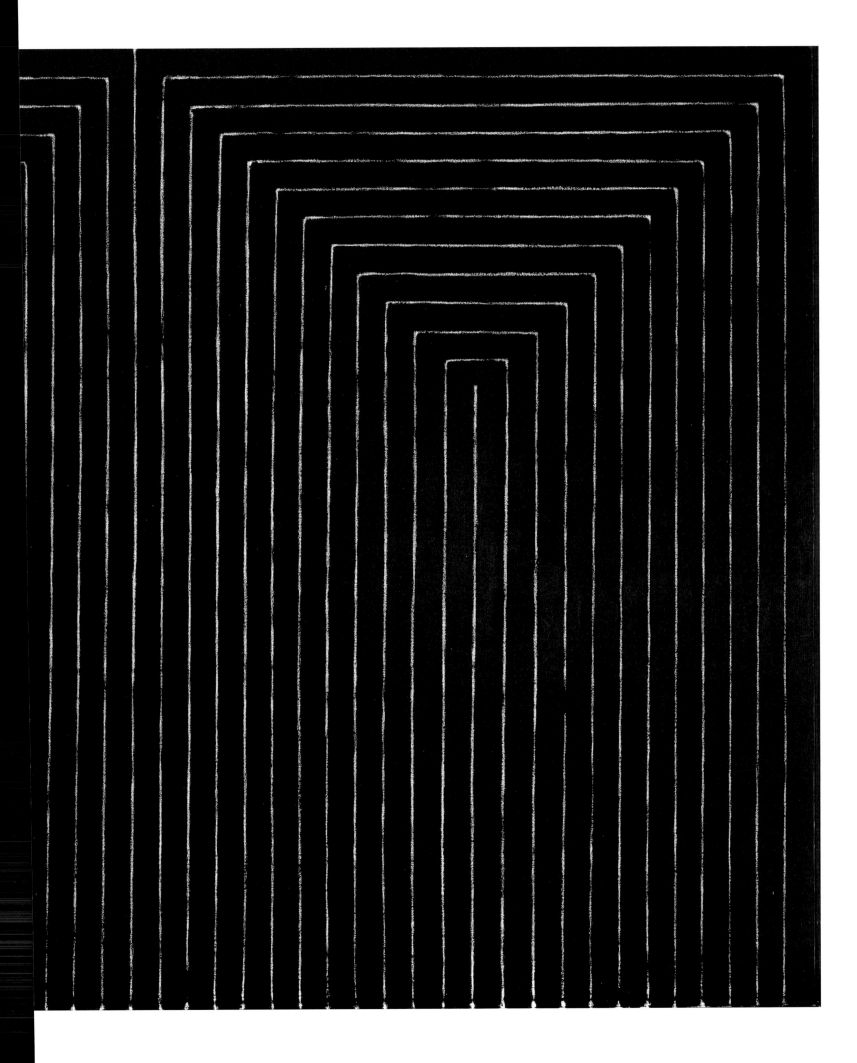

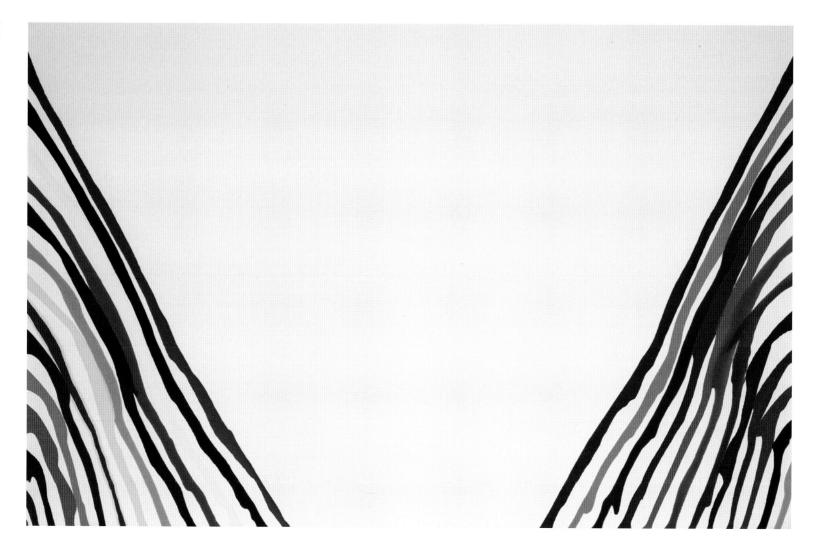

Beta Lambda. 1960
Synthetic polymer paint on canvas,
8' 7³/₈" x 13' 4¹/₄" (262.6 x 407 cm)
Gift of Mrs. Abner Brenner

Beta Lambda belongs to Louis's Unfurled series, in which diagonal bands of paint at each picture's sides are widely separated by the expanse of bare canvas between them, a powerful emptiness. Each band contains multiple rivulets of color, which now progress evenly through the spectrum, now pop with contrast, like the blue at the right of *Beta Lambda*. The pared-down simplicity of Louis's work focused a concern in the painting of the time: a concentration on the art's essential elements—line, color, ground.

Chronologically, Louis came from the Abstract Expressionist generation, but he mostly worked at a geographical and psychological remove from the New York School, and although he was crucially influenced by a member of that circle—Helen Frankenthaler—she was rather younger than its pioneers. As a result, his work both reflects and departs from Abstract Expressionist ideas. Like Frankenthaler, Louis used unprimed canvas, which absorbs paint into its fabric, so that it retains a presence in the finished work. (Primed canvas, conversely, takes paint as a discrete layer resting on and hiding its surface.) Louis also invented brushless techniques of applying paint, leaning the canvas against the wall and pouring the liquid down the tilted plane. The method deflates the Abstract Expressionist stress on the artist's hand and psyche, making *Beta Lambda* a visual field to be appreciated for its own sake.

facing page:
Roy Lichtenstein,
Girl with Ball
(see entry on page 220)

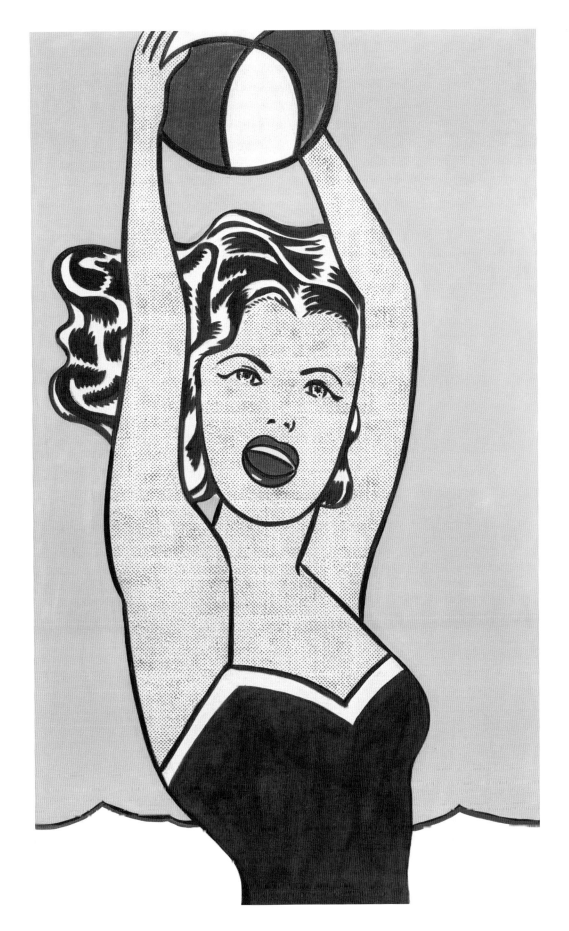

Girl with Ball. 1961

Oil and synthetic polymer paint on canvas,
60¹/₄ x 36¹/₄" (153 x 91.9 cm)
Gift of Philip Johnson

Lichtenstein took the image for *Girl with Ball* straight from an advertisement, for a hotel in the Pocono Mountains. In pirating the image, however, he transformed it, submitting the ad's photograph to the techniques of the comic-strip artist and printer—and transforming those techniques, too, into a painter's versions of them. The resulting simplifications intensify the artifice of the picture, curdling its careful dream of fun in the sun. The girl's rounded mouth is more doll-like than female; any sex appeal she had has become as plastic as her beach ball.

In choosing the banal subject matter of paintings like *Girl with Ball*, Lichtenstein challenged the aesthetic orthodoxy of the time, still permeated by the spiritual and conceptual ambitions of Abstract Expressionism. The moral seriousness of art, and art's longevity, seemed foreign to this cheap, transient ad from the consumer marketplace, a sector of roiling turnover.

Startling though the image was as an artwork, in fact, as advertising it was already old-fashioned—so that Lichtenstein's painting admits of a certain nostalgia. His simulation of printing similarly robs the technology of the polish it had already achieved: overstating the dots of the Benday process, and limiting his palette to primary colors, he exaggerates the limitations of mechanical reproduction, which becomes as much the subject of the painting as the girl herself.
(See illustration on page 219)

Pin-up. 1961

Oil, cellulose, and collage on panel, 48 x 32 x 3"
(121.9 x 81.3 x 7.6 cm)
Enid A. Haupt Fund and an anonymous fund

"Popular (designed for a mass audience), transient (short-term solution), expendable (easily forgotten), low cost, mass-produced, young (aimed at youth), witty, sexy, gimmicky, glamorous, big business." So Hamilton once described modern consumer culture—the culture that he and the other Pop artists (whether British, like Hamilton, or American) felt art had to confront. No surprise, then, that the sources of *Pin-up* include what Hamilton calls "girlie pictures," both "the sophisticated and often exquisite photographs in *Playboy*" and the more "vulgar" images found in that magazine's "pulp equivalents." Less obvious, perhaps, are the references to art history—the passages, for example, that Hamilton asserts "bear the marks of a close look at Renoir."

The nude, or the more provocative odalisque, is of course an enduring theme in art, and *Pin-up* advances an argument over what an appropriate contemporary treatment of a classic art-historical theme might be. Such a treatment, Hamilton believes, would demand a "diversifying" of the languages of art, so that he approaches the odalisque tradition through a variety of pictorial modes: the hair, for example, is a stylized cartoon, the breasts appear both in drawing and in three-dimensional relief, and the bra is a photograph applied as collage. "Mixing idioms," Hamilton has said, "is virtually a doctrine in *Pin-up*"—an image both tawdry and extraordinarily sophisticated.

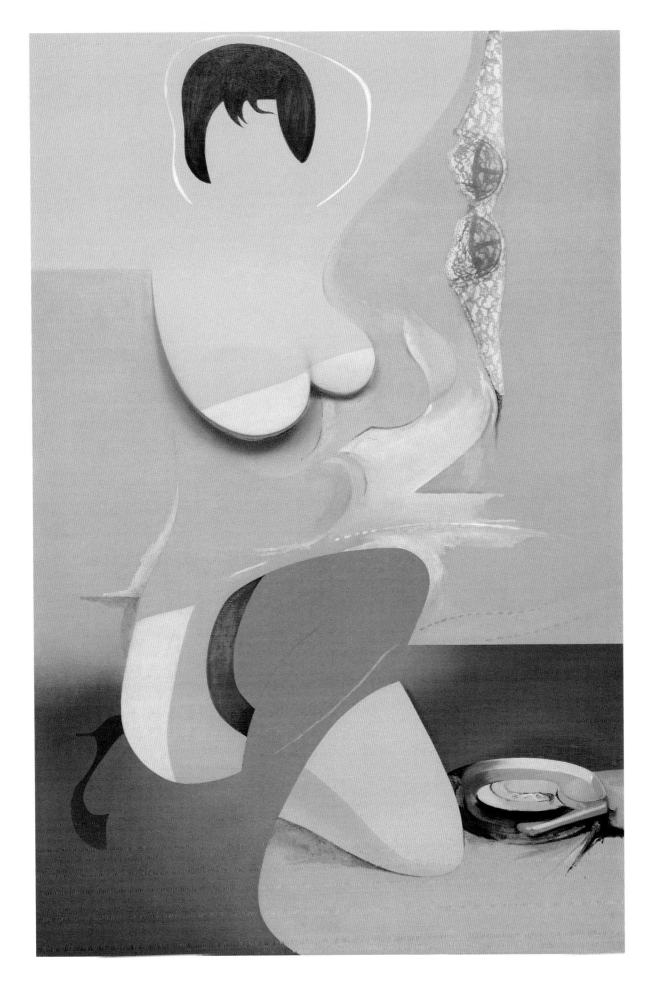

221

Blue Monochrome. 1961

Dry pigment in synthetic polymer medium
on cotton over plywood, 6' 4⅞" x 55⅛"
(195.1 x 140 cm)
The Sidney and Harriet Janis Collection

"*Yves le monochrome,*" as Klein called
himself, saw the monochrome painting as an
"open window to freedom, as the possibility
of being immersed in the immeasurable
existence of color." Although he used a
range of colors before concentrating on
three—blue, gold, and a red he called
Monopink—he is most associated with a blue
he named International Klein Blue, which he
arrived at by working with a chemist to
develop a binding medium that could absorb
pure color pigment without dimming its

brilliant intensity. A student of Rosicrucianism
and of Eastern religions, Klein entertained
esoteric and spiritual ideas in which blue
played a vital role as the color of infinity.
Keenly aware that pigment is a substance of
the earth, Klein also devised methods to
make paintings using the other three
elements—air (in the form of wind), water (in
the form of rain), and fire.

Kazimir Malevich's *Supremalist
Composition: White on White* (1918) is the
major historical precedent for recent
monochrome, but Klein argued that the
Russian artist's primary concern had been
with form—the square—rather than with
color. As a result, Klein felt that "Malevich
was actually standing before the infinite—I
am in it."

Line 1000 Meters Long. 1961

Chrome-plated metal drum containing a roll of
paper with an ink line drawn along its 1000-meter
length, 20¼" x 15⅜" (51.2 x 38.8 cm) diam.
Gift of Fratelli Fabbri Editori and Purchase

Manzoni began his career as a painter, but
his later work anticipated the Conceptual art
of the 1960s. *Line 1000 Meters Long* reflects
both sides of his thought. Regarding a
painting not as "a surface to be filled with
colors and forms" but as "a surface of
unlimited possibilities," he imagined in that
"total space" a line going "beyond all
problems of composition and size." This was
what he produced in his many works on the
pattern of *Line 1000 Meters Long*—each a
tube or drum containing a roll of paper
marked with a single continuous line. The
length of the roll varies from work to work,
but in theory, Manzoni believed, the line
could stretch to infinity.

Despite its relationship to painting, *Line
1000 Meters Long* is more conceptual than
visual. Indeed the line that is its heart eludes
the eye, for these canister works are usually
shown closed. Art that is invisible raises the
act of thinking above the act of seeing, as
Manzoni also did when, for example, he
signed eggs with his thumbprint and asked a
show's visitors to eat them. A line in a can is
itself a conceptual conundrum. Playful but
acute, *Line 1000 Meters Long* invites us to
question our expectations of the artwork, and
our responses to it.

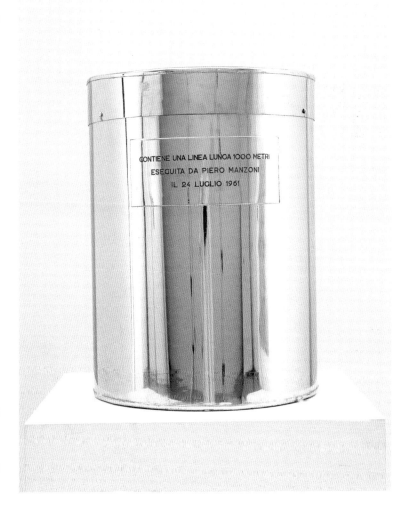

The Bus Driver. 1962

Figure of plaster over cheesecloth; bus parts including coin box, steering wheel, driver's seat, railing, dashboard, etc.; figure, 53^1/$_2$ x 26^7/$_8$ x 45" (136 x 68.2 x 114 cm), overall 7' 5" x 51^5/$_8$" x 6'4^3/$_4$" (226 x 131 x 195 cm)
Philip Johnson Fund

The idea for *The Bus Driver* came to Segal on a late-evening bus from New York to New Jersey. The driver was grim, sullen, and arrogant, and Segal caught himself thinking, "My God, dare I trust my life to this prig?" Soon afterward he found a derelict bus in a junkyard and hacked out the driver's platform. Incorporated in *The Bus Driver*, this metal armature pens in a plaster figure—a life cast. (The model was Segal's brother-in-law.)

When they first appeared, in the early 1960s, Segal's plaster molds of people in fragments of real environments were considered Pop art, since they described the everyday life of public places. But where Pop often focused on mass-media images and mass-produced objects, Segal was interested in individuals, their gestures, statures, stances, and also their inner, psychological or spiritual condition. He often left his plaster molds unpainted, valuing their whiteness for "its special connotations of disembodied spirit, inseparable from the fleshy corporeal details of the figure." In the bus driver (who has been likened to Charon, the ferryman of Greek myth who guides dead souls to the underworld), Segal saw "the dignity of helplessness—a massive, strong man, surrounded by machinery, and yet basically a very unheroic man trapped by forces larger than himself that he couldn't control and least of all understand."

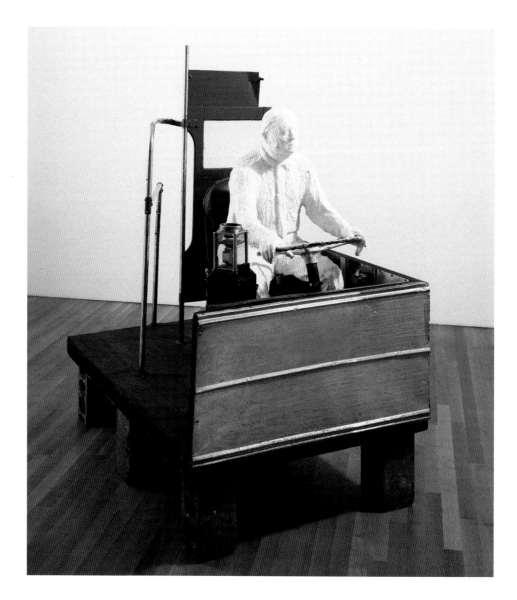

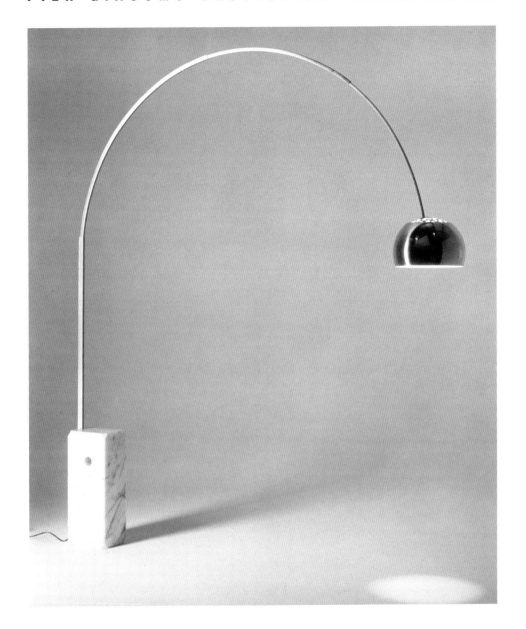

1962

Arco Floor Lamp. 1962

Marble and stainless steel, 8' 2¹/₂" x 6' 7" x 12¹/₂"
(2.5 x 2 x .32 m)
Manufacturer: Flos S.p.A., Italy
Gift of the manufacturer

Castiglioni designed more than sixty lamps and a host of other objects, working from 1945 until 1968 with his brother Pier Giacomo and then on his own. One of their best-known lamp designs, Arco, came about through the challenge of a practical problem: how to provide a ceiling lamp that would not require drilling a hole in the ceiling.

Castiglioni's motto, "design demands observation," proved accurate, for it was a street lamp that gave the brothers the inspiration for this fixture. Street lamps, affixed to the ground, have a shape that enables them to project their light beams several feet away from their bases.

In this domestic adaptation, the Castiglionis were able to illuminate objects eight feet away from the lamp's base—far enough to light the middle of a dining table—by inserting a steel arch into a heavy Carrara marble pedestal. They studied the span of the arch to be sure that its form would provide enough space for one person carrying a tray to pass behind someone sitting at the table. In addition, they made sure the heavy lamp could be moved by two people by inserting a broomstick through the hole in the marble base. Arco is a prime example of the Castiglionis' rigorous approach in design solutions.

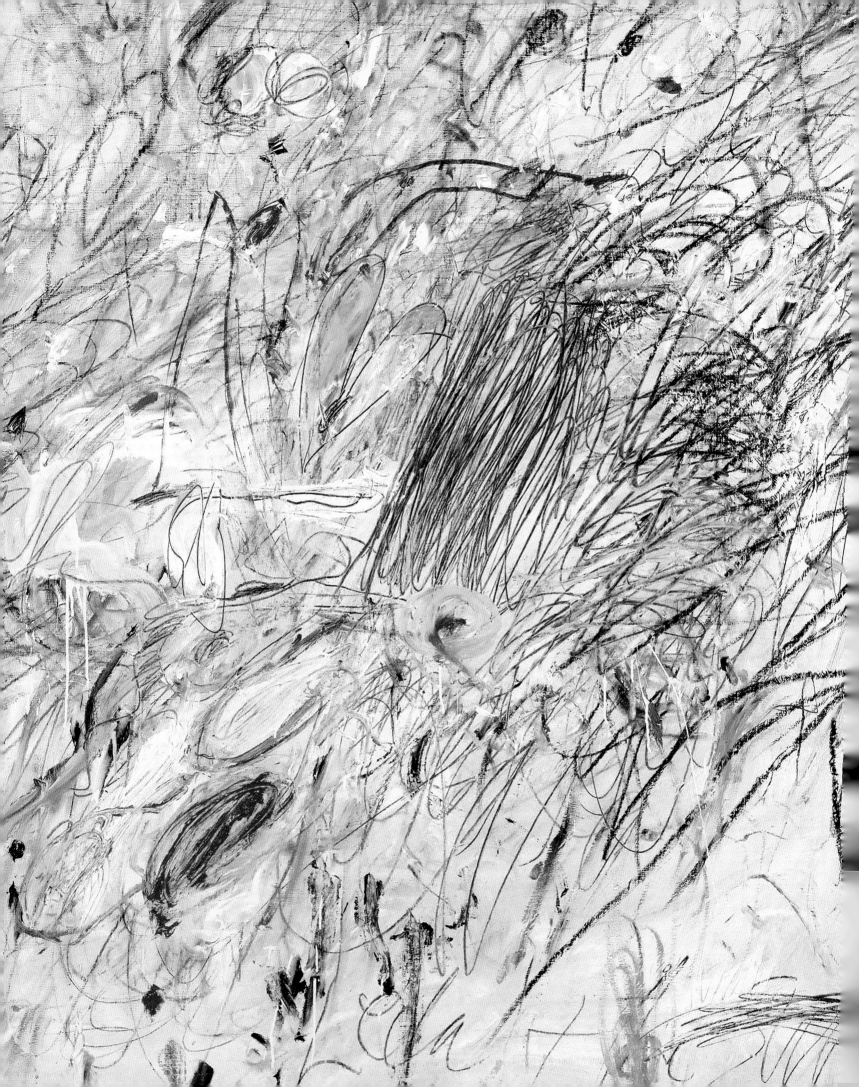

Leda and the Swan. 1962

Oil, pencil, and crayon on canvas, 6' 3" x 6' 6¾"
(190.5 x 200 cm)
Acquired through the Lillie P. Bliss Bequest (by
exchange)

Interest in the mural form was widespread
among the Abstract Expressionists, who
often worked on a scale far larger than that
of most easel paintings. Twombly, a member
of a younger generation, transposed that
interest in the wall into a different register: no
painter of his time more consistently invites
association with the language of graffiti. His
scrawled calligraphic markings may recall
the automatic writing of Surrealism, another
inheritance passed on to him through
Abstract Expressionism, but they also evoke
the scratches and scribbles on the ancient
walls of Rome (his home since 1957).

Rome supplies another touchstone for
Twombly through his fascination with
classical antiquity. Here he refers to the myth
in which Jupiter, lord of the gods, took the
shape of a swan in order to ravish the
beautiful Leda. (This violation ultimately led
to the Trojan War, fought over Leda's
daughter Helen.) Twombly's version of this
old arthistorical theme supplies no contrasts
of feathers and flesh but an orgiastic fusion
and confusion of energies within furiously

thrashing overlays of crayon, pencil, and
ruddy paint. A few recognizable signs—
hearts, a phallus—fly out from this explosion.
A drier comment is the quartered, windowlike
rectangle near the top of the painting, an
indication of the stabilizing direction that
Twombly's art was starting to take.

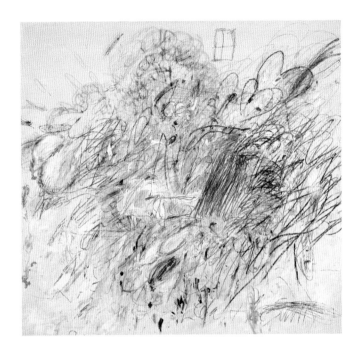

Campbell's Soup Cans. 1962

Synthetic polymer paint on thirty-two canvases,
each 20 x 16" (50.8 x 40.6 cm)
Gift of Irving Blum; Nelson A. Rockefeller
Bequest, gift of Mr. and Mrs. William A.M.
Burden, Abby Aldrich Rockefeller Fund, gift of
Nina and Gordon Bunshaft in honor of Henry
Moore, Lillie P. Bliss Bequest, Philip Johnson
Fund, Frances Keech Bequest, gift of Mrs. Bliss
Parkinson, and Florence B. Wesley Bequest
(all by exchange)

"I don't think art should be only for the select
few," Warhol believed, "I think it should be for
the mass of the American people." Like other
Pop artists, Warhol used images of already
proven appeal to huge audiences: comic
strips, ads, photographs of rock music and
movie stars, tabloid news shots. In
Campbell's Soup Cans he reproduced an
object of mass consumption in the most
literal sense. When he first exhibited these
canvases—there are thirty-two of them, the

number of soup varieties Campbell's then
sold—each one simultaneously hung from
the wall, like a painting, and stood on a shelf,
like groceries in a store.

Repeating the same image at the same
scale, the canvases stress the uniformity and
ubiquity of the Campbell's can. At the same
time, they subvert the idea of painting as a
medium of invention and originality. Visual
repetition of this kind had long been used by
advertisers to drum product names into the
public consciousness; here, though, it
implies not energetic competition but a
complacent abundance. Outside an art
gallery, the Campbell's label, which had not
changed in over fifty years, was not an
attention-grabber but a banality. As Warhol
said of Campbell's soup, "I used to drink it. I
used to have the same lunch every day, for
twenty years, I guess, the same thing over
and over again."
(See illustration on pages 228, 229)

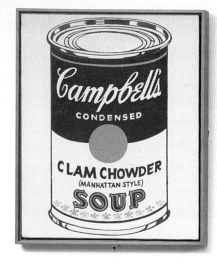

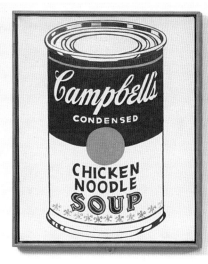

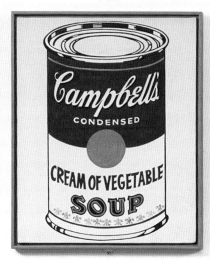

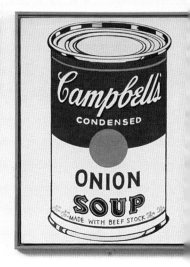

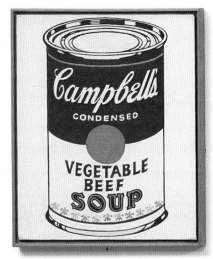

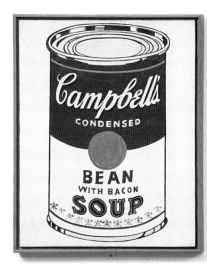

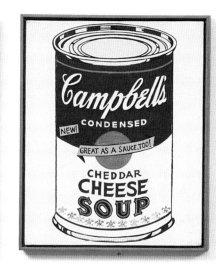

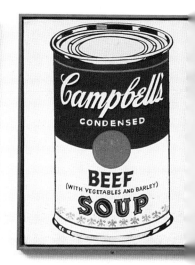

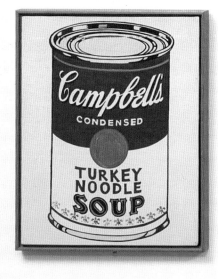

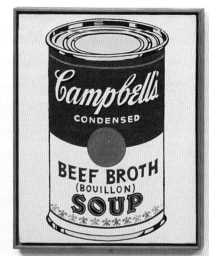

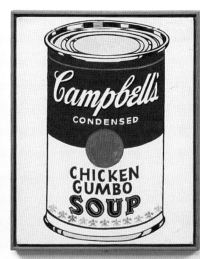

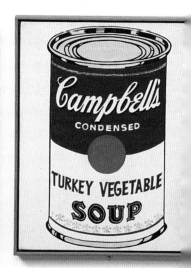

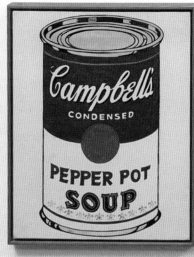

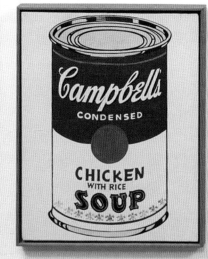

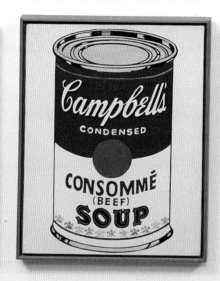

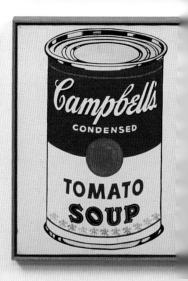

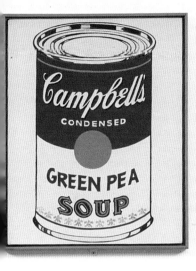
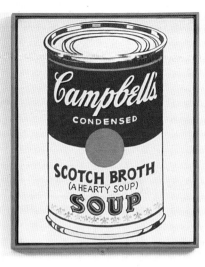
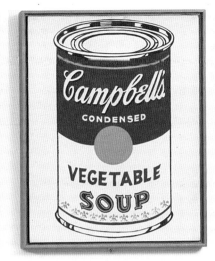
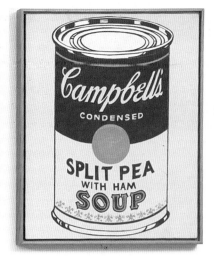
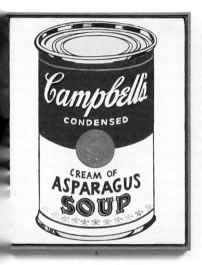
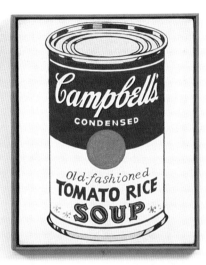
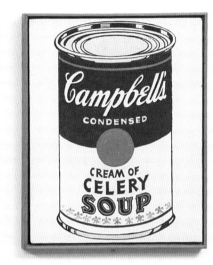
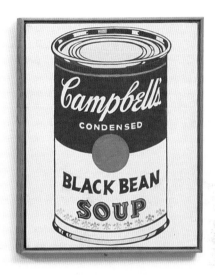
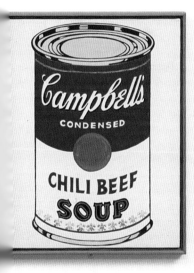
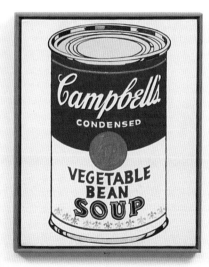
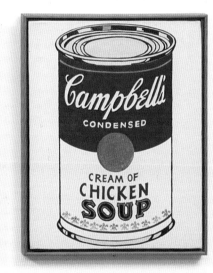
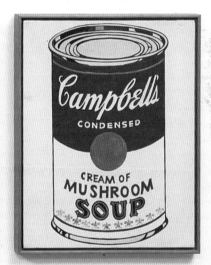
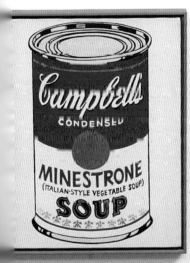
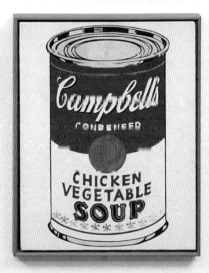
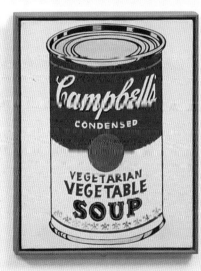
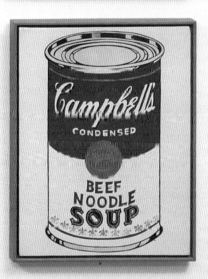

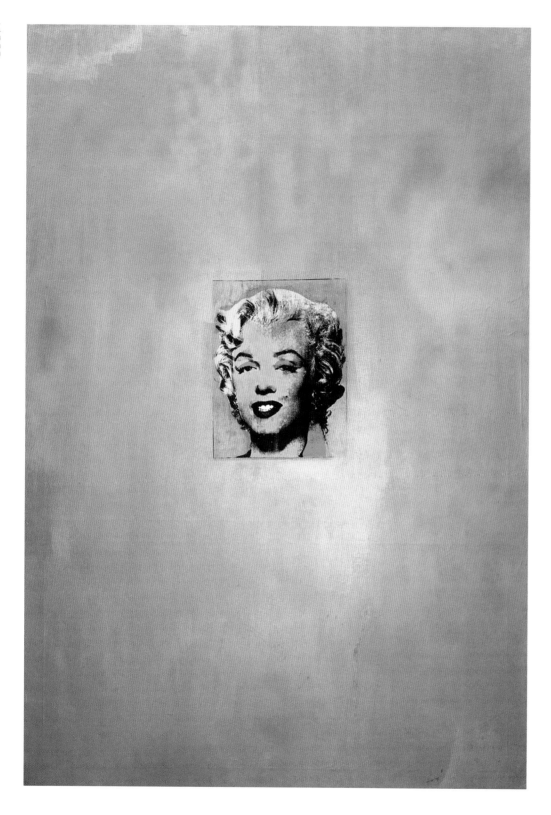

Gold Marilyn Monroe. 1962

Synthetic polymer paint, silkscreened, and oil on canvas, 6' 11¼" x 57" (211.4 x 144.7 cm) Gift of Philip Johnson

Marilyn Monroe was a legend when she committed suicide in August of 1962, but in retrospect her life seems a gradual martyrdom to the media and to her public. After her death, Warhol based many works on the same photograph of her, a publicity still for the 1953 movie Niagara. He would paint the canvas with a single color— turquoise, green, blue, lemon yellow—then silkscreen Monroe's face on top, sometimes alone, sometimes doubled, sometimes multiplied in a grid. As the surround for a face, the golden field in *Gold Marilyn Monroe* (the only one of Warhol's Marilyns to use this color) recalls the religious icons of Christian art history—a resonance, however, that the work suffuses with a morbid allure.

In reduplicating this photograph of a heroine shared by millions, Warhol denied the sense of the uniqueness of the artist's personality that had been implicit in the gestural painting of the 1950s. He also used a commercial technique—silkscreening—that gives the picture a crisp, artificial look; even as Warhol canonizes Monroe, he reveals her public image as a carefully structured illusion. Redolent of 1950s glamour, the face in *Gold Marilyn Monroe* is much like the star herself—high gloss, yet transient; bold, yet vulnerable; compelling, yet elusive. Surrounded by a void, it is like the fadeout at the end of a movie.

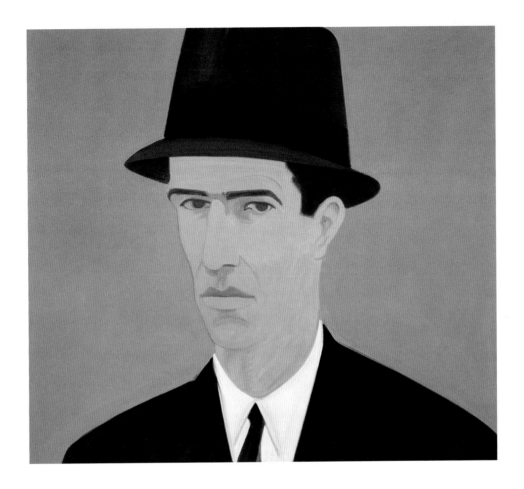

Passing. 1962–63
Oil on canvas, 71³/₄" x 6' 7⁵/₈" (182.2 x 202.2 cm)
Gift of the Louis and Bessie Adler Foundation,
Inc., Seymour M. Klein, President

Ambitious, elegant, impersonal, large in
scale, and simultaneously timeless and
reflective of its time—these, according to
Katz, are the qualities of "high style" in
painting, and they are also the qualities of
many of his own works. Believing that "you
have no power unless you have traditional
elements in your pictures," Katz achieves
high style by integrating familiar traditions
with avant-garde practice. *Passing* belongs
to a venerable genre—it is a self-portrait—
but has the scale of Abstract Expressionism.
Another inspiration is the advertising
billboard; like the Pop artists, Katz pays

attention to the cultural scene. Meanwhile,
his reductive approach and his conception of
pictorial space match those in the formalist
painting of the 1960s.

The ground in *Passing* is a flat
monochrome, and Katz's face and shoulders
are so simplified that it is mainly their clarity
as parts of a figure that insinuates their
volume. Neither smiling nor frowning, Katz
meets our gaze frankly, but his character is
muted by the artifice of the painting's design:
the perfect ellipse of the hat brim; the
asymmetry in the height of the shoulders; the
limited palette, all near-flat blacks, whites,
and grays except for the face. Far from the
bohemian artist, Katz looks coolly
imperturbable in his businessman's suit and
hat—stylish not only in his painting but in his
person.

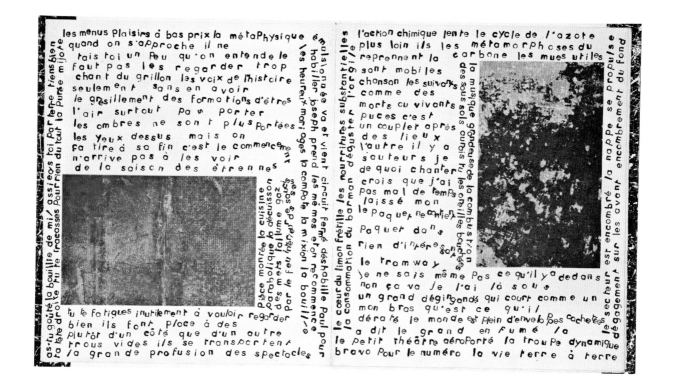

La Lunette farcie by Jean Dubuffet. 1962–63
Illustrated book with 11 lithographs, page:
17³/₁₆ x 14¹⁵/₁₆" (43.4 x 38 cm)
Publisher: PAB (Pierre André Benoit), Alès
and Paris. Edition: 55
Gift of Mr. and Mrs. Ralph F. Colin

This double-page spread from the book *La Lunette farcie* (*The Stuffed Lunette*) offers immediate immersion into the fanciful, haphazard world of Dubuffet. He created the atmospheric abstractions by chance, experimenting with a variety of "accidental" happenings to produce textures on the lithographic plates, which might include indiscriminate scratching and the random exposure of the plates to fire, liquid, dirt, or other elements. Otherworldly images are surrounded by the artist's nonsensical ramblings that consist of French words arranged more by sound or look than by meaning. The unpunctuated writing, reproducing the artist's own stenciled words, is placed in different orientations around the pages, making the text even more problematic. The inane title is virtually untranslatable. Dubuffet's relaxed, playful attitude reflects his admiration for children's art, the art of the insane, and that of the untrained. He was among the first artists to appreciate "visionary" or "outsider" art, which he called l'art brut (rough art).

La Lunette farcie was one of several books Dubuffet made with the poet-publisher Benoit. This man, whimsical by nature, would send blank etching or lithographic plates to artists such as Pablo Picasso and Max Ernst to tempt them to make images for his innovative publications.

OOF. 1962–63

Oil on canvas, 71¹/₂ x 67" (181.5 x 170.2 cm)
Gift of Agnes Gund, the Louis and Bessie Adler
Foundation, Inc., Robert and Meryl Meltzer, Jerry
I. Speyer, Anna Marie and Robert F. Shapiro,
Emily and Jerry Spiegel, an anonymous donor,
and purchase

"The single word, its guttural monosyllabic
pronunciation, that's what I was passionate
about," Ruscha has said of his early work.
"Loud words, like *slam*, *smash*, *honk*." The
comic-book quality of these words reflects
the Pop artists' fascination with popular
culture. (This interest is even more explicit in
Ruscha's images of vernacular Los Angeles
architecture.) Lettered in typography rather
than handwriting, the words are definite and
impersonal in shape; unlike the Abstract
Expressionists of the 1940s and 1950s,

Ruscha had no interest in letting a painting
emerge through an introspective process: "I
began to see that the only thing to do would
be a preconceived image. It was an enormous
freedom to be premeditated about my art."

Words like *oof*, *smash*, and *honk* all evoke
sounds, and loud and sharp ones. They also,
as Ruscha says, have "a certain comedic
value," and their comedy is underlined by the
paradox of their appearance in the silent
medium of paint, and with neither an image
nor a sentence to help them evoke the
sounds they denote. *Oof* is particularly
paradoxical, as a word describing a
wordless grunt. In Ruscha's hands, its double
O's also pun on recent paintings—the Targets
and Circles of Jasper Johns and Kenneth
Noland. Works like this one wryly point up
the arbitrariness of our agreements on the
meanings of our visual and verbal languages.

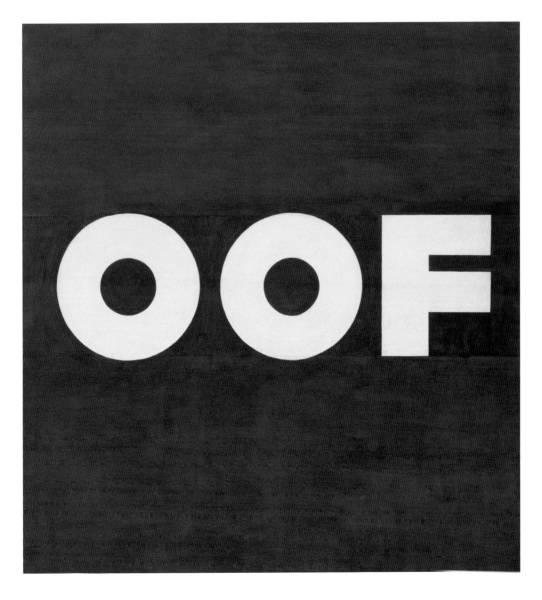

1962–63

233

P. D. Zeichnung. 1963

Ink and pastel on two sheets of paper, overall:
33½ x 24¼" (85 x 61.5 cm)
Purchased with funds given by Jo Carole and
Ronald S. Lauder and Leon D. Black

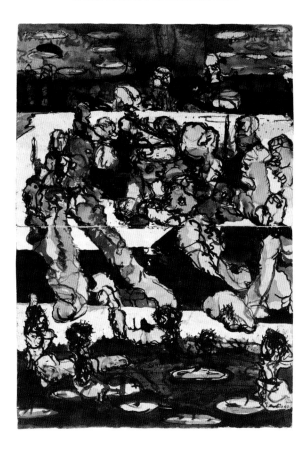

Baselitz described this drawing as "the depiction of a table with knots of figural motifs. Above and below landscape formation." The bulbous, knotted forms, spread over two sheets of paper in disjointed and contorted spaces, signal the artist's desire to formulate his own pictorial language. They also point to his fascination with the Mannerist painters, such as the Italians Jacopo da Pontormo and Parmigianino, as well as with what he considered "outsider" art, namely, the work of Antonin Artaud, Vincent van Gogh, and August Strindberg, for example, and the expressive visual language of the art of the insane. These nightmarish, amorphous, distorted, almost putrefying shapes express a sense of anger, alienation, disease, and decay that informed the artist's vision in the early 1960s.

Several of Baselitz's paintings of 1962–63 include similar knotted forms, which continued to populate his work throughout most of the decade, culminating in the famous Heroes series. These works mark his search for symbols and vocabulary that assert his own identity and iconography, which, at the time, expressed themselves through the introduction of disjointed fragments of the body, placed in irrational spaces. This drawing is also related to the artist's early iconoclastic texts, the *Pandemonium* manifestos, published in 1961 and 1962.

HENRY MOORE BRITISH, 1898–1986

Large Torso: Arch. 1962–63

Bronze, 6' 6⅛" x 59⅛" x 51¼"
(198.4 x 150.2 x 130.2 cm)
Edition: 3/7
Mrs. Simon Guggenheim Fund

Invited by the title of this sculpture to expect a description of a human torso, the viewer may notice a striking absence of the solid body that lies below the shoulders, at least in a living being.

Basing the piece on the shoulder-bone structure of a male torso, Moore actually made a simplified skeleton. The shapes of bones fascinated Moore. He was also one of the many artists of his generation who wanted to escape the classical tradition—in his words, to remove "the Greek spectacles from the eyes of the modern sculptor"—and who therefore studied objects of many eras and areas, from Cycladic art to pre-Columbian art to the African and Oceanic art of relatively recent times. "Keep ever prominent the world tradition—the big view of Sculpture," Moore once wrote, and the near-abstract forms of his art show how far he left classical naturalism behind.

In its scale and weight, *Large Torso* evokes a natural form—perhaps an arch of wind-smoothed rock. The word *Arch* in the work's title also asks viewers to look at that central vacancy, as important formally as the solid bronze. Stripping the skeleton of flesh, and melding it with landscape, Moore gives his work the sense of having been shaped by the long passage of time.

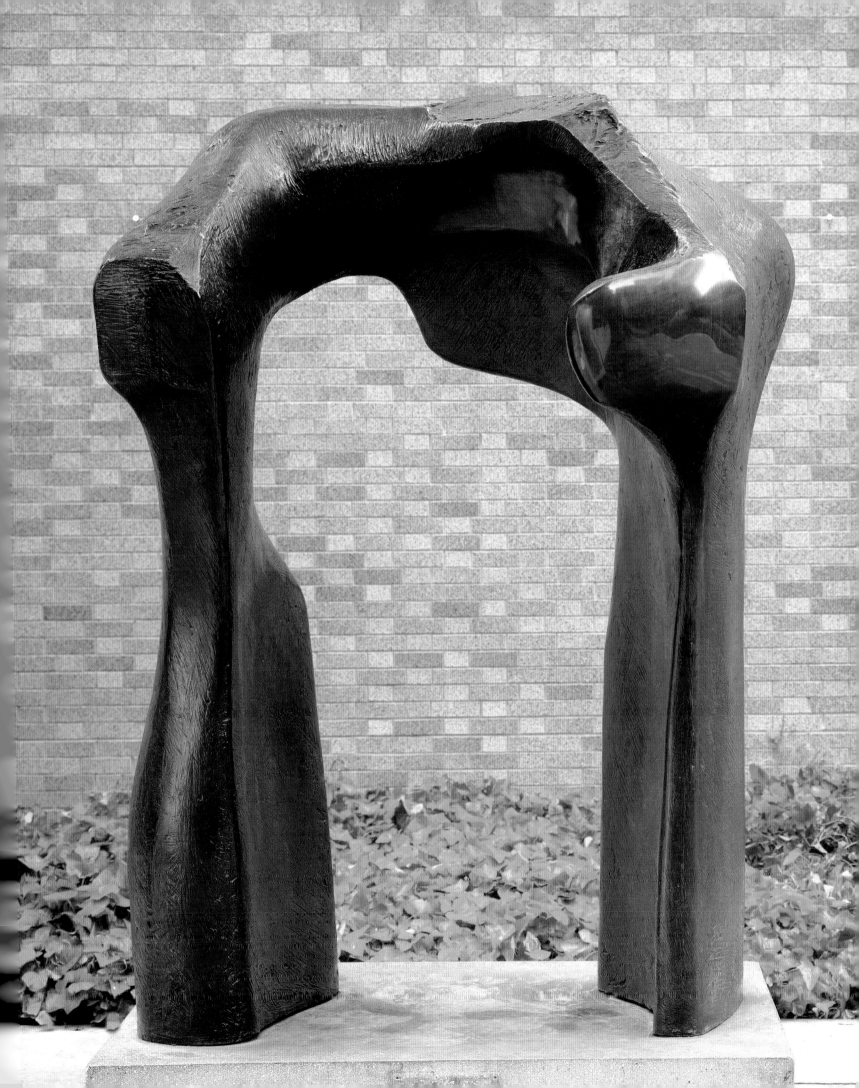

1963

Abstract Painting. 1963

Oil on canvas, 60 x 60" (152.4 x 152.4 cm)
Gift of Mrs. Morton J. Hornick

To the hasty viewer, *Abstract Painting* must present a flat blackness. But the work holds more than one shade of black, and longer viewing reveals an abstract geometrical image. Reinhardt has divided the canvas into a three-by-three grid of squares. The black in each corner square has a reddish tone; the shape between them—a cross, filling the center square of the canvas and the square in the middle of each side—is a bluish black in its vertical bar and a greenish black in its horizontal one.

Works like this were strongly influential for the Minimalist and Conceptual artists of the 1960s, who admired their reductive and systematic rigor. But the poetry of their finely handled surfaces, and their deeply contemplative character, tie them to the Abstract Expressionist generation of which Reinhardt was a member, if a dissident one. Insisting on the separation of art from life, Reinhardt tried to erase from his work any content other than art itself. In the late black canvases that include *Abstract Painting* (he called them his "ultimate" paintings) he was trying to produce what he described as "a pure, abstract, non-objective, timeless, spaceless, changeless, relationless, disinterested painting—an object that is self-conscious (no unconsciousness), ideal, transcendent, aware of no thing but art."

1964

Ale Cans. 1964

Lithograph, sheet: 22⁷/₈ x 17³/₄" (58.1 x 45.1 cm)
Publisher: Universal Limited Art Editions, West Islip, New York. Edition: 31
Gift of the Celeste and Armand Bartos Foundation

At first glance, *Ale Cans* appears to be a representation of immediately recognizable mundane objects portrayed in a realistic manner. A second look, however, reveals small details that challenge this initial assumption. The pair of cans, placed frontally with exacting care, sits on a base that seems to float in the surrounding black void. Black scribbled lines, some extending into the empty margin around the composition and others creating shadows on the cans and base, affirm the artist's touch. And while the cans have a three-dimensional presence, the black background is clearly flat. These conflicting sensations create an unsettling tension between reality and illusion.

For this print, Johns used as his subject his own 1960 sculpture *Painted Bronze*, his first work showing two Ballantine Ale cans. Since the publication of this print, the artist has periodically reinterpreted these cans in various mediums, while subjecting the image to continuing metamorphosis. The transformation of everyday "found" objects into fine art was first introduced by the Dada and Surrealist artists early in the twentieth century. Here Johns has taken this transformation one step further, manipulating the object until it becomes something other than what it is.

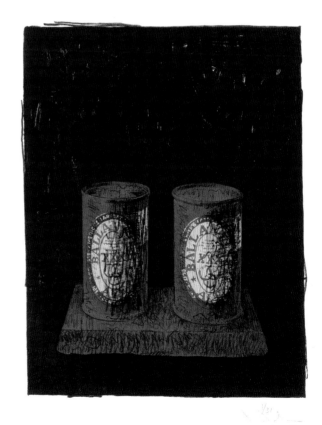

JAMES ROSENQUIST

F-111. 1964–65
Oil on canvas with aluminum, overall 10 x 86'
(304.8 x 2621.3 cm)
Gift of Mr. and Mrs. Alex L. Hillman (by exchange)
and Lillie P. Bliss Bequest (by exchange)

"Painting is probably much more exciting than advertising," Rosenquist has said, "so why shouldn't it be done with that power and gusto, with that impact." Like other Pop artists, Rosenquist is fascinated by commercial and everyday images. He also understands the power of advertising's use of "things larger than life"—he once painted billboards for a living—and even in early abstractions he borrowed the exaggeratedly cheerful palette of the giant signs. His next step was to explore the artistic potential of the billboard's scale and photographic style.

Rosenquist generally spikes that style with

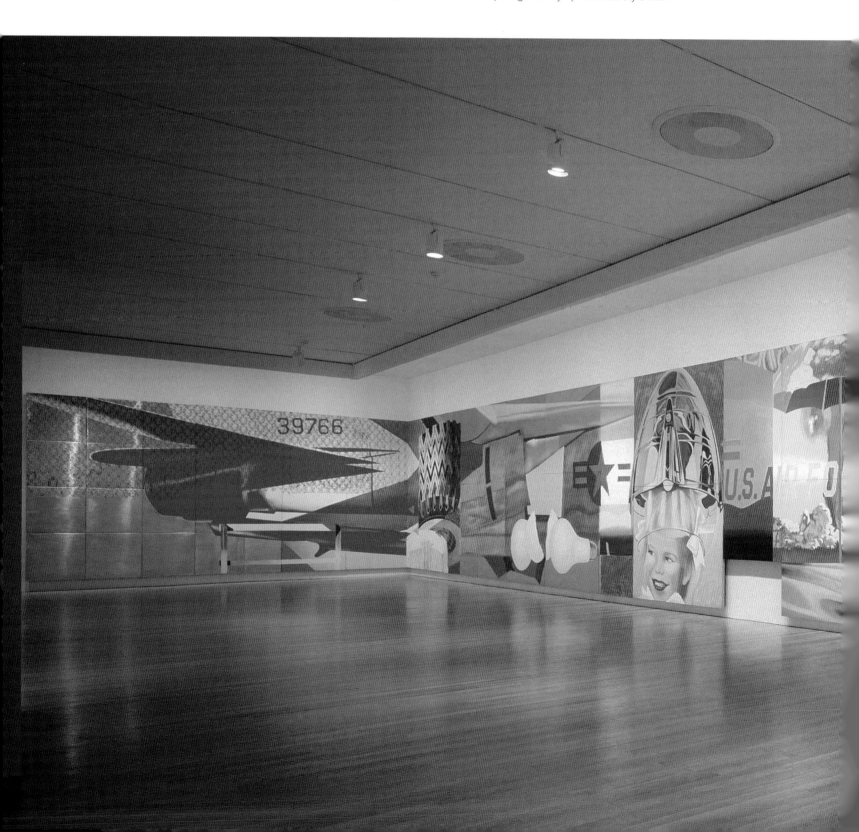

disorienting fractures and recombinations of images. *F-111* becomes still more overwhelming through its particularly enormous size and panoramic shape: it is designed to fill the four walls of a room, engulfing and surrounding the viewer—unlike a billboard, which, despite its magnitude, can be viewed all at once. Also unlike a billboard, *F-111* fuses pictures of American prosperity with a darker visual current. A diver's air bubbles are rhymed by a mushroom cloud; a smiling little girl sits under a missilelike hairdryer; a sea of spaghetti looks uncomfortably visceral; and weaving through and around all these images is the *F-111* itself, a U.S. Air Force fighter-bomber. Painted during the Vietnam War, *F-111* draws disturbing connections between militarism and the consumerist structure of the American economy.

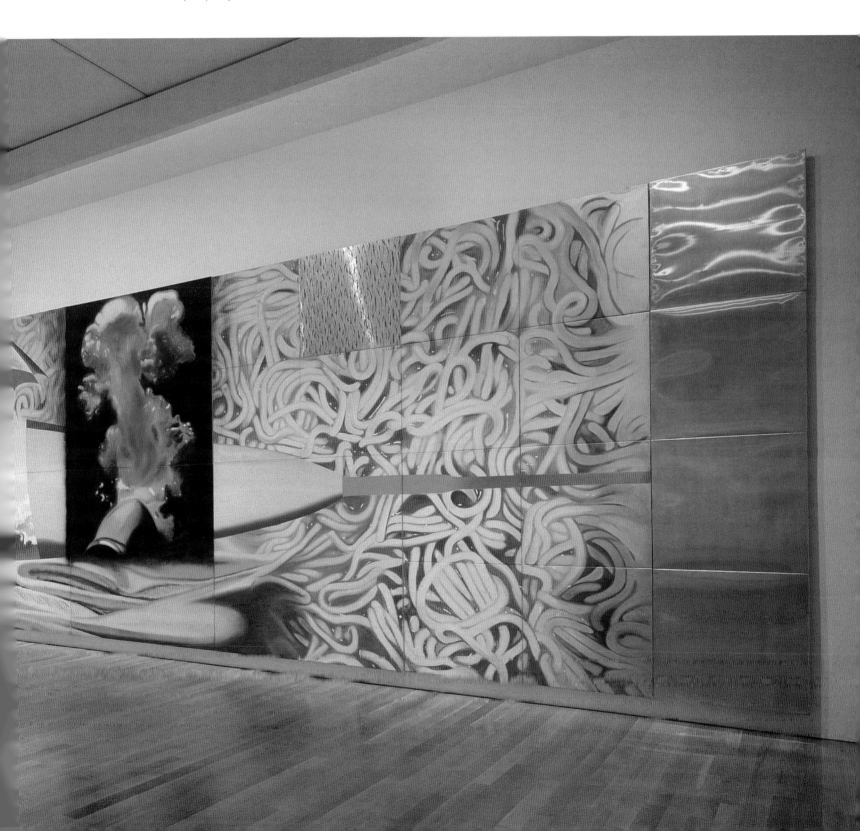

White Cabinet and White Table. 1965

Wood, oil, and eggshells; cabinet
33⁷/₈ x 32¹/₄ x 24¹/₂" (86 x 82 x 62 cm),
table 41 x 39³/₈ x 15³/₄" (104 x 100 x 40 cm)
Fractional and promised gift of Ronald S. Lauder

Explaining his beginnings in art, Broodthaers
once wrote, "The idea of inventing something
insincere ... crossed my mind and I set to
work at once." Anyone upset to find a
cabinet of eggshells presented as art might
take this to mean that the work is a joke. But
there is another possibility: Broodthaers is
warning us not to take him at face value, but
to look for hidden meanings.

White Cabinet and White Table actually
does have aesthetic ancestors, in Marcel
Duchamp's objects and in the surprises of
René Magritte. It also reflects the concern
with everyday reality in the Pop and
neo-realism of Broodthaers's own time. But
Broodthaers wanted to avoid glamorizing
modern products, and eggshells have
nothing uniquely contemporary about them.
They interested Broodthaers, rather, as
empty containers—containers "without
content other than the air."

There are other containers in *White
Cabinet and White Table*: the cabinet and
table themselves, both stuffed with content,
but an apparently empty or meaningless one.
If the table stands on the floor like a
sculpture's pedestal while the closet hangs
on the wall like a painting's frame
(Broodthaers described himself as "painting
with eggs like the primitifs"), then the work
subtly analyzes art itself: how does art
contain meaning for its viewers? Or has it
been drained of meaning, like an eggshell
minus its egg?

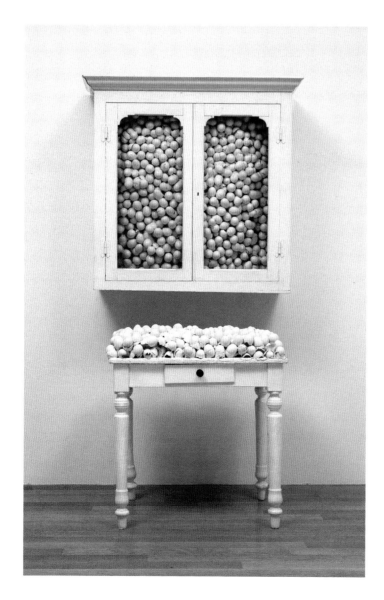

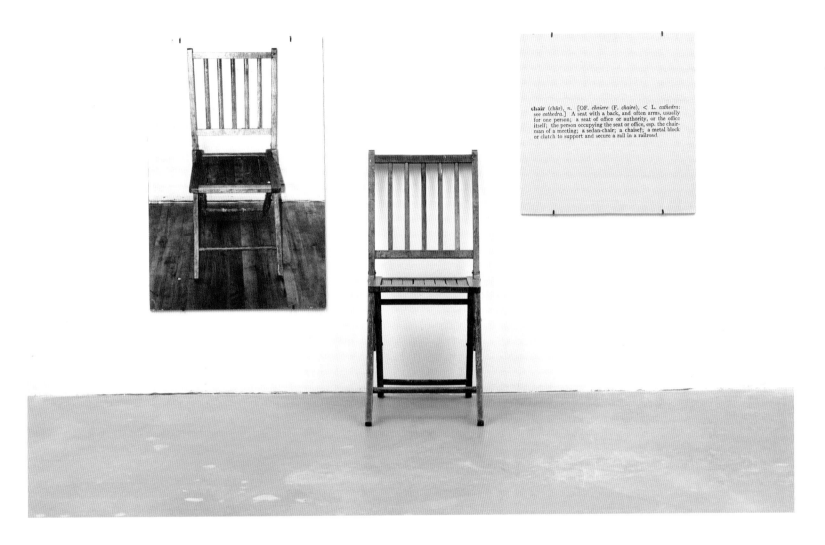

One and Three Chairs. 1965

Wood folding chair, photographic copy of chair,
and photographic enlargement of dictionary
definition of a chair; chair, $32^{3}/_{8}$ x $14^{7}/_{8}$ x $20^{7}/_{8}$"
(82 x 37.8 x 53 cm); photo panel, 36 x $24^{1}/_{8}$"
(91.5 x 61.1 cm), text panel, 24 x $24^{1}/_{8}$"
(61 x 61.3 cm)
Larry Aldrich Foundation Fund

A chair sits alongside a photograph of a
chair and a dictionary definition of the word
chair. Perhaps all three are chairs, or codes
for one: a visual code, a verbal code, and a
code in the language of objects, that is, a
chair of wood. But isn't this last chair simply
... a chair? Or, as Marcel Duchamp asked in
his *Bicycle Wheel* of 1913, does the inclusion
of an object in an artwork somehow change
it? If both photograph and words describe a

chair, how is their functioning different from
that of the real chair, and what is Kosuth's
artwork doing by adding these functions
together? Prodded to ask such questions,
the viewer embarks on the basic processes
demanded by Conceptual art.

"The art I call conceptual is such because
it is based on an inquiry into the nature of
art," Kosuth has written. "Thus, it is ... a
working out, a thinking out, of all the
implications of all aspects of the concept
'art.' Fundamental to this idea of art is the
understanding of the linguistic nature of all
art propositions, be they past or present, and
regardless of the elements used in their
construction." Chasing a chair through three
different registers, Kosuth asks us to try to
decipher the subliminal sentences in which
we phrase our experience of art.

241

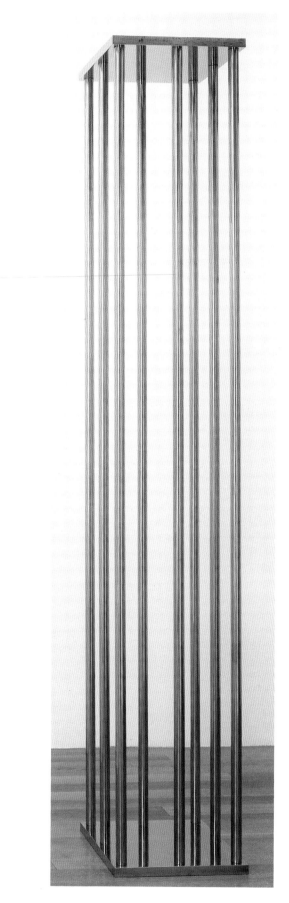

Cage II. 1965

Stainless steel, 7' 1¹/₄" x 14¹/₄" x 14¹/₄"
(216.5 x 36.2 x 36.2 cm)
Edition: 2/2
Gift of Agnes Gund and Lily Auchincloss

Cage II may seem easy to grasp: a space sealed by bars—a cage. But it would be a thin person indeed who could fit in this narrow room, and in any case, how would anyone get in? There are no doors, no hinges. The metal, too, a pristine stainless steel, is richer than brute prison iron. *Cage II* is surely a paradox: a cage made elegant and abstract.

The paradox only multiplies, for *Cage II* is also a kind of portrait. It remakes a piece from 1961, in wood, but otherwise the same except for the title: *Statue of John Cage*. The John Cage whose name gave de Maria a pun was, of course, the well-known composer and theorizer of modern music. But an aesthetic tradition is also cited here, for Cage had close links to an art-making approach associated with Marcel Duchamp (a long-standing friend of Cage's)—an approach favoring conceptual thought, and, also, a love of puns and wordplay.

The foursquare geometry of *Cage II*, meanwhile, and the purity of the work's medium, point in another direction—toward the Minimal art of the 1960s, an art of system and order. Yet in the work's enigmatic combination of openness and rigor there remains a tribute to the paradoxical artist and musician who inspired it.

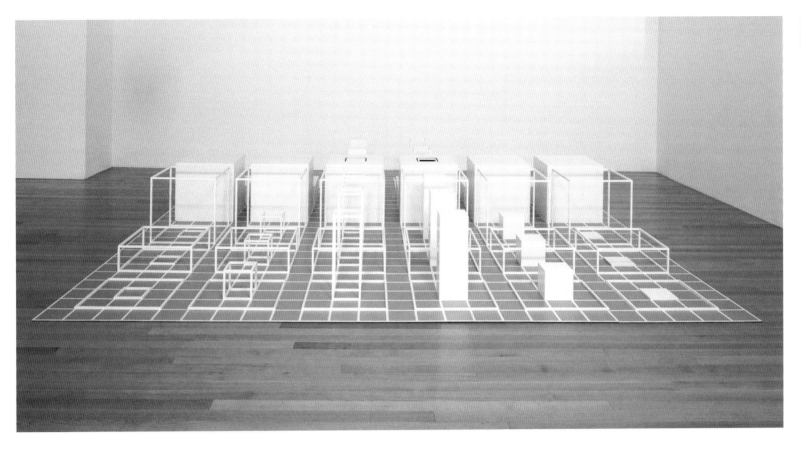

Serial Project, I (ABCD). 1966

Baked enamel on aluminum, 20" x 13' 7" x 13' 7"
(50.8 x 398.9 x 398.9 cm)
Gift of Agnes Gund and purchase (by exchange)

LeWitt's work emerged alongside the
Minimalist and Conceptual art movements of
the 1960s, and combines qualities of both.
Like the Minimalists, he often uses simple
basic forms, in the belief that "using complex
basic forms only disrupts the unity of the
whole"; like the Conceptualists, he starts with
an idea rather than a form, initiating a
process that obeys certain rules, and that
determines the form by playing itself out. The
promise of Serial Project demands the
combination and recombination of both open
and closed enameled aluminum squares,
cubes, and extensions of these shapes, all
laid in a grid. Both intricate and methodical,
the system produces a visual field that gives
its viewers all the evidence they need to
unravel its logic.

In a text accompanying Serial Project,
LeWitt wrote, "The aim of the artist would not
be to instruct the viewer but to give him
information. Whether the viewer understands
this information is incidental to the artist; he
cannot foresee the understanding of all his
viewers. He would follow his predetermined
premise to its conclusion avoiding
subjectivity. Chance, taste, or unconsciously
remembered forms would play no part in the
outcome. The serial artist does not attempt to
produce a beautiful or mysterious object but
functions merely as a clerk cataloging the
results of his premise."

ROBERT MOTHERWELL   AMERICAN, 1915–1991

Elegy to the Spanish Republic, 108.
1965–67
Oil on canvas, 6' 10" x 11' 6¼" (208.2 x 351.1 cm)
Charles Mergentime Fund

Elegy to the Spanish Republic, 108
describes a stately passage of the organic
and the geometric, the accidental and the
deliberate. Like other Abstract Expressionists,
Motherwell was attracted to the Surrealist
principle of automatism—of methods that
escaped the artist's conscious intention—and
his brushwork has an emotional charge, but
within an overall structure of a certain severity.
In fact Motherwell saw careful arrangements
of color and form as the heart of abstract art,
which, he said, "is stripped bare of other
things in order to intensify it, its rhythms,
spatial intervals, and color structure."

Motherwell intended his Elegies to the
Spanish Republic (over 100 paintings,
completed between 1948 and 1967) as a
"lamentation or funeral song" after the Spanish
Civil War. His recurring motif here is a rough
black oval, repeated in varying sizes and
degrees of compression and distortion.
Instead of appearing as holes leading into a
deeper space, these light-absorbent blots
stand out against a ground of relatively even,
predominantly white upright rectangles. They
have various associations, but Motherwell
himself related them to the display of the dead
bull's testicles in the Spanish bullfighting ring.

Motherwell described the Elegies as his
"private insistence that a terrible death
happened that should not be forgot. But," he
added, "the pictures are also general
metaphors of the contrast between life and
death, and their interrelation."

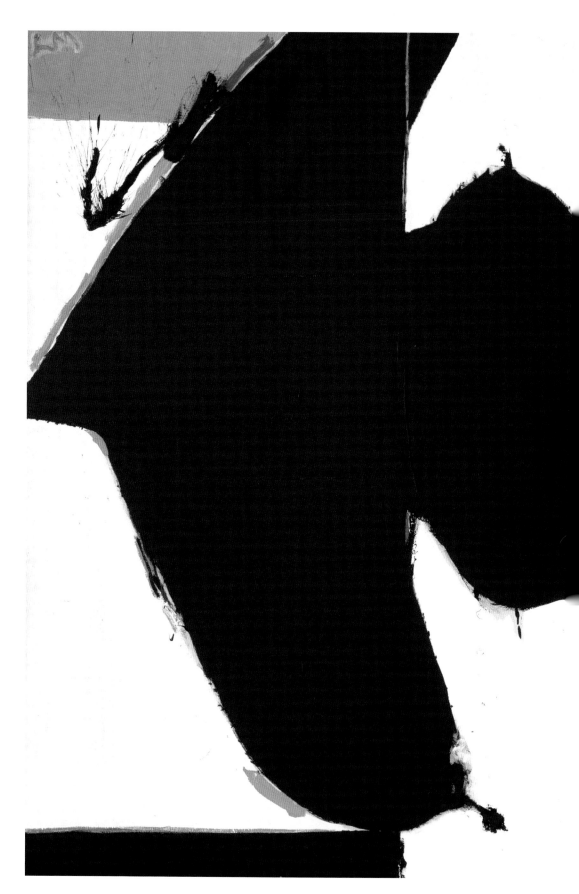

244

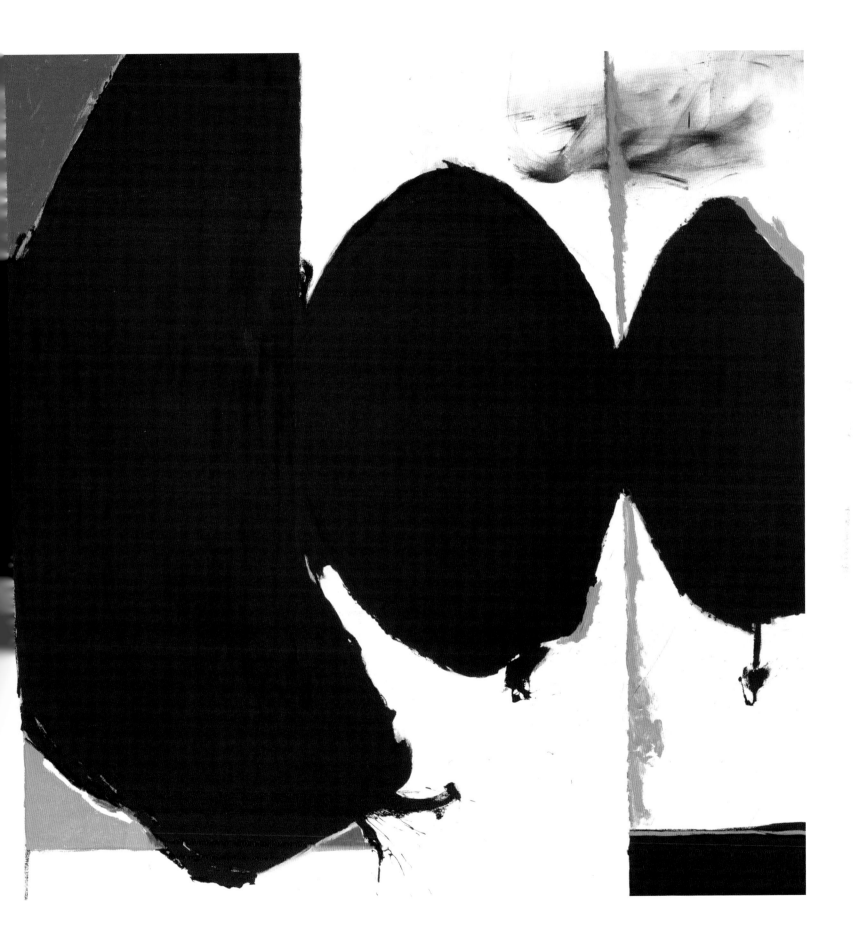

LARRY BURROWS AMERICAN, 1926–1971

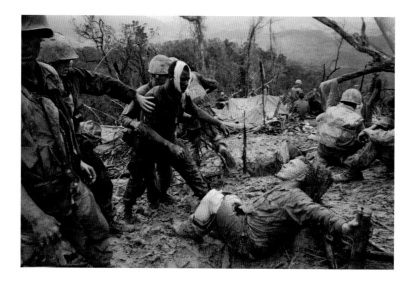

At a First-Aid Center during Operation Prairie. 1966

Dye transfer print, 19¹/₄ x 29³/₄" (48.9 x 75.5 cm)
Gift of Time, Inc.

An expert at photographic technique, Burrows was the first photographer to cover a war comprehensively in color. In this scene, the white and bloodied bandages and the vulnerable pale flesh of the wounded man on the ground are all the more striking because they stand out against the muted grays and browns of the devastated landscape. The composed drama of the photograph recalls the stylized choreography of history painting from earlier centuries. Yet the picture's power lies no less in its vivid description of utter ruin and existential exhaustion than in our knowledge, through photography, that these are real men in a real place.

Burrows covered the Vietnam War for *Life* magazine from 1962 until his death at the age of forty-four, in 1971, when the helicopter carrying him to the invasion of Laos crashed. In his work, Burrows sought the center of violent action and attempted to describe its effects on people. He hoped that his photographs would "penetrate the hearts of those at home who are simply too indifferent" and that they would "show people what others go through."

CLAES OLDENBURG AMERICAN, BORN SWEDEN 1929

Giant Soft Fan. 1966–67

Construction of vinyl filled with foam rubber, wood, metal, and plastic tubing; fan, 10' x 58⁷/₈" x 61⁷/₈" (305 x 149.5 x 157.1 cm), variable; cord and plug, 24' 3¹/₄" (739.6 cm) long
The Sidney and Harriet Janis Collection

Pop art's gaze on the universe of commercial products is often deadpan and cool. With Oldenburg, though, it becomes more comically disorienting: sculptures like *Giant Soft Fan* challenge our acceptance of the everyday world both by rendering hard objects in soft materials, so that they sag and droop, and by greatly inflating their size. (There are also Oldenburg works that make soft objects hard.) The smooth, impersonal vinyl surfaces of *Giant Soft Fan* are Oldenburg's knowing inversion of the hard-edge aesthetic of the 1960s. There is humor in this transformation of a hard machine into a collapsible object, which, like Salvador Dalí's limp watches, has a not too elliptical bodily and sexual connotation. There is also a subtle nostalgia: in its focus on the culture of its time, Pop art seemed jarringly up-to-date in the 1960s, but this fan's design was old-fashioned even then.

Oldenburg often makes monumental public sculpture, enlarging his everyday objects to a scale far more enormous than even the *Giant Soft Fan*. Notes he wrote in 1967 show him playing with that idea: "The Fan's first placement was on Staten Island, blowing up the bay. Later, I sited it as a replacement for the Statue of Liberty ... [guaranteeing] workers on Lower Manhattan a steady breeze."

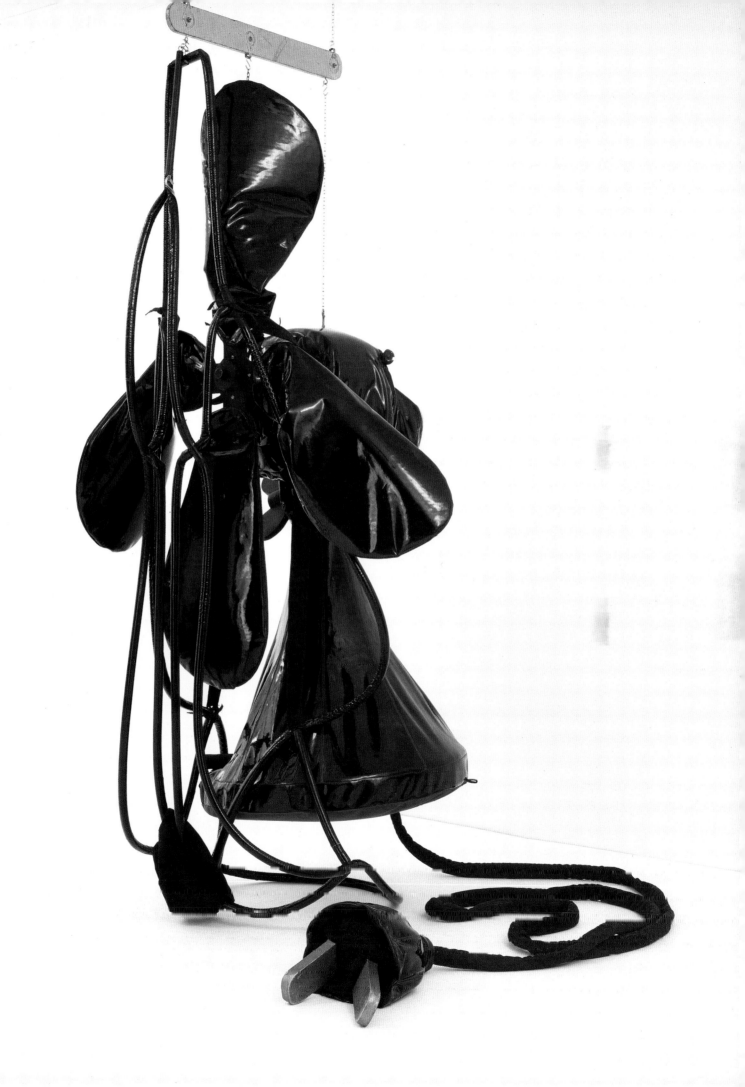

1967

Boy in a Straw Hat Waiting to March in Pro-War Parade, New York City. 1967
Gelatin silver print, 14³/₄ x 14¹/₂" (37.5 x 36.8 cm)
The Ben Schultz Memorial Collection.
Gift of the artist

Arbus approached photographic portraiture as a two-way street, through which a relationship is established between the viewer (who has taken the place of the photographer) and the subject. To experience the picture is to enter into that relationship, whose candor and depth may be assessed in just the same way that we gauge the sincerity of others every day—and as they judge ours.

Many of Arbus's subjects are outcasts of one sort or another, and many viewers are at first repelled or merely fascinated by her pictures. Only after these defenses are set aside are we able to see that the vulnerability of her people invites us to recognize our own.

Apart from a handful of pictures, including this one, Arbus did not address political issues directly. But her unsparing frankness in confronting human frailty is one of the signal achievements of American art in the dark days of the Vietnam War.

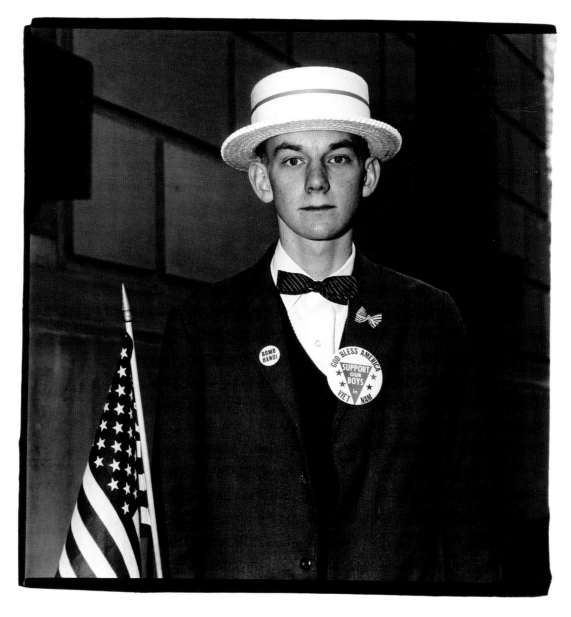

Untitled (Stack). 1967

Lacquer on galvanized iron, twelve units,
each 9 x 40 x 31" (22.8 x 101.6 x 78.7 cm),
installed vertically at 9" (22.8 cm) intervals
Helen Acheson Bequest (by exchange) and gift
of Joseph Helman

Sculpture must always face gravity, and the stack—one thing on top of another— is one of its basic ways of coping. The principle traditionally enforces a certain hierarchy, an upper object being not only usually different from a lower one but conceptually nobler, as when a statue stands on a pedestal. Yet in Judd's stack of galvanized-iron boxes, all of the units are identical; they are set on the wall and separated, so that none is subordinated to another's weight (and also so that the space around them plays a role in the work equivalent to theirs); and their regular climb—each of the twelve boxes is nine inches high, and they rest nine inches apart—suggests an infinitely extensible series, denying the possibility of a crowning summit. Judd's form of Minimalism reflected his belief in the equality of all things. "In terms of existing," he wrote, "everything is equal."

The field of Minimalist objects, however, is not an undifferentiated one—Judd also believed that sculpture needed what he called "polarization," some fundamental tension. Here, for example, the uniform boxes, their tops and undersides bare metal, suggest the industrial production line. Meanwhile their fronts and sides have a coat of green lacquer, which, although it is auto paint, is a little unevenly applied, and has a luscious glamour.

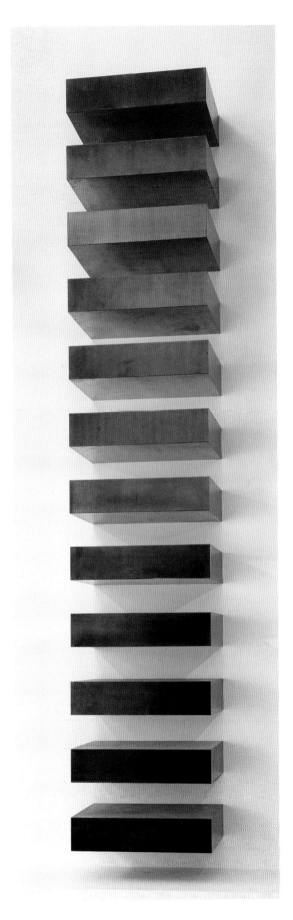

1967

1968

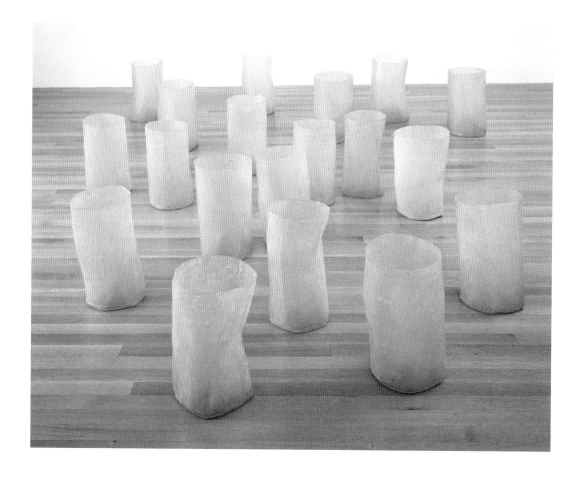

Repetition 19, III. 1968

Nineteen tubular fiberglass units, 19 to 20¹/₄" × 11 to 12³/₄" (48 to 51 cm × 27.8 to 32.3 cm) diam. Gift of Charles and Anita Blatt

Repetition 19, III comprises nineteen bucketlike forms, all the same shape but none exactly alike. Nor do they have a set order, since Hesse allowed latitude in placing them: "I don't ask that the piece be moved or changed, only that it could be moved and changed. There is not one preferred format." The Minimalist artists, who emerged a little before Hesse did, had explored serial repetitions of identical units. Hesse loosened that principle: *Repetition 19* is simultaneously repetitive and irregular. She also tended to work on a humbler scale than the Minimalists often had, and her forms and materials are less technocratic; she herself called the

forms in *Repetition 19* "anthropomorphic," and recognized sexual connotations in these "empty containers."

This fiberglass version of *Repetition 19*, is the third Hesse planned. (The first is in papier-mâché; the second, which she imagined first in metal, then in latex, was never completed.) Besides beautifully modulating the light, the fiberglass seems both soft and hard, contributing to the richly paradoxical character of these subtle objects: nonconformist individuals somehow make a group; the arrangement, whatever it is, is both random and coherent, unified by the similarity preserved through difference. And paradox is fitting here: Hesse wanted, she said, to make an art object that "accedes to its nonlogical self. It is something, it is nothing."

Untitled. 1968
Synthetic polymer paint on metal, 60³/₈"
(153.2 cm) diam.
Mrs. Sam A. Lewisohn Fund

This untitled work is a convex, spray-painted disk held a foot or so out from the wall by a central post. Its subtle, tactile surface modulates delicately from center to edge, and it is softly lit from four angles, creating a cloverleaf pattern of shadow. The white center of the disk can seem to lie level with the white wall, so that the eye spends time trying to understand what it sees—what is nearer and what is farther, what is solid and what is immaterial light, or even light's absence. For Irwin, the result is "this indeterminate physicality with different levels of weight and density, each on a different physical plane. It [is] very beautiful and quite confusing, everything starting and reversing."

Evading confinement by the rectangle of the conventional painting, Irwin's disks literally extend past their own boundaries—spread out into their environment, which is as much a part of them as their own substance. The idea, in part, extends the Abstract Expressionist notion of an infinite, all-encompassing, allover field, but with the qualification that for Irwin, "To be an artist is not a matter of making paintings or objects at all. What we are really dealing with is our state of consciousness and the shape of our perceptions."

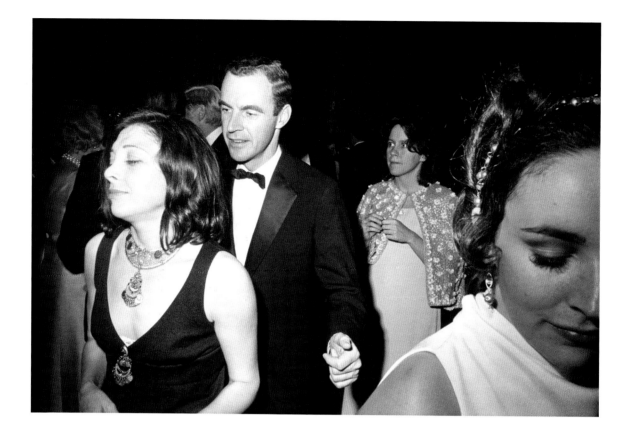

Centennial Ball, Metropolitan Museum, New York. 1969

Gelatin silver print, 10⅝ x 15⅞" (27 x 40.3 cm)
Purchase

This photograph invites any number of scenarios to explain the intimate drama at this fancy party, but declines to endorse any single one. Who, for example, might be romantically involved with whom? What has provoked the anxious stare of the woman in the background? We shall never know the answers to these questions.

Winogrand loved to observe the behavior of humans and other animals, and he loved photography's voracious capacity for description, but he did not confuse the two.

In his pictures he created a parallel theater of experience, the force of which resides not in the reliability of its facts but in the liveliness of its fictions.

This picture belongs to a long series, begun in the late 1960s, made at demonstrations, press conferences, and other gatherings whose participants expected to be noticed and, often, photographed. For the photographer Tod Papageorge, Winogrand's series vividly evokes the 1960s by offering "a unilateral report of how we behaved under pressure during a time of costumes and causes, and of how extravagantly, outrageously, and continuously we displayed what we wanted."

JACQUES MAHÉ DE LA VILLEGLÉ FRENCH, BORN 1926

122 rue du Temple. 1968
Torn-and-pasted printed papers on linen,
62⅝ x 82½" (159.2 x 209.6 cm)
Gift of Joachim Aberbach (by exchange)

The title of this work derives from the street in Paris from which these torn posters were taken. The layers of fragmentary color, words, and images of faces were pasted onto linen in a technique called *décollage* (literally, un-collage). In this technique, posters or other promotional materials are torn up to create new compositions, with one image often superimposed over another. Villeglé stated that *122 rue du Temple*, a combination of movie posters and political advertisements for a legislative election instigated by the events of May 1968 in Paris, is a reflection of reality. Thus, not only

is he interested in the visual impact and pictorial construction of his works, but he also confers upon them a sociological status.

Villeglé has devoted his entire career to *décollage*. He was affiliated with *Nouveau Réalisme*, a French art movement of the late 1950s and early 1960s devoted to transforming everyday objects and detritus into art in the belief that painting was incapable of conveying the actually of postwar society. Villeglé sees the street as a repository of ready-made art. He invented the persona of the anonymous passerby, or common man, whose random tears are "discovered" by the artist and thereby poeticized. Through this incorporation of chance and choice, Villeglé assumes the role of a conservator of works of art unconsciously created by others.

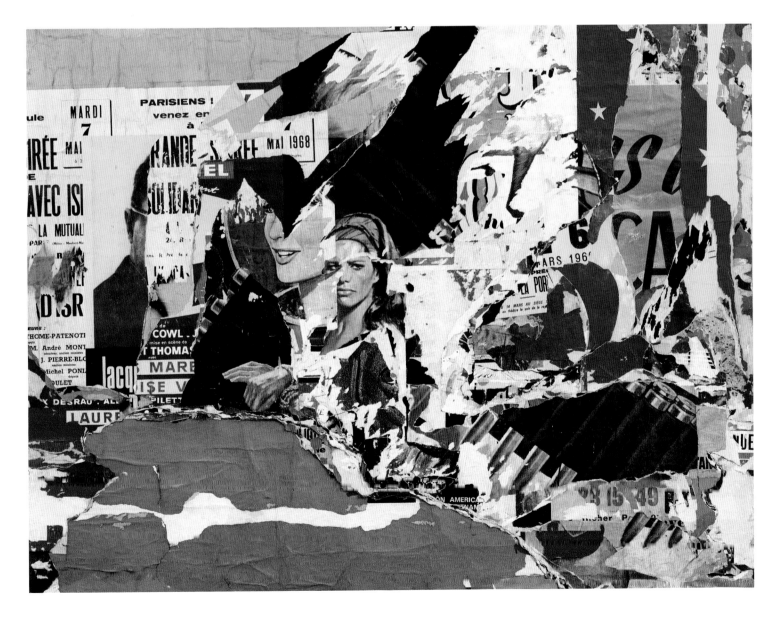

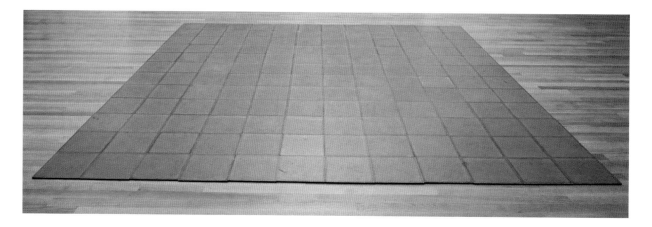

144 Lead Square. 1969

144 lead plates, each approx. ³/₈ x 12 x12"
(.9 x 30.5 x 30.5 cm), overall ³/₈" x 12'7⁄₈" x 12'1¹/₂"
(.9 x 367.8 x 369.2 cm)
Advisory Committee Fund

144 Lead Square is one of several works in which Andre abuts twelve-by-twelve-inch metal squares to form a larger square, also based on the number twelve (twelve feet to a side). In this case the metal is lead; elsewhere Andre uses aluminum, steel, zinc, copper, magnesium, and tin. What is fascinating is the complexity of the aesthetic ideas enforced in this simple plan.

Simplicity, after all, is itself an idea. *144 Lead Square* implicitly argues with the sculptural conventions that it refuses: an elevating base or pedestal, the craft and talent of shaping, high finish, even three-dimensionality. (Only marginally volumetric, *144 Lead Square* rises a mere ³/₈ of an inch off the floor.) Instead, Andre uses a straightforward system to organize flat modules of basic materials. It is the system, and the shape and size of the materials themselves, that determine the work's form. Each part of this Minimalist work is the same proportion of the whole, and no part commands more attention than any other.

"My works are not the embodiments of ideas or conceptions," Andre has said. "My works are, in the words of William Blake, 'The lineaments of Gratified Desire.'" There is indeed a sensuousness in Andre's approach to materials, and to the artwork's relationship with the surrounding space. Like Minimalism generally, however, his sculpture is fundamentally impersonal, and evinces a solemn austerity.

Untitled. 1969

Gray-green felt, draped, 15' ³/₄" x 6' ¹/₂" x 1"
(459.2 x 184.1 x 2.5 cm)
The Gilman Foundation Fund

Although Morris helped to define the principles of Minimal art, writing important articles on the subject, he was also an innovator in tempering the often severe appearance of Minimalism with a new plasticity—a literal softness. In works like this one, he subjected sheets of thick industrial felt to basic formal procedures (a series of parallel cuts, say, followed by hanging, piling, or even dropping in a tangle), then accepted whatever shape they took as the work of art. In this way he left the overall configuration of the work (a configuration he imagined as temporary) to the medium itself.

"Random piling, loose stacking, hanging, give passing form to material," Morris wrote. "Chance is accepted and indeterminacy is implied. ... Disengagement with preconceived enduring forms and orders for things is a positive assertion."

This work emphasizes the process of its making and the qualities of its material. But even if Morris was trying to avoid making form a "prescribed end," as a compositional scheme, the work has both formal elegance and psychological suggestiveness: the order and symmetry of the cut cloth is belied by the graceful sag at the top. In fact, a work produced by rigorous aesthetic theory ends up evoking the human figure. "Felt has anatomical associations," Morris has said, "it relates to the body—it's skinlike."

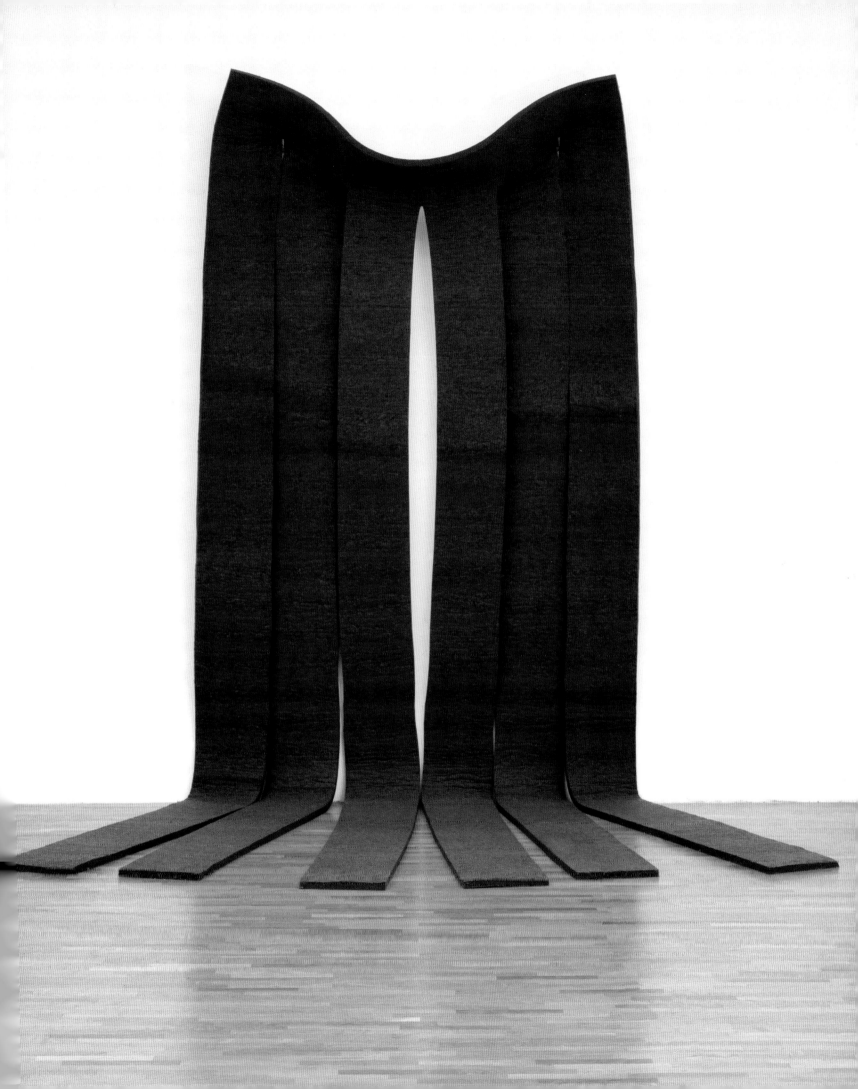

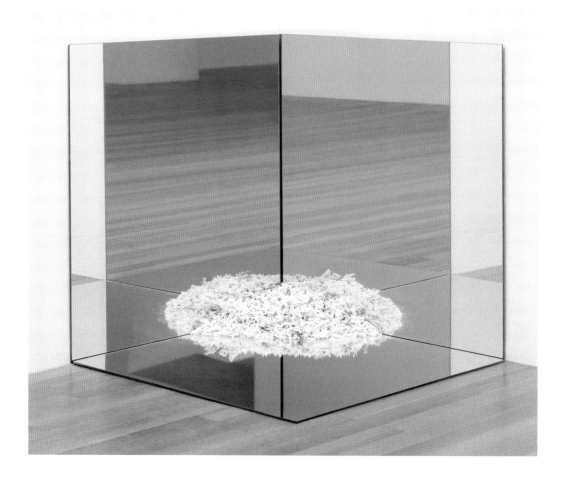

Corner Mirror with Coral. 1969

Mirrors and coral, 36 x 36 x 36"
(91.5 x 91.5 x 91.5 cm)
Fractional gift of Agnes Gund

Smithson's three mirrors in a corner create a structure both lucid and elusive: as each mirror reflects the space around it, it multiplies the reflections in the other mirrors, creating an image with the symmetry of a crystal. Mirrors appear often in Smithson's art, as do fragments of the natural world—here, there are pieces of coral piled in the angle where the mirrors meet. Smithson also combined mirrors with heaps of sand, gravel, and other rocks, matching nature's brute rubble with its precise visual twin. (The delicacy of the lacy pink coral is unusual in his work.) The pairing of matter and reflection corresponds to another duality: on the one hand, unshaped shards of stone or reef; on the other, art, sculpture, and the indoor space of the gallery.

One of the earthworks artists of the 1960s and 1970s, in other pieces Smithson manipulated the natural landscape, sometimes simply and temporarily, through mirrors, sometimes drastically, with a bulldozer. *Corner Mirror with Coral* relates to his "Non-Sites," indoor works containing substances from an outdoor site elsewhere. Both cerebral and powerfully material, his art shows a fascination with entropy, the tendency of all structures and energies to lose their integrity. In this work a perfect form—the mirrors make three sides of a cube—is made illogical and illusory, for the coral seems to float in midair.

Tizio Table Lamp. 1971
ABS plastic and aluminum, max. 46³/₄ x 42¹/₂"
(118.7 x 108 cm)
Manufacturer: Artemide S.p.A., Italy
Gift of the manufacturer

Sapper claimed that he designed the Tizio
lamp because he could not find a work lamp
that suited him: "I wanted a small head and
long arms; I didn't want to have to clamp the
lamp to the desk because it's awkward. And I
wanted to be able to move it easily." The
designer's dream lamp, the Tizio is an
adjustable table fixture that can be moved in
four directions. It swivels smoothly and can
be set in any position, its balance ensured by
a system of counterweights. The halogen
bulb, adjustable to two different light
intensities, is fed through the arm from a
transformer concealed in the base. In 1972,
when the Tizio lamp was first produced, the
use of the arms to conduct electricity was an
innovation seen in few other lamp designs.

From a formal point of view, the Tizio lamp
was revolutionary. Black, angled, minimalist,
and mysterious, the lamp achieved its real
commercial success in the early 1980s, when

its sleek look met the Wall Street boom. Found
in the residences of the young and successful
and in the offices of executives, the lamp has
become an icon of high-tech design.

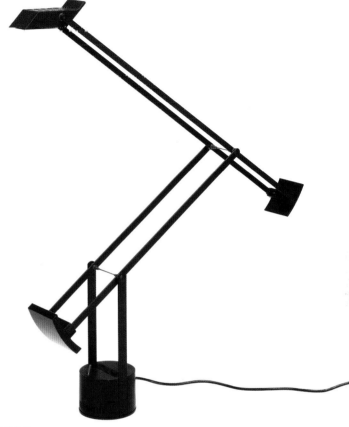

**Divisumma 18 Electronic Printing
Calculator**. 1972
Cast-injected ABS plastic body, flexible
synthetic rubber, and melamine, 1⁷/₈ x 9³/₄ x 5"
(4.8 x 24.8 x 12.7 cm)
Manufacturer: Ing. C. Olivetti & C., S.p.A., Italy
Design collaborators: Dario De Diana, Alessandro
De Gregori, Derk Jan De Vries, Antonio Macchi
Cassia, Gianni Pasini, and Sandro Pasqui
Gift of the manufacturer

It was hard to resist touching the Divisumma
18 calculator when it first appeared on the
market. Produced by Olivetti, for whom Bellini
began working as a chief
industrial design consultant
in 1963, it proved to be
enormously popular.
The Divisumma 18
was small and
portable, in contrast
to earlier computing
machinery, much of which looked

like heavy cabinetry. The keyboard, with its
nipplelike buttons, is encased in Bellini's
typical rubber skin, which in this design is a
playful yellow.

In the 1960s, Bellini began his career at a
turning point in the history of twentieth-
century design: the transition from
mechanical to microelectronic technology. To
accommodate rapidly changing technology
and increasing miniaturization, new products
had to be designed. Bellini was able to link
the necessities of the developing electronics
industry to contemporary visual culture by
emphasizing tactile qualities and taking
advantage of the expressive possibilities of
such new materials as plastic. Bellini made
industrial products desirable by injecting into
his designs subtle anthropomorphic
references, which stimulate emotional
responses. Plastic, leather, or rubber, for
example, may have the sensual properties of
human skin.

257

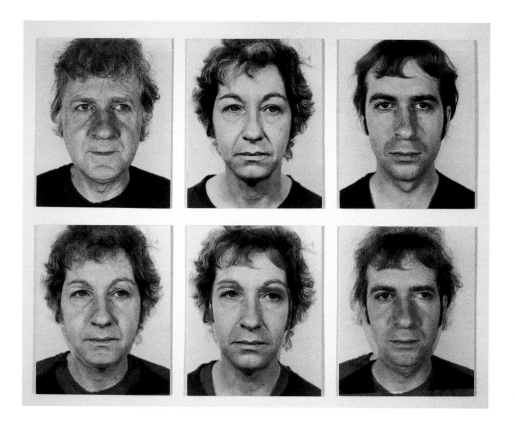

Family Combinations. 1972
Six gelatin silver prints, each 12⁷/₈ x 10³/₁₆"
(31.6 x 25.9 cm)
Gift of Robert and Gayle Greenhill

The top row of this tableau of six pictures represents, from right to left, Wegman, his mother, and his father. The bottom row consists of superimpositions of all possible combinations of any two of the three images above. The combinations resemble the sorts of pictures that once circulated as scientific illustrations of racial and social types. The humor of Wegman's tableau derives from the deadpan sincerity with which he has reenacted this absurd operation.

Photographs perform many banal functions in our everyday lives, so banal that we rarely stop to think about them. The head shots that appear on identity cards and drivers' licenses are good examples. In the early 1970s Wegman helped to lead an artistic movement that emulated the look of such photographs but short-circuited their functions. The idea was to invite us to consider the meanings we attach to these pictures, and so to explore our habits of thought and our social arrangements. Wegman's talent for comedy has been evident from the beginning, but it took a while to see that his playful wit is colored by kindness and warmth.

Grove Group, I. 1973
Oil and wax on canvas, 6' x 9' ¹⁄₈"
(182.8 x 274.5 cm)
Treadwell Corporation Fund

The beautiful blue-gray-green of *Grove Group, I* was inspired by the colors Marden saw in a stand of olive trees in Greece, and he has described works like this one as referring to nature. Yet this monochromatic painting is far from the "window on the world" of the conventional landscape, and even from the sense that many abstract pictures allow of opening onto another space. Working in a sensuous mix of oil paint and wax, Marden creates a surface of substance and mass, opaque and dense. At the same

time, that mass seems weightless, that density luminescent: it is as if, in carefully building up the surface, Marden had been able to trap within its layers the light that saw its making.

The painting comes from a series of five, dating from 1973–76. In each of the other four works, monochrome panels, in different but related colors, abut to produce an overall format of the same size and shape as the single-panel *Grove Group, I*. This modular and methodical design recalls the strategies of Minimal art, but few Minimalists would call their work "highly emotional," as Marden has. "The paintings are made in highly subjective states," the artist says, though he adds, "within Spartan limitations."

Robert/104,072. 1973–74

Synthetic polymer paint and ink with graphite
on gessoed canvas, 9 x 7' (274.4 x 213.4 cm)
Gift of J. Frederic Byers III and promised gift
of an anonymous donor

"No work of art was ever made without a
process," Close has said, and
Robert/104,072 was made by a painstaking
process indeed: it is composed of tiny black
dots, each set inside a single square of a
104,072-square grid. The sense of shape
and texture—of the distinction between metal
and skin, between knitted sweater and bushy
mustache—depends on the density of the
paint, which Close applied with a spray gun,
revisiting each square an average of ten
times. Not surprisingly, the work took fourteen
months to make.

When Close began to paint portraits, in
1967–68, figurative painting was widely
considered exhausted. The figures in Pop art
were coolly ironic; and other artists were
painting abstractions, or were abandoning
painting altogether for more conceptual
systems of art-making. Close preferred to
apply a conceptual system to a traditional
mode of painting. The aggressive scale
makes the system clear—close up, the
gridded dots in *Robert/104,072* are quite
apparent—and the black-and-white palette
reflects the image's source in a photograph.

Robert/104,072 announces itself as less
illusion than code. For Close, a picture like this
one is not "a painting of a person as much as
it is the distribution of paint on a flat surface.
... You really have to understand the artificiality
of what you are doing to make the reality."

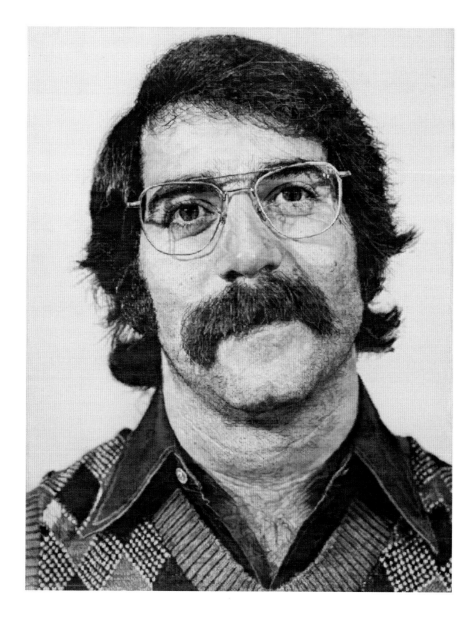

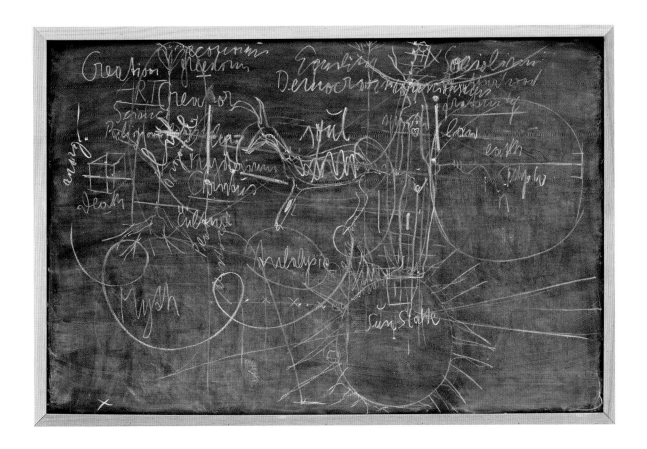

Untitled (Sun State). 1974
Chalk on painted board with wood frame,
47¹/₂" x 6' (120.7 x 183 cm)
Gift of Abby Aldrich Rockefeller and acquired
through the Lillie P. Bliss Bequest (by exchange)

This drawing unites the cosmic and
terrestrial, as it maps an ideal state in which
the social order is conceived as a living
organism, intimately linked to a balanced
natural order. Each motif is a metaphor: the
sun creates energy, which circulates by
means of a looping line; through alchemy it
takes form in a threefold system of culture—
art, science, and religion—and travels toward
the ideal state; this life principle is balanced
by the death principle, and the earth by the
primary actor, Man, an androgynous figure
accompanied by an emblem of his
animalistic and spiritual nature—the stag.

Untitled (*Sun State*) is one of Beuys's
Blackboard drawings, which were created
during his lectures at educational institutions
and museums. This drawing evolved during
his participation in the public dialogue, "Art
into Society, Society into Art" at The Art
Institute of Chicago in 1974. Here Beuys
demonstrates, with a thin looping line and
verbal descriptions, the connections among
myth, alchemy, astrology, anthropology, and
the social and political sciences. The result is
a work described by the artist as a kind of
astrological chart embodying his ideas of the
ideal state, in which democratic principles
inform cultural life (freedom), law (equality),
and economics (fraternity). It is a constellation
delineating a structure for a harmonious social
body, or, alternatively, a social sculpture—an
evolutionary process whose goal is to "sculpt
new models for the entirety of life."

1976

Axes. 1976

Synthetic polymer paint, gesso, charcoal, and pencil on canvas, 64⁵/₈" x 8' 8⁷/₈" (164.2 x 266.4 cm)
Purchased with the aid of funds from the National Endowment for the Arts

"By the middle of the '70s," Rothenberg has said, "I sensed that people were tired of Minimal and Conceptual art. It made sense to paint an image of something you could recognize and feel something about." Having found herself doodling a horse on a bit of canvas in 1973, Rothenberg shortly began a series of full-scale paintings of horses. These works anticipated the powerful return of figurative and subjective content in American and European art of the late 1970s and 1980s.

Rothenberg, however, runs the emotional immediacy of figurative art through the filter of abstraction. In *Axes*, her working of the paint favors its material presence over its illusionistic or expressive possibilities. The body of the horse is a largely flat white—there is little modeling to give it volume or detail to give it character. It shares that white with the ground around it, which it traverses improbably slantwise, and straight lines cross both body and ground, insisting that they are constituents of the same flat surface. The result is neither wholly representational nor wholly abstract, and reflects the ideas of its time even while it breaks from them: "I was able to stick to the philosophy of the day—keeping the painting flat and anti-illusionist—but I also got to use this big, soft, heavy, strong, powerful form."

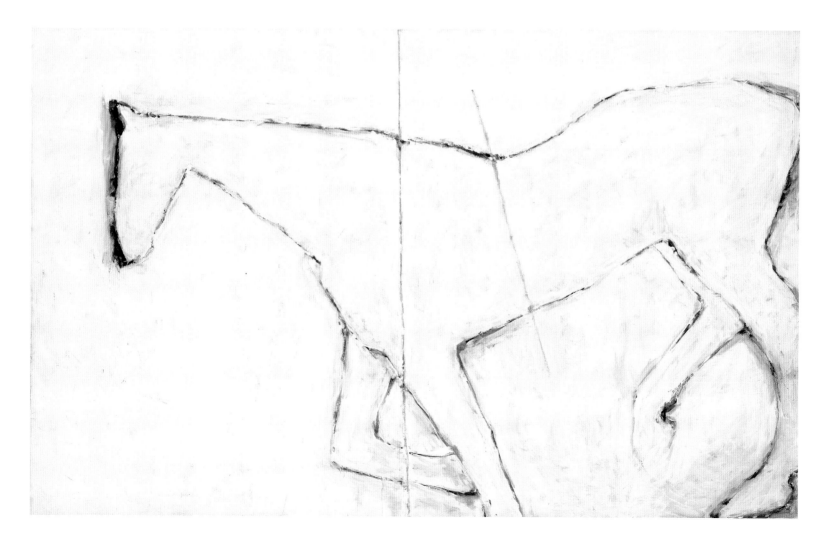

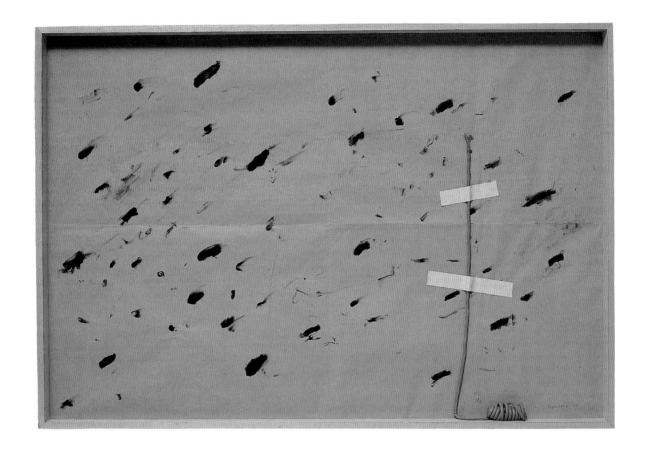

Untitled. 1977
Synthetic polymer paint, tallow, and adhesive
tape on brown paper, 39¹/₄ x 58¹/₈"
(99.6 x 147.6 cm)
Gift of Barbara G. Pine

In this drawing, a thin roll of tallow with a
wick, symbolizing an extinguished candle,
is attached with two strips of white tape to a
sheet of brown paper. The background is
splattered with irregular dark blue smudges
of paint that recall smudges of smoke. These
irregular spots evoke marks made by the
burning wick of the tallow cord. The work
invites the viewer to question its very
structure and the meaning of its unusual
combination of composite elements.

Always confrontational and forceful, yet
beautiful and often poetic, Kounellis's work
engages the viewer on several levels: visual,
emotional, and physical. It represents the
artist's commentary on the surrounding reality
and reflects his political attitudes. For
example, his Fire installations of the late
1960s related his optimistic belief in
revolutionary fervor, whereas the Smoke
works of the early 1970s are symbolic of
extinguished revolutionary zeal. According
to Kounellis, "Smoke creates ghosts" and
is a metaphor for history and the passage
of time.

Kounellis's art is closely identified with the
Italian Arte Povera movement of the mid-
1960s. Encompassing both an aesthetic and
a political dimension, the movement
emphasized the use of everyday, poor
(*povera*) non-art materials raised to the level
of art through the artist's intervention, thus
attempting a merger of art and life.

1978

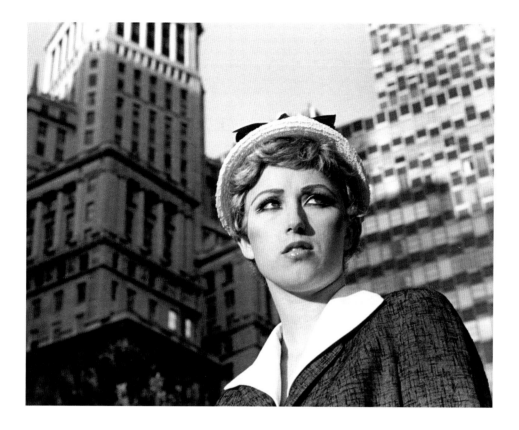

Untitled Film Still #21. 1978
Gelatin silver print, 7¹/₂ x 9¹/₂ " (19.1 x 24.1 cm)
Purchase

Each of Sherman's sixty-nine *Untitled Film Stills* (1977–80), presents a female heroine from a movie we feel we must have seen. Here, she is the pert young career girl in a trim new suit on her first day in the big city. Among the others are the luscious librarian (#13), the chic starlet at her seaside hideaway (#7), the ingenue setting out on life's journey (#48), and the tough but vulnerable film noir idol (#54). To make the pictures, Sherman herself played all of the roles or, more precisely, played all of the actresses playing all of the roles. In other

words, the series is a fiction about a fiction, a deft encapsulation of the image of femininity that, through the movies, took hold of the collective imagination in postwar America— the period of Sherman's youth, and the crucible of our contemporary culture.

In fact, only a handful of the *Untitled Film Stills* are modeled directly on particular roles in actual movies, let alone on individual stills of the sort that the studios distribute to publicize their films. All the others are inventive allusions to generic types, and so our sure sense of recognition is all the more telling. It tells us that, knowingly or not, we have absorbed the movie culture that Sherman invites us to examine as a powerful force in our lives.

Cornish Stone Circle. 1978
Fifty-two stone slabs (Delabole slate), overall
19' 8³/₈" (600 cm) diam.
Gift of Barbara Jakobson and John R. Jakobson,
Junior Council, and Anonymous Funds

Ancient stone circles survive at scattered sites in many parts of Long's native England, relics of the country's distant past. In evoking these local and age-old forms, *Cornish Stone Circle* bypasses the classical tradition of sculpture in favor of "primitive" art, an influence on artists since the early twentieth century. Long's art, however, also inflects more recent ideas.

   Like certain Minimalist sculptures, *Cornish Stone Circle* has no base or pedestal, no height to speak of, nor is it even an intact mass. More, its mass is mutable: the circle must be three meters in radius, and its fifty-two rough stones must be stably situated, evenly distributed and separated, and randomly arranged, but otherwise their placement is open to change. Long's most searching revision of the character of the art object, however, has to do with his relationship with the natural environment. Like other earthworks artists, he is attracted to outdoor, often remote, terrain, where he may pile stones, mark a path, or simply take a long walk; later he may exhibit photographs, maps, or written descriptions of these actions, for his work shares Conceptual art's concern with the different experiences conveyed by different visual and verbal systems. In this context, *Cornish Stone Circle* becomes not only a sculptural configuration but a way of representing a far-off place, through the presence of materials gathered there.

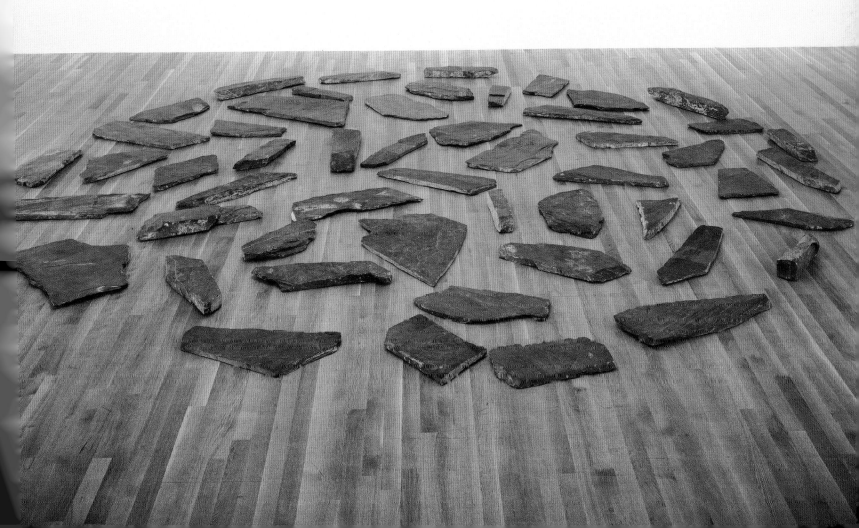

BILL VIOLA AMERICAN, BORN 1951

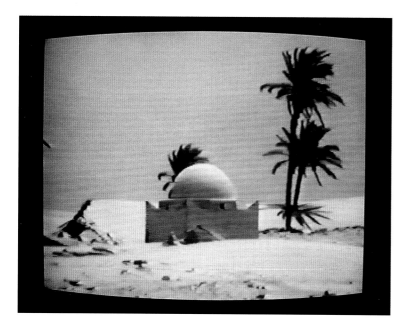

Chott el-Djerid (A Portrait in Light and Heat). 1979

³/₄" video, color, sound, 28 minutes
Gift of Catherine V. Meacham

Chott el-Djerid (A Portrait in Light and Heat) almost magically captures the optical and acoustic distortions of nature. Focused on landscape, the video work dwells briefly on

the snowy plains of midwestern America and Saskatchewan, then abruptly switches to the arid Tunisian desert. Viola investigates the world of illusion and how it is made. He works by slowly discovering the distinctive character of a place, probing its power and energy, drawing upon the associations it evokes, and searching instinctively for its archetypal symbols. In Tunisia, he was fascinated by the pastel-colored desert mirages floating mysteriously near the horizon.

To shoot *Chott el-Djerid*, the artist used one video camera set on a tripod and meticulously framed his subject from a fixed vantage point. He would only begin filming when he considered ideal atmospheric conditions to have occurred; at times he waited up to several days. He moved his camera only a few inches forward or backward between many shots so that he could fabricate a zoom during editing. In his studio, Viola carefully developed the rhythm of this nonverbal narrative of ordinary events happening in real time. Its pace compels viewers to assume a mindset of dreamlike suspended animation. It is filled with ambient natural sounds that temper its sense of otherworldliness: for example, the viewer first identifies an oncoming pair of motorcycles through aural, rather than visual, cues.

RICHARD DIEBENKORN AMERICAN, 1922–1993

Ocean Park 115. 1979

Oil on canvas, 8' 4" x 6' 9" (254 x 205.6 cm)
Mrs. Charles G. Stachelberg Fund

Diebenkorn's Ocean Park series, begun in 1967, makes general reference to the beachside land- and cityscape of the neighborhood in Santa Monica, California, around the artist's studio. The series is the work of an artist who synthesized the principal currents of the twentieth century's most rigorous abstract art (after painting representationally), joined it to a painterly 1950s sensibility, and created a new style with both the seriousness and the decorativeness of his exemplars, and with a gentle but firm sensuousness that is entirely his own. The work uses the components of

Piet Mondrian's mature art, but escapes from the form of geometry that Mondrian had adapted from Cubism to learn more from the less confining structures, and the breathing surfaces, of Barnett Newman and Mark Rothko. But Diebenkorn recomplicates the spareness of those artists' fields, reintroducing a searching, durational record of the work's creation.

The influence of another touchstone for Diebenkorn, Henri Matisse, is apparent in *Ocean Park 115*, as in the rest of the series, in the way the space is divided into flat planes and bands of color. Built up of successive layers of pigment, the painting's blues and greens shift in their density, invoking a translucent luminosity.

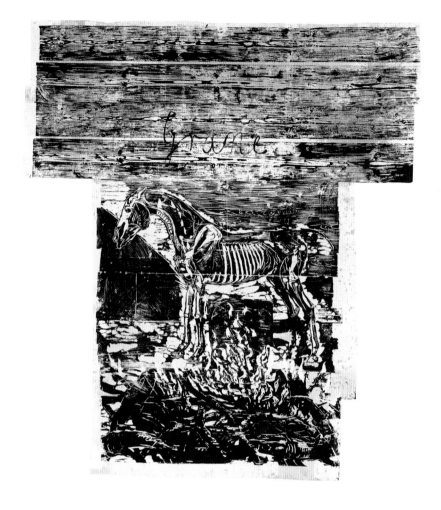

Grane. 1980–93

Woodcut with paint additions, comp.:
9' 1¹/₁₆" x 8' 2¹/₂" (277.1 x 250.3 cm) (irreg.)
Edition: unique

Purchased with funds given in honor of Riva Castleman by The Committee on Painting and Sculpture, The Associates of the Department of Prints and Illustrated Books, Molly and Walter Bareiss, Nelson Blitz, Jr. with Catherine Woodard and Perri and Allie Blitz, Agnes Gund, The Philip and Lynn Straus Foundation Fund, Howard B. Johnson, Mr. and Mrs. Herbert D. Schimmel, and the Riva Castleman Endowment Fund

The title of this work refers to Brunhilde's horse in the renowned operatic cycle, *The Ring*, by Richard Wagner. Near the opera's end, Brunhilde, in grief over the murder of the hero Siegfried, makes a funeral pyre for him and rides her horse, Grane, into the flames to join her beloved in death. The rigid skeletal horse positioned over flames, the primeval scorched landscape, and the tombstonelike format of the composition directly allude to death.

Much of the power of this image derives from Kiefer's forceful use of the woodcut medium; in the jagged edges of the white areas we sense the artist's bold cutting of the woodblock. For climactic drama, he applied white paint to heighten the flames and orange-brown staining for the smoldering glow surrounding the scene. The monumental size of this work required thirteen sheets of paper to be joined together and mounted on linen.

Kiefer has created a large body of work exploring his nation's identity and the moral and philosophical issues facing post–World War II Germany. His imagery contains references to his country's historical and cultural past but also serves as a metaphor for universal suffering, sacrifice, and destruction.

Pair of Rock Chairs. 1980–81
Gneiss, a: 49$^1/_4$ x 43$^1/_2$ x 40"
(125.1 x 110.5 x 101.6 cm); b: 44 x 66 x 42$^1/_2$"
(111.6 x 167.7 x 108 cm)
Acquired through the Philip Johnson, Mr. and
Mrs. Joseph Pulitzer, Jr., and Robert
Rosenblum Funds

From behind, these sculptures resemble
nothing so much as half-buried boulders, or
the tips of submerged outcrops of living rock.
It is only from the front that they show the
results of human artifice: two simple cuts,
one horizontal, one vertical. In each stone
the result is a flat and ample ledge with an
upright back—an invitation to sit.

The opportunity extended by *Pair of Rock
Chairs* is actually not only physical but social,
for two seats will tempt two people to rest
and talk. Burton had a deep interest in social
exchange—in fact, his first artworks were
performances in front of an audience. His
sculpture developed out of the furniture he
used as props in these performances, and
always remains part furniture, undermining
the common notion that art is somehow
separate from everyday life. Burton admired
the Russian Constructivist artists who, earlier
in the century, had linked innovative forms to
a concern with their practical social
applications. The natural shapes of these
chairs, and their beautiful surface—variously
rough and smooth, and veined in gray and
white—inject aesthetic pleasure into their
obvious usefulness.

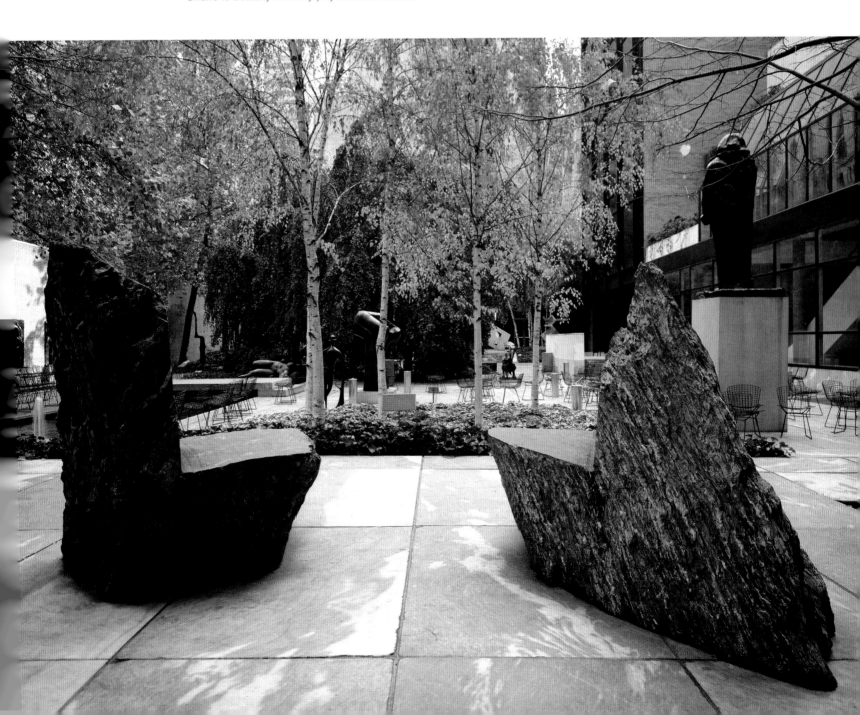

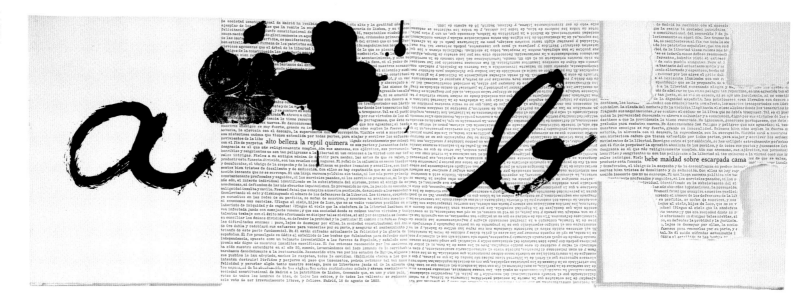

Anular by José-Miguel Ullán. 1981
Illustrated book with 23 etchings, page: 12⁷/₈ x
9⁷/₁₆" (32.7 x 24 cm) (irreg.)
Publisher: R.L.D., Paris. Edition: 150
Abby Aldrich Rockefeller Fund (by exchange)

Anular—the word means to nullify or
invalidate—presents a copy of an early
Spanish constitution displayed as a single-
spaced typewritten manuscript overlaid with
Ullán's short poetic phrases and Tàpies's
cryptic alphabet letters and symbol-like forms.
Tàpies's super-imposed letters, looking like
graffiti strewn across the pages, derive from
the first character of the poet's adjacent
words. Frequently portions of the text are torn,
turned upside-down, or even obscured by
Tàpies's "graffiti," possibly suggesting a
disregard for the constitutional rights of
individuals. The overall visual effect produces

a sense of contradiction and dissent, while
also implying an act of nullification. Tàpies
had lived through the many years of Franco's
rule in Spain, and, at the time of the book's
execution, Ullán was living in exile due to his
refusal to serve in the military.

As seen in the four-page spread displayed
here, each sheet is attached at its left and
right edges to the next sheet. The pages are
assembled in an accordion fold, making
possible various panoramas. Pages can be
turned one by one in the conventional
manner, revealing a double-page spread; the
continuous ensemble can be completely
unfolded to show the entirety of text and
images; or selected segments can be
opened and spread out, as here. The
resulting effect of this unusual book format is
the creation of a world of words, an ongoing
dialogue between painter and poet.

The Departure of the Argonaut

by Alberto Savinio. 1983–86

Illustrated book with 49 photolithographs,
page: 25⁹/₁₆ x 19¹¹/₁₆" (65 x 50 cm)
Publisher: Petersburg Press, New York
and London. Edition: 288
Gift of Petersburg Press Inc.

Clemente's composition flows across this
double-page spread, overlapping and almost
obscuring the text beneath. The large figure
in the center is echoed in the smaller
figures—resembling paper dolls joined at the
hands and feet—that radiate from it. The
careful placement of turquoise ink allows the
text to be decipherable.

This text, a poetic diary titled *The
Departure of the Argonaut*, was written in
1917–18 by the Italian artist Savinio (an alias
of Andrea de Chirico, the younger brother of
the celebrated painter Giorgio de Chirico). It
recounts Savinio's travels as a soldier from
northern Italy to the Macedonian front near
Salonika. The title alludes to another voyage
in the same part of the world, the
mythological journey of Jason and the
Argonauts in search of the Golden Fleece.
Clemente's enormous admiration for Savinio's
book, which he referred to as his Bible, led to
his decision to illustrate it.

Clemente has been associated with a
1980s avant-garde movement known as Neo-
Expressionism, in which the figure played a
significant role. In this work the human form
assumes center stage, offering a visual
complement to the written text.

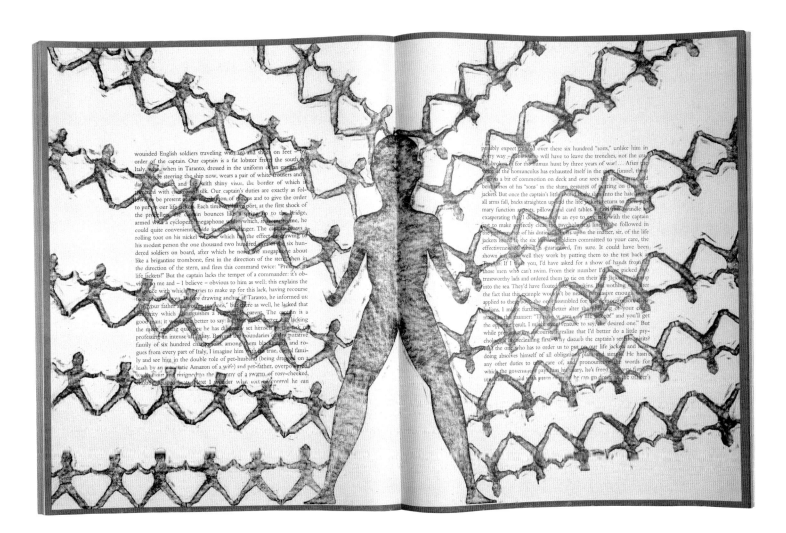

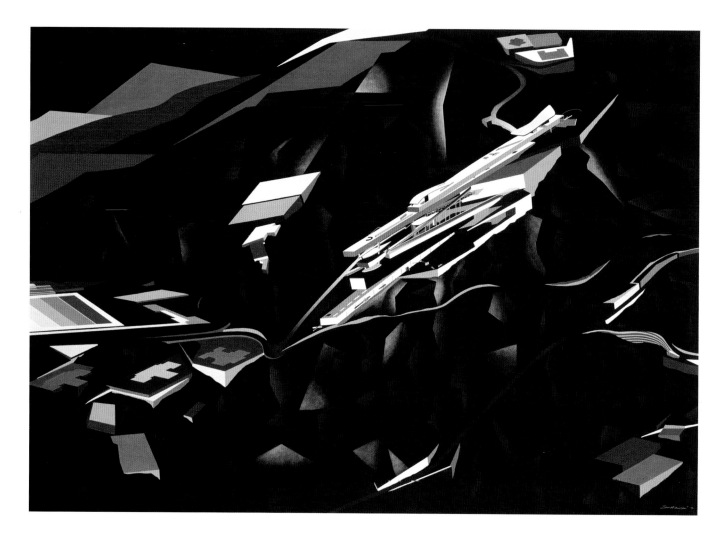

The Peak, Kowloon, Hong Kong. Project, 1983
Exterior perspective, 1991: acrylic on paper, mounted on canvas, 51" x 6' (129.5 x 183 cm)
David Rockefeller, Jr. Fund

This project by Hadid, whose work has been called "deconstructivist," was the winning design in a competition for a private club to be located in the hills of Kowloon, overlooking Hong Kong. Hadid proposed a transformation of the site itself by excavating the hills and using the excavated rock to build artificial cliffs. Into this new topography, she interjected cantilevered beams, shardlike fragments, and other elements that seemed to splinter the structure into its myriad constituent parts, as if it had been subjected to some powerful destabilizing force.

Seemingly defiant of gravity, the forms of Hadid's project hover and float, animated by the same visionary power that marked the ground-breaking Constructivist structures that Vladimir Tatlin, El Lissitzky, and Moisei Ginzburg imagined would arise in a new, postrevolutionary Soviet society. That seeming instability, which can also be found in the works of a number of other architects active in the 1980s, has been related to the literary movement of deconstruction, whose principal interpreter, the French philosopher Jacques Derrida, has become a familiar figure within contemporary debates on architectural theory.

White Anger, Red Danger, Yellow Peril, Black Death. 1984

Two steel beams, four painted metal chairs, and cable, overall 62³/₄" x 17' 11¹/₈" x 16' (159.4 x 546.4 x 487.7 cm)
Gift of Werner and Elaine Dannheisser

Two steel girders hang in an X-shape. Slid over them are three chairs (variously seatless, backless, and legless) in different metals, one red, one yellow, one black, while a fourth metal chair, in white, hangs adjoining—the girders may hit it if they swing or spin. Usually designed for rest and comfort, chairs here grow precarious, both menaced and menacing.

Escaping convenient labeling by school or style, Nauman has explored many materials and art forms—fiberglass, video, neon, installation, drawing, and more. He emerged alongside the Conceptual artists of the 1960s, and although his work is often more concretely physical than theirs, he shares their interest in the functioning of language. Nauman sees artmaking not primarily as the creation of aesthetic form but as a question of picking apart the habits of perception and structures of language that dictate the meaning of the work of art.

The title *White Anger, Red Danger, Yellow Peril, Black Death* invokes perennial fears and prejudices: racism, xenophobia, plague. Nauman's art, he says, "comes out of being frustrated about the human condition. And about how people refuse to understand other people." Given the animosities and anxieties cited in the work's title, the chairs' tensely dangling balance can be seen as conjuring the instability of the global equilibrium, but with a stringency surpassing verbal metaphor.

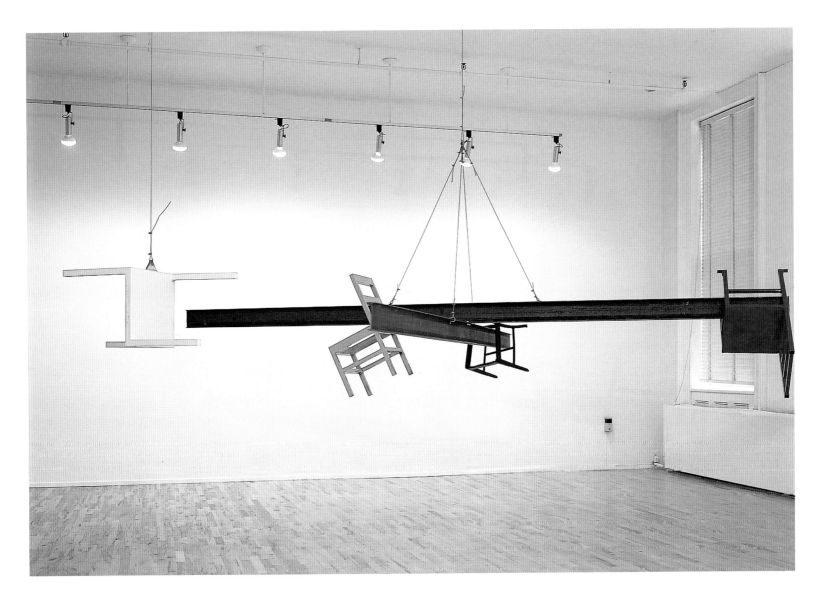

1984

Pace. 1984
Synthetic polymer paint on fiberglass on wood
with aluminum, 59¹/₂ x 26 x 28"
(151.2 x 66 x 71.1 cm)
Gift of an anonymous donor and gift of
Ronald S. Lauder

Like his Minimalist contemporaries, Ryman is
a carefully systematic artist, but he has a
painter's respect for the qualities of surface
and touch. To examine the medium
methodically, he imposes two limitations: his

paintings are white, and square. Yet white,
Ryman shows, changes dramatically
depending on what paint is used and how it
is applied. Paint lies differently on different
supports, and Ryman has used a gamut of
materials besides canvas, including
cardboard, wood, and aluminum. The scale
of his works varies widely. Exploring the way
the painting stands against the wall, Ryman
has used all the stages between near flush
and deep relief. He has also made the
painting's hanging devices integral to the
composition.

In *Pace* the painting is horizontal. The
narrow edge of the work is unpainted
redwood. The upward plane is fiberglass,
and is painted in a reflective white enamel,
while the underside, also white, has a soft,
light-absorbent surface. The painting is
supported by wall fasteners and aluminum
legs.

Paintings are always hung vertically
against the wall, Ryman realized, because
pictures "need to be seen that way. I thought
... since I'm not really making pictures, a
work could possibly not be vertical. It could
be just the opposite. ... I thought I was a little
crazy, but I thought, 'I'll try it; it'll be
interesting, a challenge.'"

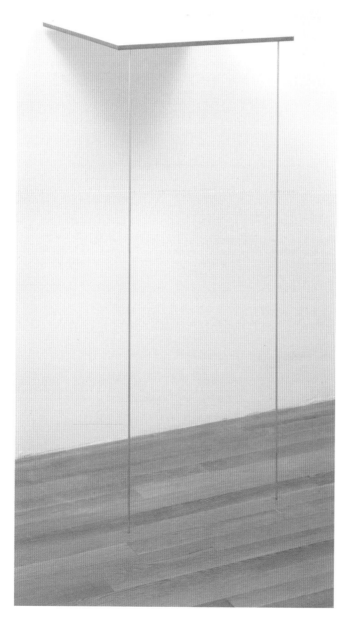

274

FRANK O. GEHRY AMERICAN, BORN CANADA 1929

Bubbles Chaise Longue. 1987
Corrugated cardboard with fire-retardant coating,
27³/₄" x 29" x 6' 4³/₈" (70.5 x 73.7 x 194 cm)
Manufacturer: New City Editions, USA
Kenneth Walker Fund

Gehry worked with an unexpected, throwaway material—corrugated cardboard—in two series of surprisingly sturdy and humorous home furnishings. The instant success of the first series, Easy Edges, introduced in 1972, earned him national recognition. Gehry conceived its cardboard tables, chairs, bed frames, rocking chairs, and other items to suit the homes of young as well as old, of urban sophisticates as well as country dwellers. The Bubbles Chaise Longue belongs to Experimental Edges, the second series, which was introduced in 1979. These objects

were intended to be artworks; yet they are sturdy enough for regular use. As the cardboard wears, it begins to appear suedelike and soft. Gehry's material lends itself to the curving form of this chair, its rollicking folds are, perhaps, a play on the corrugations themselves.

Heavily marketed and intentionally inexpensive, this furniture epitomized Gehry's interest in promoting affordable good design. The choice of "lowbrow" cardboard for Bubbles reflects Gehry's broad interest in using industrial, commercial, and utilitarian materials. An award-winning architect, he has worked with exposed chainlink fencing, corrugated metal, and plywood in concurrent architectural projects. In both the furniture series and the buildings, Gehry has given value to seemingly worthless materials by using them to create lasting designs.

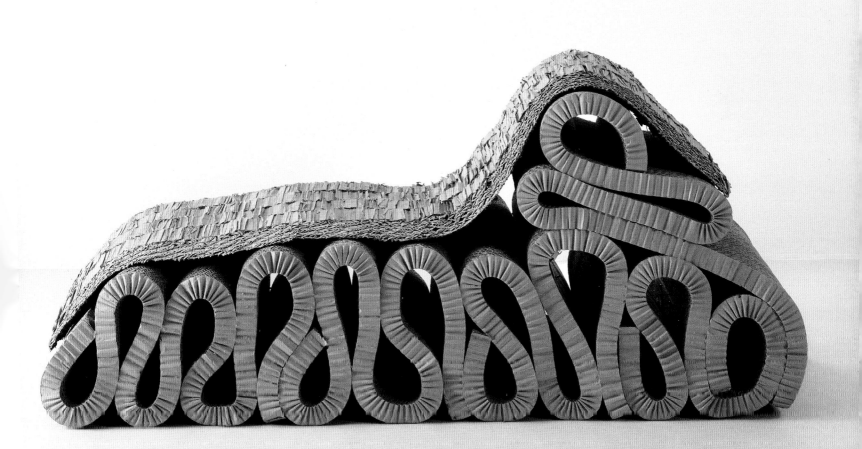

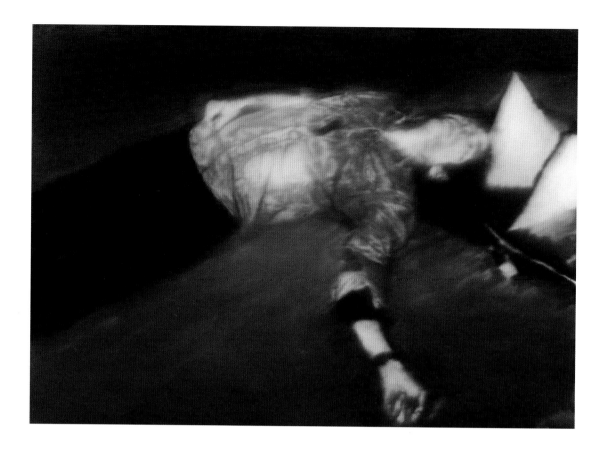

October 18, 1977. 1988

Fifteen paintings, oil on canvas, installation
variable, from 13³/₄ x 15¹/₂" (35 x 40 cm)
to 6'6³/₄" x 10' 6" (200 x 320 cm); shown: *Man
Shot Down*, 39¹/₂ x 55¹/₄" (100.5 x 140.5 cm)
Purchase

On *October 18, 1977*, Andreas Baader, Jan-
Carl Raspe, and Gudrun Ensslin were found
dead in their cells in a Stuttgart prison. The
three were members of the Red Army
Faction, a coalition of young political radicals
led by Baader and Ulrike Meinhof, who had
earlier hung herself in police custody. Turning
to violence in the late 1960s, the Baader-
Meinhof group had become Germany's most
feared terrorists. Although the prisoners'
deaths were pronounced suicides, the
authorities were suspected of murder.

The fifteen works in *October 18, 1977*
evoke fragments from the lives and deaths of
the Baader-Meinhof group. Richter has
worked in a range of styles over the years,
including painterly and geometric abstraction
as well as varieties of realism based on
photography; the slurred and murky motifs of
this work derive from newspaper and police
photographs or television images. Shades of
gray dominate, the absence of color
conveying the way these second-hand
images from the mass media sublimate their
own emotional content. An almost cinematic
repetition gives an impression, as if in slow
motion, of the tragedy's inexorable unfolding.
Produced during a prosperous, politically
conservative era eleven years after the
events, and insisting that this painful and
controversial subject be remembered, these
paintings are widely regarded as among the
most challenging works of Richter's career.

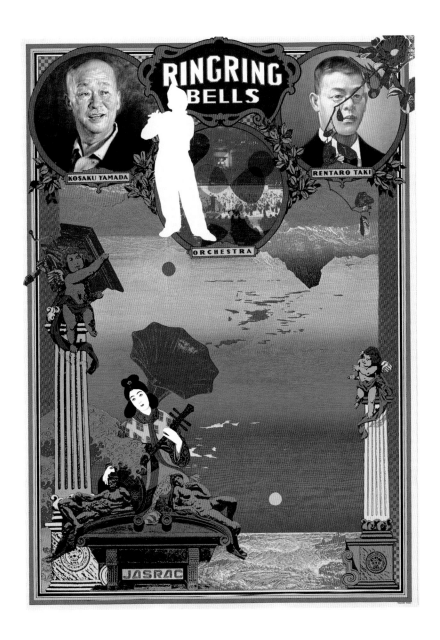

Japanese Society for the Rights of Authors, Composers, and Publishers.
1988
Poster: silkscreen, 40¹/₂ x 28⁵/₈" (102.9 x 72.7 cm)
Gift of the designer

Yokoo's designs characteristically possess a level of personal expression that is remarkable within the graphic arts; the subjects being publicized frequently seem only incidental to the overall design. Craftsmanship is also of paramount importance to Yokoo, who utilizes an elaborate silkscreen process that is unusual in the production of posters, which are ephemeral. His challenges to the commercial nature of the poster are in many respects an homage to traditional Japanese *ukiyo-e*

prints, woodblocks produced for the popular market.

In contemporary culture, the individual is increasingly inundated and bombarded with vast amounts of visual information relayed by a variety of means, including television, film, digital media, and print. Combining visual motifs from a multiplicity of cultures and periods, Yokoo's eclectic graphic art reflects this complexity. Included in this poster are references to Édouard Manet's painting *The Fifer*, Michelangelo's Medici tombs, and traditional and contemporary Japanese images.

The complicated appropriation in Yokoo's work echoes Japan's evolution in the 1960s and 1970s from an insular culture to an economic world power.

JOHN BARNARD BRITISH, BORN 1946
FERRARI S.P.A. ESTABLISHED 1946

Formula 1 Racing Car 641/2. 1990
Body materials: composite with monocoque
chassis in honeycomb with carbon fibers
and Kevlar, 40^1/$_2$" x 7' x 14' 8^1/$_2$"
(102.9 x 213.4 x 448.3 cm)
Manufacturer: Ferrari S.p.A., Italy
Gift of the manufacturer

This Formula 1 Racing Car—with an exterior
body designed by Barnard and interior
chassis engineered and designed by the
Ferrari company—clearly illustrates the
modernist dictum "form follows function." The
shape of its exterior has been determined by
the laws of physics and aerodynamics, and
falls within the rules and guidelines set up by
the governing body of the sport of
automobile racing. The sleek and sculptural
silhouette of this Ferrari allows air to pass
over the body with minimal drag and
maximal down-force, which ensures
precision handling even at speeds in excess
of two hundred miles per hour.

High-performance racing cars represent
the ultimate achievement of one of the
world's largest industries. Painstakingly
engineered to go faster, handle better, and
stop more quickly than any other kind of
automobile, they are the most technologically
rational and complex type of motorcar
produced. Experimentation and innovation in
design, stimulated by the desire to win, are
constants in the ongoing quest for the
optimal racing machine.

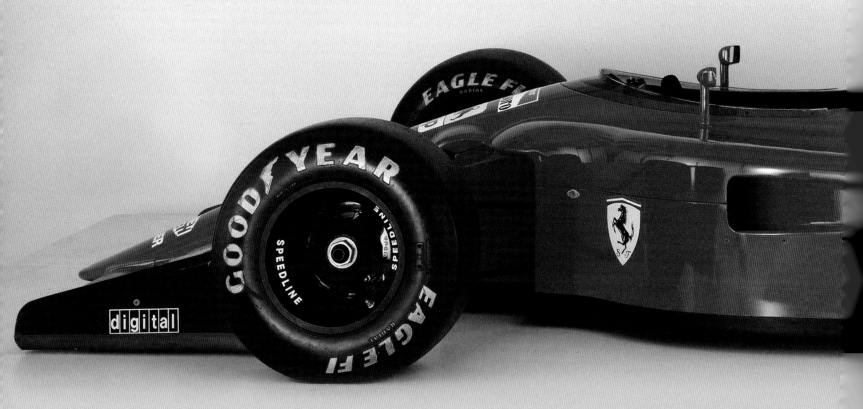

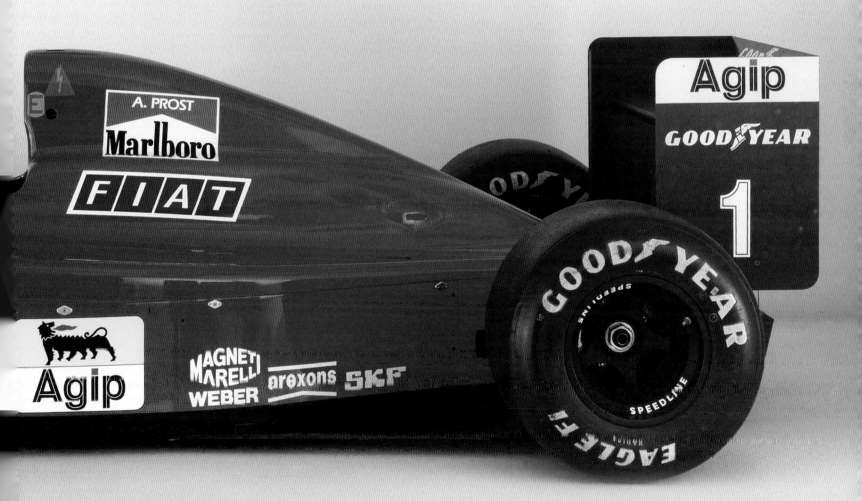

FELIX GONZALEZ-TORRES AMERICAN, BORN CUBA, 1957–1996

"Untitled" (Death by Gun). Begun 1990
Nine-inch stack of photolithographs, sheet:
44¹⁵/₁₆ x 32¹⁵/₁₆" (114.1 x 83.6 cm)
Purchased in part with funds from Arthur
Fleischer, Jr. and Linda Barth Goldstein

The viewer's first reaction to "Untitled" (*Death by Gun*) is one of uncertainty. Is this stack of papers on the floor meant to be walked around and viewed from different angles, like sculpture? Or did the artist intend these papers to be picked up and examined? Listed on the sheets are the names of 460 individuals killed by gunshot during the week of May 1-7, 1989, cited by name, age, city, and state, with a brief description of the circumstances of their deaths, and, in most cases, a photographic image of the deceased. These images and words, appropriated from *Time* magazine, where they first appeared, reflect Gonzalez-Torres's interest in gun control.

Conceptually, *Death by Gun* is an ongoing work of art. Viewer participation is an important element, and the public is encouraged to read the sheets and take them away to keep, display, or give to others. While Gonzalez-Torres determined that the stack is "ideally" nine inches high, he arranged for the depleted sheets to be continually reprinted and replaced, thus insuring that *Death by Gun* can be distributed indefinitely. From its beginnings, printed art has been made in multiple copies for dissemination to a wide audience. Here that idea is expanded with an edition that is "endless."

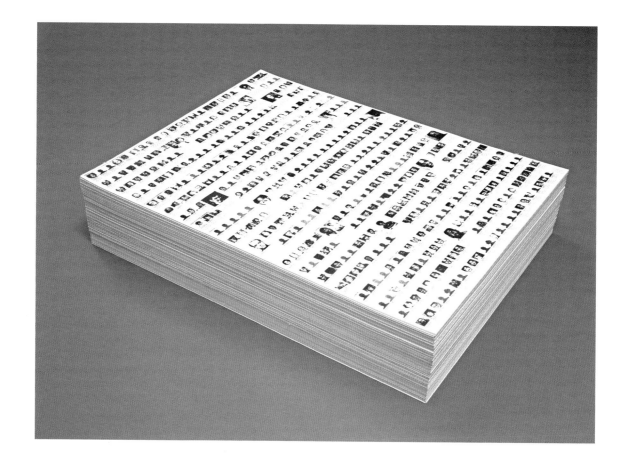

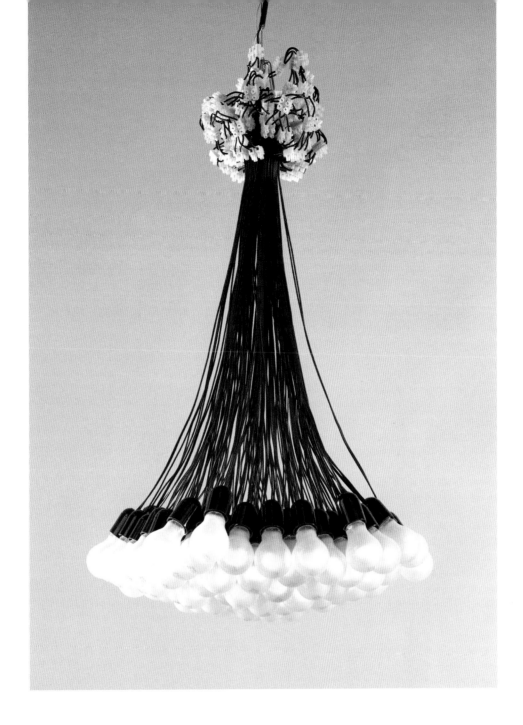

R O D Y G R A U M A N S DUICH, BORN 1968

85 Lamps Lighting Fixture. 1992
Standard lightbulbs, cords, and sockets,
39³/₈ x 39³/₈" (100 x 100 cm) diam.
Manufacturer: Droog Design, the Netherlands
Patricia Phelps de Cisneros Purchase Fund

Contemporary Dutch designers have been
markedly innovative in experimenting with
materials, a trend that crosses International
boundaries. Readily available at any
hardware store, Graumans's simple
materials—eighty-five black cords, sockets,
and lightbulbs—yield a grand chandelier
through the strength of his design. Gathered
in a unified bundle at the ceiling, the cords

flare out to accommodate the mass of
lightbulbs below.

Graumans's 85 Lamps was selected for
inclusion in the first design collection offered
by Droog Design, established in 1994 by
designers and theorists Gijs Bakker and
Renny Ramakers. It is a firm that has
captured much attention for its stance
against consumerism and its use of industrial
and recycled materials. The diverse works of
the talented young designers chosen for The
Museum of Modern Art design collection
celebrate ingenuity, economy of form, and a
minimalist aesthetic, as does this lamp by
Graumans.

RICHARD SERRA
AMERICAN, BORN 1939

Intersection II. 1992
Cor-Ten steel, four plates, each
13' 1¹/₂" x 55' 9³/₈" x 2" (400 x 1700 x 5 cm)
Gift of Ronald S. Lauder

Slightly younger than the Minimalist artists, Serra has intensified a quality of their work—a heightening of the viewer's physical self-awareness in relation to the art object. In early works of Serra's, heavy metal slabs stood in precarious balance; any close look at them was a charged affair. *Intersection II*, similarly, sensitizes its visitors, inviting them under and between its massive walls—which, they will find, exert an enormous psychic pressure.

That pressure arises from the weight, height, and leaning angles of the walls, and from their variously dark and rusted surfaces. It is tempered by the elegant precision of their lines and the satisfying logic of their arrangement. The slopes and placements of the great steel curves produce two outer spaces that invert each other at floor and ceiling, one being wide where the other is narrow. Meanwhile the central space is a regular yet biased ellipse. Whether these spaces are experienced as intimate or threateningly claustrophobic, what Serra has said of his earlier work applies: "The viewer in part became the subject matter of the work, not the object. His perception of the piece resided in his movement through the piece, [which] became more involved with anticipation, memory, and time, and walking and looking, rather than just looking at a sculpture the way one looks at a painting."

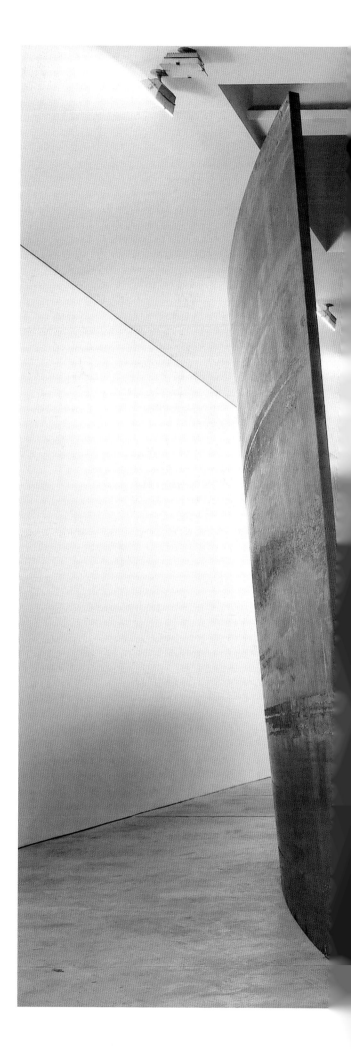

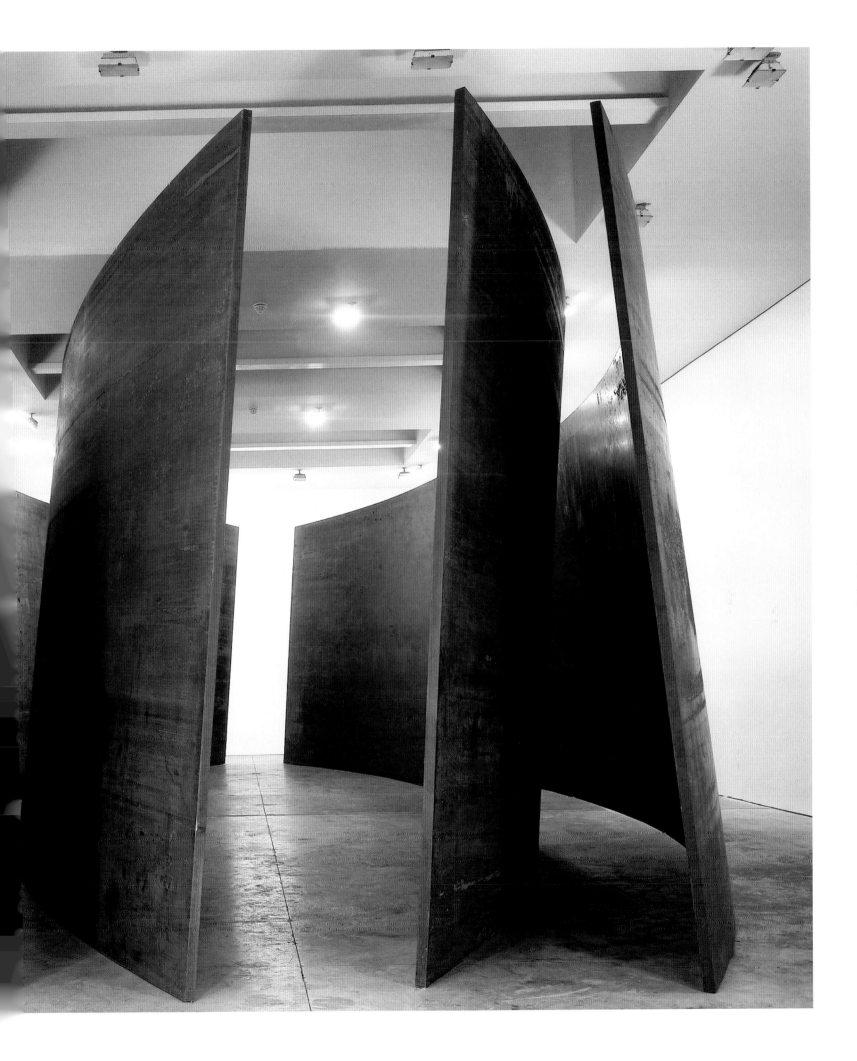

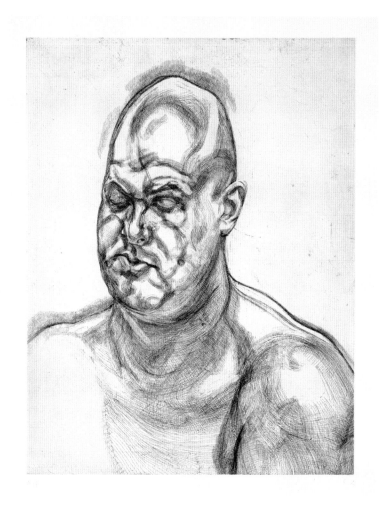

Large Head. 1993
Etching, plate: 27⁵/₁₆ x 21¹/₄" (69.4 x 54 cm)
Publisher: Matthew Marks Gallery, New York.
Edition: 40
Mrs. Akio Morita Fund

The large man depicted here with great intensity and keen observation is Leigh Bowery, a favorite model of the German-born British artist and grandson of Sigmund Freud. Bowery's brief career as a brilliant but abrasive performance artist was cut short by his early death in 1995. He performed mainly in London, where Freud first saw him, but he also appeared in New York and elsewhere. His distinctive physiognomy and massive physicality attracted Freud, who depicted Bowery in a series of paintings and prints over a period of four years. The calm repose of the figure seen here contrasts sharply with more provocative and disturbing representations of this brash eccentric artist, as shown in several large paintings.

Freud is not a traditional printmaker. Instead, he treats the etching plate like a canvas, standing the copper upright on an easel. He delineates his meticulously rendered composition across the plate, working day after day until the tightly woven representation is complete. The image is created with lines alone, which intersect, swell, and recede.

Family Romance. 1993
Mixed mediums, 53" x 7' 1" x 11"
(134.6 x 215.9 x 27.9 cm)
Gift of The Norton Family Foundation

Two parents, two young children: "It's a nuclear family," as Ray says, the model of American normalcy. Yet a simple action has put everything wrong: Ray has made all of them the same height. They are also naked, and unlike the store-window mannequins they resemble, they are anatomically complete. This and the work's title, the Freudian phrase for the suppressed erotic currents within the family unit, introduce an explicit sexuality as disturbing in this context as the protagonists' literally equal stature.

Early works of Ray's submitted the forms and ideas of Minimalism to the same kind of perceptual double-take that *Family Romance* works on the social life of middle-class Anglo-Saxon America. He has worked in photography and installation as well as sculpture, and his art has no predictable style or medium; but it often involves the surprise of the object that seems familiar yet is not. Like other works of Ray's involving mannequins, *Family Romance* suggests forces of anonymity and standardization in American culture. Its manipulations of scale also imply a disruption of society's balance of power: not only have the children grown, but the adults have shrunk.

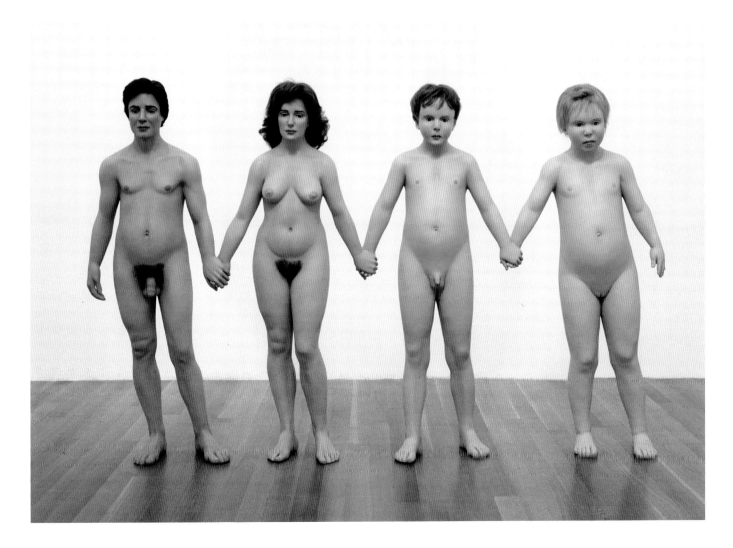

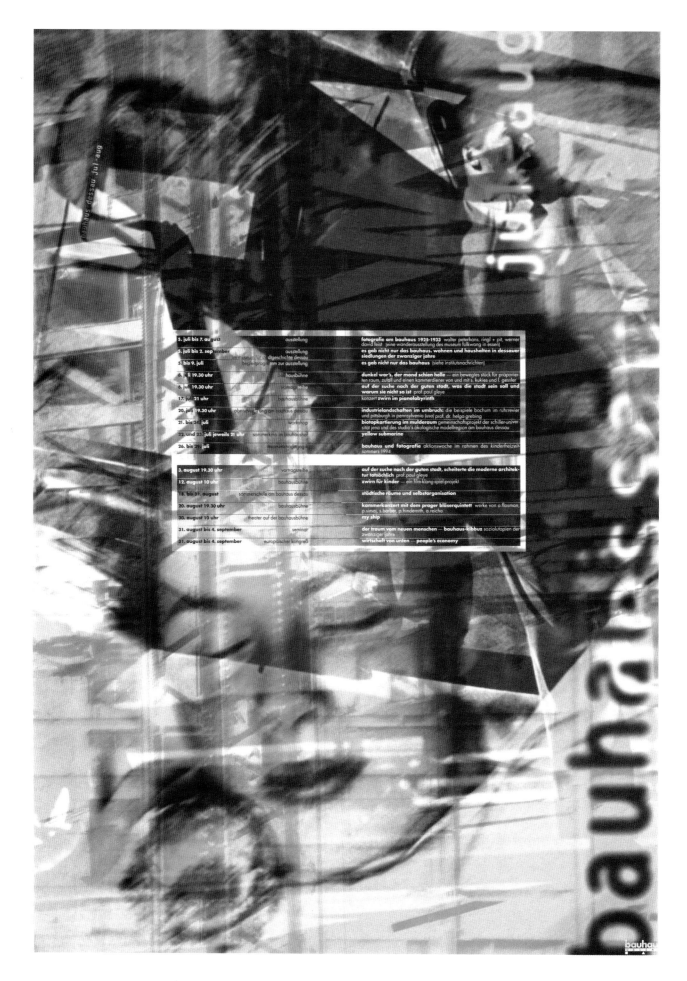

Bauhaus Foundation Dessau, Jul–Aug. 1995

Poster: offset lithograph, 33 x 23³/₈"
(83.8 x 59.4 cm)
Members: Sophie Alex (German, born 1967), Wilhelm Ebentreich (German, born 1952), Detlef Fiedler (German, born 1955), Daniela Haufe (German, born 1966), Siegfried Jablonsky (German, born 1950)
Gift of the designers

Cyan's images frequently evoke the past through the use of a complex layering of disparate historical images. Its posters and other graphic designs suggest the hazelike state of memory from which only bits and pieces can be retrieved. The innovative use of collage, made possible by the use of computer software, is an extension of the photomontage and photogram experiments performed by many modernist designers in the 1920s and 1930s. In addition, cyan frequently uses simple sans-serif type organized in a grid that appears to follow many of the rules of the "new typography" practiced at the Bauhaus in the 1920s.

Computer technology was not available to this five-person design collective from the former East Berlin until after the fall of the Berlin Wall in November 1989. Since then, they have skillfully mixed new visual forms —produced with the aid of sophisticated technologies—and more traditional modernist typography, creating posters that are extremely inventive and yet true in spirit to the modernist concern for clarity. Much of their work has been for German cultural institutions; among them, appropriately, is the Bauhaus Foundation Dessau.

VIK MUNIZ BRAZILIAN, BORN 1961

Mass. 1997

Two silver dye bleach prints (Cibachrome), each 60 x 48" (152.4 x 122 cm)
The Fellows of Photography Fund and Anonymous Purchase Fund

Seeing and believing are two sides of the same coin, which is why the eye can so easily fool the mind and vice versa. Muniz has made a large body of art, at once intelligent and funny, exploring this interdependence.

Here, for example, he began by copying a black-and-white photograph of a crowd, drawing it carefully in chocolate syrup on a small piece of paper. He then photographed the drawing in color and greatly enlarged it in the final print. The enlargement invites us to enjoy the delicious viscosity and gleaming highlights of the sticky-sweet stuff (and the skill with which Muniz has handled it). But the surprise and satisfaction of the picture lie in the stubbornness with which the photographic image reasserts its legibility despite the artist's playful depredations.

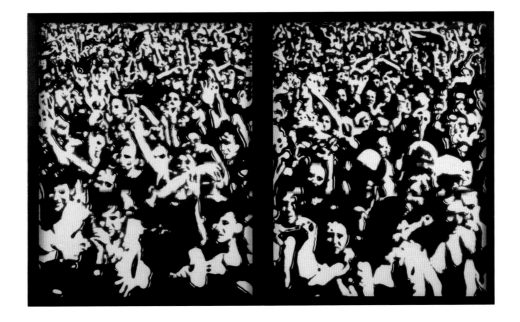

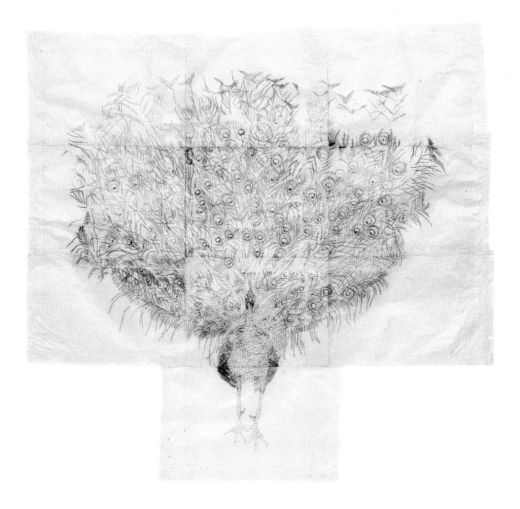

Peacock. 1997
Etching, composition and sheet: 7¹/₂" x 6' 4³/₈"
(181.6 x 194 cm)
Publisher: unpublished. Printer: Columbia
University, New York. Edition: several known
variants
Lily Auchincloss Fund

Peacock is the most monumental and
commanding example of the many works by
Smith based on sketches made in natural
history museums and then printed on sheets
of textured handmade paper. After emerging
in the 1980s with confrontational sculptures
of human figures and body parts, Smith
shifted her focus in the mid-1990s to the
natural world, depicting birds, other animals,
and the cosmos in sculptural works as well
as prints and books. For Smith, who was
raised a Catholic, birds have a particular
significance, both as a reference to the
poignant beauty of the environment and as a
symbol of the Holy Spirit. Here, the
authoritative majesty of the peacock's frontal
stance reflects the artist's appreciation of this
rare and magnificent creature.

Smith considers printmaking a vital part of
her work, and she has become one of the
most innovative and committed printmakers
of the last two decades. She has said,
"I could just make prints and be satisfied."
To date, Smith has published over 150 prints
and books, in formats ranging from
monumental multimedium prints and
elaborate *livres d'artiste* to screenprinted
tattoos and rubber stamps. When she began
working with imagery of birds and other
animals, Smith discovered the detailed,
refined line available in etching, and found it
an irresistible medium for describing feathers
and fur. In *Peacock*, her markings are so
dense as to almost obscure the bird's face
and body and turn the image into an
abstraction. The formal delicacy of this work
is enhanced by Smith's overt passion for the
inherently tactile qualities of paper—a
material that she has explored extensively in
sculpture. Smith likes to work with
translucent, skinlike sheets of handmade
paper, folding them, pasting them together,
and otherwise manipulating them in inventive
and unexpected ways.

Times Square, New York. 1997
Chromogenic color print, 6' 1" x 8' 2"
(185.4 x 248.9 cm)
The Family of Man Fund

This picture is large for a photograph—six by eight feet. It measures itself not against its mammoth subject but against the human viewer, and against other works of art. Gursky emerged from art school in Düsseldorf, Germany, in the mid-1980s, just as photographers were beginning to compete successfully with painters for attention and space on the walls of galleries and museums. In the process they discovered new opportunities in scale. Here the viewer is assaulted from afar by the eye-popping bands of color but, upon approaching, is invited to study in detail the vast atrium of the Marriott Marquis Hotel, built in New York's Times Square in 1985.

In fact, the picture is, to a considerable degree, an invention—a seamless image derived from photographs but recomposed and otherwise manipulated in Gursky's computer. It is at once hyper-real and unreal, an indelible image of our artificial world, made with the aid of the tool of our time.

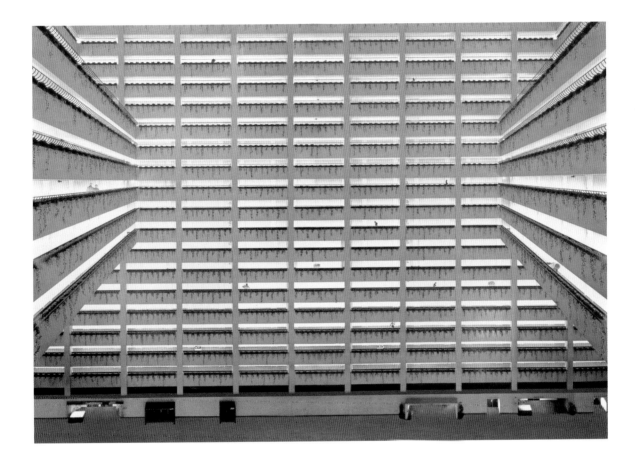

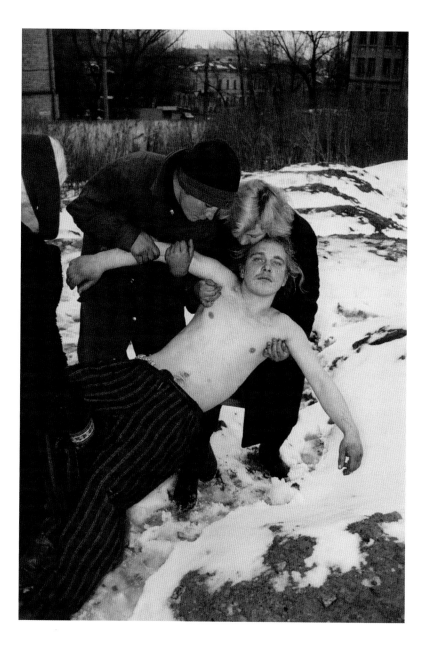

Untitled. 1997–98
Chromogenic color print, 58⁷/₁₆ x 39³/₁₆"
(148.5 x 99.5 cm)
Gift of Howard Stein

The demise of the Soviet Union in 1991
spelled disaster for many citizens of
Mikhailov's native Kharkov, in Ukraine.
As the state apparatus collapsed, bleak
predictability rapidly gave way to chaos and
want. The photographer, whose earlier work
includes sympathetic records of communal
pastimes, responded with a bitter series that
starkly evokes the squalor of desperation,

drink, and despair. In the same years, but in
another photographic mode altogether, he
experimented with flagrantly staged political
and sexual satires.

A decade later, as a few made millions, the
least fortunate Ukrainians were more
desperate still. This untitled work belongs to
Mikhailov's bold and risky series Case
History, for which he paid Kharkov's outcasts
to pose and perform. The best of his new
photographs improbably blend the opposing
poles of his art. No-nonsense realism and
impromptu playacting seamlessly conspire in
a persuasive theater of wrenching misery.

Smart Car ("Smart & Pulse" Coupé).
1998
Steel frame and thermoplastic body panels,
61" x 59³/₈" x 8' 2³/₈" (154.9 x 150.8 x 254.9 cm)
Manufacturer: Micro Compact Car Smart GmbH,
Renningen, Germany, and Hambach, France,
2002
Gift of the manufacturer, a company of the
DaimlerChrysler Group

Size matters. As its clever marketing slogan "reduced to the max" suggests, the Smart Car has been developed to maximize the convenience, comfort, and safety of driver and passenger, while minimizing the impact on the environment. Low fuel consumption (averaging 49 miles per gallon) and eco-friendly methods of production distinguish this two-passenger car from the others on the market.

The Smart Car was developed in the early 1990s at the Mercedes-Benz design studio in Irvine, California, where a team of engineers and designers, led by Gerhard Steinle, created the prototype. The design and marketing strategy was further developed with input from the Swatch watch company.

Cars are sold at "Smart Centers" throughout Europe, where the brightly colored vehicles are stacked in towers like objects in a display case, clearly aimed at youthful, style-conscious consumers seeking an affordable car.

The Smart Car's body reveals a clear, functional, modular design. The black frame of reinforced steel—the so-called Tridion safety cell—gives the vehicle its inherent strength. The safety cell defines the car as an integral unit, enabling the Smart Car to be conveniently short for a city car, without the front and back ends that project beyond the passenger compartment in a conventional vehicle. The steel frame is coated with powder paint, considerably less harmful to the environment than conventional painting processes. Colorful, lightweight body panels made of recycled plastic are virtually dent-resistant and rust-free. They are easily exchanged for a new set whenever the owner wants to change color. The interior is unexpectedly spacious. The engine is located below the passengers, allowing space to be conserved and seats to be given additional height.

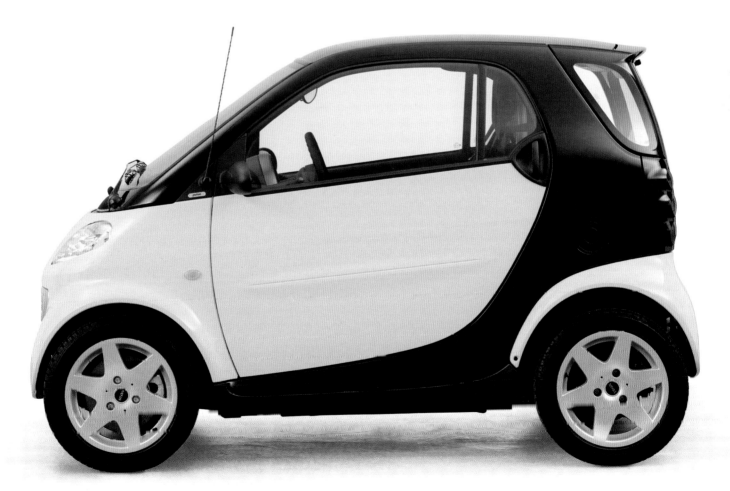

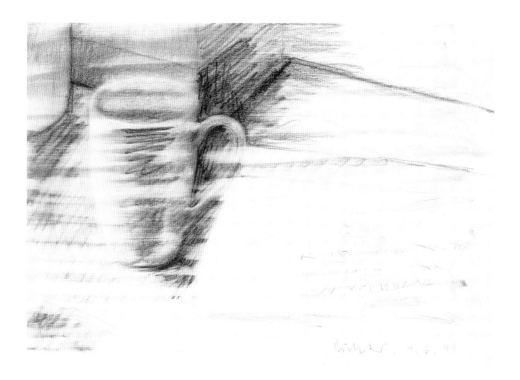

4.6.1999 (99/45). 1999

Graphite on paper, sheet: 8¹/₄ x 11³/₄"
(21 x 29.8 cm)
Purchased with funds provided by The Edward
John Noble Foundation

At first glance, this modest pencil drawing appears to be a simple image of a teacup—a memento, perhaps, of a quiet morning at a kitchen table, in the manner of a traditional still-life. On closer inspection, however, it unravels and becomes something else entirely. The flat tones, sharp contours, and regular shading suggest that the artist's source for the drawing was a photograph of a cup rather than a cup itself. Indeed, no simple sketch taken from life, *4.6.1999* is an image of an image. Most likely derived from one of Richter's own snapshots, the drawing bears the pictorial imprint of the impersonal and mechanical language of the camera. The erased marks that run across the center of the sheet further complicate the drawing. Slicing the motif into strips, these striations disrupt the "transparency" of the image,

calling special attention to the process of the drawing's making. Like the use of photographic source material, these erasures register the artist's hand negatively, as something absent or canceled.

The tension between the apparent simplicity of the motif and the pregnant implications of the means by which it was rendered points to the critical charge in Richter's art, which over the last four decades has probed the myriad ways in which images are made and perceived. Working in many different mediums and styles (indeed, this drawing was executed concurrently with another work done completely abstractly), Richter has consistently examined the contingency of representation, fashioning a body of work of tremendous variety, versatility, and import. By underscoring the constructed nature of illusionism, Richter's work invites viewers to reflect on how they perceive the world, and, in the process, invests his personal visions with public implications.

Torus House, Old Chatham, New York.
Project, 1999
Interior perspective: Digital Duraflex print,
24 x 32" (61 x 81.3 cm)
Barbara Pine Purchase Fund

Torus House represents a contemporary revision of the artist's house, a type of residence rooted in the nineteenth-century Arts and Crafts movement. The two largest spaces in the house will be painting studios. The space pictured in this computer-generated print will be used for easel painting and will also serve as a gallery and a living space. The glass walls provide generous views of the partially wooded field in this remote, contemplative setting. Spatially and visually, the vertical circulation in the center of the studio links all the principal elements of the house.

The formal character of the Torus House design is remarkable for its melding of seemingly incompatible geometric languages. The architect hopes to reinvigorate the historical tension between the orthodox and the radical: "The dialectic between norm and exception in architecture relies on the persistence or memory of social and building conventions on the one hand and formal transgression on the other." In this instance, the norm is a courtyard house, which is transformed by the use of nonarchitectural, seamless, curvilinear forms derived from the torus. That topological form is generated by rotating one circle along the path of a second, larger circle, usually producing a doughnutlike shape.

Amplifying the ambiguity between the house's interior and exterior, a stair, which occupies what would be the hollow core of the torus, bypasses the interior of the house by running directly from the parking area at ground level to the roof above. The architect explains that "the curvilinear lines and undulations blend the individual components into an unbroken surface that resembles features of the landscape beyond."

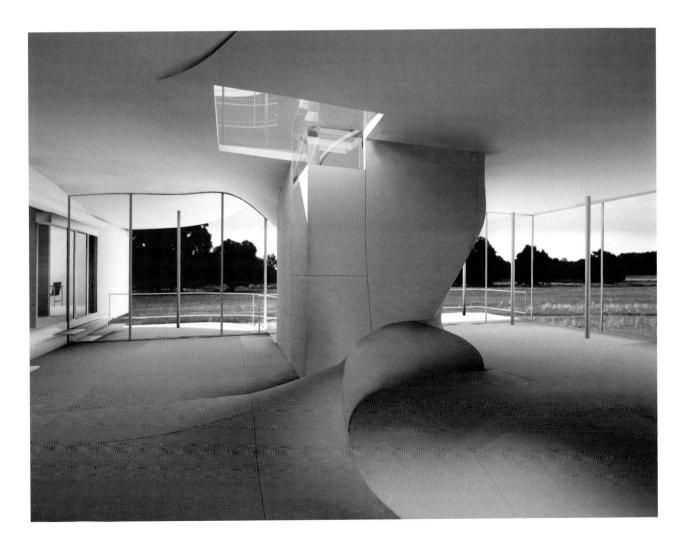

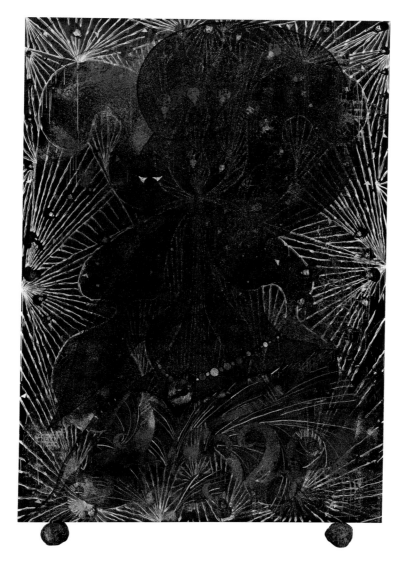

Prince amongst Thieves. 1999

Synthetic polymer paint, collage, glitter, resin,
map pins, and elephant dung on canvas, 8 x 6'
(243.8 x 182.8 cm)
Mimi and Peter Haas Fund

Ofili's intensely worked, vibrant paintings
combine a wide range of referents, from
African burlesque to Western popular culture.
Using a cut-and-mix technique and repetitive
patterning, the works evoke the anarchic
rhythm of hip-hop lyrics and performance.
Prince amongst Thieves features the
caricatured yet regal profile of a bemused
man of African descent, set against a
densely ornate background dotted with
countless minute collages of the heads of
illustrious black figures. The work's
shimmering, psychedelic surface of sprayed
pigment, synthetic polymer paint, glitter,
elephant dung, and splashes of translucent
resin produces a ritualistic effect that
parodies stereotypes of black culture while
celebrating difference. The lacquered
clumps of elephant dung on which the
canvas rests have become a signature for
Ofili, and they confer on the painting a
sculptural and perhaps even totemic
presence, invoking African tribal art, with
which Ofili (who is of Nigerian descent)
became familiar during a visit to Zimbabwe,
in 1992.

The artist uses elephant droppings for its
traditional associations but procures it from
the London Zoo, thereby probing his cultural
heritage and urban experience in ways that
confound identity typecasting. Ofili's mix of
hybrid sources culled from popular
magazines, music, folk art, and the tough
streets around his Kings Cross studio, in
London, epitomizes a new form of
counterculture that subtly reworks Western
perceptions of blackness.

Geezer. 2002

Oil, cut-and-pasted printed paper, and pencil on wood, 31⁷/₈ x 29¹/₂" (81 x 74.9 cm)
Purchased with funds provided by The Buddy Taub Foundation, Dennis A. Roach, Director

Geezer is part of a large body of work by Lucas dedicated to Charlie George, a star player of one of the top London soccer clubs during the 1970s. Lucas grew up in the same gritty working-class neighborhood as George, who in the artist's youth represented dreams of stardom and escape. Here, in a portrait comprised primarily of collaged pizza-parlor advertisements, Lucas uses her relationship with the soccer star as a touchstone for a complicated investigation of identity, success, and marketing.

While George is the ostensible subject of the portrait, the figure bears an uncanny resemblance to Lucas, whose work typically explores androgyny, the hybridity of personal identity, and double meanings. Indeed, *Geezer* can be understood as a kind of self-portrait connecting the artist's personal history with that of the soccer star's. However, *Geezer* is infused with a biting political critique as well. By rendering the face of the portrait from advertisements—the only legible identifying characteristic in the drawing is the logo of George's team, Arsenal—Lucas seems to speak to the commodification of bodies in sports, and in society generally. Not only are the fans' identities molded by their identification with sports stars, but those models to which they aspire are themselves just blank screens for the projection of logos. In this light, the letters "NANZA," which emblazon the absolute center of the subject's forehead, stand as a poignant symbol for the fragmentary nature of the "BONANZA" of success. For as much as *Geezer* celebrates Charlie George and represents dreams and their realization, it also depicts the underbelly of certain aspects of late-stage capitalism—a stance perfectly attuned to the tradition of political commentary in much collage, to which Lucas knowingly nods with this work.

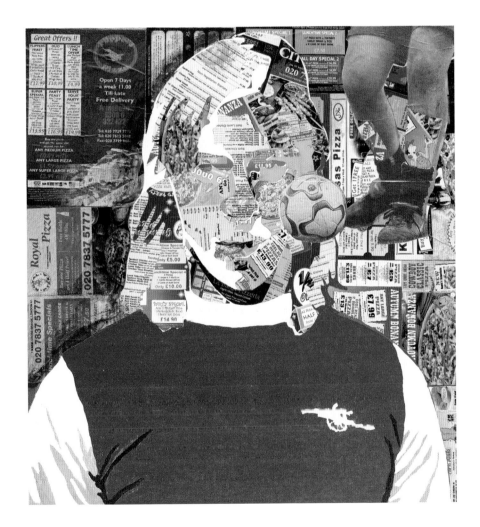

INDEX OF ARTISTS

The photographs in this book were taken by the staff photographers of The Museum of Modern Art, with the exception of the following: © 2005, Digital Image, Timothy Hursley/The Museum of Modern Art, New York/SCALA, Florence: pp. 14, 18 19. Seth Joel: pp. 81, 135, 143, 257. Thomas Powel, pp. 282-283. Friedrich Rosenstiel, Cologne: p. 276. Sperone Westwater, New York: p. 273.

Individual works of art appearing herein may be protected by copyright in the United States of America or elsewhere, and may thus not be reproduced in any form without the permission of the copyright owners.

Every effort has been made to locate copyright holders for the photographs used in this book. Any errors or omissions will be corrected in subsequent editions.

Certain credits appear at the request of the artist or the artist's representatives.

Adams: Collection Center for Creative Photography, University of Arizona, © 1981 Center for Creative Photography, Arizona Board of Regents. *Albers*: © 2005 The Josef and Anni Albers Foundation/Artists Rights Society (ARS), New York. *Álvarez Bravo*: © Manuel Álvarez Bravo. *Andre*: © Carl Andre/Licensed by VAGA, New York, NY. *Arbus*: © Diane Arbus. *Arp*: © 2005 Artists Rights Society (ARS), New York/ADAGP, Paris. *Avery*: © 2005 Milton Avery Trust/Artists Rights Society (ARS), New York. *Bacon*: © 2005 Estate of Francis Bacon/Artists Rights Society (ARS), New York/DACS, London. *Balla*: © 2005 Artists Rights Society (ARS), New York/SIAE, Rome. *Balthus*: © 2005 Artists Rights Society (ARS), New York/ADAGP, Paris. *Baselitz*: © Georg Baselitz. *Bayer*: © 2005 Artists Rights Society (ARS), New York/VG Bild-Kunst, Bonn. *Beckmann*: © 2005 Artists Rights Society (ARS), New York/VG Bild-Kunst, Bonn. *Beuys*: © 2005 Artists Rights Society (ARS), New York/VG Bild-Kunst, Bonn. *Bonnard*: © 2005 Artists Rights Society (ARS), New York/ADAGP, Paris. *Brancusi*: © 2005 Artists Rights Society (ARS), New York/ADAGP, Paris. *Braque*: © 2005 Artists Rights Society (ARS), New York/ADAGP, Paris. *Brassaï*: © Brassaï. *Broodthaers*: © 2005 Artists Rights Society (ARS), New York/SABAM, Brussels. *Burrows*: © Larry Burrows. *Burton*: © 2005 Estate of Scott Burton/Artists Rights Society (ARS), New York. *Calder*: © 2005 Estate of Alexander Calder/Artists Rights Society (ARS), New York. *Cartier-Bresson*: © Henri Cartier-Bresson. *Chagall*: © 2005 Artists Rights Society (ARS), New York/ADAGP, Paris. *Clemente*: © Francesco Clemente. *Close*:

© Chuck Close, courtesy PaceWildenstein, New York. *Cornell*: © The Joseph and Robert Cornell Memorial Foundation/Licensed by VAGA, New York, NY. *D'Albisola*: © Tullio d'Albisola. *Dalí*: © 2005 Salvador Dalí, Gala-Salvador Dalí Foundation/Artists Rights Society (ARS), New York. *De Chirico*: © 2005 Artists Rights Society (ARS), New York/SIAE, Rome. *De Kooning*: © 2005 The Willem de Kooning Foundation/Artists Rights Society (ARS), New York. *De Maria*: © Walter de Maria. *Delaunay*: © L & M SERVICES B.V. Amsterdam 20050508. *Derain*: © 2005 Artists Rights Society (ARS), New York/ADAGP, Paris. *Diebenkorn*: © The Estate of Richard Diebenkorn. *Dix*: © 2005 Artists Rights Society (ARS), New York/VG Bild-Kunst, Bonn. *Dubuffet*: © 2005 Artists Rights Society (ARS), New York/ADAGP, Paris. *Duchamp*: © 2005 Artists Rights Society (ARS), New York/ADAGP, Paris/Succession Marcel Duchamp. *El Lissitzky*: © 2005 Artists Rights Society (ARS), New York/VG Bild-Kunst, Bonn. *Ensor*: © 2005 Artists Rights Society (ARS), New York/SABAM, Brussels. *Ernst*: © 2005 Artists Rights Society (ARS), New York/ADAGP, Paris. *Evans*: © Walker Evans Archive, The Metropolitan Museum of Art. *Fontana*: © Fondazione Lucio Fontana. *Francis*: © 2005 Estate of Sam Francis/Artists Rights Society (ARS), New York. *Frank*: © Robert Frank, from *The Americans*, courtesy Pace/MacGill Gallery, New York. *Frankenthaler*: © Helen Frankenthaler. *Freud*: © Lucian Freud. *Giacometti*: © 2005 Artists Rights Society (ARS), New York/ADAGP, Paris. *González*: © 2005 Artists Rights Society (ARS), New York/ADAGP, Paris. *Gonzalez-Torres*: © The Felix Gonzalez-Torres Foundation, courtesy of Andrea Rosen Gallery, New York. *Gorky*: © 2005 Artists Rights Society (ARS), New York. *Gottlieb*: © 2005 Esther and Adolph Gottlieb Foundation/Licensed by VAGA, New York, NY. *Grosz*: © 2005 Estate of George Grosz/Licensed by VAGA, New York, NY. *Gursky*: © 2005 Andreas Gursky/Artists Rights Society (ARS), New York/VG Bild-Kunst, Bonn, courtesy Monika Sprüth/Philomene Magers, Cologne/Munich. *Hadid*: © Zaha Hadid Architects. *Hamilton*: © 2005 Artists Rights Society (ARS), New York/DACS, London. *Hesse*: © The Estate of Eva Hesse. Hauser & Wirth Zürich London. *Höch*: © 2005 Artists Rights Society (ARS), New York/VG Bild-Kunst, Bonn. *Irwin*: © 2005 Robert Irwin/Artists Rights Society (ARS), New York. *Johns*: © Jasper Johns/Licensed by VAGA, New York, NY. *Johnston*: © Frances Benjamin Johnston. *Judd*: © Judd Foundation/Licensed by VAGA, New York, NY. *Kahlo*: © 2005 Banco de México, Diego Rivera & Frida Kahlo Museums Trust. Av. Cinco de Mayo No. 2, Col. Centro, Del. Cuauhtémoc 06059 México, D.F. *Kahn*: Reprinted with permission of Sue Ann Kahn. *Kandinsky*: © 2005 Artists Rights

Authors

Introduction, Glenn D. Lowry
Painting and Sculpture texts, Fereshteh Daftari,
David Frankel, Claire Henry, Roxana Marcoci,
Angela Meredith-Jones, María José Montalva,
Lilian Tone, Anne Umland
Drawings texts, Mary Chan, Magdalena
Dobrowski, Kristin Helmick-Brunet, Laura
Hoptman, Jordan Kantor, Angela Meredith-Jones,
Margit Rowell, Rachel Warner
Prints and Illustrated Books texts, Starr Figura,
Carol Smith
Architecture and Design texts, Paola Antonelli,
Bevin Cline, Luisa Lorch, Matilda McQuaid,
Christopher Mount, Peter Reed, Terence Riley
Photography texts, Peter Galassi, Susan Kismaric
Media texts, Barbara London

Design
Studio Contri Toscano, Florence

Color separations
Professional Graphics, Inc., Rockford, Illinois
Fotolito RAF, Florence